*Law and State
in Papua New Guinea*

# LAW, STATE AND SOCIETY SERIES

*Editors*

Z. BANKOWSKI, *Department of Public Law, University of Edinburgh, U.K.*
M. CAIN, *Department of Law, London School of Economics and Political Science, U.K.*
W. CHAMBLISS, *Department of Sociology and Anthropology, University of Delaware, Newark, U.S.A.*
M. MCINTOSH, *Department of Sociology, University of Essex, Colchester, U.K.*

# Law and State
# in Papua New Guinea

## PETER FITZPATRICK
*University of Kent at Canterbury*

1980

## ACADEMIC PRESS
*A Subsidiary of Harcourt Brace Jovanovich, Publishers*
London · New York · Toronto · Sydney · San Francisco

ACADEMIC PRESS INC. (LONDON) LTD.
24/28 Oval Road
London NW1

*United States Edition published by*
ACADEMIC PRESS INC.
111 Fifth Avenue
New York, New York 10003

**British Library Cataloguing in Publication Data**
Fitzpatrick, Peter
  Law and state in Papua New Guinea.
  1. Papua New Guinea — Economic conditions
  2. Underdeveloped areas — Economic conditions — Case Studies
  3. Underdeveloped areas — Law — Case studies
  4. Law — Papua New Guinea
  I. Title
  330.9′ 95′ 3        HC687.P3        80-49982

  ISBN 0-12-257880-5

Typeset by Colset Ltd.,
Singapore

Printed in Great Britain by
Whitstable Litho Ltd., Whitstable, Kent

# Preface

It is necessary to say something of how this book came about. It is grounded in particular and often practical concerns; to appreciate these will help mark the book's limits and, I hope, invest it with meanings beyond my intentions.

The book appears straightforward enough in structure. It presents, firstly, a Marxist perspective on law and state in the third world, which is then applied and refined in a historical class analysis of the Papua New Guinea case. Matters did not proceed in such a straightforward way, however. The book emerged initially as a reaction against several things — against much academic work in the third world, against theorizing about so-called law and development in particular, against the colonial experience in Papua New Guinea and against the post-colonial. I will outline these reactions and indicate how they led to the perspective offered here. The exercise will be neither rigorous nor lengthy.

Fortunately my research in Papua New Guinea began in 1970 at a time when theories of development and modernization in the third world were coming under increasing and effective attack (for example, Frank 1971b; Griffin, 1969; Rhodes, 1968). Reacting against them imposed no strain on originality and the ground has been well worked since. In the end it became clear that, even in their own terms, these theories were ahistorical, and merely prescriptive or predictive. The third world was to evolve, or be made to evolve, in the direction of the social formations of western capitalism. The process would take place by the introduction of capital trailing along with western values and institutions. The outcome would be the transformation of resident social formations and thereby the elimination of backwardness and of the cause of underdevelopment. I will consider this doctrine in its political and ideological aspects when looking at law and state in Chapter Two, but enough has been said about it here.

Theorizing about law and development operated implicity within the confines of this doctrine. It merely added an instrumental perspective. Introduced or "modern" law was to be used to bring about this transformation of backward social formations — to change the behaviour of the backward residents and to provide a supportive frame for the intervening progressive influences (Trubek, 1972, pp. 2 – 9). Law was usually viewed as an effective and "value-neutral" means of achieving these given ends (Trubek and Galanter, 1974). Because law was or would be effective in this, history was irrelevant: law could transform existent reality and shape the future. Since history, with its determining effect on law, was out of the picture, law could be seen as standing apart and therefore as neutral. Society could thus justifiably be considered from within the focal sanctum of law. So, to take the most highly elaborated example of theorizing about law and development, Seidman can present a supposed "theory about the relationship between the state, the legal order, and social, political and economic development" in which the relevance of social forces is illustrative and consequential (Seidman, 1978, p. 9). This general stance — essentially the view from within law — enabled studies in law and development to remain comfortably bound by such accepted academic ideologies as law and the policy sciences and sociological jurisprudence. That this internal stance has implications for law as ideology is a point made in Chapter Two. The basic message, in summary, that I have to extract and carry on with here is that this stance serves the existing order (see Hunt, 1979, Chapters 1 and 2). More generally, Baran has put it that an "intellect worker" working within a particular compartment of knowledge, lacking a "concern with the whole" and "leaving this concern to others ... *eo ipso* accepts the existing structure of the whole as a datum and subscribes to the prevailing criteria of rationality, to the dominant values, and to the socially enforced yardsticks of efficiency, achievement and success" (Baran, 1967, p. 7).

I shall now follow this "concern with the whole" into the context of Papua New Guinea. Lloyd's criticism of "evolutionary theories" of development in the third world can serve as an introduction to typical academic concerns with development and "social change" in Papua New Guinea. He notes that, with these theories:

> A greater concern is shown for the internal structure of the traditional society, at an early stage of development, than for its relationship with the external environment. Change is seen as deriving from processes within the structure rather than as a response to environment and demands. The study of the development of traditional into modern society takes precedence over an examination of the conflict between the two. (Lloyd, 1973, p. 68)

Hence one finds T.S. Epstein's much cited study of a Tolai society put vaguely in terms of "primitive capitalism" when the society would fit no rigorous definition of capitalism. Yet this perspective does enable Epstein to emphasize aspects of that society making for capitalist development and to present other aspects as hinderances to development (Epstein, 1968). In an influential study, Finney finds that the society which concerns him is "preadapted to capitalism" but this finding stems from his prime concern with "entrepreneurship", rather than from the wider reality which he subordinates (Finney, 1973, pp. x – xi). History, or Lloyd's "external environment", provides little more than a sketchy background to these studies. These are only two examples among many, but they are notable. It is a small step along this "internal" path to the view that underdevelopment is not created historically but issues from the backward people themselves — perhaps from their irrationality and their lack of understanding of the wider world (see for example, McSwain, 1977). From this it followed, roughly, that academics aligned themselves with the intervening influences that would, in the name of development, advance these backward people and help in the creation and sustaining of an emergent, fragile "new nation". In particular there was great sympathy with the state even in the colonial period, and a willingness, even in sensitive scholarship, to accept its prescription of the tasks to be done and to view the manifestly malign effects of state action as unintentional (see for example, Howlett et al., 1976, pp. 249 – 250). Thus, to give a legal example, supposed criminologists focused on the efficacy of coercive legal controls, taking the officially defined content and purposes of the controls as axiomatic (Boehringer, 1976).

These academic stands tended, in a negative way, to set my initial and rather inept research perspective. This perspective was confirmed when, after the elections of 1972, I worked with the first national government on policies and programmes that were allegedly decolonizing. Both the research and the work with the government required an alternative framework to the dominant academic and colonial frames. The work on dependency and underdevelopment, which was then rapidly expanding, was pitched at an international level, and thus seemed too remote from my initial concern with legal aspects of economic enterprises at the village level — a concern defined by the body sponsoring the initial research. It was also too remote as well as too pessimistic, in its effects, to be compatible with involvement in reformist politics. At the political level there was no strong guiding ideology or highly specific impetus for radical change. The "solutions" found for the research and at the political level were broadly similar and broadly wrong.

As for the research, the solution was greatly influenced by a libertarian academic ethos of the late 1960s. In the third world, this appeared as a distrust of imposing any kind of outside research structure. Research into what "the people" were concerned with was advocated, as was helping "dominated cultures" to survive and effectively confront the wider forces buffeting them (Hymes, 1974). To study what "the people", including their elected representatives, wanted — to give their concerns this validity — seemed to turn the existing academic and colonial stands upside down and this was satisfying. This approach was, however, riddled with insoluble difficulty and much of this book could be read as a criticism of it. Nevertheless, my research was conducted on this basis for several years and it must be said here that this extreme relativism led to some patchiness. The patches comprise much of the research presented here — research on group economic enterprise, on laws restrictive of small scale economic enterprises, on the legal regulation of foreign investment and on several smaller topics.

At the political level, operative guides came from two sources. One was a highly influential report on general development policy by a visiting advisory mission (Overseas Development Group, 1973). In retrospect it is very easy to see that its apparently radical proposals were merely concerned to deal with some of the symptoms of underdevelopment without confronting the structural underpinnings of this underdevelopment. Being reactive and diffuse this source provided little that was ideologically comprehensive and coherent. The other source was an attempt to provide this — a kind of specific socialism called Papua New Guinea ways. Like other specific socialisms, such as African socialism and Arab socialism, this was an anodyne populism that obscured as well as legitimized the continuation of existing structures of exploitation. Both these sources are described in more detail in Chapter Eight. The point here is that the assertion of Papua New Guinea ways and some similar aspects of the mission's report fitted and supported the essentially populist basis of my research.

As Chapter Eight indicates, the bankruptcy of populism soon became evident: reforms that sought to counter dominant class interests were either not carried out or were fundamentally restrained in their implementation. Former radicals and nationalists found comfortable niches within ongoing social forces. A new research framework was called for not only to replace the one discredited by events but also to explain these events. A populist frame, it became evident, was flawed because it relied on the concerns of "people" who were largely subordinated to dominant views. It could not begin to question these views, and at best it could generate only sniping discontents.

Marxism provided a substantial alternative, and the introduction to it came through "neo-Marxist" theories of underdevelopment. These often did not appear to have much to do with Marxism, but they did provoke some enlightening debates clarifying the relevance of Marxism to the third world context (see for example, Laclau, 1971). Marxist explanations proved able to put together the seemingly disparate evidence that was puzzling me at that stage of my research and enabled me to see this evidence in a new way. This helped me to identify new areas of research which were needed to get something like a whole view. This is not to suggest that I have a comprehensively assured epistemological stance operating from within Marxism.

I should like to say something of the particular Marxist framework being used. The first two chapters do this in some detail and for the present I will continue to discuss two main and related themes — the concern with the whole and the limits of reformism. With Marxism, as I understand it, the concern with the whole does not and cannot involve the seeking, much less the finding, of some formular element that will finally encompass or explain reality. It provides an operatively integrated set of concepts which, to borrow the terms of Thompson's argument, "are brought to bear upon the evidence as 'expectations'. They do not impose a rule, but they hasten and facilitate the interrogation of the evidence" (Thompson, 1978, p. 237). A basic exception to this must be the primary importance, but not the exclusiveness, of the determining effect of the economic element. Perhaps this can be justified as a given factor because production is necessary for survival — "the simple fact ... that mankind must first of all eat, drink, have shelter and clothing, before it can pursue politics, science, art, religion, etc." (Engels in Marx and Engels, 1970, p. 249). I do not follow this up here but merely mention it as an assumption underlying the present work, and one well established by work in the Marxist tradition.

Of course, the Marxist tradition itself is far from homogeneous. It seems that it is becoming less, and some matters of disagreement are quite fundamental. Marxism has also developed in varying ways in its application in different social formations. There are three points here that seem particularly relevant to the present work. The first concerns the particular development of Marxism in relation to social formations of the third world. The second could be called, in short, the debate between capital and class, and the third involves the efficacy of political action.

To consider the first point, it is a fact that Marx provided little on the third world that was consistent or developed, and classical Marxist theories of imperialism focus predominantly on the imperialist social formations (Foster-Carter, 1974, pp. 69 – 75). "Neo-marxist" theories tend to be concerned with the process of underdevelopment caused by the "first world" exploiting the third. Although this process is seen as giving rise to particular class elements within the social formations of the third world, these theories have proved less than perceptive on the detailed and dynamic operation of social forces within these formations. In particular, little attention was paid to the place and effect of pre-capitalist modes of production. Recent work by French Marxist anthropologists has pointed out the necessity of giving a central place to the operative combination of pre-capitalist modes and the introduced capitalist mode (D. Seddon, ed., 1978). This is the main focus for the present work. It is first presented generally and then developed in its relation to class formation, to state action and especially to law. In particular, this focus serves to identify what is distinctive about the form and function of law within social formations of the third world. This is outlined in Chapter Two and then refined considerably in its application to the Papua New Guinea case.

Commenting on "the economic structure" and "the theoretical primacy accorded this category [and] its alleged ultimacy as an explicator", Cain and Hunt discern:

> .... a contradiction endemic to Marx' and Engels' work. Sometimes — and this is increasingly and predominantly true of Marx — it is capital as such, as it is conceived, which provides this ultimate account in the elaboration of the concept of capitalism itself; at other times — and this occurs in the works of both authors — accounts are presented in terms of the bourgeois classes and their interests. (Cain and Hunt, 1979, p. xviii)

Although the present work talks generally of the movement and impact of capital, it comes down heavily on the class side of this divide. To attempt to do otherwise is tempting. For example, some of what Marx said on "the law of the tendency of the rate of profit to fall" is so fresh in its application to the third world that it could have been written today (Marx, 1973, p. 751). To continue with the example, such a "law" has a predominant part in several theories of imperialism (see for example, Mandel, 1968, pp. 453 – 454). However, little confident use is made here of such "laws of motion". I do not know enough about them or about how to use them, but even advocates of these laws seem uncertain about how to establish their primacy and their effect (see for example, Hirsch, 1978, pp. 75, 83 – 84). So perhaps my concern with the whole has to be seen as narrowed by a partial emphasis on class and class struggle.

The emphasis on class and class struggle provides an operational link between economy and political action. Given its setting, the book has to stress the subordinate place of political action. This is certainly not meant to deny the utility of such action, however. Indeed, I take it that the efficacy of voluntary action has a central part in the particular dialectical nature of Marxism. The focus on class should at least indicate an integral emphasis on political action. Emphasis on the contraints that bind and interact with political action can be seen as a step in seeking for what can be done. There is an implicit positive in much of the seem-

ingly destructive analysis. For example, in the context of the social forces it
serves, populism in Papua New Guinea is the precise opposite of a basis for radical
change. Only when it is seen as a support for the existing order and a diversionary
dead-end for radical activists will the necessity for action alternative to that shaped
by it be necessary. Yet such a line of argument can be taken as insulting to those
who are dedicated to populist ideologies and programmes, as many in Papua New
Guinea are. This line can be seen as a questioning of intelligence or motives — an
implicit assertion that these people are fools or fiends. The point can be a particularly sensitive one in the politics of ''development'' where good intentions and
asserted capability have to count for so much. All I can say is that, in this, I do not
mean to insult and we are all fools and fiends. I only wish my theory could more
adequately accommodate my affection and gratitude.

My gratitude is profound. People generally, many political and community
leaders and state officials were extremely generous in giving time to interview and
discussions, in providing liberal access to documentary information and in
providing exciting opportunities for work on legal and other projects (people
who provided particular information are acknowledged in footnotes or in the
text). As the book amply illustrates, I have relied on many academics who have
worked in Papua New Guinea. Disagreement does not, of course, detract from
my great debt to them. The same is true for others who have directly supported or
encouraged the research in various ways most notably, Moi Avei, Tos Barnett,
the Commonwealth Foundation, Michael Grey, John Kaputin, John Ley, Sir
John Minogue and Iambakey Okuk. Colleagues who have supported and helped
me include Lesley Andrews, John Ballard, Zen Bankowski, Loraine Blaxter, Ken
Buckley, Maureen Cain, Ian Grigg-Spall, Robin Luckham, Susie McGowan,
Abdul Paliwala, Julie Southwood, Barry Stuart and Robert Wanji. Without
implicating them in my errors, and borrowing Synge's elegant tribute to the
Aran Islanders, I appreciate ''their kindness and friendship, for which I am more
grateful than it is easy to say''. To Shelby Fitzpatrick I am more grateful than it is
possible to say.

*June 1980*                                                                 Peter Fitzpatrick

For Shelby Flowers Ferris

# Contents

# 1 Underdevelopment

These initial chapters provide a sketch, so far as I am able, of the theory underlying the account that follows of the Papua New Guinea case—an account partly intended to reflect back supportively on the theory. It may help at the outset to present the main lines of this sketch and to show what academic niches it could fit into.

At its most general, the approach used here has been described by Gutkind and Wallerstein as "the model of 'political economy'" (1976, p. 7). The overall focus is historical. As with underdevelopment theory, capitalist penetration is seen as creating and shaping the social formations of the third world—those social formations usually described in terms of colonies, countries and nations (Frank, 1971a). However, the perspective here is more one internal to these social formations: "emphasis is given to how indigenous structures articulate with external influences" (Gutkind and Wallerstein, 1976, p. 10). This internal perspective has yet to be provided with much flesh in detailed analysis and research (Long, 1977, p. 92; Meillassaux, 1972, p. 97). The present work develops this perspective both theoretically and in describing the Papua New Guinea case. The necessary account taken of external influences has, then, to be brief. This adds a further difficulty to the already enormous ones involved in grappling with these influences. There is no shortage of general and formular accounts available ranging from classical theories of imperialism to a plethora of current debate (see for example, Banaji, 1977; Brenner, 1977; Frank, 1974; Owen and Sutcliffe, 1972). Perhaps evasively, a broad and not greatly theorized account is provided here. This may leave a gap but the 'line' I adopt is at one with Leys when he advocates that:

> . . . the *general* question about exploitation in the third world needs

to be dissolved in a series of more particular questions about the forms, degrees and effects of different kinds of exploitation in different national and international contexts, and the way these relate to forms, degrees and effects of domination and oppression and the struggles waged against both. (Leys, 1977, p. 102)

In this light, the theoretical perspective is sometimes refined and narrowed as we go along. In particular, the present work is based largely on the historical experience of those social formations created as colonies in the 'second imperialism' of the later nineteenth century. With them, capitalist penetration was usually not strong enough to transform the resident or traditional social formations.[1] Capitalism did have profoundly disruptive effects but it also made for the conservation of traditional modes of production largely because they served to subsidize capitalist production and to counter potentially disruptive class organization. From this, a central theme of the present work emerges: such conservation of the traditional gives a distinctive cast to many functions of law and state in the third world and to the forms taken by law and state—distinctive, that is, in comparison with the functions and forms found in the so-called first world. For example, law and state played a forceful and leading role in the establishment of capitalism in the first world when the economic determinants associated with the capitalist mode were not yet fully developed (see for example, Marx, 1974, Vol. I, Chapters 27 and 28). With the second imperialism, law and state played a broadly similar role in colonization. Since capitalist penetration was weak at the economic level, law and state had the function of integrating the overall colonial social formation. They had to tie the traditional mode of production and the capitalist mode together into an operative whole. Yet, and here is the distinctive element, they had to keep the two modes sufficiently apart to conserve the traditional. Even the weak presence of the capitalist mode would, without more, have had too solvent an effect on the traditional. So, the function here of law and state was more structurally enduring than with the establishment of capitalism in the first world. This function is oriented towards the conservation and continuing exploitation of the traditional mode whereas, in the context of the first world, the leading role of law and state was oriented more to the elimination of pre-capitalist modes. To take a particular if crucial aspect, the conservation of the traditional mode in the colonial situation involves, as we shall see, maintaining the tie between the producer and the means of production whereas Marx could remark of the establishment of capitalism in the first world that "the so-called primitive accumulation . . . is nothing else than the historical process of divorcing the producer from the means of production'' (Marx, 1974, Vol. I, p. 668). Initial summary of a complicated argument runs the risk of condensed obscurity and to say even this little has involved plodding over delicate theoretical constructs and fine formalisms that are treated in more detail and with more respect now.

As Worsley says with reassuring forcefulness, ''it is no ideological assertion but a simple generalization rooted in empirical observation, that the prime content of colonial political rule was economic exploitation'' (Worsley, 1967, p. 45). However, as Magdoff can add, this does not mean that ''unadulterated economic motives'' can be found ''for *each and every* act of political and military policy'' (Magdoff, 1969, p. 13). Nor is this to deny that the individual instigators and agents of colonial rule may have held to other purposes (national security, the civilizing mission, the conversion of the heathen). The present study starts with that colonization, known as the new imperialism, of the late nineteenth century when in this context ''there are good and sufficient reasons for clearly marking off a new period in the affairs of world capitalism'' (ibid., p. 27). The advent of this period sees the emergence of monopoly capitalism and the resulting and increased ''pressures from industrial and finance capital to obtain guaranteed privileged markets for goods and capital and [especially—P.F.] sources of raw materials against the threat to these from economic rivals'' (Barratt Brown, 1972, p. 58). Consequently, previous and limited forms of trading, treaty and consular penetration gave way to a more concerted and formal colonization in Asia, in the ''scramble for Africa'', and in a smaller scramble for Oceania. Resident social formations were disrupted in the forcing and the organizing of them to fit the economies of the metropolitan countries. The overall economy of a colony basically complemented the domestic metropolitan economy. Thus the colonial economy was only integrated externally and relied on the metropolitan economy for its maintenance or reproduction. In the result, the colonial economy provided too few internal linkages to stem the outflow of surplus value and it was usually too weak to sustain anything but the most fitful and limited growth.

The particular characteristics of colonial social formations differed with the varying nature of capitalist penetration and of the resident social formations. Penetration could exceptionally result in the marginalization of resident social formations so that once deprived of their land they were not a significant factor in the colonial economy. Somewhat at the other extreme there was a type that could be called a colony of administration where the concern is merely to "hold down" the territory and not directly to exploit resident social formations but rather to keep them intact and self-regulating. Apart from these two types, the resident social formations were exploited in different degrees and in different ways. The settler colony, although it involved the conservation of traditional modes of production for their subsidizing of the labour supply, usually entailed a comparatively intense and disruptive exploitation. Colonies of what can be called peasant formation, including, for example, the 'culture system' on Java and the indigenous peasant cash-crop production of the Gold Coast, were based in direct reliance on the conservation of the traditional mode of production. The varying nature of resident social formations also had its effect. In some colonies there were already elaborate, highly organized and highly stratified systems of economic exploitation and political control and often these were integrated functionally into the colonial social formation, one example being the so-called indirect rule of much British colonization. With other colonies, resident social formations were smaller and more informal and egalitarian in organization. Here colonial rule tended to be more direct and penetrating. This account is obviously not exhaustive and even these few broad types, as well as others, can interact in many combinations in different colonies.

One largely consistent aspect, if one varying in its intensity, is that of the conservation of the traditional mode of production. That 'Western' impact is supposed to have disintegrated resident social formations is "a commonly held notion" (Morkovitz, 1977, p. 77). The prognostic equivalent is supplied by modernization theory which has it that resident "economic systems are to be transformed and the remnants of backwardness wiped from the slate" (Finkle and Gable, 1966, p. 205). As for the direction of this transformation, "it is confidently assumed that the rest of the world will not only become like the United States but that it wishes to do so" (Lloyd, 1973, p. 69). Marx and Engels of the *Communist Manifesto*, in a similar if potentially more incisive vein, saw the bourgeoisie comprehensively creating "a world after its own image" (Marx and Engels, 1970, p. 39). Reality so far appears largely otherwise. As Kay has argued, capitalism's penetration of what is now called the third world was not economically strong enough to transform and shape resident social formations in its own image and likeness (Kay, 1975). The special aptness of this argument to those colonized in the second imperialism has already been suggested. As a slight excursus and to narrow the application of the argument further, in anticipation of its particular relevance to Papua New Guinea, it fits particularly those colonies created by Britain during the second imperialism. In that period, the international dominance of Great Britain was being increasingly challenged by the United States, Germany and France and by "the end of the century, both the United States and Germany surpassed Britain in industrial production" (Barratt Brown, 1972, p. 47). Hymer has summarized subsequent situations in a way that will prove helpful:

> It is well to remember that the 'New Imperialism' which began after 1870 in a spirit of Capitalism Triumphant, soon became seriously troubled and after 1914 was characterised by war, depression, breakdown of the international economic system, and war again, rather than Free Trade, Pax Brittanica and Material Improvement.
>
> A major, if not the major, reason was Great Britain's inability to cope with the byproducts of its own rapid accumulation of capital; *i.e.*, a class conscious labour force at home; a middle class in [some of—P.F.] the hinterland; and rival centres of capital on the Continent and in America. Britain's policy tended to be atavistic and defensive rather than progressive, more concerned with warding off new threats than creating new areas of expansion. (Hymer, 1972, p. 130)

It now remains to look within the colonial and post-colonial social formation and in so doing to provide a more extensively theorized account of the conservation of the traditional mode of production and of its operative combination with the capitalist mode. This conversation and combination are then related, firstly, to the contemporary involvement of capitalism in the third world and, secondly, to class formation in the third world.

In short, "the main tendency is not to dissolution of the non-capitalist modes of production but to their *conservation-dissolution*" (Bettelheim, 1972, p. 298). In contrast to transforming the traditional mode, capitalism has, for its own purposes, "imparted a certain *solidity*" to it, as Banaji has put it (1973, p. 395). As for mainstream academe, McSwain has noted that ". . . examples of persisting tradition abound in the literature on modernization in contemporary societies" (McSwain, 1977, p. xv). References on this score from the literature of modernization or development, of underdevelopment and of recent French Marxist anthropology could be multiplied to the point of banality. The general formulations so far leave many necessary questions unanswered about the conservation of the traditional mode of production and its combination, or 'articulation', as it is more usually called, with the capitalist mode. Before looking at these necessary questions it may help to provide a summary of the main functions served by this conservation and combination. These, and other, functions are also considered in more detail later.

For Meillassoux, "the agricultural self-sustaining communities" form "an organic component of capitalist production" in, basically, performing the "functions of social security" that capitalism avoids in the colonial situation (Meillassoux, 1972, p. 102). More particularly, for many workers, such as those on plantations, the traditional mode of production will provide a basis of support for their families as well as for themselves when they are returned to their traditional environment, or when they cannot find wage-work or when they are too sick or old to be able to work. Peasant production for the capitalist market will be subsidized through the support the peasant derives from subsistence production within the traditional mode (Meillassoux, 1972, p. 102). It is with these instances that some operative effect could possibly be given to Marx's prime "law of the tendency of the rate of profit to fall" in the capitalist mode of production (Marx, 1974, Vol. III, Part III). Such a law has a central part in several Marxist theories of imperialist expansion (Kemp, 1972). With the combination or 'articulation' of modes of production, this law could help further explain why capitalism sought out and used, yet conserved, these 'agricultural self-sustaining communities'. Since the communities subsidized the provision of labour, this presumably allowed the extraction of surplus value at a rate in excess of that obtainable in the domestic metropolitan context and so offset the tendency of the rate of profit to fall. As for other functions served by the conservation of the traditional mode, I also argue, and attempt to establish in the Papua New Guinea context, that this conservation serves the distinct function of maintaining ethnic division in the countering of class consolidations that would challenge the dominance of metropolitan capitalism. This function, as we shall see in the next chapter, is heightened in the weakness of the colonial state and in the weakness of many a post-colonial one as well.

Returning to the combination of the capitalist and traditional modes of production, there remain many disturbingly large questions to be confronted. If one talks of a combination of modes, what is holding the whole together? Perhaps one mode is dominant and provides this integrative element, but if the capitalist mode is on the scene, some would say that it tolerates no strange modes before it (Frank, 1971a; Hindess and Hirst, 1975). In such a case, the idea of combination seems out of the picture. However, if we can only talk of the capitalist mode, then in most social formations of the third world we have a capitalism that, for example, involves much production for use, much collective or communal control of property and much control by direct producers of the means of production. This is a puzzling kind of capitalism. Perhaps the puzzle can be resolved by finding a transitional or 'colonial' mode of production as Dupré and Rey have done and as Banaji once did (Dupré and Rey, 1973; Banaji, 1973, p. 395). Or there may be some other integrative key—something larger than or transcending modes of production—such as, perhaps, the idea of the social formation. If so, how do we theorize its transcendent position? In grappling with these questions, I will look critically at a recent and ambitious attempt to establish a position that could answer them: Banaji's account of "modes of production in a materialist conception of history" (Banaji, 1977). This provides a somewhat contrary basis for my perspective which, in summary, is that two modes can co-exist and combine with one occupying a dominant, integrative position. Further, for the period since the second imperialism the capitalist mode has obviously been dominant at the level of the world capitalist social formation. Since that period also, the capitalist mode has been making the running with third world social formations *qua* colonies, countries or nations. At the level of resident or traditional social formations it can be the case that the capitalist mode is not dominant.

In a penetrating analysis, Banaji has argued the position that one can speak only of a single mode of production (ibid.). He sets out to deliver us from a "chaos of simple abstractions" into something of a chaos of complex ones. For this deliverance the root of the problem seems to be what counts as a mode of production. The basic confusion in this area has arisen, in Banaji's view, because "in the neo-populist currents of 'third world political economy' " (ibid., p. 35) and elsewhere, people equate a mode of production with a form of labour process—a simple abstraction. Thus the capitalist mode is equated with the presence of wage-labour. It is only in such narrow focus that one mode can be seen as combining or 'articulating' with another. Distinguishing semantically the numerous instances where Marx defined a mode of production in terms of labour process, Banaji says that a mode of production is very much more but what precisely it is is never entirely clear. For Banaji, a mode of production is a broad, historical or epochal category. Pitched at this very general level, the capitalist mode can be dominant yet tolerate diverse or even seemingly contradictory forms within it. Thus the slave plantations of the West Indies are seen as capitalist, or as part of the wider capitalist mode of production, even though the form of labour was a slave form and not a capitalist form. Thus, again, peasant production for the market in the third world is not seen as a combination of the traditional and capitalist modes of production. Peasants are really disguised proletarians. The conditions under which they produce for the market are so straited by the capitalist mode, with its determination of prices and its imposition of conditions as to output and quality, that peasants are not selling 'their' crop but rather their labour power. As this last example serves to illustrate, the general issue is more than doctrinal. If the capitalist mode is exclusive and so dominates 'peasant' production that it is rendered not basically peasant but proletarian, then such a conclusion would have profound consequences for class action.

This summary doubtless does not do justice to Banaji's complex and valuable analysis. I would now like to use it as a provocative basis for elaborating on the problem in three ways. One involves the idea of transition; the second concerns the relevance of the idea of the social formation; and the last returns to the varying functions being served by the conservation of the traditional mode.

As for the idea of transition, a mode of production does not, of course, appear fully-formed, peremptorily displacing a preceding mode. A new mode (or its precursory forms) will often have a long, sometimes tentative, precarious or even reversible history in its drive towards dominance or exclusiveness during which it will, as Banaji recognizes, take "distorted and incomplete transitional forms" (ibid., p. 9). Given this, how can it be known that one mode has been definitively displaced by another? A simple, and not uncommon, answer is provided by Banaji: a mode has been displaced when it is no longer 'self-sufficient' or cannot maintain itself under its own 'laws of motion' but, rather, is dependent for 'its' maintenance on another mode of production (ibid., e.g., pp. 33 – 35). Thus, for example, a traditional 'mode' may become so reliant on inputs from the capitalist mode, such as wages remitted by plantation workers, that 'it' cannot exist independently of these inputs; so it then ceases to exist and all that remain are dependent forms of the previous mode. But what of the reverse situation—the dependence of the capitalist mode on the conservation of the traditional? For example, could it not be, complex as the question is, that if the subsidizing effect of conservation were removed, and no longer available, for instance, to counter the tendency of the rate of profit to fall, then the capitalist mode would find itself in a terminal crisis? This implicit objection can be somewhat outflanked by resorting to the idea of transition and saying, in Banaji's terms, that there are historical 'laws of motion' which show that one mode is, or is in the process of becoming, the enduringly dominant one and that the other has a purely provisional and declining existence. This may be so and it is good to postulate and ponder on these laws of motion, but as far as I know they have yet to be discovered. Perhaps, for example, and in woolly terms, in the long run the inherent restlessness and expansionary dynamic of capitalism will disintegrate resident social formations, and thoroughly displace traditional modes of production. However, this is to make huge predictive assumptions about the nature and development of world capitalism, and transitions and the long run can be very long (see for example, ibid., p. 12). In short, as Saul and Woods argue for Africa, the course of any transition here and its realization should be considered "most problematic, and, in any event [it] remains a very long-term proposition" (Saul and Woods, 1971, p. 107). What the present argument suggests, then, is that a mode of production may remain a mode even though it is dependent on another. Further, the argument suggests that in situations of the combination or, as it is usually put, articulation of two modes of production, what is involved is an interaction and interdependence of the two modes. It does not follow from this that, if there are two extant modes in operation, some concept 'bigger' than 'mode of production' is needed to encompass the combination of the modes. One mode, I will argue, can be dominant and integrative of the two modes.

These broad conclusions need much supporting refinement. Some can be provided by the idea of the social formation. The idea can be used to mark off different social wholes, some of which can yet be seen as parts of another, and more particularly, the capitalist mode of production *in toto* can be seen as the basis of a capitalist world social formation. Within this there are numerous social formations of the colony, country and nation variety. Within these, at least, within most countries of the third world, there are integral social formations of lineage, clan and various other descriptions which I have called here resident or traditional social formations. The question whether the capitalist or the traditional mode of production is dominant can receive different answers for different social formations. Take, as a basis for analysis, the classifications provided in the African context by Dupré and Rey (1973). The first period of contact between capitalism and what they call the lineage mode of production is the trade period in which the lineage or traditional mode is seen as dominant. Then comes a phase of transition, the colonial period, in which neither mode is seen as dominant but, rather, they are seen as integrated into a distinct mode of production which involves "using the economic basis characteristic of lineage society to establish the conditions of transition to capitalism" (ibid., p. 147). This transition is completed with 'neo-colonialism' when the capitalist mode is dominant and the traditional mode plays a varying and supplementary role. Now the adequacy of this account depends upon its implicitly not going beyond an internal view, that is, beyond a view internal to particular and partial social formations. So, viewed from within the resident or traditional social formation, the trade period is one in which the traditional or lineage mode is clearly dominant. Capitalism has only a very limited trade, treaty or consular presence. It appears from this perspective almost marginal. When such a social formation as the colony comes on the scene, it becomes possible to see, from within it, the two modes in some balanced combination and this makes, as they see it, for this new, transitional mode of production. Finally, the capitalist mode is dominant, but not exclusive, in its operation within the post-colonial social formation. Viewed from an outside perspective, from the total capitalist world social formation or from Banaji's epochal perspective, the picture becomes very different. From this perspective, even in the trade period, the capitalist mode of production could be seen as dominant; in the combination of the two modes, capitalism was the prime mover (Thomistic terms are perhaps getting close to appropriate) and with its greater overall power and expansionary dynamic it continued to make the running. Still from this external perspective, with colonialism, at least since the colonization of the second imperialism, one does not have an equal balance of the capitalist and traditional modes; the capitalist mode is by now clearly dominant. With the post-colonial period, the external and internal perspectives come closer together. Even so, from an internal perspective the domination of the capitalist mode will, as we shall soon see, vary greatly from one country to another. It can even be the case that if we look from within the resident or traditional social formation, the traditional mode will still be pervasively dominant.

Focusing now on the social formation *qua* colony or country, the question of the combination of modes of production needs to be refined further by looking at the various concrete functions the combination serves. With the colony of administration mentioned earlier, the easiest way of holding down the territory was to leave it as it was, so far as this was compatible with colonial political control. The qualification often involved the containing or breaking down of troublesome concentration of traditional power. When capitalist enterprise intervenes, there is a closer involvement with the traditional mode. The returns to a plantation worker, for example, were little more than enough for his sustenance whilst working on the plantation and for his and his family's tax. The traditional mode was conserved to support the worker when he was sent back or when he returned to his traditional environment, to support him when he could not get work or was ill or old, to support the worker's family and to nurture a new supply of labour. If the demand for labour for the capitalist mode grew to the extent that the level of labour needed for the conservation of the traditional mode was not maintained, then the traditional mode would start to break down and would no longer be so available to subsidize capitalist production. This issue, although still present, was not posed so starkly in those colonies where peasant production for the market was promoted but integrated with subsistence production at the level of the traditional mode. This "line of least resistance" (Wallerstein, 1976, p. 41) had a similar subsidizing effect, making possible low prices of goods exported to the metropolis. We will consider in the next chapter how the combination of the capitalist and traditional modes was effected, but it should be mentioned here that the traditional mode was not merely passive in the face of the capitalist mode. It was often the basis of fierce resistance, and, more pertinently here, it was rarely inflexible and conservative. It adapted in the cause of its own survival to the pressures of capitalist production and was able in this way to sustain heavy demands on it for labour (Long, 1977, p. 94; Salisbury, 1962). However, there were limits and if the contrary forces of capitalist penetration became sufficiently intense, the traditional mode tended to decline. In pursuing this point as well as the variety of situations served by the conservation of the traditional, we have briefly to complete the general historical picture which so far has gone little beyond the early stage of the second imperialism.

As Kay has noted of the period between the two world wars:

> [The] . . . success of capital, its ability not only to ride the crisis of the inter-war period, but use it as a basis for a far-sweeping recomposition, should not blind us to its intensity, or even less to its pervasiveness. For the crisis of the inter-war period overwhelmed the whole capitalist world to an unprecedented degree. It was a genuinely international crisis engulfing both developed and underdeveloped countries alike, illustrating more vividly than any other single event, the extent to which capital had unified the world economy by the beginning of the twentieth century. (Kay, 1975, p. 176)

This inter-war depression, after what had been considerably more favourable terms of trade for most colonies, created considerable unrest. Decreased demand for agricultural products served to encourage urban migration and the emergence of an urban proletariat and the usually weak structures of colonial control were strained. The withdrawal of many European capitalists from colonial trade and agriculture created some space as it were for a national bourgeoisie to emerge. Whether or not with a view to ultimate 'independence', most colonial powers attempted to channel these changes by promoting new structures most comprehensively described as 'neo-colonial'. The trend began to make most colonial state bureaucracies more indigenous. Hopefully compliant bourgeois class formations were promoted and generally policy and some resources were committed to economic and political 'development' (Foster-Carter, 1974, p. 77).

This so-called development fitted in with, and served as justification for, the huge increase in capitalist investment in the third world in the period following the second world war. This involved some investment in secondary industry but there was considerably more in natural resource extraction and export agriculture, responding to the great increase in demand in these areas from the first world. The international enterprise or, as it is usually called (but not often accurately), the multinational enterprise, supported by metropolitan states and new international agencies such as the World Bank, replaces trade as the dominant way of integrating the third world into the capitalist world social formation. This change is associated with the growth in the scale and complexity of capitalist production, the intensification of monopoly and the consequent need for planning and for 'stability' (Murray, 1972). These factors made for a tighter integration of the third world into the capitalist world social formation. At the same time these factors made for the further development of class forces within colonies, and the breaking down of the 'undifferentiated mass' of the colonized (Amin, 1974, p. 386). Class demands for liberation and independence increased, these usually taking nationalist and populist forms. The effectiveness of these demands was added to by the new rivalry from 'socialist' countries and the perceived possibility of communist inspired revolution (Magdoff, 1969, pp. 53–54). Bitter and enduring struggles for liberation did result but the predominant response of a still weakly embedded capitalism was to co-opt potentially compliant class elements —the makings of a resident 'ruling class'.

The thesis of neo-colonialism and some theories of underdevelopment consider that third world countries are now typically independent in political form only and that effective structures of economic dependency and external domination persist with the neo-colony being, basically, sub-ordinated to the metropolitan economies. National bourgeois elements are labelled comprador or lumpen in their abject service of the metropolitan bourgeoisie. Such a picture fails to catch the considerable variety that now characterizes third world countries. Generalization here is particularly hazardous, being not only necessarily and immensely wide but contemporary as well. It is, however, important here to make an attempt. As with colonies, summary discussion can only be in terms of very general types of social formations and economies with actual ones sometimes involving a mixing of these types.

Countries where export agriculture remains dominant appear to fit the models of neo-colonialism and underdevelopment most closely. Colonial structures are basically undisturbed. The economy remains comprehensively controlled by the metropolitan bourgeoisie, which is not restricted in integrating it into their wider enterprise. In this the national bourgeoisie and the post-colonial state play a facilitative and subordinate role, incapable of changing the very exploitative structure on which they rely. Countries dominated by natural resource extraction are usually in a broadly similar position. As Rollins has shown, mining companies are now capital intensive in their operations and employ few people (Rollins, 1970). The great bulk of their inputs are imported, they generate few linkages internal to the third world country and as its development would increase their costs, they "have . . . a vested interest in the continued backwardness of the economy in which their production operations are carried out" (ibid., p. 197). Bairoch has also shown that for the third world "the great extension of mining, so far from encouraging the development of manufacturing industry, has actually hindered it" (Bairoch, 1975, pp. 57 et seq.). With the increasing resort to capital-intensive production in these economies, there is less significance in conserving the traditional mode to subsidize the provision of labour. It continues to be conserved none the less, partly because an element of subsidy remains, partly because it is still there and there is no dynamic immediately undermining it, and partly because, in terms of later argument, its conservation functions in class containment. However for economies of resource extraction the contemporary situation is becoming more complex with some countries being able apparently to use large revenues for some internal accumulation and development.

Probably the most significant exceptions are those social formations which could be called countries of longer industrialization, such as Brazil, Mexico and India. These were usually also social formations of longer colonization and tend to fall outside the immediate concern here with the offspring of the second imperialism. In these countries industrialization has by now become comparatively extensive, growth rates are considerable and internal class formations are quite highly developed. This is not to say that such growth is unequivocally or predominantly beneficial. It can entail the increasing impoverishment of much of the population. Accelerating class conflict often leads to draconic political repression. Moreover, although the state and the national bourgeoisie do assume some significant independence of the metropolitan bourgeoisie, they still operate in close conjunction with this element of the bourgeoisie which continues to provide the bulk of the capital, technology and key management. There is increasing resort to 'nationalization', 'fade-out' requirements, turnkey agreements and joint-ventures (see for example, Evans, 1977). Even where the stake of the metropolitan bourgeoisie is being restricted in terms of ownership, such bourgeoisie derives compensatory returns from management contracts, the licensing of know-how and in other ways. These returns will often be inflated through transfer pricing mechanisms (Vaitsos, 1974). As well, the development of internal class conflicts and the resulting instabilities have often enabled the metropolitan bourgeoisie to manipulate the situation and contain national forces that sought to dominate it (Petras, 1975).

In these countries the more intense penetration of capitalism tends to undermine or marginalize the traditional mode. With most other social formations of the third world, such as those dominated by export agriculture or by natural resource extraction, the conservation of the traditional tends to persist. The basic structure of these social formations appears to remain immune even to the infusions of capitalist investment that have increased so much recently. (The growing interest of large-scale capitalist 'agribusiness' in the third world could lead to more direct onslaughts on the traditional mode (see for example, Feder, 1977).) The persistence of this conservation now assumes more complex and contradictory dimensions. The emergence of internal class forces and ensuing political independence tend to rule out the crudity of many colonial controls aimed at conserving the traditional mode. To a large extent this conservation is now more structurally set and so can rely less on direct regulation. For example the worker does not have to be forced so much to labour and then be compulsorily reintegrated into the traditional mode since he and his family are now more dependent on wages and "through low wages and precarious employment the labourer is periodically expelled from the capitalist sector and sent back to the rural areas" (Meillassoux, 1973, p. 89). Aspects of the traditional mode, as we shall see shortly, come to take root and to sustain people within the urban areas (Evers, 1977). The vagaries of world prices and general economic instability underline for the peasant the necessity of maintaining subsistence production. To a significant degree colonial controls aimed at conservation are retained and variants introduced—these are matters considered in the next chapter. Generally, I have already referred to McSwain's remark about "examples of persisting tradition which abound in the literature on modernization in contemporary societies" of the third world (McSwain, 1977, p. xv). The "alternation model" originated by Gluckman sees the African as supposedly 'detribalised' when living in town but as becoming retribalized on returning to the rural area (Epstein, 1967, p. 276). As well, there is much work on 'circular migration' between urban and rural areas, on the provisional nature of 'urban commitment' and on 'peasants in cities' (see for example, Mangin, ed., 1970). The (profoundly sensible) 'conservatism' and 'backwardness' of the peasant in the face of efforts at 'development' and 'modernization' are recurrent themes in the sociology of development (Long, 1977, pp. 41 – 70). One illuminating analysis of the literature shows that, far from being wiped off the slate as the theorists of modernization would have them, peasants persist and multiply and will continue to do so in the foreseeable future (Mortimer, 1975).

The continuing conservation of the traditional mode takes place side by side with emerging internal class formations which are, in many ways, inimical to this conservation. The situation is further complicated in that aspects of resident social formations prove conducive to the emergence of some inimical class elements. For example, with political independence on the horizon the colonist promoted hopefully compliant bourgeois class elements by building on hierarchies and inequalities within resident social formations. Those in dominant positions within these formations had opportunity thrust upon them, becoming 'enterpreneurs' and 'businessmen'. Their sons monopolized educational opportunities and 'leadership training' and, hence, monopolized advancement in the state system. This process "unleashed hitherto contained antagonisms" within resident social formations, straining mechanisms that had traditionally linked wealth with a "counterpart in social responsibilities" (Balandier, 1965, pp. 388 – 389). However, the outcome is not necessarily the creation of a pure bourgeoisie. Balandier's account of an African group can be generalized:

> The existence of behaviour referring to two essentially different economies appears quite clearly in the two strategies between which an individual who has saved some capital must choose. He can make true "economic investments", and seek profit and personal advantage; but this entrepreneurial mentality cuts him off from his original social milieu. Therefore these cases remain rare, and are found almost only in urban centers and their vicinity. He can, on the contrary, choose to make "sociological investments"; in this case, he uses new economic conditions to achieve or to reinforce a traditional type of prominence. The size of his "clientele" and the extension of his generosity will reveal his degree of success; his profit will be expressed in prestige and authority. This second option is the more common: the economic "game" is still only a method to achieve goals determined by the old social and cultural system. (Balandier, 1965, pp. 392 – 393)

This outcome is reflected in the widespread existence of brokerage and patronage roles. The broker or patron mediates between resident social formations and the outside world and such formations are maintained as the basis of the broker's or patron's economic and political power (see for example, Hale, 1978, pp. 272 – 273). In this way the conservation of the traditional mode serves to contain elements of a national bourgeoisie, to contain them especially in the potentially competitive aspects of their relation with the metropolitan bourgeoisie. This aspect of class containment can be extended to include other class elements, as we shall see shortly. For example, conservation of the traditional mode and circular migration makes the class organization of a proletariat extremely difficult.

With the increase in urbanization, conservation of the traditional mode comes to play another distinctive role. Urban residence is no longer so subject to the colonial system of controls that limited periods of residence and effected periodic repatriation to rural areas. Such a system is incompatible with the need for more skilled labour that comes with industrialization, albeit usually very limited, and with the growth of an indiginous public bureaucracy and certain sectors of the economy. Evers has argued that, just as production for the capitalist mode is subsidized by the traditional mode operating in the rural areas, a "similar process takes place in the urban economy and that similar principles apply here as well as in the rural sector'' (Evers, 1977, p. 4). He identifies a 'subsistence sector' in this urban economy in household food processing, the maintenance and running of the home and, sometimes, in the provision of services. It could be added that the production of food and housing are often provided for in an urban 'subsistence sector'. Capitalism, he finds, is also subsidized in utilizing ''a large 'proto-proletariat' that provides cheap services and food (typically hawkers)'' (ibid., p. 7). This ''proto-proletariat'', it could be further added, tends to operate within a pre-capitalist mode that can be seen as akin to or a part of this 'subsistence sector'. These matters are considered further when looking at classes. The argument is capable of much refinement and contention but it is broadly supported by work on what McGee calls the 'ruralization' of the third world city (1971, p. 58). At least it could be concluded that processes operate in urban areas in subsidizing the capitalist mode that have affinities to and links with the traditional mode and that are often a carry-over of this mode to the urban areas. It is in this perspective that one can also interpret the widespread reliance in urban areas on ethnically based associations of mutual aid which provide some security for people against sickness and unemployment (Meillassoux, 1972, p. 103). Often exchanges of savings and food will take place between a worker and members of his traditional group in the rural area. In this way and through circular migration the traditional mode operates over considerable separations in space and time.

Finally, the contemporary situation suggests a particular need to conserve the traditional mode for the purpose of social control. Since capitalist penetration has not comprehensively transformed the social formations of the third world, the multinational enterprise, Hymer argues, has a problem to ''keep the excluded two-thirds of the population under control'' (Hymer, 1972, p. 132). The conservative economist H.G. Johnson has attributed something like a line of least resistance to the objectives of the multinational enterprise in the third world, which objectives:

> . . . are not to transform the economy by exploiting its potentialities—especially its human potentialities—for development, but to exploit the existing situation to its own profit by utilization of the knowledge it already possesses at minimum cost of adaptation and adjustment to itself. (As quoted in Barnet and Müller, 1974, pp. 159 – 160)

The conservation of the traditional mode could well fit these objectives. This perspectives may throw light on an ostensibly new approach of influential institutions concerned with 'development' policy, such as the World Bank. This approach involves putting less emphasis on economic growth and more on 'redistribution' and rural development including popular access to credit and extension services and, sometimes, 'self-reliance' in subsistence food production (see for example, McNamara, 1973; ILO, 1972; cf. Feder, 1977). This approach also looks like a line of least resistance, promoting a dispersed peasantry integrated into the tradi-tional mode instead of the former emphasis on promoting an accumulating and socially disruptive 'progressive farmer'.

The conservation of the traditional mode of production is basic to class formation in the third world. It helps explain much of the oft-noted 'incompleteness' of class formation, of the 'inchoate' and 'emerging' nature of classes (for use of such terminology, see for example, Gutkind and Wallerstein, 1976, p. 13; Mamdani, 1976, p. 10). This incomplete-ness prompts some to assert that class is of relatively minor significance in the third world and that racial and ethnic divisions are more crucial (for example, Kuper, 1974, pp. 203 – 234; Klinghoffer, 1974). In broadly similar vein, third world politicians, especially in populist appeals to national unity, often assert that there are no classes or 'opposed classes' in their country (Mair, 1967, p. 126). Even those sympathetic to the use of class analysis seem to find it difficult to apply class categories without the use of more or less exotic adjectives such as 'bureaucratic' or 'organ-izational' bourgeoisie, 'big' peasantry and 'lumpen' proletariat (see for example, Markovitz, 1977; Shivji, 1976). Admittedly, there are special problems with class analysis in the third world context but these are prob-lems of the complexity of the context, not of the relevance of class. In par-ticular, racial and ethnic decisions are seen in the present work as sub-ordinate to class division. It is perverse to assert the dominance of race and ethnicity when the purpose of the maintenance of these divisions is to contain class formation.

Problems in contemporary class analysis are not, of course, confined to the third world. Voluminous debates have taken place on, for example, where, in class terms, to locate the so-called new middle class or middle stratum—the salariat of wage earning executives, professionals and white collar workers whose affinities to the proletarian mould are widely variable. With the celebrated divorce between ownership and control of corporate property, strains are placed on classic formular accounts of class in terms of ownership of the means of production. The emergence of the welfare, managerialist, corporatist etc. state shows the salariat *qua* state operatives making regulating and controlling decisions about property in general, that often override the power associated with private ownership. These debates have their third world twists and counterparts. Senior state operatives have such an apparent ascendancy in many social formations of the third world as to qualify, in some views, as a bureaucratic bourgeoisie, or they are seen vaguely as a 'petty bourgeoisie'. They do, however, seem proletarian in that they are wage earners. Some members of this class element do set up economic enterprises as well but this is far from invariable. They do have some regulative control over property and sometimes run state economic enterprises. They have some control over the allocation of surplus especially in the dispensing of the state's economic favours. These aspects are significant, but do they amount to such a strong controlling relation to the means of production as to make these state operatives members of a bourgeoisie? Probably the aspect that most impels people to apply the label of bourgeoisie here is the huge volume of surplus drawn off by this class element in most social formations of the third world. The surplus comes in as state revenue, including taxes paid by peasants and workers, and goes out in large degree as high wages paid to members of this class element. Yet their employment is not property and, in all, they do not appear to have that structural security of purchase on production that characterizes the classic, owning bourgeoisie. Indeed, to contain this class element completely within a bourgeois mould obscures one of the most significant facts about them and about political life in third world social formations—the fact that this class element has no strong economic base. There are, as we will see shortly, other class elements which raise difficulties of categorization. For example, the issue of whether a peasant is a peasant or a disguised proletarian has already been raise.

Something of a summary, if controversial, resolution to such problems can be got from Wright's notion of contradictory class location (Wright, 1976, 1978, Chapter 2). He argues "that not all positions in the social structure can be seen as firmly rooted in a single class; some positions occupy objectively contradictory locations between classes" (Wright, 1976, p. 4). He relates these positions in the social structure to several definitional criteria of class. Some of these positions, such as 'managers' and 'semi-autonomous employees', are then seen as occupying locations that are contradictory as between the proletariat, the bourgeoisie and the petty bourgeoisie. More particularly, the definitional criteria cover ideological and political aspects as well as the economic, with the last being emphasized and seen as ultimately effective (ibid., p. 28). The economic is refined to take account of three processes of control: "control over the physical means of production; control over labour power; control over investments and resource allocation" (ibid., p. 30). It is in terms of these three processes that "the central class forces of capitalist society—the bourgeoisie and the proletariat—can be seen as representing polar class positions" (ibid., p. 39). It is in this same perspective that "certain positions can be thought of as occupying a contradictory location around the boundary of the proletariat; others as occupying a contradictory location around the boundary of the bourgeoisie" (ibid., p. 32). This argument is applied in a thorough way to various such positions commonly found in the first world. Presumably because, with these positions, economic determinants can be inconsistent, "it is at the political and ideological levels, [that] class struggle pushes contradictory locations closer to or further from the working class" and "the more a position coincides with the basic class division of bourgeoisie and proletariat the less weight political and ideological forces have in determining class position" (ibid., pp. 41 and 40).

This rather bald summary hardly does justice to Wright's incisive analysis and acute supporting observation but I hope its richness and aptness will become more apparent as we proceed. One particularly fitting aspect of the analysis should be mentioned at the outset and that is its ability to comprehend the situation where two modes of production are operating. The point is that the contradictory location need not only be contradictory between class positions within a mode of production, it can be contradictory also as between positions in different modes. Hence third world peasants may be disguised proletarians in the context of the capitalist mode of production but they will usually retain a peasant-type basis within the traditional mode.

I will now apply this analysis in more detail describing different class elements within social formations of the third world. Because there is a multiplicity of terms applied to these class elements I will emphasize the particular terms I intend to use as they come up. Dealing first with the internal or *national bourgeoisie*, it is usually seen in three groups—the commercial or economic or *urban bourgeoisie* for one, the kulak class or *big peasantry* or *rural bourgeoisie* for another, and, finally, the petty or organizational or *bureaucratic bourgeoisie*. I will be indicating shortly that the big peasantry and bureaucratic bourgeoisie cannot be placed unequivocally in the bourgeois mould. Leaving them there for the time being, the national bourgeoisie as a whole typically occupies a weak and subordinate economic position with the metropolitan bourgeoisie, that "great absent member" (Amin, 1974, p. 393), remaining dominant. Given the comparative advantage of metropolitan-style factors of production there remain few areas in which the national bourgeoisie can base itself economically (Arrighi, 1970, p. 242). Even these areas tend to be interstitial or supplementary in an economy oriented to metropolitan needs. Given this, it is usually difficult to find any economic activity of the national bourgeoisie that does not mark it as dependent and comprador in character. There are exceptions to this in the more assertive stance of the bureaucratic bourgeoisie in some countries. This assertiveness, based in the operation of state enterprises and the extraction of state revenue, often places the bureaucratic bourgeoisie in competition not only with the metropolitan bourgeoisie but with other elements of the national bourgeoisie. However, there usually remains an underlying co-operation among these various elements of the bourgeoisie. Any restiveness here on the part of the urban and rural bourgeoisie can be stilled in their frequent reliance on the state for their own promotion and maintenance. One area in which the national bourgeoisie has developed considerably is in the production and, to a limited extent, processing of export crops. In this the rural bourgeoisie and big peasantry often emerge in an ambiguous or contradictory relation to the traditional mode of production, relying on an advantaged position within that mode for capital accumulation and for the supply of labour, but being dogged by distributive demands of the less advantaged—demands that result from the very reliance on the traditional mode. The argument to "let the kulaks run" (Arrighi and Saul, 1973, p. 22), and hence break down these inhibitions, is not always a practicable one where the overall and conflicting emphasis is on the conservation of the traditional mode, mainly in the interests of the metropolitan bourgeoisie. Also, conditions making for increasing agricultural intensity within the traditional mode (growing density of population, soil fertility, crop suitability and limiting technologies) often constrain the kulaks' run. The result is that the bourgeoisie in the rural areas has often not fully or uniformly emerged but is bound in a continuing relationship with the traditional mode. Such a relation is reflected in the structures of patronage and brokerage mentioned earlier.

The position of the proletariat has also to be related to the dominance of the 'great absent member' and the low level of industrialization in the third world, although, as I mentioned earlier, the picture is changing in some social formations. Even the limited industrialization as well as the presence of enterprises of natural resource extraction provide very little employment because of their capital-intensive nature (Arrighi, 1970, p. 252; cf. Barratt Brown, 1974, pp. 264 – 272). The proletariat's class impact can be further diminished in its relation to the traditional mode. Because of economic instability, intense competition for jobs, seasonal variations in the supply of jobs, and the continuing commitment of many workers to the traditional mode, the worker periodically returns to his traditional area. In this situation the class organization of the proletariat is stunted because of enormous difficulty. This analysis applies particularly to the unskilled and semi-skilled workforce. The skilled workforce is more stable and urban-oriented. Too much has been invested in the development of their skills to allow their return to rural areas with the loss of these skills to capitalist production. This skilled element therefore has comparatively high incomes and superior urban living conditions. Some have even argued that this element is a labour aristocracy, its interests being more with the ongoing order than with other proletarians and exploited class elements. On the other hand, it has been suggested that the income gap between these workers and others is not so great, especially when account is taken of the costs of living in an urban context and of the meeting of continuing obligations to family and kin (Cohen and Michael, 1973, p. 36; Jeffries, 1975). This does not succeed, however, in depriving the labour aristocracy argument of all validity.

To return to the bureaucratic bourgeoisie, its members can now be seen in a contradictory location between the proletarian and bourgeois poles. A part of this 'particular' bourgeoisie would comprise the national executives of metropolitan enterprises—a part that extends into the skilled reaches of the proletariat. These executives have little or no independent power. Their advance within the metropolitan enterprise never goes beyond the national sphere. In terms of economic criteria their class position is close to the proletarian pole although ideologically and politically they will tend towards the bourgeois. The position of senior state operatives is more complex and more significant. I will use the term bureaucratic bourgeoisie to apply only to them in future. It is something of a truism—and one developed in the next chapter—that the economic power of the national bourgeoisie tends to flow from political power rather than *vice versa*. This is somewhat overdrawn but it serves to bring out several dimensions of the bureaucratic bourgeoisie's class position. First, the bureaucratic bourgeoisie is sometimes directly involved in the control of the means of production through governmental regulation, the running of state economic enterprises and involvement in governmental joint ventures with the metropolitan bourgeoisie. Second, the bureaucratic bourgeosie has charge of the allocation of state resources which often play a significant part in the promotion of other elements of the national bourgeoisie. Third, much of the public revenue, a revenue derived in varying parts from the peasantry and the proletariat as well as from the bourgeoisie, is used to pay the comparatively high wages of the bureaucratic bourgeoisie; as a proportion of public revenue these wages are, in some social formations, massive (see for example, Markovitz, 1977, p. 208). Fourth, these wages and their advantaged position within the state system are sometimes used by members of the bureaucratic bourgeoisie to set up their own enterprises and so to become part-time members of the urban or rural bourgeoisie (see for example, Amin, 1974, p. 372; Mamdani, 1976, p. 10). These enterprises may be set up in co-operation with members of the bureaucratic bourgeois' traditional group, thus maintaining links with the traditional mode, and so increasing the complexity of the contradictory location by extending it over two modes of production. In the same vein, the members of the bureaucratic bourgeoisie may be part of the patronage and brokerage links to the traditional mode, which links operate in the allocation of state resources (see for example, Markovitz, 1977, pp. 315 – 316). The situation is further complicated in Markovitz's general comment on the African situation:

> To draw sharp distinctions among the administrative bourgeoisie, the politicians, and the businessmen can be misleading because power and class are not necessarily matters of individuals, but of families. The same men can play many roles and take part in politics, administration, and commerce. Their brothers, cousins, fathers and sons can do the same. The result is a web of relations that brings the holders of power into overlapping and sustained contact. (Markovitz, 1977, p. 210)

All this makes the class position of the bureaucratic bourgeoisie a matter of complexity and one difficult to resolve confidently and generally in its effect on class action. To many observers, this class element is the dominant exploiting one internal to social formations of the third world. As state operatives, and like their first world counterparts (Wright, 1976, p. 25), the bureaucratic bourgeoisie shows a strong affinity to the bourgeois in the exercise of political and ideological domination. In this it can be seen as serving in particular the interests of the metropolitan bourgeoisie. However, in many instances its concern to extract state revenue from the enterprises of the metropolitan bourgeoisie, has made it more assertive in its relation with this 'great absent number', than other elements of the national bourgeoisie (see for example, Evans, 1977). This assertiveness is in its own interest but it may also be a response to growing working-class pressure together with the bureaucratic bourgeoisie's partial location in the proletarian mould. It should also be remembered that in the struggles to oust colonial rule and in peasant revolutions, this class element has often played a leading role, which can probably be related in part to the proletarian aspect of its location and to some continuing links with the peasantry.

There remains two class elements which overlap and which occupy a position that straddles the capitalist mode of production and the traditional or other pre-capitalist modes. One of these is the *peasantry* and the other an urban-based class element of *petty commodity producers*. 'Peasantry' as a class category is a disputed and difficult one (Foster-Carter, 1974, pp. 89 – 90). The peasantry is usually defined in terms of some exploitative relation to an overlord or the state (which can here include the bureaucratic bourgeoisie) or to the market or to any combination of these. In terms of this element, the peasantry produces surplus for others. A peasant also has significant independent control of the means of production. The basic production unit is usually the household but this unit tends to be maintained in the context of a wider peasant community. With much of the third world, the peasantry can be further delineated as having an operative commitment to both the capitalist mode of production and the traditional mode. Production for use or subsistence production takes place in the traditional mode and production for the market is realised in the capitalist. One who produces wholly within the traditional mode is not a peasant, although the term is so extended by some. Nor is one who operates wholly within the capitalist mode a peasant, although the term 'big peasant' is sometimes used by people to include certain members of the rural bourgeoisie. The term 'big peasant' is more generally used to describe something like a stratum of comparatively wealthy peasants. As a class category the big peasantry can be seen as having a contradictory location within the bourgeoisie: although having a significant operative commitment to the traditional mode, the big peasant will often hold property within the capitalist mode and employ labour on a proletarian basis. Also, as we have seen already, some view peasant production as so bounded by externally imposed conditions that the peasant is considered a proletarian selling his or her labour power rather than an independent producer (Banaji, 1977, pp. 34 – 35). From the perspective of the traditional social formation, however, the peasant's reliance on production for the market will vary from the great to the small and supplemental. Through seasonal wage-labour and through circular migration to and from urban areas, the peasant will often become a proletarian *pro tem*.

All of which, again, makes the generalization of a class position difficult. In terms of class action, classical Marxism is at one with the theorists of modernization in viewing the peasantry as a reactionary, politically apathetic and declining class element (see Marx and Engels, 1970, pp. 623 – 626; Mortimer, 1975), but the peasantry persists and effects twentieth century revolutions. In such optimistic vein, some acute observers see the possibility of a 'worker – peasant alliance' (for example, Shivji, 1976, pp. 116 – 120). Wolf finds a promise of revolutionary activity in "the development of an industrial workforce still closely geared to life in the villages" (Wolf, 1970, p. 292).

The class element of urban-based petty commodity producers is perhaps the most awkward, the difficulty and range of class locations being reflected in the profusion of titles it attracts such as petty bourgeoisie, lumpen proletariat and urban peasantry. Petty commodity producers are self-employed artisans and traders operating on a small scale who have control of their often scant means of production. They rely on their family and wider kin in setting up their enterprises, as well as for labour and, often, for custom. They largely operate within that "urban subsistence sector" identified by Evers and described earlier (Evers, 1977). Within this broad category there is a considerable range covering, for example, the classic petty bourgeois hovering hopefully on the fringe of the bourgeoisie, the 'disguised' proletarian as an out-worker for capitalist enterprise, the back-yard manufacturer and food grower, and the street and market trader. Through the provision of cheap necessities for the workforce, through out-work and in subcontracting, petty commodity producers function in support of the capitalist mode. They do so less directly in providing and maintaining a reserve army of the urban unemployed and in the absorbing or involving of otherwise dissident elements (McGee, 1971, p. 88; Mkanda-wire, 1977, pp. 34 – 35). On the other hand, petty commodity producers can be too efficient as competitors in areas occupied by bourgeois enterprise and so efforts are often made to suppress them through state action.

Although Marx saw petty commodity producers declining with the advance of capitalism (see Scott, 1979), their number in the third world city seems very much on the increase. With population growth and the accompanying decline of the rural option, more such 'urban peasants' are remaining in the urban area and capitalist production has proved incapable of absorbing many of them as wage labourers. Their class position (and its implications for class action) is, then, an issue of growing importance. Gerry and Birkbeck argue aptly and incisively for a refined analysis that would take account of the variety of class positions in which petty commodity producers stand (Gerry and Birkbeck, n.d.). As for general assessments, some have discerned a revolutionary potential in petty commodity producers (see Foster-Carter, 1974, p. 89). Most observers, however, are thoroughly sceptical, considering the petty commodity producer to be at best uncertain and unreliable in this (see for example, Cohen and Michael, 1973). Given the relations that petty commodity producers have to the capitalist mode of production, this scepticism can be seen as having some basis, but these relations are widely varying and often close to the proletarian and peasant moulds. With the growing repression of the proletariat in many third world countries, there may well be scope for an alliance here comparable to that foreseen between proletarians and peasants.

Class analysis, then, does not make for a simple theoretical structure to carry over into the analysis of law and state in the next chapter. The defining reality is too involved for this. However, despite a complex of contradictory locations I would suggest that the main lines of class analysis can be presented in terms of a bourgeoisie, a proletariat, a peasantry and a class element of urban based petty commodity producers. The bourgeoisie can be divided in some ways into a metropolitan and a national bourgeoisie. Less distinctly, the latter can be seen as an urban bourgeoisie and a rural bourgeoisie with the big peasantry attendent as something of an aspirant bourgeois but as occupying a position that straddles the bourgeoisie and the peasantry. The unsatisfactorily titled bureaucratic bourgeoisie must be seen as strongly linked to the bourgeoisie but with some significant location within the proletariat. The main complicating contradiction to be carried over into the analysis in the next chapter is that capitalist penetration brings with it forces that are corrosive of the traditional mode of production, including the class formations typical of capitalism. Yet the traditional mode is also conserved in the cause of capitalism and this conservation serves to stunt and contain these class formations. This results in various compromised and combined forms of ideology, law and state action which are now considered.

## Notes

1. 'Traditional' may connote something static. As later analysis will show, I do not intend this here or in using the term throughout this work.

# 2 Law and State in The Third World

I try here, first, to provide a theory of law and state. This is then related to the concerns of the first chapter in an account of law and state in the third world. Except where it is explicitly extended, the theory applies only to law and state in the mode of production dominant at the level of the colonial or national social formation—the capitalist mode of production.

Here, and in the rest of the book, the focal concern is with what can formally be marked off as 'law'. Law is seen as a type of state action, distinctive in certain operational ways, but sharing its functions with other types of state action. This sharing of functions is signified here in the term 'law and state'. In the following chapters dealing with the Papua New Guinea case, the term 'law and state' signifies, as well, a more central part for state action generally. In dealing with this concrete context, I found it usually impossible to give even the most superficial descriptive content to laws without seeing them as integral parts of various sets of state action. So, the applied chapters, while giving most space to law, approach it through a consideration of wider state action.

Law and state are seen as having two broad functions—one being described as the economic and the other as the political. To consider the economic function first, very generally it is a service function. Law and state, effectively if often indirectly, give normative form and coercible content to relations of production. They thus help secure the immediate conditions necessary for production. Here, law and state are ''deeply imbricated within the very basis of productive relations'' (Thompson, 1977, p. 261). This is not to say that law and state in this economic function (much less in the political) merely reflect economy or are merely subordinate to it. Law is also a product of the specific social formation. Within a social formation the effect of different economic forces will not be unidirectional. The state performs essential tasks of adjustment and integration. This will be especially the case where social formations are, as it is said, in transition or in transformation and there are considerable conflicts of economic forces. In such a situation the part of law and state is particularly influential (Anderson, 1974, p. 403). In particular, law and state can in this situation provide a framework that is 'in advance' of or fits one of competing economic forces and helps secure conditions favourable to its dominance. Hence the 'capitalist' absolutist state and "juridical relations of private property" had a part in effecting the transition from feudalism to capitalism (Poulantzas, 1973, pp. 157 – 167).

For purposes of the present work, this aspect of law and state as being in advance of economic forces can be refined by Pashukanis' theory of law (Pashukanis, 1978). He builds creatively on Marx's idea of the commodity to erect what can be called an exchange theory of law:

> Marx reveals that the fundamental condition of existence of the legal form is rooted in the very economic organization of society. In other words, the existence of the legal form is contingent upon the integration of the different products of labour according to the principle of economic exchange. In so doing, he exposes the deep interconnection between the legal form and the commodity form. (ibid., p. 63)

This leads Pashukanis to put basic emphasis on the idea of the legal subject: "it is in the exchange transaction in particular that the subject figures for the first time in all the fullness of its definitions" (ibid., p. 117). Thus "the contract is a concept central to law" (ibid., p. 121). (The following is a gloss on Pashukanis via Neumann (1957, Chapter 2) but it is supportable in Pashukanis' general theory.) With contract the (free and equal) legal subjects voluntarily agree on the terms of exchange. Law and state have no concern with the substantive fairness of exchange. They will enforce contracts and they will provide a framework for the exchangers or legal subjects to operate within. Legal rules making up this framework are general in content, that is, they are not tailored to specific or actual instances. These rules are stable and predictable to the effect that a legal subject can orient his or her conduct around them. Contracts and the rules are upheld by the state through impartial courts which apply existent and limited principles and standards. Law, in short, is not concerned to pre-define or to regulate comprehensively the position of the individual but, rather, to provide a generalized frame in which individuals are free to find themselves and to create relations with each other which the state will enforce—"the element of will pays . . . a decisive role in constructing the concept of the legal subject" (Pashukanis, 1978, p. 116). Relying on Arthur's summary, the perspective I want to stress here, and take up later in relation to the third world, is that:

> Historically . . . it was precisely commodity exchange which furnished the idea of the subject as the abstract bearer of all possible legal claims. It is only in the conditions of commodity production that the abstract legal form is necessary—it is only there that the capacity to have a right in general is distinguished from specific claims and privileges. It is only the constant transfer of property rights in the market that creates the idea of an immobile bearer of these rights . . . Pashukanis argues that property attains its highest development (in the shape of unimpeded possession and alienation) only in modern society, and that this freedom of disposition may be closely related to the category of legal subject or legal person. (Arthur, 1978, pp. 14, 16)

Pashukanis' theory, as we shall see, does have as well an important bearing on the political function of law and state, as an account and explanation of a powerful ideology.

Others have supplied historical perspectives that would broadly support Pashukanis and that underline the point being stressed here. For example, Horwitz summarizes his account of "the transformation of American law, 1780 – 1860" this way:

> By around 1850 that transformation was largely complete. Legal rules providing for the subsidization of enterprise and permitting the legal destruction of old forms of property for the benefit of more recent entrants had triumphed. Anticommercial legal doctrines had been destroyed or undermined and the legal system had almost completely shed its eighteenth century commitment to regulating the substantive fairness of economic exchange. Legal relations that had once been conceived of as deriving from natural law or custom were increasingly subordinated to the disproportionate economic power of individuals or corporations that were allowed the right to "contract out" of many existing legal obligations. Law, once conceived of as protective, regulative, paternalistic and, above all, a paramount expression of the moral sense of the community, had come to be thought of as facilitative of individual desires and as simply reflective of the existing organization of economic and political power. (Horwitz, 1977, p. 253)

With the emergence of capitalist or proto-capitalist law, Dumont observes that "there is no longer anything ontologically real behind the particular being, [and] . . . the notion of 'right' is attached not to a natural and social order, but to the particular human being" (Dumont, 1965, p. 22). Law thus becomes the expression of the 'power' or 'will' of the legislator or legal subject (ibid.). Von Jhering has put the point particularly vividly in remarking that "the progress of law consists in the destruction of every natural tie, in a continued process of separation and isolation" (as quoted in Diamond, 1973, p. 326).

With the advent of monopoly capitalism, Pashukanis' theory does not cover the new form of law that emerges in addition to the exchange-based form, as he does recognize (Pashukanis, 1978, Chapter 4). His theory has its typical application to competitive or market capitalism. Its relevance is lessened in the emergence of monopoly capitalism with its status-based economic positions and the greater intervention of the state and of law in securing the immediate conditions necessary for production (R. Murray, 1971). The state under monopoly capitalism plays a more supportive role in the economy and, to some extent, a directive one. In doing this the state assumes flexible powers under broad, discretionary legal provisions. These provisions are applied in particularized ways. Legal subjects no longer operate outside the state's sphere orienting their conduct by fixed rules of general applicability. Rather, if they have effective power or are otherwise recognized by the state, they bargain with the state for particularized outcomes in the context of these broad, discretionary legal provisions.

As for the political functions of law and state, these are what can be called particular and general functions. The particular is a constitutional function. Law constitutes itself and much of the state. Nothing more is said about this function in this theoretical part. The general function has two aspects: securing the overall coherence of relations within the dominant class and containing the subordinate class or classes. There are two broad ways in which the general function is performed. One way is by direct coercion. The other way is by securing consensus through popular involvement in or identification with processes of domination.

The bare function is well recognized and amply illustrated later. Its aspects need not be elaborated on here except perhaps to emphasize, for its particular relevance later, that securing the overall coherence of relations within the dominant class is a necessity because, in terms of economic interests, different elements of the bourgeoisie are not always at one. In this, the state has to 'hold the ring', to ensure the victory, in Marx's words, of 'the big material interests of the bourgeoisie (even against the will of the bourgeoisie)'' (see Poulantzas, 1973, pp. 258 – 259). Marx and Engels see law as having a distinctive part ''as representing the 'average interests' of the ruling class—the interests of the class conceived as a whole rather than of particular sections or individuals'' (Cain, 1974, p. 143).

To move on to ways of performing the general political function, direct coericon is straightforward enough and is much illustrated later. A particular point about direct coercion and the form of law should be made here. Even under competive capitalism the exchange theory of law could not account fully for the form of law. Laws dealing with class regulation, especially with the containment of subordinate classes, often take the form of broad, discretionary provisions giving officials power to define in particular ways what situations will be subject to legal coercion, such as laws dealing with public order and emergency powers (see Hunt, 1976, pp. 180 – 181.) A universalist, normative encompassing of precisely pre-defined behaviour cannot accommodate the future variety of potentially disruptive class action.

The securing of consensus is more complex. It is largely an ideological process, especially in obtaining the consensus of subordinate classes. Tangible benefit will help generate consensus more among the dominant class than among the subordinate, but there can be no enduring ideology in the air. It must have some grounding in social practice. The legal will be one ideology among many, sharing with others common supports in social practice. However, law also contains its own distinctive supporting social practice. Law actually does (at least in part) what its ideology represents. I use the term legality to cover the coincidence of legal ideology and this distinctive supporting practice. Using the simplifying exaggeration of its ideological aspect, legality, generally, entails the limitation of personal and public power. Power is contained in a normative frame within which all members of society are treated in objectively consistent ways. It contrasts with the arbitrary and the idiosyncratic use of power. Its historical extreme is bourgeois legality or the rule of law. For law to rule, its rules must be stable, universally applicable and relate to precisely but generally pre-defined behaviour; people must be free to orient their conduct around these rules and equal in so doing (no element of personal power or personal status must come between the individual legal subject and the law). The rules must be upheld by impartial officials, themselves bound by and bound to apply the rules; finally, for law to rule, the state itself must be bound by law and law can only be changed in ways allowed by law.

To what extent is the exaggeration of ideology supported in social practice? At its most fundamental there is a minimal legality, some minimal normative ordering, involved in the very existence of a human society (Hart, 1961, pp. 187 – 195). Legality thus contains a necessary universalism or reflects the commonalty and hence it can be that ''legality . . . celebrates and elevates the law to an exalted status as the expression of unity in the nation'' (Sumner, 1979, p. 293). This minimal legality does not extend very far; it does not cover a wide range of social practice. For example, Genovese's deft analysis of the slave society of the Southern United States shows both how minimal legality can be and how it exists none the less (Genovese, 1975, pp. 25 – 49). Some universalism seems necessary to support an element of consensus, for direct coercion is never invariably practicable: ''it is possible'', said Talleyrand, ''to do many things with a bayonet, but one cannot sit on one'' (as quoted in Nwafor, 1975, p. 44). Hence, legality involves giving subordinate elements in society some purchase on law (see Sumner, 1979, p. 264). It involves ''guaranteeing at least a modicum of equality and security for the whole society'' (Marcuse, 1971, p. 101).

The ideological aspect of bourgeois legality is supported in this under-lying necessity for legality. But it must have further supports. The most obvious support is that bourgeois legality includes social practice that actu-ally operates in conformity with the ideology. Structurally, bourgeois legal-ity is functional to competitive capitalism and historically it played a key part in the emergence and consolidation of bourgeois rule (Neumann, 1957, Chapter 2). For reasons which Poulantzas outlines, the bourgeoisie's ''lack of political capacity'' meant that this rule was specifically limited:

> Marx and Engels . . . explain the reasons why the bourgeoisie expe-
> riences this difficulty in the realisation of its hegemony *over the*
> *dominated classes*. These are: the internal fractioning of the bourgeois
> class; the continued existence of the classes of the small producers in
> capitalist formations and their complex reflection at the political
> level; the rise and organised struggle of the working class; the institu-
> tions of the capitalist state (for example, universal suffrage), which
> hurl all the classes or fractions of society on to the political scene, etc.
> *In short, everything happens as if the specific co-ordinates of the struggle of the*
> *dominant classes contribute to prevent their political organisation.*
> What then is the role of the capitalist state in this context? It can be
> stated as follows: it takes charge, as it were, of the bourgeoisie's
> political interests and realises the function of political hegemony
> which the bourgeoisie is unable to achieve. But, *in order to do this, the*

> *capitalist state assumes a relative autonomy with regard to the bourgeoisie.*
> (Poulantzas, 1973, pp. 284 – 285)

This "relative autonomy" entails a universalist form of state. This universalism is buttressed by bourgeois legality, for with it law rules, law is the rule of or for all and law binds the state. Law provides an involving normative frame in which conflicts arising from the limited rule of the bourgeoisie can, in part, be settled in a neutral yet controlled way. Returning to ideology, bourgeois legality can now be seen as having a minor branch in the academic ideology of legal positivism with its emphasis on the neutrality and self-contained or self-sufficient nature of law.

Supports in social practice which extend beyond legality are, of course, numerous. Supports within and without of legality will interact and combine and can only be distinguished analytically. Perhaps the most significant general support is that subordinate elements do sometimes affect and benefit from state action, a famous example from law being Marx's account of the Factory Acts (Marx, 1974, Vol I, Chapter 10). Another support can be derived from the exchange theory of law. The identity of the legal subject is rooted in commodity exchange with its implication of equality and freedom and commodity exchange is essential to the capitalist mode of production. Thus there is an element of involving voluntariness or an 'element of will' (Pashukanis, 1978, p. 116). The proletariat is implicated, for labour is a commodity.

To say that legal ideology is supported in social practice is not to say that the ideology accurately represents or accurately reflects the social practice. I have said it exaggerates the social practice. More specifically, this means that not only is the ideology more roseate than the practice warrants, but also that the ideology operates by taking or relying on part of the practice and then by generalizing and presenting this part as the relevant whole. Hence, to continue with the example of the exchange theory, exchange based relations are generalized in legal ideology to show that all legal subjects are free and equal. Bourgeois legality does not extend directly to immediate relations of production which are based on economic inequality and economic coercion. Formal legal equality and freedom thus mask and serve to legitimate exploitative economic relations. In particular, law structures the apparently fundamental social relation as commodity exchange—as an exchange of equivalents—so serving to conceal the extraction of surplus, especially through wage-labour. Further, and in terms of bourgeois legality, the free and equal legal subject stands, and need only stand, in an individual or one-to-one relation with the state, without the potentially disruptive mediation of class and class action, which would tend to result from recognition of the exploitative nature of economic relations (Sumner, 1979, p. 262). Bourgeois legality also does not present a whole picture of law itself. Laws relating to public order and emergency powers are in many ways incompatible with it. The working class has been singled out specifically in prohibitions on combination. Women and children had and have a restricted status in law. Generally, bourgeois legality serves to conceal the fact that, under the rule of the bourgeoisie, law acts very much for the dominant class and against or upon the subordinate elements (Black, n.d., 1976).

The most wide-ranging derogation from bourgeois legality comes with the broad, discretionary legal powers the state acquires under monopoly capitalism. The extent to which bourgeois legality has been displaced by this form of law is usually overdrawn, for polemical purposes (see for example, Hayek, 1944, Chapter 6). Even with this broad, discretionary form of law, bourgeois legality applies to the extent that the state and state operatives are bound by law. But with this form of law state operatives are seen as having such broad powers to make particularized decisions as to obviate law in its form of universally applicable rules and so on. Law becomes less effective as a guide to and constraint on how officials can behave. However there are other factors which serve to maintain still images of the rule of law. With monopoly capitalism ideologies of pluralism and corporatism emerge. These present the state as an impartial arbiter between the competing forces pressing upon it. Law as state action and even as broad discretion thus retains something of its aspects of neutrality and universalism. In a related vein, academic legal ideology comes in aid to modest effect with sociological jurisprudence and its balancing of 'interests' in the creation of law and with other doctrines that see law in the service of 'values' or 'interests' or state policy, such as the so-called policy sciences (Hunt, 1978, Chapters 1 and 2; Lasswell and McDougal, 1943). Pluralist ideology does have support in social practice in that 'interests' do obtain some benefits from the state and are often integrally involved in processes of state action. In this the state can now be seen not only to relate or respond to the individual legal subject but also to social groups. As a result the cohesion of social groups may be reinforced for, there being strength in both unity and numbers, the individual cannot "legitimately claim the right to act for himself if by so doing he might undercut the ability of his group to represent itself effectively in competition with other organized interests" (Fraser, 1976, p. 154).

I will now apply and qualify this analysis in the third world context. The main qualifying theme is, I argue, that law and state have a role that is more structurally central and structurally enduring in the third world. This role can be related to the conservation of the traditional mode of production. Law and state have to conserve this mode in the face of destructive economic forces introduced with the capitalist mode. Because the two modes have in this to be kept significantly apart, they cannot be integrated 'naturally' or economically and so law and state have to tie them into an operative combination. Such conservation also means that integrative economic forces remain inhibited, thus maintaining the reliance overall on law and state. In particular, indigenous class forces characteristic of capitalism are stunted and, indeed, this marks one function of conserving the traditional mode. In the end, law and state continue to be particularly and predominantly responsive to the interests of the only coherent and potent class element affecting it, the metropolitan bourgeoisie. Such interests include, of course, the conservation of the traditional mode. But in the post-colonial situation this class element is the 'great absent member'. It can no longer rule directly and there has to be some indigenous bourgeois element as a resident 'ruling class'. As this ruling class is not 'naturally' emergent (because indigenous class forces have ben stunted and so on) law and state come to play a central role in its promotion. However, this promotion tends to contradict the conservation of the traditional mode, which conservation is in the interests of the metropolitan bourgeoisie. Law and state then have a regulating or mediating part in relations between the resident bourgeoisie and the metropolitan, a part that, predominantly, subordinates the resident element.

I will look firstly at the colonial situation as typified in those colonies created in the second imperialism. This account focuses initially on the functions of law and state, then on the resulting forms of law and then on ideologies. In the colonial situation "economic exploitation is based on the seizure of political power—the two characteristic features of colonialism" (Balandier, 1970a, p. 37). With both economic exploitation and political power, law and state played a central role (see for example, Hunter, 1966, p. 67; Woddis, 1967, p. 15). The colonial state creates and maintains the whole colonial social formation. Here "the state pre-exists society" and "law may serve to constitute society" (Smith, 1974, p. 109). Where a social formation has to contain two diverse modes of production, where it is, as is commonly put, in transition, law and state have a central part in overall social cohesion (Anderson, 1974, p. 403; Ghai, 1976, pp. 33 – 34).

However, it cannot be asserted that in this situation "it is the political relations which appreciably determine the relationship to the means of production, rather than the reverse" (Kuper 1974, p. 415). This appears so if one focuses only on the colonial social formation, but the colonial state is rarely more than an administrative section of the metropolitan, and the colonial economy is dependently integrated into the metropolitan. "Political relations" as well as law and state have to be seen as rather abjectly reflecting the wider metropolitan economy. For example, the British Colonial Office built up an array of prototype laws used to create and integrate the colonial social formation—something of "an *imperial* legal culture" (Luckham, 1978, p. 237)—laws which were drawn on with minimal modification in various colonial situations. Whether it was the indentured labour laws of Rhodesia or the peasant culture system imposed by the Dutch on the Javanese, the appropriate political relations and legal provisions were responses identifiable in the needs of the metropolitan economy.

The colonial social formation itself is critically unintegrated in terms of economy. As Luckham notes for Ghana, "the legal system was particularly important in incorporating pre-colonial social formations in the colonial framework" (ibid., p. 207). These social formations contained little or no 'free' labour, so the producer had to be separated from the traditional means of production and legally coerced to work in various systems of forced and indentured labour. Taxes were introduced as an incentive to labour to get cash for the tax. Alternative means of getting cash for taxes which would reduce this incentive, such as cash-cropping, were often legally prohibited or restricted, especially in settler colonies. Alternatively, with colonial economies based on the creation of a peasantry, peasants often had to be legally coerced into controlled and compulsory schemes of cash-cropping. The colonial state takes special measures to acquire or to validate the acquisition of land for plantations and mines.

However the traditional mode is not only to be exploited but to be conserved. Law and state have to confront and contain the destructive effect of capitalist economic forces. Hence law provided for the periodic repatriation of workers to their traditional areas. It restricted and controlled migration to and residence within towns and dealings in land (see for example, Wolpe, 1975, p. 249). The entering into of contracts of commodity exchange by the colonized is often strictly limited. In the cause of conserving the traditional mode, law and state have also to mediate between the resident colonist and the metropolitan bourgeoisie as a whole. The resident colonist has sometimes to be restrained by law, for the traditional mode would tend to be undermined if resident planters and miners were allowed to go to disruptive lengths in promoting and expanding their individual enterprises (see for example, Gluckman, 1971, p. 394). Large scale investment by members of the metropolitan bourgeoisie was on occasion prohibited (Kay, 1975, p. 106). In restraining these forces and conserving the traditional mode, law and state also have a related but distinctive function in countering the formation of classes that could challenge colonial rule and metropolitan domination generally. This function was served by laws aimed at conserving the traditional mode, since this conservation maintained ethnic division which, in turn, countered class consolidation. This function of class containment was served more particularly by laws of the public order variety and by laws containing any organization outside of the context of traditional social formations.

In this situation, legal form followed function. Law and state had to combine the capitalist and traditional modes of production into an operative whole yet keep them sufficiently apart to conserve the traditional. The colonized had to operate within the capitalist mode and often had to be forced to do so, yet they had also to be forced to stay outside of it when they wanted to stay in. This resulted in an authoritarian system of legal administration. Writing of the colonial situation, Balandier notes that "the country had to be controlled, 'held down', so that the administrative system becomes an integral part of all colonized societies" (Balandier, 1970a, p. 29). Elsewhere he notes that "colonization transformed every political problem into a technical problem to be dealt with by the administration. It contained every expression of communal life and every action that seemed to limit or threaten its grip, irrespective of the forms of the native political society and the colonial regimes that organised their domination" (Balandier, 1970b, p. 160). The necessity for such containment is heightened in the numerically small presence of the colonists and their objectively weak position, resulting from the limited penetration of capitalism. Law and bourgeois legality were often presented by the colonist as a justifying part of the civilizing mission (Huttenback, 1976, pp. 13 – 16; Rheinstein, 1963; p. 220; Seidman, 1978, p. 201). Whatever else colonial law was, it certainly was not an exemplar of bourgeois legality (see for example, Ghai and McAuslan, 1970, p. 34). Given what had to be done to structure the colonial economy and to maintain it, universalism, freedom and equality of any significant kind are quite out of the question. "Strictly contractual relations are not possible", as Maquet had said (1972, p. 232). Law was explicitly based on divisions in terms of racially ascribed status with the colonized being subject to a distinct legal system that gave colonial officials wide and comprehensive, discretionary powers over their charges. In analysing the claims of an apologist that bourgeois legality was a great boon to the African, Seidman finds that none of the following (using his description) applied to the colonized: equality before the law, access to the courts, fair trial and independence of the judiciary, or the courts as guarantors of governmental regularity (Seidman, 1978, pp. 201 – 210). Most elements of bourgeois legality were, however, present in regulating relations within the bourgeoisie, including the resident colonists. Some laws, mainly the basic criminal law, applied formally to the whole colonial population. Even this limited universalism was adulterated in its application. To give examples, if colonists committed serious crimes they were often given the option of leaving the territory; and generally, colonial judges, formally impartial and separate from the colonial administration, could be relied upon not to 'rock the boat' (see Luckham, 1978, p. 210). Because of the weakness of colonial rule, solidarity among the colonists was a prime value. Sometimes law took a form compromised between bourgeois legality and authoritarian coercion, the most notable example of this being the widely used indentured labour system. There was formally a contract of employment and entry into it was, at least in theory, free. However, the 'terms' of the contract were almost wholly laid down in legislation giving officials considerable controlling power over the worker. Breach of these 'terms' would usually be a criminal offence, the most notable offences being refusal to work or 'desertion' before expiry of the period of indenture.

Another type of formal compromise is rooted in the weakness of colonial rule and the conservation of the traditional mode. With the rapid colonization of the second imperialism resources of rule were greatly stretched. Political power within traditional social formations is therefore co-opted in the 'indirect rule' of British colonialism and variants elsewhere. Although overstating the case, Robinson has noted that, with colonial rule, "its administrative, constitutional, land and economic policies were largely institutionalizations of the indigenous, political alliances which upheld it" (Robinson, 1972, p. 139). In this, systems of 'native' or 'customary'' law are often formally recognized and incorporated into the overall legal system, although the colonist insists on the supremacy of the introduced law (see, Burman n.d.). Even where the colonist formally prescribes these resident systems of law in the name of the civilizing mission, they are recognized *de facto* none the less.

In the colonial situation race is the fundamental ideological category:

> In certain conditions of imperialist development, ideological and political domination tend to be expressed not in terms of the relations of class exploitation which they must sustain but in racial, ethnic, national, etc., terms and, in all cases, this is related to the fact that the specific mode of exploitation involves the conservation, in some form, of the non-capitalist modes of production and social organization, the existence of which provides the foundation of that exploitation. Indeed, it is in part the very attempt to conserve and *control* the non-capitalist societies in the face of the tendency of capitalist development to disintegrate them and thereby to undermine the basis of exploitation, that accounts for political policies and ideologies which centre on cultural, ethnic, national, and racial characteristics.
>
> In certain circumstances capitalism may, within the boundaries of a single state, develop predominantly by means of its relationship to non-capitalist modes of production. When that occurs, the mode of political domination and the content of legitimating ideologies assume racial, ethnic, and cultural forms and for the same reason as in the case of imperialism. In this case, political domination takes on a colonial form, the precise or specific nature of which has to be related to the specific mode of exploitation of the non-capitalist society. (Wolpe, 1975, p. 244)

Closely related ideologies of racial superiority, social evolution and imperialism went hand-in-hand justifying the exploitation of colonized peoples (Harris, 1968, pp. 106 – 134). Authoritarian rule was the only way in which people so inferior and so lacking in moral control could be governed. In this, law was a part of the whole "civilizing mission" (Huttenback, 1976, pp. 13 – 16), but it was a special part because it provided a legitimated form of coercion. Much of colonial government in British Africa, for example, was "carried on through the forms of a criminal trial" (Seidman, 1978, p. 207). 'Law' thus assumed potent symbolic dimensions. Missionary activity provided supporting ideologies and an inexpensive manifestation and legitimation of the civilizing mission. Despite its wrecking of traditional cultures, such activity had a strong conserving tendency for, with the second imperialism, it came to be premised on the innate and unalterable inability of the colonized to proceed beyond the most rudimentary levels of civilization (Fyfe, 1973, p. 28). Overall, the disruption of the traditional mode of production was justified in terms of the civilizing mission, a boon presented by the colonist as an alleged return for being able to exploit the resources of the colony (Lee, 1967,

p. 44). Coercion of the 'native' to work for the colonist was a convenient part of the civilizing mission. Various, ostensibly benign ideologies of 'trusteeship' and 'protection' justified the conservation of the traditional mode.

In the post-colonial situation the functions of law and state and the forms of law came to resemble more, but far from entirely, the position of law and state within the capitalist mode of production. Some presence now of the class formations characteristic of capitalism indicates that economic determinants are of more effect and that there is less need for direct legal controls to force production and to maintain the economy. The operative combination of the capitalist and the traditional modes of production is now more structurally set; workers and their families are more reliant on wages; peasants are more tied to production for the market; and there is the ruralization of the cities. There remains a strong tendency towards the conservation of the traditional mode and a need for some continued protective regulation—a need added to somewhat now by disruptive aspects of the emergence of the national bourgeoisie. This emergence and the more intense involvement of the national bourgeoisie give a greater part to bourgeois legality. However, the conservation of the traditional mode and the limited transforming effect of capitalism result in the retention by law and state of their colonial, authoritarian cast as well.

Bourgeois legality, naturally enough, is strengthened by and serves the greater presence of a bourgeoisie. As the economist Harry G. Johnson put it in writing of "economic policies toward less developed countries":

> To establish a modern society capable of self-sustaining economic growth at a reasonable rate requires, in broad cultural terms, the attainment of political stability and a reasonable impartiality of governmental administration, to provide a political institutional framework within which individuals and enterprises (whether working for their own gain or within the public sector) can plan innovations with maximum certainty about the future environment. It requires the establishment of a legal system defining rights of property, person and contract sufficiently clearly, and a judiciary system permitting settlement of disputes sufficiently predictably and inexpensively, to provide a legal institutional framework within which production and accumulation can be undertaken with a minimum degree of noneconomic risk. And it requires the establishment of a social system permitting mobility of all kinds (both allowing opportunity and recognizing accomplishment), and characterized by the depersonalization of economic and social relationships,

> to provide maximum opportunities and incentives for individual
> advancement on the basis of productive economic contribution.
> (Johnson, 1967, pp. 44 – 45).

Allowing for the inept ideological element, this is a valuable summary of
the operative aspects of modernization doctrine. In all these aspects bourgeois legality performs, in various ways, a service function. Probably the
most significant aspect is the securing of some stability in an unstable
environment. There are now several studies underlining the prime
emphasis placed on stability by the metropolitan bourgeoisie, shorter term
profits, for example, being traded off for longer term stability (Aharoni,
1966; Girvan, 1970).

The system of capitalist law and state exists in advance of the emergence
of the resident or national bourgeoisie. The system is, as it were, ready-
made for use by this class element and assists in its emergence. Most of the
colonial laws based on differences of racially ascribed status are repealed,
thus doing away with many of the restrictions on the emergence of a
national bourgeoisie. The system of capitalist law and state can now be
used to enforce capitalist relations often in opposition to relations rooted in
the traditional mode of production. This new economic man—"the idea
of the subject as the abstract bearer of all possible legal claims" (Arthur,
1978, p. 14)—can seek to have his 'will' override the personalized obligations of traditional community, and to liberate 'private' property from the
integral ties of the collective order (see for example, Galanter, 1968,
p. 70). As well as serving as a pole-star for the emergence of the national
bourgeoisie, law and state play a more specifically purposive part in this.
Here political power can again be seen as leading to economic power. The
state, partly influenced by the emergent national bourgeoisie, fosters this
class element through management and technical (extension) services,
development grants and easy credit. New land laws will often facilitate the
obtaining of individual ownership of communal land. Laws relating to the
'indigenization' of some economic activity, to trade licensing and to
import controls create artificial and highly profitable monopolies for the
national bourgeoisie (see for example, Seidman, 1978, pp. 412 – 413). It is
also through the state that the bureaucratic bourgeoisie assumes its
economic power and indeed very identity. Because of their dependence on
it, the state is of focal importance in mediating between different elements
of the national bourgeoisie.

This dependence is also effective with the state's shaping and limiting
the emergence of the national bourgeoisie in the interests of the

metropolitan bourgeoisie. The national bourgeoisie remains weakly based economically. It is stunted by the dominance of the metropolitan bourgeoisie. Since a large political presence of the metropolitan bourgeoisie is no longer acceptable and since the national bourgeoisie has little economic power to support the political, there tends to be considerable political instability. This makes any concerted or sustained assertion of the national bourgeoisie against the metropolitan difficult. Because of this weakness, the state relies on the maintenance of ethnic divisions to fragment and obviate opposition and so the state shares a strong interest with the metropolitan bourgeoisie in the conservation of the traditional mode. Despite its weakness, the national bourgeoisie will have considerable comparative advantage over the metropolitan in some economic activities that the metropolitan bourgeoise wishes to preserve for itself. There is also potential for conflict between the metropolitan bourgeoisie and the bureaucratic bourgeoisie, with the latter wishing to extract more state revenue from the former. Since some of this revenue goes, as extension services, grants, and loans, to benefit the national bourgeoisie generally, this issue can give some focus to pressures from the national bourgeoisie. In this more complex situation law and state come to mediate between the metropolitan bourgeoisie and the national. On the face of it, there are now often broad, discretionary legal provisions enabling the state, and the bureaucratic bourgeoisie, to control the metropolitan bourgeoisie. These include trade licensing and 'indigenization' measures, natural resource regulation and investment codes. Increasingly, the state requires some involvement of national elements in enterprises with the metropolitan bourgeoisie or nationalizes the enterprises of the metropolitan bourgeoisie but leaves them with the benefit of management contracts and of the licensing of technology and know-how. Whilst there is doubtless at times a genuine assertiveness on the part of the national bourgeoisie at the back of these measures (particularly in these social formations of longer industrialization), the measures also serve to legitimate the continuing presence of the metropolitan bourgeoisie and to mask its persisting dominance. Since the presence of the metropolitan bourgeoisie is apparently so subject to restrictive conditions and apparently so controlled, their presence is rendered more acceptable. In this, the position of the ostensible controllers, the bureaucratic bourgeoisie, is also legitimated. Law and state also play a large part in containing competition from the national bourgeoisie (Weeks, 1973, p. 79). This function no longer takes the form of the direct legal prohibitions and controls of the colonial period; rather, bourgeois legality and the imposing of universal, 'modern' or 'modernizing' standards serve to favour those who can comply with them. Laws attuned to metro-politan-style factors of production impose health, safety, environmental, quality control and packaging standards on production and these standards serve to restrict the national bourgeoisie (see for example, Kanyeihamba, 1979, pp. 7 – 9). The big peasantry tend to be contained by the conserva-tion of the traditional mode. There still often remain legal restrictions on dealing with rural land so as to prevent its being taken out of the traditional mode. Traditional obligations and traditional law are maintained. In parti-cular, the reproduction of the big peasantry is often undermined by the persistence of traditional laws of inheritance (see for example, Okoth-Ogendo, 1979).

Other classes and class elements are contained in a wide variety of mea-sures which make for the continuation of colonial structures. There are often still controls on urban migration in 'pass' and 'vagrancy' laws. Laws relating to housing standards, urban planning and the obtaining of urban land tend to make urban existence precarious and provisional for the unskilled and semi-skilled elements of the proletariat as well as for the bulk of petty commodity producers. These class elements are also the ones primarily affected by laws of the public order variety. Such laws are often taken over intact from the colonial period and it is not uncommon for them to become even more draconic. Petty commodity producers are as well restricted and harassed through laws relating to trade licensing, health standards, traffic obstruction and to many other things. In this, their urban existence is not only made precarious but they are restrained in competing with the bourgeoisie. The proletariat, especially its more skilled element, is contained by laws restricting and even prohibiting trade union activity and in laws which provide alternative, controlled forms of 'industrial relations'. The peasantry continues to be largely self-regulating although, and especially with pressure for state revenue, underdevelopment does place strains on traditional law and resident mechanisms of control (Snyder, 1978; Thomson, 1975, 1979). On the other hand, new legal forms of local government and co-operative marketing tend to buttress the existent structure of the peasantry.

As for the form of law, bourgeois legality plays a more prominent part in the post-colonial situation. This reflects the more effective presence of the metropolitan bourgeoisie and the emergence of the national bourgeoisie. The metropolitan bourgeoisie can be particularly well served by bour-geois legality. The third world worker and the member of the national bourgeoisie are formally equal in law to, for example, the large multi-national enterprise but both are even less able than their first world counterparts to correct the basic inequality which bourgeois legality masks. Moreover, in terms of bourgeois legality the multinational enterprise in its relation to the third world state is, on the whole, an individual legal subject much like any other. The state deals with it in the restricted and diffuse legal-regulative categories that apply to all legal subjects: criminal law, contract law, company or corporate law, natural resource regulation, taxation law, exchange control and so on. This 'overmightly subject', the multinational enterprise, can easily manoeuvre around these fixed and limited categories and, in the result, the state's response to the multinational enterprise is organizationally dispersed, uncoordinated and ineffectual. With the emergence of the national bourgeoisie most colonial legal controls based on socially ascribed status are repealed, including laws which restricted the legal and contractual capacity of the colonized and including the system of special courts for them.

However, the national bourgeoisie is only weakly based economically and provides little support for bourgeois legality. This weak base and the inability of the metropolitan bourgeoisie now to rule directly makes for considerable political instability and 'pure' force in the form of military government, tends to be a frequent option. Thus in writing of Africa, Nwabueze could conclude that bourgeois legality in its constitutional aspect had failed (Nwabueze, 1973, pp. 300 – 301). Further, dominant internal class elements are not secure enough to allow of institutionally set and enduring limitations on their political power. In its support of the metropolitan bourgeoisie, however, bourgeois legality appears to flourish. In the post-colonial period introduced capitalist law continues much as it was, and even has conscientious updatings to keep it in line with metropolitan legal changes (see for example, Pooley, 1972). Maitland-Jones can observe that "the state of law in African countries today seems remarkably healthy" (Maitland-Jones, 1973, p. 95). Nwabueze's account of the failure in Africa of bourgeois legality in its constitutional aspect has to be qualified to exempt largely the independence of the judiciary, something crucial to the maintenance of bourgeois legality generally (see Nwabueze as cited in Seidman, 1978, p. 359). This judiciary is conservative, as befits one operating under the settled dominance of a class or class element, in this case the metropolitan bourgeoisie. It is not restless, progressive and creative in the cause of such as change, development and the establishment of a struggling, emergent class.

The form of broad, discretionary law fitted to colonial authoritarian rule continues also. This is partly because many colonial-type controls persist not only for the same reasons but also to deal now with political instability and with the presence of the urban 'unemployed' and 'dispossessed' (Kay, 1975, p. 187). The broad, discretionary form of law acquires a further significance in the mediation of relations within the bourgeoisie and in this the state assumes the general interventionist and ostensibly pluralist form characteristic of monopoly capitalism. The most significant mediation is that between the metropolitan and the national bourgeoisie. As we have just seen, law and state appear to be significantly concerned here with the control and subordination of the metropolitan bourgeoisie and the state assumes a wide range of legal powers for this purpose, but these powers are not used extensively or effectively (Wallerstein, 1974, p. 356). Such evasion can be hidden in this form of law since, in its breadth and flexibility, it does not entail any specific accountability on the part of officials operating it. This flexibility and the interventionist, plural form of the state serve to identify the national bourgeoisie with the state, for they allow of involvement in the processes of state decision making, in such ways as memberships of consultative committees and marketing boards.

The interventionist, plural form of the state also serves to accommodate elements of traditional social formations. Although the state is predominantly responsive to the capitalist mode of production, it is not unaffected by the persistence of the traditional mode. On the one hand, the third world state has been seen as a national, universalist ordering force in the cause of capitalism (see for example, Markovitz, 1977, pp. 118 – 119). On the other, it can be seen as shot through with 'primordial loyalties' and organizationally irrational influences emanating from the traditional mode (Riggs, 1964). These influences are seen most clearly in the state's role as provider of resources (Weeks, 1973, p. 76). People compete for these resources often on the basis of traditional groupings which, in this, are structured as relations of brokerage or patronage and as legal forms of local-level political and/or economic organization. The competition for resources helps reinforce the groupings. Such involvement in the state system is, however, too small and too oblique to lend much popular support to legality at the national level. The conservation of the traditional mode and the fact that most people have only a precarious or limited stake in the capitalist mode of production undercuts the establishment of bourgeois legality as a popular phenomenon. These same reasons and the weakness of the state tend to make people look to traditional relations, including traditional law, for security of life and property. The peasant village and the urban shanty town are rarely penetrated by the national law in ways likely to win the inhabitant's gratitude or support. In these areas the police are characteristically disliked and distrusted (Clinard and Abbott, 1973, pp. 24 – 26). Legality at the national level and bourgeois legality in particular extend little mediating involvement to such people and must appear largely oppressive in upholding the interests of dominant class elements.

In the post-colonial situation, ideology is ostensibly less paternalistic and even celebrates freedom and the virtues of liberal democracy. Ultimately, however, it is saying the same things as colonial ideology if in different and more elaborate ways.

The ideology of the civilizing mission now finds a counterpart in that of development and modernization. Such doctrines have it that the introduction of modern or western values and institutions will transform third world social formations into a metropolitan likeness and in this way they will eradicate the backwardness that causes underdevelopment (Frank, 1971b). This transformation, "though so radical, will be a peaceful process, one that does not affect the dominance and stability of the guiding modern values and institutions" (Rhodes, 1968). As well as obviously serving the interests of metropolitan capital, the ideology of modernization, and its sub-branches of 'nation building' and 'planning', serve to legitimate the position of the national bourgeoisie, the 'new elites', the resident agents and the indigenous vanguard of modernization. This ideology also helps legitimate the arrogation of tremendous state power for the Herculean task of development and helps legitimate the broad, discretionary form of law. Such legitimations underlie the emphasis in academic theorizing about law and modernization on the efficacy or ever omnipotence of law as an instrument of development (Trubek and Galanter, 1974). As with the general ideology of modernization, this theorizing sometimes explicitly sets a better, modern, western world towards which transforming law is to aim (Galanter, 1965). This is more usually done implicity if crudely. Thus, for example, the State Department of the United States financed expeditions by legal academics to several third world countries to gauge receptivity to US-style law (Franck, 1972). Resident social formations and their law "cannot lead to development" and indeed are "the cause of underdevelopment in all its forms" (respectively, Seidman, 1972, p. 315; David as quoted in Costa, 1969, p. 367). However for many theorists law is legitimated in being 'value-free' (see references in Franck, 1972, pp. 787, 789). Even absurdly granting an absence of directive aims or values, legal scholarship as ideology remains well adapted to serving given, exogenous 'values' or 'interests' (Merryman, 1977, p. 465). The outer limits of acceptable change allowed for by theorizing on law and modernization is that law must somehow be more responsive to 'the disaffected' and 'the poor', basically to reconcile them to existent structures of power (Hager, 1972, p. 37; Franck, 1972, p. 779; Valdez, 1975). To borrow Santos' incisive summary, "law and development studies" emphasize "the positive role of law—an ideological bias in favour of lawful social transformation and against revolutionary processes. And thus they become, whatever the intentions of their cultivators, little more than a rhetoric of legitimation" (Santos, in press).

The conservation of the traditional mode of production has a somewhat opposed ideological effect. Various resident ideologies import a modified traditionalism such as the specific socialisms (Arab socialism, African socialism, Kenyan socialism), programmes of cultural authenticity (Zaire providing a recent example), ujamaa in Tanzania and African humanism in Zambia. In a similar vein are numerous assertions of a convenient classlessness. Law, in Nkrumah's view, must "embody our traditional social attitudes of communal endeavour, or a classless society" (Nkrumah, 1962, p. 104). Law must reflect the customs of "the people" (Nyerere as quoted in Cotran, 1969, p. 140). A significant practical manifestation of this line is the various projects of "unification" of customary law (Cotran, 1966, pp. 84 – 92). Several scholars have seen the preservation of aspects of traditional law as being compatible with or conducive to modernization (Deng, 1971; Elias, 1956; Gluckman, 1966, p. 66; Rudolph and Rudolph, 1967).

Returning to modernization theory proper, it does contain a damning contradiction. Since it entails development towards the "western" ideal, it entails also some commitment to liberal democracy. Hence there is, or was, great emphasis on "training for democracy" (Lee, 1967; Nettl and Robertson, 1968, pp. 45 – 50). Liberal democracy and bourgeois legality, with their emphasis on freedom, equality and universalism, provided apt weapons for use by the emergent national bourgeoisie in struggles against the colonist (Ake, 1976, pp. 203 – 204). Their utility persisted, for the emphasis or racial equality enabled glaring indigenous inequalities to be tolerated: bluntly, social equality and ethnic self respect demanded there be rich and successful nationals to stand comparison with rich and successful colonists (Markovitz, 1977, p. 213). For scholars of law and modernization, the introduced law itself, through some process of ethical infection, was to induce behaviour in conformity with bourgeois legality

(Trubek, 1972). If results in that direction were less than spectacular, some consolation could be had in the progressive effect of legal education, "the wedge leading to the reform of the entire legal system" which reform would "stimulate economic growth and political democracy" (ibid., p. 10).

On the other hand modernization theory does have an authoritarian tendency. These backward societies have to fit an externally determined and imposed frame. For this a strong state, order and stability are needed (Geertz, 1963, pp. 109 – 110; O'Brien, 1972). Law is often seen as having a central role in ensuring this strength, order and stability (Braibanti, 1968, p. 3; Gardner, 1978, p. 14). As O'Brien has shown, modernization theory has tended to conform more to the dictates of order and stability (that is, repression) than to liberal democracy (O'Brien, 1972). Modern law and modern legal education have rarely been seen to stand apart from this. On the contrary, law is often seen as rightly associated with the preservation of order—any order (see for example, Paul, 1962 – 63, p. 193). Gardner instances how legal education with a 'progressive', instrumentalist emphasis produced efficient operatives for military dictatorships in Latin America (Gardner, in press).

In all, this account of law and state does not pretend to be a picture of coherence and consistency. Law and state function to mediate and regulate wider contradictions. Law and state are not always and continually successful in this. They themselves reflect these wider contradictions. Some broad explanatory consistency is derived from the effect of the wider setting on law and state – a setting sketched in the first chapter—and particularly from the dominance of the metropolitan bourgeoisie and the related conservation of the traditional mode of production. I will now apply and somewhat refine this account of law and state in the Papua New Guinea context. It would prove tedious to underline continually the relevance of the numerous aspects of this account. I often, then, leave their relevance implicit in the presentation of the facts. Generally, the Papua New Guinea case is presented as an historical class analysis. Sometimes there is a leaping ahead in time to tie up particular aspects of the analysis.

# 3 The Colonists[1]

This chapter looks at the metropolitan bourgeoisie, including their frontiersmen in Papua New Guinea—the "conquistadores of the coconut" (Reed, 1943, p. 126) and the miners—and at law and state in the securing of their interests and in the regulation of relations among themselves. The next chapter looks at law and state in the control and containment of the colonized. Predominant emphasis is given to colonization by Australia as this was far and away the most significant. The account in these chapters covers the period up to the second world war and on some points beyond. In the chapters that then follow, the continuing and changing functions of law and state are related to the class formations that emerge after the second world war and with the advent of the post-colonial situation: the peasantry, the proletariat and the bourgeoisie. This provides a basis for the analysis that follows of contemporary law and state.

With the second imperialism the spreading effect of inter-imperialist rivalry in the assumption of direct colonial rule in Asia and Africa took little time to reach Oceania. From about the middle of the nineteenth century, this area had been penetrated through trade and the limited exploitation of gold, sandalwood, *bêche-de-mer* and pearls. In this initial period imperial rule took such limited forms as criminal jurisdiction over nationals of the imperialist power and the gunboat (Scarr, 1967, p. 22). However, the growth of industry in Europe and the United States created a demand for products of plantation agriculture which could be supplied from this area, such as cotton, sugar and copra. The increased efficiency of shipping now enabled these products to be marketed profitably. The resulting demand for land and, especially, labour led to more intensive penetration.

This happened in significantly different degrees with different imperialist powers. Initially Britain was the dominant power in the area, but its dominance, as elsewhere, was being challenged by rising industrial powers—the relevant ones in Oceania being Germany, France and the United States—and its capabilities were being stretched to the limit by its success in the scramble for Africa. Hobsbawm summarizes the situation well:

> Imperialism was not a new thing for Britain. What was new was the end of the virtual British monopoly in the undeveloped world, and the consequent necessity to mark out regions of imperial influence formally against potential competitors; often ahead of any actual prospects of economic benefits, often, it must be admitted, with disappointing economic results. (Hobsbawm, 1969, p. 131)

Again, Hymer has noted of British imperialism at this time:

> Instead of embarking on a "big push" to develop the vast hinterland of Empire, colonial administrators often adopted policies to slow down rates of growth and arrest the development of either a native capitalist class or a native proletariat which could overthrow them. (Hymer, 1972, p. 130)

The interests of Germany and the United States were somewhat more positive. As expanding powers, they were actively seeking new sources of supply, some of which Oceania could provide. This difference in interests and in, as we shall see, the nature of direct colonization, is vividly reflected in Britain's effort to secure agreement with Germany and the United States on laws banning the provision of arms, dynamite and alcohol to labour recruits and their kin. The provision of these things was a successful inducement for the supply of labour, but it also had profoundly disruptive effects on the people of the area. Britain could afford a moral posture: she had little need of this labour and she wanted to restrain others in obtaining it. Germany and the United States wanted the labour and although they could not explicitly reject overtures in such a humanitarian cause, they effectively refused in procrastination (Firth, 1973, pp. 34, 45 – 46; Scarr, 1967, pp. 189 – 190).

As for what is now called Papua New Guinea, Britain was certainly a reluctant colonist. In addition to the general reluctance to further extend herself, Britain was concerned that the people of Papua New Guinea would probably not face colonization amiably and that there would thus be considerable costs of 'pacification' (Oram, 1976a, p. 18; Ruhen, 1968, p. 17). The Australian colonies, especially Queensland which is geographically close to Papua New Guinea, put pressure on Britain to annex Papua New Guinea because of a concern that Germany was about to colonize it. An act of the Queensland parliament, the New Guinea and Pacific Jurisdiction Contribution Act of 1884, expressed the view in the name of the Australian colonies:

> That further acquisition of dominion in the Pacific south of the Equator by any foreign Power would be highly detrimental to the safety and well-being of the British possessions in Australasia and injurious to the interests of the Empire. (Whittaker et al., 1975, p. 457)

Reflecting the pressure of Australian traders to annex the territory (Joyce, 1971, p. 9), the act also gave as a reason for annexation:

> . . . the certainty that the island will shortly be the resort of many adventurous subjects of Great Britain and other nations, and the absence or inadequacy of any existing laws for regulating their relations with the native tribes . . . . (Whittaker et al., 1975, p. 457)

Some few German nationals had already settled in the north-east of the territory. As well as being an assertive colonizer, Germany was further spurred on in this context because it believed Queensland wanted the territory as a source of cheap labour for its sugar plantations. The same belief made Britain even more reluctant to colonize Papua New Guinea on behalf of its Australian offspring (Docker, 1970, p. 189). Britain's reluctance was fuelled, also, it seems, by the near genocidal impact the Australian colonists had had on the indigenous population of Australia (Oram, 1976a, p. 19). Nevertheless, when Germany moved to annex the northern part of the territory (New Guinea) in 1884, Britain, with the financial backing of the Australian colonies, established a 'protectorate' over the southern part (Papua—then referred to as British New Guinea). In 1885 and 1886, Britain and Germany formally agreed on a partition of the territory. Britain's initial involvement in Papua reflected the reluctance to colonize it. The protectorate form did not ever give Britain formal sovereignty over the area. Britain had intervened merely in a protective capacity, or, more accurately, a holding capacity, so that "evil-disposed men will not be able to occupy your country", as "Queen Victoria's representative" explained the position to some of the people (Whittaker et al., 1975, p. 462). Penetration by settlers and economic enterprise was severely restricted (Mayo, 1972). However, in 1888 Britain formally declared the area a colony opening the way for the more extensive involvement which we will consider shortly.

German colonization of New Guinea was on the other hand more vigorous, reflecting as it did the different interest that Germany had in the process. Germany was an expanding industrial power with a colonial empire much smaller than Britain's and there was considerable domestic pressure at the economic level for greater imperial expansion (Townsend, 1964). Theories of German 'social imperialism' have also emphasized that expanding colonization served to legitimate the regime within Germany and to mute class tensions arising from rapid economic change (Wehler, 1972). (Of course it is a common assertion as well that British imperialism served at this time to divert the proletariat.) The German 'protectorate' declared in 1884 did not, unlike the British variety, involve a limited juris-diction but was the same as full colonization. Most rights of sovereignty were delegated to a concessionary company which, in effect, ruled New Guinea for periods totalling about 13 years. For the rest of German rule, until the takeover of the colony by Australia in 1914, the Imperial govern-ment ruled directly. For a variety of reasons the concessionary company was not successful (Firth, 1972). Under the rule of the Imperial govern-ment a more intense and effective colonization took place so that by the end of German rule there was a vigorous settler colonization of a few par-ticular areas.

Before considering the Australian takeover of these colonies, it may help to have some overview of her performance as a colonist in relation to her general position at this time. Australia as a colonist could rarely be described as vigorous, at least until the rapid expansion of Australian involvement in Papua New Guinea after the second world war. Australia, it has been said, lacked the "surplus energy" necessary for colonization (Eggleston, 1928, p. 7). There are several aspects to this metaphorical defi-ciency. First, it was simply the case that opportunities for pastoral and agri-cultural settlement were more attractive in underdeveloped Australia than outside (Rowley, 1972, p. 119). The second aspect is that, for the period of its colonization of Papua New Guinea until 1940, Australia's own economic performance was unimpressive and presumably not capable of sustaining colonial expansion (Clark, 1975, p. 61). Thirdly, for much of the period of its rule over Papua New Guinea, Australia could fairly be described as a neo-colony of Britain. In this role, it was basically a supplier of raw materials and foodstuffs with a very limited industrialization. There was little Australian demand for the materials that Papua New Guinea could produce. Further, Australia was a typical colonist in restricting economic development when this fitted her own interests. These restrictions, which will be considered shortly, also limited the attractiveness of Papua New Guinea for settlers and investors.

Australia had always been closely included in the running of Papua. It took charge fully in 1902 and formally in 1906. Its takeover of New Guinea was more abrupt and dramatic being the result of mild military conquest in 1914. Australia's control was formally established in 1921 when it took charge of New Guinea as a mandate of the League of Nations. It is something of a commonplace that Australia's colonization of Papua New Guinea was for military-strategic reasons (Hasluck, 1976, p. 215). If this were so, Australia's interest would take form as a colony of administration and analysis could proceed on that simple basis. However, matters were far more complicated and interesting. Until the second world war no bases or resident military forces were established and, in fact, the area was considered to have little strategic importance (Simington, 1977). With New Guinea, it is quite clear that Australia's interest was basically economic (Joyce, 1971, pp. 8 – 9; Territory of New Guinea, 1914 – 21, p. 14; Rowley, 1971, pp. 59 – 68). On the Australian takeover in Papua every effort was made to promote white settlement (Legge, 1971, p. 38; Power, 1974, pp. 82 – 86, 140). It was only with the early failure of these efforts that some emphasis was given to so-called native development. Settler colonization in New Guinea was comparatively more vigorous. It built on the German base—a base which Germans were encouraged to expand during the first world war in anticipation of Australians' taking it over. This takeover was near to completion by the late 1920s. Even though plantation agriculture did remain more expansionary and more vigorous in New Guinea, New Guinea tended gradually to join the Papuan case in the trough of the inter-war years when the world market for primary products was depressed. In both territories plantation agriculture was, overall, the most significant part of the colonial economy. This was mainly a matter of copra production. Gold-mining did have a considerable if erratic impact; on occasion it employed more than did plantation agriculture and it was for some periods the main export earner (Mair, 1970, pp. 112 – 113, 132 – 134).

Apart from the external influence of low world prices, Australia imposed further restrictions on the development of Papua New Guinea and these restrictions, in turn, contributed to the weakness of capitalist penetration. Australia, being itself a tropical and sub-tropical primary producer, restricted the production of competitive crops in Papua New Guinea (Gadiel, 1973, pp. 110 – 111; Hasluck, 1976, p. 294; Joyce, 1971, p. 30; McKillop, 1977c, pp. 33 – 34). Most significantly, demand for copra was limited by measures preferring Australian dairy products including butter and lessening Australian demand for Papua New Guinea copra for margarine making. Demand from elsewhere was curtailed through the application for a time of the Australian Navigation Act to Papua New Guinea. By requiring, in effect, that certain shipments from Papua New Guinea for overseas be routed through Australia, the act tended to give a monopoly to Australian shippers and to increase freight costs (Brookfield, 1972, p. 67; Power, 1974, p. 162). This effect of monopoly was concentrated further when the Australian government subsidized, for the carriage of mail, the shipping arm of one of the Australian companies trading in the Pacific (Power, 1974, pp. 161 – 162). Finally, in 1936 a new Australian shipping law virtually excluded foreign shipping from the profitable Pacific trade (Power, 1974, pp. 122 – 123). In its typical colonial concern to protect its own monopoly, Australia prevented others doing what it would not. Company law in New Guinea did not allow of companies' "engaging in agricultural, pastoral or forestry pursuits, . . . aerial nagivation" or certain types of mining unless at least two-thirds of their shares were held by "British subjects", Australians being such British subjects (Fairbairn, 1969, p. 37; Wolfers, 1975, pp. 143 – 144). A company seeking a licence under the New Guinea law regulating mineral exploitation had to meet a similar requirement. The body which dealt with land seized from the Germans could only sell it to British subjects or to companies the majority of whose shareholders were British subjects. In Papua, even whilst the colony was formally under British control, the Australian colonies intervened to prevent planned British investment of substantial proportions (Legge, 1956, pp. 92 – 98). It was a symptom and a further cause of the weakness of capitalist penetration that Australia devoted only small administrative resources to the colonization of Papua New Guinea. Brookfield, writing of the colonization of the larger land masses in the Pacific, summarizes other relevant matters this way:

> . . . universally prevalent local warfare not only made the areas dangerous for visitors, but also greatly limited the mobility of potential [labour] recruits toward the recruiter. Hence it was necessary to pacify areas, develop a basic infrastructure, and create the conditions leading towards a demand for money, before a sufficient

supply of labour could be tapped. Government activity in this area was constrained by a minimal administrative staff and budget, hence pacification could only be achieved by establishing private agents of the colonial system, as missionaries, traders or planters. So the economy continued to spread, and by spreading aggravated its problems of transport, and denied itself the economies of concentration. Foci of plantation activity did develop, but they were fed with labour from an enormous area . . . . High fixed costs, due to remote location and small size, have reinforced pressures to hold down wages, and hence to continue use of unskilled migrant labour recruited from an ever-more-distant labour frontier. (Brookfield, 1972, pp. 51 – 52)

These forces which pushed back the labour frontier in Papua New Guinea, overspreading and weakening the economy, were added to by others. Migratory workers were generally unwilling, especially in the earlier part of colonization, to engage in plantation labour when they had once tasted it (Ward, 1971). Laws aimed at the conservation of traditional society, which are considered later, prevented the build-up of a permanent workforce within the labour frontier. To the extent that opportunities for Papua New Guineans to grow cash crops did increase within the frontier, there was less incentive to work for the colonist in order to earn the money to pay the native tax and school fees (Brookfield with Hart, 1971, p. 264).

For a cumulation of reasons, then, capitalist penetration in Papua New Guinea was weak. It was left to the colonial state, especially in legal measures, to take the leading part in bringing the key factors of production, labour and land, into operation within the colonial economy. This process was subject to three broad and related constraints. First, as we have just seen, the economy was comprehensively subordinated to the Australian economy. Second, the economy depended upon the traditional mode of production to subsidize its labour supply. Hence the economy had to be restrained in its destructive impact upon this mode. Often, as we shall now see, one finds the colonial state asserting "the big interests of the bourgeoisie" against particular groups of settlers who wished to burgeon in the more thorough exploitation of Papua New Guineans and their land. The third related constraint, which is elaborated on in the next chapter, was that the colonial political presence was too weak to control or contain potentially hostile class forces that would emerge with a more intense exploitation. (Elsewhere, perhaps most conspicuously in South Africa, it has been possible to combine a more vigorous capitalism with a continuing emphasis on conserving the traditional mode through use of a huge, legal-administrative apparatus.) I will now look at how the key factors of production of labour and land were brought into operation and regulated within the colonial economy.

Judging from the amount of law and the amount of time in colonial legislatives devoted to it, the provision of labour for plantations and mines was the prime concern in the colonial situation in Papua New Guinea. Land, as we shall see, was a less complicated matter. Labour was supplied for plantations and mines through the indenture system. The system was premised on the recognition that 'natives' had to be coerced by law to work because they were 'lazy' (Nelson, 1969, pp. 600 – 601). It is clear that coercion was needed because Papua New Guineans preferred their own way of life to the boring and arduous work on plantations and mines, especially after they had experienced such work (Ward, 1971). Even academic apologists for the system acknowledge that the so-called primitive affluence of the traditional mode was a constraint on the supply of labour (see for example, Smith, 1975, p. 10). So, the worker in the indenture system had to be subject to criminal penalties if, among other things, he 'deserted' his employer or failed to work diligently. To this extent the system was "really rather like slavery" as Lieutenant-Governor Murray of Papua conceded (Murray, 1931, p. 9). Unlike slavery, the entry into employment was, in theory, voluntary. The other main aspect of the system—"the gesture at justice" as Rowley has put it (1971, p. 66) —comprised measures that purported to protect the 'native' and to assure his welfare. In terms of the Covenant of the League of Nations (which was binding on Australia in the case of New Guinea and accepted as policy in Papua) "the well-being and development of such peoples form a sacred trust of civilisation" (Jinks, *et al.*, 1973, p. 121). So, labour law in Papua and in New Guinea made provision for such things as maximum hours of work and minimum wages and for health, dietary and accommodation standards. The law also provided for the protection of the worker against fraud and cruelty on the part of employers and labour recruiters. A recent academic study says that the law was mostly complied with and so the system "on the human level . . . . was neither brutal nor particularly oppressive" (Smith, 1975, pp. 31, 33, 37). As the same account shows, Australia was also concerned to preserve traditional social formations, to prevent "detribalisation" and the creation of a "landless proletariat" (ibid., Chapter 2). Hence labour law provided that after a certain period in employment the worker had to be returned to his village and not 're-engaged' under indenture for a certain further period. The law on this changed often but, generally, in Papua a worker had to be returned to his village after no more than three years and, in New Guinea, after no more than four and a half years. The colonial administration basically only ever allowed the 'signing-on' of 'single' men and this despite a professed concern with homosexuality on plantations and despite occasional pressure from employers to promote the recruitment of families. The law did make provision for wives to accompany workers but this provision was so hedged about and put such greater obligations on the employer that it was rarely availed of. Such wives could be recruited to work, but apart from this, women could not be recruited except for domestic duties. Allowing families and women to reside near the workplace would, of course, tend more towards the dissolution of the traditional mode and the creation of a permanent wage-labour force. As well, limitations were from time to time imposed to prevent over-recruiting of labour.

As we shall see later, the various protective provisions in the individual labour system often did not fit the reality of its operation. However, even the mere content of the legal provisions themselves were hardly always beneficent and humane. For much of the period that concerns us here, the legal minimum (and, in practice, maximum) wage was five shillings a month in New Guinea and ten in Papua. In Australian New Guinea, a protective law provided that "the capacity of each recruiting vessel for each native carried shall be an area of not less than one square metre and an air space of not less than one and a half cubic metres below deck" (Territory of New Guinea, 1914 – 21, p. 45). The provision of quite abject living conditions was sufficient to comply with the law (Nelson, 1975, p. 349; Oram, 1976a, pp. 33 – 34). To take only one more of many possible instances, the death rate among labourers, especially on the goldfields, was frequently extremely high. For example, "expressed as a percentage of the average number of labourers in the Northern Division [of Papua] the death rate varied from about thirty per cent in 1898/99 to ten per cent in 1903/04, and even in later years it was probably never less than five per cent" (Nelson, 1975, p. 313). This was mainly because of the inadequate dietary standards in the law. Despite official recognition of this, little was done to correct the situation (Legge, 1971, p. 89; Roe, 1971, p. 144; Territory of New Guinea, 1924 – 25, p. 11; Territory of Papua, 1915 – 16, p. 25).

Mair has said of 'conditions in practice' in Australian New Guinea:

> Where conditions of work were concerned the pressure of economic demand was stronger than humanitarian considerations. Rapid development, it was argued, was in the interests of the whole

country, and therefore of course in those of the native population; it must not be hampered by pedantic insistence on the letter of the law. The plantations had had to encounter every kind of difficulty, and should not have their burdens increased beyond what they could bear. Inspection was in any case inadequate, and officers who were anxious to enforce the prescribed conditions felt that they could not count on support from headquarters. (Mair, 1970, p. 184)

Papua was basically no different (Rowley, 1972, pp. 60 and 92). It is sometimes said that the Germans were not as draconic or at least no worse than the Australians in the operation of the indentured labour system (Jinks, et al., 1973, pp. 180 – 181; Lawrence, 1964, p. 45; Rowley, 1971, p. 65). Certainly when the Australians took over from Germany in New Guinea and from Britain in Papua, they modified the indenture laws in the interests of the employers (Legge, 1956, pp. 156 – 157; Salisbury, 1970, p. 70; Territory of New Guinea, 1914 – 21, p. 12). However, it should be added that the relative vigour of German colonization was not easily restrained by protective laws and planters were often able to override the German administration with disastrous results for some New Guinea social formations (Firth, 1973). Under all regimes, in Papua and in New Guinea, breaches of the law by employers were flagrant, widespread and usually uncorrected and labour-related atrocities were common (see for example, Nelson, 1975; Willis, 1974, pp. 70 – 71; Rowley, 1972, p. 115). Officially recorded complaints by workers that on the face of them could warrant prosecution ran into hundreds and sometimes thousands each year but prosecutions of employers were few (see for example, Territory of New Guinea, 1959 – 60, pp. 237 – 238).

The ethos in which the law operated was hardly conducive to compliance with it or to its adequate enforcement. The employer had ready access to a colonial official or a colonial court to enforce his side of the labour laws but the Papua New Guinean had, in practical terms, almost no access to officials or to courts to enforce his side. Enforcement of his side depended on a system of official inspection which was grossly inadequate. For example, the New Guinea law for much of its history provided merely for an annual inspection of the plantation or mine but even this requirement was often not complied with. As Rowley has noted, it was "all too commonly the case for officials to regard as their duty assistance to employers" (Rowley, 1971, p. 104). Generous allowance was made, sometimes in the law and always by officials in its enforcement, if employers found it difficult or impossible to comply (see for example,

Territory of New Guinea, 1914 – 21, pp. 48 – 49; Territory of New Guinea, 1950 – 51, p. 131). Even where they were inclined to take action officials have always operated on a 'warning' basis that gave the employer a chance to rectify his breach of the law and courts would not convict an employer if such a warning had not been given (Utz Wellner, personal communication). If the law or the officials were not adequately sympathetic then planters could resort to their pressure group associations and their usually strong representation in colonial legislatures (Power, 1974, pp. 180, 188 – 189; Radi, 1971, p. 121). As in other colonies, the plantation itself (and to a lesser extent, the mine) was a 'small state' with the employer as close to autocratic ruler (Beckford, 1972, p. 19). As an illustration of this, there was legal power given to employers for a time in German and Australian New Guinea to mete out 'disciplinary punishments'—confinement or fines as well as corporal punishment under the Germans (Territory of New Guinea, 1914 – 21, p. 51). The worker could only participate in the wider economy through the employer. The worker depended on the employer for the basics of life (provided as part of his wage in kind) and, besides tax, often the only outlet for his cash wage was the employer's store. This dependence was further emphasized in the law which said that whilst indentured the worker could not enter into any other contract apart from his contract of employment. Generally, and in terms of preserving a correct order in the 'small state', it was for some time an offence for a worker "to create or foster a bad influence among his fellow workers" and such has usually been a sufficient ground for terminating the employment contract.

The practice of the system is vividly reflected by the people's response to it. Usually they chose not to 'sign on' again after a period under indenture, and, on the available figures, almost 4% of the indentured workforce 'deserted' each year.[2] Desertion is particularly significant for there were so many pressures on the labourer to stay: as well as the standard criminal sanctions against 'desertion', the 'deserter' stood to lose his deferred pay (half of his wages were, by law, accumulated for payment on expiry of the indenture); he would usually find himself in a strange and hostile area; even if he got home he could be in trouble with the traditional leader who perhaps had him recruited and there would still be the economic pressure of the native tax forcing him to return or to find work elsewhere.

Turning to enforcement and taking the available figures for the whole colonial period (which means confining the figures to New Guinea), the 'native labour' laws were, up to and including the year 1950 – 51, enforced ten times more against workers than against employers. After 1950 – 51 (most of the penal sanctions against workers having been abolished at the end of 1950) convictions of employers decreased sharply. The average number of convictions of employers then was 7·56 a year with long periods when there were hardly any at all. Nor did conviction for an offence under the indenture laws hold much terror for an employer. He was fined but never imprisoned. For the available figures from New Guinea the average fine per conviction of an employer was Australian $5·80.[3]

There were, however, two areas where the indenture laws were more rigorously applied. It is indicative of the emphasis on the conservation of the traditional mode that, in stark contrast to other obligations, the employer's obligation periodically to repatriate the worker was scrupulously administered (Hasluck, 1976, p. 156). It is indicative of effective enforcement that the employers constantly complained about the repatriation aspects of the indenture laws. The other area of rigorous application was in the obligations placed on workers. Convictions of New Guineans under the indenture laws averaged (up to 1950 – 51) 652 a year and 93% of these convictions were for 'desertion' or failure to work or 'perform duty'. The number of workers convicted in any year was only a small proportion of the total number under indenture but this factor does not exhaust the significance of these laws. As I tried to show earlier, the law in its enforcement and administration generally was almost totally biased in favour of the employer. This patent bias would have made the isolation of the worker more than geographical and would have underscored his dependence.

There were other legal measures influential in securing a supply of labour. Perhaps the most significant was the native tax, quite clearly introduced to create a need for cash and thus force people into wage-labour, even though it was sometimes claimed officially that this was not the intention (Legge, 1971, pp. 46 – 47; Murray, 1931, p. 4; Reed, 1943; p. 149; Sawai, 1977, p. 299). Also, and in contrast to the German record, for much of the colonial period Australian legal measures discouraged cash-cropping and cash-crop processing among New Guineans and this restricted a source of money to pay the tax, a source that successfully competed in attractiveness with wage-labour (Lawrence, 1964, pp. 45, 227; McCarthy, 1963, pp. 79 – 81; Radi, 1971, pp. 107 – 108). Perhaps similar supply considerations lay behind the provision for a time of a legal maximum wage (ten shillings a month) in New Guinea since a higher wage would enable the tax of more people to be paid and thus decrease the pressure on the people to seek wage-labour (cf., Seidman, 1973, p. 562).

Land law, as with laws relating to labour, was concerned to bring a key factor of production within the capitalist mode, yet to preserve sufficient land for the continued viability of the traditional mode. A too vigorous land acquisition by settlers would have to be restrained if the traditional mode, with its reliance on a land-intensive type of subsistence agriculture, were to be preserved as a base for the supply of labour. The conflict involved here would be considerably blunted if, as is a common view, land was a plentiful resource. This view is at best questionable. Of the land area, 2·08% was alienated to the colonist and most of this was alienated in the early days of colonization; it is probable that only about 12% of the land area is suitable for cultivation and of course a great deal of this area would have been used for subsistence production (Barnett, 1976). Indeed, conservation-oriented laws did restrain land alienation and the fact that these laws were resented by resident colonists is evidence that they were needed and largely effective (McSwain, 1977, p. 55; Rowley, 1972, p. 118). All of the colonial regimes subjected land dealings between colonists and 'natives' to approval and control including provision for inspection to ensure that enough land was left for subsistence agriculture. The efficacy of this system varied, however, from regime to regime and from time to time. With the more intense colonization of German rule, the extent of protection was in practice often not great (see for example, Salisbury, 1970, p. 28). However, German rule did come to entail a strong emphasis on the control of land and dealings in the conversation of the traditional mode (Jinks et al., 1973, p. 175). In Australian New Guinea settlers were sometimes allowed their heads and officials were then more concerned with promoting a land-grab than with protection. Such were "the days of 'have a yarn with the district commissioner and he will fix you up' " (Hasluck, 1976, pp. 121 – 122). The district commissioner and his officers could on occasion be too busy setting up their own plantations. The colonial administration, being close to the settlers in such and various other ways, would be inclined to facilitate land acquisition and so would sometimes have to be restrained by the metropolitan government (ibid., pp. 120 – 123). Both the British and the Australians in Papua had a reputation for a more consistently scrupulous concern to protect 'native rights' in land, a reputation born more of a weaker colonization than a superior subjective morality. In the early days of Australian rule in Papua, land law was modified in favour of prospective settlers resulting in a mild land boom

(Legge, 1971, p. 38; Power, 1974, p. 140). At this time there were so few officials and so much land alienated in such short time, that it would have been impossible to comply with the protective provisions in the law.

No matter how land was acquired and no matter whether protective provisions were complied with, law and state tended to uphold and to provide legitimation for the settlers' occupation of land. This legitimacy was sought even before formal colonization when settlers used make-shift systems of registration (Oram, 1976a, p. 18; Ruhen, 1968, p. 100). Indeed, legitimation has been most needed and its bestowal has caused most controversy with the dubious, deceitful and brutal ways in which settlers acquired much land in pre-colonial and early colonial times. The New Guinea case has been especially well documented in this (see for example, Rowley, 1958; Sack, 1973; Salisbury, 1970). There are indications that the situation was basically similar in Papua even if there was less subservience to the settler whose presence and influence was not, in any case, as strong (Oram, 1976a, pp. 23 – 24). Generally, land was often acquired for the proverbial axe and beads or a petty monetary equivalent. It was sometimes awarded by the colonial administration as compensation for wrongs supposedly done to settlers by the 'natives'. It was often acquired after a perfunctory effort to determine ownership and such effort, naturally, tended to result in error. Land boundaries were frequently only roughly drawn and were conveniently self-expanding. The colonial administration took land which it categorized legally as 'waste and vacant'—land that was neither waste nor vacant. The validity of these land acquisitions raised a fundamental legal issue about property relations in the colonies. Many Papua New Guineans claim that they accepted small payments in land transactions and initially tolerated land-grabbing because they thought the land was only to be used for a very limited period. Cycles of land use in their own agriculture were short (unlike the long cycles involved with copra growing, for example) and the idea of absolute ownership of land was one totally alien to their own social relations. Land was something integrated into the total complex of social relations. Although rights in land were, in some areas, quite highly elaborated, land was never a commodity. Land use was regulated through personalized social relations. Evidence that Papua New Guineans saw these early land transactions in terms of limited use is overwhelming (Firth, 1972, p. 367; Howlett *et al.*, 1976, p. 112; Lawrence, 1964, p. 67; Rowley, 1972, pp. 116 – 117; Sack, 1973). In recent times Papua New Guineans have mounted challenges in the courts to some of these early acquisitions. The main line of argument was derived closely from an apt and ample British case law to the effect that 'primitive' people have no notion of ownership in land and hence were unable to transfer ownership. However there was another stream of case law, based on the experience of settler colonies where much plantation land was acquired from 'primitive' people, and such law has it that these people do have and can transfer ownership. The cases reflect the characteristics of different kinds of colonies and not of different kinds of 'primitive' peoples (James, 1974). Australian courts followed the latter line of cases and upheld the property rights of the settlers. German law as applied in New Guinea took a similar view of the matter (Sack, 1973, p. 134).

In the creation and operation of the colonial economy, then, law and state served the interests of the colonists and served to check the resident colonists in too vigorous or disruptive a development. Various laws, such as the indenture laws, provided rights for or protected the colonized, but these were inadequately enforced except where they also served the interests of the colonists. This point is followed up in more detail in the next chapter. As a bridge to that chapter and as a concluding aspect of the present one I will now describe something of the constitutional function of law and state and of the form of law in the colonial context as well as something of the attendant ideologies that supported the colonist.

As is typical of colonial regimes, those in Papua New Guinea were basically regimes of administration. They implemented political decisions made elsewhere. A Papua New Guinean official described the position to his people thus:

> The Queen tells Number One in Canberra what to do; he tells Number One in Port Moresby [the capital] what to do. Number One in Port Moresby tells the District Commissioner what to do, and he tells the Number One Kiap what to do [a kiap being a patrol officer or local level colonial official]. The Number One Kiap tells me what to do, and I tell you what to do. So you had better do it. (Brookfield, 1972, p. 101)

However, like most settler colonies, internal political forces were given some constitutional recognition. Colonial legislatures, although dominated by members appointed from the ranks of the colonial administration, did allow of planter, trader and, to a lesser extent, miner representation. Representatives of these interests were also appointed usually but some provisions was made for the election of a small number. 'Native' members were a relatively recent phenomenon and elected 'native' members a more recent one still. Community-level representative government was also allowed only recently. In the early stages of colonization, however, efforts were made to promote indirect rule. Such efforts eventually had to come to grips with the smallness of scale of Papua New Guinea social formations and with the indeterminacy of their social and political structures (see Langness, 1973, pp. 153 – 154; Sankoff, 1972, p. 561). Indirect rule then had to assume the modest proportions of using traditional leaders or their agents in the implementing and policing of the more detailed aspects of 'native administration'. Rather than being indirect 'rulers', they were "dependent upon seemingly omnipotent white administrators" (Loveday and Welfers, 1976, p. 1). The basic operative at the local level was the European patrol officer who combined wide administrative powers and judicial functions.

Law was a fundamental instrument and an ideology of colonial rule. An Administrator of Papua New Guinea (the leading resident official) wrote generally of the patrol officers:

> . . . to whom Australia owes so much in the exploration and basic development of the country, added to which is the even more significant side of their work—the establishment of law and order in areas which were hitherto uncontrolled.
>
> Their task has not been an easy one, but it is one which has always been carried out by those concerned with tenacity, honesty of purpose, and above all with the supreme desire to bring peaceably to the people they contact the benefit of law and order and an advancing civilization. (D.M. Cleland in Sinclair, 1966, p. vii)

As with other colonists, 'justice' was seen as "a gift that we have brought to them" (Hasluck, 1976, p. 189). With acute insight one noted anthropologist described "the essential features of our legal system" thus:

> It was associated with a concept of universalist morality and the view of an individual as a citizen-unit, who, before the law, was identical with all other such units, who had equal rights, privileges and obligations guaranteed and enforced by the law. It stressed impartial or abstract justice, handing out standard decisions, and punishments, according to the nature of the issue or offence, irrespective of economic, social or political considerations.

and noted that:

> What the [Papua New Guinea] villager found difficult to understand about our legal system was the concept of universalist moral obligation and impartial justice emphasising the nature of the wrong rather

than the sliding scale decisions according to the relationships involved. (Lawrence, 1970, pp. 72 – 73)

Perhaps the villager's difficulty could be noted with some tolerance because "our legal system" as it was applied in Papua New Guinea was certainly not one where the "concept of universalist moral obligation and impartial justice" held sway. Not only was there a distinct system of law which applied only to Papua New Guineans but, even when law was formally universal, it was applied in ways that systematically discriminated against Papua New Guineans. As for the distinct system of law, Papua New Guineans were subjected to a coercive regime of 'native administration' which in the form of broad, discretionary legal provisions gave low-level colonial officials comprehensive control over their charges, a control that was often exercised (Mair, 1970, p. 66). This regime, as well as general law and order matters and obligations under the indentured labour system, were enforced in separate Courts of Native Affairs or Courts for Native Matters (Chalmers and Paliwala, 1977, pp.74 – 82). With these courts, the judge, prosecutor and chief prosecution witness would often be a low-level official trying someone for failure to comply with an order he gave in the first place.

As for law formally applicable universally, it only had relevance to Papua New Guineans when acting upon them, that is, when they were tried for offences under the general criminal law. Even so, many of these offences were rarely made applicable to the colonists, particularly petty offences of public order. However, discrimination persisted also in cases where both the colonist and the colonized were tried. The relatively humane Judge Winter in a case in Papua in 1902 found that "racial feeling is so general and so strong in this country, that I cannot regard the defendant morally culpable in taking the life of a native" (Nelson, 1975, p. 388). Hubert Murray, also relatively humane and the leading resident official in Papua for most of its colonial history, considered that it was "quite impossible to administer even-handed justice . . . public opinion is so strong against it and one has to be so certain one is right; and a native must have a very strong case indeed to get a conviction against a white man" (Inglis, 1974, p. 79). Crimes by colonial officials very often went unprosecuted (Zorn, 1975, p. 58). A colonist suspected of serious crime was sometimes allowed the option of leaving the colony (Fitzpatrick, 1974, pp. 44 – 45). In a similar vein, if somewhat out of the category of universally applicable law, we have just seen that the indentured labour system placed obligations on both the colonized and the colonist but these obligations were discriminatorily enforced against the colonized to a massive degree.

There were other ways in which the notion of 'impartial justice' could be seen not to pertain. I have already mentioned that low-level colonial officials combined the roles of administrator, prosecutor and judge. For much of colonial rule full-time administrators manned the superior courts. The performance of judicial and administrative functions by one person does not necessarily mean that there is no judicial impartiality but it does strongly suggest what was in fact the case, that the judicial element was subordinated to the administrative (Bayne, 1975, pp. 14 – 15; Hasluck, 1976, pp. 176 – 177, 180, 344). Even in recent times this was much the case and then "even in higher circles in [the capital] Port Moresby and in the Crown Law Office itself" (Hasluck, 1976, p. 177). In terms of popular images, 'law', as we will see in the next chapter, comes understandably to be synonymous with coercive, restraining authority.

In all it is not surprising to find that, when convenient, colonial authority was exercised with scant regard to colonial law, much less to bourgeois legality. 'Rough justice' and 'punitive expeditions' involving an abundance of illegality were the order of the day with early colonial rule (Nelson, 1976). As Bayne has summarized the situation, "in making initial contact or in patrolling 'difficult' areas, Administration Officers respected neither the property of the villagers nor, in several cases, their lives" (Bayne, 1975, p. 21). Illegal assault by patrol officers was a standard technique of good government (John Kaupa, personal communication). In New Guinea, the Australian administration persistently extracted forced labour from the people for its own purposes and contrary to its own laws (Paliwala et al., 1978). Nor were legal niceties, such as the absence of any legal prohibition of the conduct in question, allowed to inhibit the colonial administration in its draconic suppression of emergent class action (Gammage, 1975, p. 25).

German law and the British "principles and rules of common law and equity" were "received" with the various colonizations (Gibbs, 1945; Sack and Sack, 1975, p. ix). This reception provided the frame and some content for an overall colonial legal system. It also provided a law personal to the colonist grounded in bourgeois legality and largely untouched by the authoritarian aspect of colonial law. Colonial officials saw law grounded in bourgeois legality as necessary to encourage metropolitan investment (Paliwala et al., 1978). Traditional law (dealt with in Chapter 5) remained as the law personal to the colonized and colonial law's relation to it was distinctly ambiguous. Traditional law could hardly be ignored or suppressed, as it was the law of the vast bulk of the people. It was embedded in and supportive of the traditional mode of production which the colonist sought to conserve. Yet traditional law was also seen as uncivilized, arbitrary and partial and, in short, contrary to bourgeois legality (Bayne, 1975, pp. 18 – 19). This delicate conflict was resolved by extracting something called 'native custom' from the operative dynamic of traditional dispute settlement. The perceived vices of traditional law could then be attached to dispute settlement. Provision was usually made for the recognition of 'native custom' in colonial courts, subject to broad exceptions including one that the custom concerned must not be inconsistent with colonial law. Even where there was no such formal recognition, as was the case with Papua for much of its colonial history, custom was allowed "in every case where it can be reasonably fitted in with our idea of good government" (Murray as quoted in Oram, 1976a, p. 50). Traditional dispute settlement was, on the other hand, beyond tolerance and perhaps illegal. This stance was basically fiction: there were imaginative efforts by some individual officials to extend the colonial court system to take over functions of traditional dispute settlement (see for example, Quinlivan, 1975). However, it was not possible for colonial courts to do this in anything approaching a comprehensive way.

As for ideology, Australia as a colonist claimed a particular, humanitarian virtue (Nelson, 1974, p. 84; Territory of New Guinea, 1914 – 21, p. 14). As a colonial power Australia was, of course, far from unique in the belief in its superior benevolence. Indeed, the exploitative relations of any colonialism were so manifestly at odds with the egalitarian nature of Australians' self-image, that they appear to have to deny that they were colonists at all (Hudson, 1971; Wolfers, 1972, p. 72). Perhaps this evasion exempted the Australians from making any original contribution to colonial ideology. The rhetoric of their rule was much the same as that of the Germans and the British and was in large part directly derived from the latter (Legge, 1971, p. 33; Rowley, 1972, p. 75).

Colonial ideology, as we saw in Chapter 2, contained a convenient duality. On the one hand, the ideology of protection justified conserving the traditional mode of production. On the other, the civilizing mission or the ideology of improvement, to use the Spencerian idiom of the day, justified the adaptation and exploitation of resident social formations. In Papua New Guinea, the "preservation of the colonized people" and the "protection of their rights and privileges" were given great emphasis (see for example Jinks *et al.*, 1973, p. 90; Oram, 1976a, p. 43). Despite being commonly seen as a disruptive element, the activity and the ideology of the missions were very much geared towards the conservation of the traditional mode (see for example Townsend, 1978, pp. 11, 47). The ideology of protection also had, and was meant to have, a legitimating impact on the colonized. For example, on the annexation of Papua by the British, the people were assured (and this remains deeply embedded in the folk memory) that "your lands will be secured to you, your wives and children will be protected" (Whittaker *et al.*, 1975, p. 462). For any wrong by a colonist there would be a fair enquiry, justice would be done and "evil-disposed men . . . promptly punished by the officers of the Queen" (ibid., p. 462). However, and in the justifying terms of Article 22 of the Covenant of the League of Nations, the sacred trust of civilization also extended to effecting change and development. Requiring people to work on plantations and at mines was part of the sacred trust because to so work was a civilizing influence and the best sort of education 'the native' could get (Firth, 1977, pp. 240 – 241; Jinks *et al.*, 1973, pp. 91, 94; Nelson, 1969, p. 601). More generally, Murray had put it that the Papuan must be raised "eventually to the highest civilization of which he is capable" (Jinks *et al.*, 1973, p. 118), but the process was not to be rushed (Woolford, 1974, p. 15). Indeed, the process could not be rushed, for as "the great Murray in 1906 put it . . . 'the abysmal difference between the Stone Age and the twentieth century forms a chasm which it is almost impossible to span' " (Hastings, 1969, p. 37). Hence, for "people at so low a stage of evolution . . . argument and moral suasion [do not] have very much influence . . . [and] advance must be made with the sanction of Ordinances and Regulations" (Territory of Papua, 1919 – 20, p. 111). As Ake says of Africa, the colonist made his victims what they would be to deserve the treatment they got (Ake, 1976, p. 202). That theme is now pursued into the actuality of the Papua New Guinea situation.

## Notes

1. Some of the material relating to labour in this chapter and to a few aspects of the containment of the working class in Chapter 6 has been used in Fitzpatrick (1978). I am grateful to E.L. Wheelwright and Ken Buckley for being able to use it here.
2. This figure and the rest of the New Guinea figures in this chapter are derived from a necessarily hefty sample of half the years of Australia's rule in New

Guinea. The figures (where available) for the years so selected were then extracted from the Annual Reports covering those years and the various calculations in the text were derived from those figures.

3. This average figure includes a few cases where there was a conviction but a nil fine.

# 4 The Colonized

This chapter deals with law and state in the class containment of the colonized. A large part of this function is performed by those aspects of law and state which conserve the traditional mode in its subsidizing of capitalist production. Such conservation also serves class containment. For example, those laws which ensure the periodic repatriation of the worker also make the class organization of a proletariat next to impossible. There are, in addition, laws that have a distinct function of class containment, such as, as we will see, many laws regulating urban residence. Further, conservation-oriented laws were enforced in areas where conservation did not act in subsidizing capitalist production. The political power of the colonist was, objectively, weak in the extreme and the colonist perceived it as such. The colonized had little reason to support the exercise of this political power. More particularly, they had little reason to conform either because of the benefits they received from the exercise of this power or because of their participation in it. The weakness of colonial power meant that pervasive and direct repression was not an option. Hence the traditional mode had to be conserved for its maintenance of existent ethnic division, a division that was, in Papua New Guinea, helpfully extreme. In its conservation generally, the traditional mode is not simply acted upon: it adapts purposively to capitalist penetration in ways that make for its own conservation, and that thus support law and state in their function of conservation. I will now lend some detail to this line of argument and in so doing somewhat qualify it.

In the colonial situation

> There is a great imbalance between the mass of the ''colonizers'' and
> the mass of those ''colonized''. And there is a more or less persistent

> fear of seeing the hierarchy re-established on the sole basis of the size
> of the masses. (Balandier, 1970a, p. 47)

As for Papua New Guinea:

> At the turn of the century there were about 500 Europeans, mostly
> Germans in New Guinea—missionaries, traders and planters. After
> 1900, when Papua had become an Australian Territory (in 1906) and
> the Germans had settled down to serious colonization of New
> Guinea, the European population increased steadily. In 1914, at the
> outbreak of World War I there were 1,027 Europeans in New
> Guinea and 1,186 in Papua. At the outbreak of World War II the
> figures were 4,399 and 1,822 respectively. (Utrecht, 1977, p. 4)

This was in a population of the colonized that, prior to the second world
war, was probably close to two million. (Current total population is close
to three million.) The population under 'government control' in New
Guinea alone in 1920 was 177,620 and in 1940 it was 662,724 (Kaa, 1970,
pp. 2 – 3).

The Australian colonists, with some accuracy then, perceived their position as weak and precarious. A certain siege mentality becomes under-
standable, such as the view in Papua, that "the position of the European is
that of a small garrison, upholding the cause of civilization among a more
or less hostile or indifferent population of primitives; and obviously the
lives of this small garrison and the honour of the women must be
protected" (see Nelson, 1976, p. 29). The relatively enlightened Murray
wrote, in justifying capital punishment, of "the Territory of Papua, where
a small white community is surrounded by a barbaric population hardly
out of the stone-age" (see Inglis, 1974, p. 109). In Australian New
Guinea, the colonists felt themselves to be "among a sea of barbarians
whom they never doubted would cheerfully cut their throats if it could be
done" (Gammage, 1975, p. 20). Gammage brings out the central point
that the colonists saw their security as based ultimately "on the obvious
mistrust and animosity which divided the natives" (ibid., p. 20). That the
point is central is vividly illustrated by what is called the Rabaul strike of
1929. This was a scrupulously restrained, "peaceful and purposeful" strike
(ibid., p. 23). It was a strike of almost all the New Guinean workers,
including the New Guinean police, in the major town of Rabaul. It was so
effectively organized in terms of solidarity that no white resident knew of
it until it had happened. The colonists' response was swift, fearful and
furious. Draconic punishments were inflicted on leaders of the strike—

punishments resulting from charges not adequately authorized in law (ibid., pp. 25 – 28). The colonists' response indicated that what concerned them was the ability of the people to combine across ethnic divisions:

> . . . the entire episode indeed must have been highly disconcerting to those who, like the Administrator himself, "knowing anything of the native mentality" found it "quite inconceivable that the natives who belong to different tribes, and who nurse hereditary enmities against each other should sink their differences and combine in a general demonstration". (Epstein, 1969, p. 29)

The *Rabaul Times*, in the same vein, said "the alarming thing is that the matter was well organized" (Woolford, 1974, p. 16; see also Ford, 1972, p. 1207). So, although they claimed no more than a benevolent claim to protect the colonized, the colonists did sometimes make explicit a certain self-interest in preventing "detribalization" and the creation of a "landless proletariat", to use the terminology of numberless official pronouncements to this effect (see for example, Smith, 1975, Chapter 2).

The colonized had a definite and a subordinate place in the colonial order. They were, as we saw, viewed by the colonist as inferior. They were seen and treated as only capable of playing a part in the colonial economy in dependent relation to the colonist. In Papua, and the position was the same in New Guinea, government staff were directed "above all to prepare the country for development by Europeans. There is not and there has not been any other policy" (Power, 1974, p. 91). Although there was some formal policy emphasis on the development of "native agriculture" little was done about this and even less was effective (Oram, 1976a, p. 28; Radi, 1971, p. 102). Any independent economic initiatives the colonist moved to stultify, often proscribing them as illegal. Hence the famed 'apathy' of the colonized. Knowledgeable observers found in Papua "a passivity and an attitude of dependence" and found that government intervention "had effectively stifled or demoralised almost every source of independent iniative" (Oram, 1976a, p. 61; Wolfers, 1972, p. 73). The position was the same in New Guinea (Howlett et al., 1976, pp. 5, 336). Sankoff provides a revealing incident from New Guinea:

> In one Buang village everyone was convinced not only that any initiative in business on their part was doomed to failure because of their lack of competence, but also that it was illegal. When a government patrol arrived in the village some six months after one brave man had defied local opposition and started a trade store of substantial

proportions, everyone ran to warn the entrepreneur that the patrol
had come to arrest him for his rashness. (Sankoff, 1969, p. 72)

Others have noted Papua New Guineans' perception that the setting-up,
by them, of economic activities outside of the traditional mode was illegal,
even though this was not always formally illegal (Allen, 1979, p. 15;
McCarthy, 1963, p. 18; Salisbury, 1970, p.243). To some extent one can
see here, using Freire's terms, that the wide-ranging prescriptions of the
colonial order have been internalized by the people (Freire, 1970, p. 31;
1972, p. 11). In terms of the dominant power, Papua New Guineans can
but perceive their own societies as utterly inferior, yet they are to keep to
those societies. They are denied any personally significant part in the
superior society. Reminiscent of Fanon (1967), cases of psychiatric treatment reveal a 'status anxiety' in which delusional trappings of the
dominant society are taken on and the attributes of the inferior society
rejected (Burton-Bradley, 1975, pp. 10 – 28). A common aspect of the
'cargo cult' was the seeking of a new life and the rejection of the old.

There are more substantial ways in which colonization could command
some popular allegiance. Most especially the introduction of some dramatically effective medicines and the partial suppression of inter-group violence
were widely appreciated. Even at its best however, colonial rule and
colonial law were viewed as something negative and repressive, as authoritarian, arbitrary and limitless, even as idiosyncratically varying with the
officials who applied it (Allen, 1979, pp. 4, 10 – 11; Sam et al., 1975,
p. 162). Because of the weakness of colonial rule and the need to conserve
the traditional mode of production, the coverage of colonial law could, in
fact, only be limited. Writing of one large grouping, Warren noted that:

> The administrative and legal system barely penetrated to the day-to-
> day lives of most villagers: tax was collected, censuses were taken and
> only major crimes and serious disturbances of the peace were to be
> brought to the attention of the central authorities. Villagers other-
> wise managed their own affairs . . . . (Warren, 1978, p. 128)

From this should be excepted intrusions in the cause of health and hygiene
and other more *ad hoc* and varying effects of 'native administration'.
Simpson refers to a study of another group which shows that "law was
seen as an intruder, alien and unrelated to local traditions, thus leading to
strong village resentment" (Simpson, 1978, p. 31). Hence there was no
fundamental acceptance by the people of colonial law: they accepted it only
provisionally (Reay, 1974). The Hageners, Andrew Strathern finds:

... held that while the [colonial] administration had to carry out its own rituals they also had to carry out their own; and so a dualistic view of "law" and "custom" was created. Once such a dualistic view was established, the effects of control over violence and the introduction of new laws seen as "good" were partly nullified. The people continued to define themselves as partly "bad", i.e. still partly adhering to custom. (Strathern, 1977, p. 139)

The persistence of the traditional mode provides a basis for this 'custom' and a basis for treating the intrusions of colonial rule and colonial law as provisional. Colonial rule is thus afflicted with a continual crisis of legitimation which further underlines the need to maintain ethnic divisions. The focus on the traditional mode means that no 'universal' relations emerge—"there is little sense or understanding of a political relation with the wider concentric circles of government and administration that might be expected eventually to comprise village-state relations", says Warren of the now contemporary situation (1978, p. 125). 'Understanding' could hardly result in a more effectively involving relation for, as one 'understanding' and powerful leader sympathetic to the colonist put it to his people, "the law comes from England, then it comes to Canberra to the House of Parliament and from there it comes to New Guinea. I have told the government in Port Moresby what I want but they won't listen to me. They can't change these things in New Guinea, it rests in Canberra" (Brown, 1972, p. 118). The people perceived the 'law' as being all coercive authority whether it was colonial rule in general or law in particular and whether it was exercised by officials or by settlers (McSwain, 1977, pp. 58, 80). This was hardly surprising given, as we saw in the last chapter, the immense power of the colonist as settler, the manifestly close relation between planters and officials, the breadth of discretionary power conferred on officials and the facility with which the colonist could and did resort to illegal means of control. Relying on this image of law, a large mining company can today advise its new employees that there is "law of the Government [and] law of the Company AND both are necessary" (see Fitzpatrick, 1974, p. 41).

To say that the 'traditional' mode was conserved does not mean that resident social formations were static or that they stay much the same or that they were not profoundly disrupted (Meggitt, 1971; Worsley, 1971, p. 50). This conservation is a dynamic process in which resident social formations adapt and vigorously interact with capitalist penetration in the cause of their own survival. Elements of the social formations interact as well in ways that are destructive of these formations, but more of this in the next chapter. Broadly, much of the impact of capitalist penetration is absorbed and contained within the traditional social formation which, in turn, is somewhat assisted in this by aspects of capitalist penetration. Thus the inflow of money and new goods was largely absorbed in traditional exchange rather than in disruptive production—absorbed in a displacing of some traditional trade goods, in an inflation of exchange values and in a general intensification of exchange activities (Finney, 1973, pp. 33 – 4, 37; Howlett *et al.*, 1976, p. 16; Lawrence, 1964, p. 227; Meggitt, 1971, pp. 201 – 203; Strathern, 1971, pp. 54, 91 – 92, 109). An array of new consumption goods soaked up wages and the proceeds of cash crops. These goods were accessible in towns and in the planter's store. If the attractions of these proved limited, appropriate wants were fostered as with, for example, the "smoking schools" conducted by German traders (Firth, 1972, p. 365). New forms of exchange in gambling and prostitution became increasingly common. Recently, alcohol has become perhaps the most significant item of wasteful consumption and it plays an increasingly important part in exchange activity. The suppression of warfare and the introduction of new labour-saving means of production, such as the steel axe (much more efficient than the traditional stone axe), created time for more exchange activity and also created space, as it were, to accommodate the absence of some people in indentured labour (Lawrence, 1964, p. 228; Salisbury, 1962). To the extent that there was indigenous cash-cropping, this was accommodated within the traditional mode of production, a point illustrated in the next chapter.

Capitalist penetration and the response of resident social formations also strengthened the position of traditional leaders who could sometimes be recruited in the service of the colonial regime (Brown, 1963; Salisbury, 1964). Hence the extension of exchange also strengthened the position of leaders as they were the organizers of much exchange activity (Brown, 1963; Epstein, 1969, p. 18; Epstein, 1968, p. 39; Meggitt, 1971, p. 201; Salisbury, 1964, p. 230; Salisbury, 1970, p. 11; Strathern, 1971, p. 54). In the trade period before formal colonization, some leaders bolstered their power through acquiring arms from traders with whom they had, as a result, a certain common cause (Epstein, 1969, p. 18). Some leaders also found common cause with labour recruiters. It was the practice, and one legally regulated for a time, for labour recruiters to use persons in authority to put pressure on young men to sign-on; for this purpose a 'bonus' was paid and, it would appear, some leaders became very wealthy in the process

(Mair, 1970, pp. 193, 194; Rowley, 1958, pp. 124 – 125). Firth notes that the village 'chief' appointed by the Germans could be relied upon for a reasonable offering of 'free recruits' for planters (Firth, 1973, p. 146). Finally, leaders or agents whom they controlled were often appointed to positions of local level authority as operatives of the colonial regime especially to aid in the enforcement of colonial law, a form of limited indirect rule, although direct rule was very much the colonial policy (Oram, 1976a, p. 45). Leaders used this situation to increase their power in the traditional context (Brown, 1963; McSwain, 1977, p. 72; Salisbury, 1964). Despite the official disapproval of traditional dispute settlement, these leaders used their new positions to enhance their role as dispute settlers and this activity was informally integrated into the work of official courts. Colonial field officers encouraged these leaders to hold courts modelled on the officers' own Courts of Native Affairs or Courts for Native Matters with an appeal extending to these latter courts (see for example, Reay, 1974, pp. 206 – 207). In all, there was often a symbiotic relationship between traditional leaders and the colonial administration. The leaders relied on the administration as a basis for their greater power and the administration relied on the leaders as a means of control at the community level. In short, the conservation of the traditional enhances the position of the leader and thus facilitates the incorporation of the traditional into a regime of indirect rule.

The traditional mode is, of course, far from self-conserving. We have already seen that colonial law and state have a crucial part to play. The indentured labour law put limits on the numbers that could be recruited from particular areas, required workers to be periodically repatriated and required them to stay then for a period in their home area before signing-on again. Under the Australians this repatriation aspect of the law was adequately enforced even if this was not always the case for limits on recruitment (Hasluck, 1976, p. 156). Colonial officers often supervised signing-on and recruiters and employers had to maintain a system of records and registers that greatly facilitated enforcement of the law on repatriation. Employment outside the indenture system was only allowed by law for very brief periods or for employment within a short distance of the worker's traditional home or sometimes only allowed where both these conditions applied. The idea here was that the worker would remain integrated into his home area because he would not be far from it or long away from it, or both. Perhaps more unequivocally directed against class organization was a standard provision in the indentured labour law which made it an offence and a cause for dismissal if a worker "fosters a bad influence amongst his fellow labourers".

Class containment can also be seen as a function of those laws which made dealings in land, outside the traditional context, subject to the control of the colonial administrations. In this "the attachment of the native to his land" was a central plank of colonial policy (Hasluck, 1976, pp. 161, 226). These laws seem, on the whole, to have been effectively enforced (McSwain, 1977, p. 55; Rowley, 1972, p. 118). The metropolitan government did restrain the colonial administration when it was too indulgent to settlers on this score (Finney, 1973, pp. 46 – 47). Under the Australians these laws extended not just to transactions between Papua New Guineans and colonists but to transactions among Papua New Guineans where such transactions were not covered by traditional custom. With some involvement of Papua New Guineans in cash-cropping, to allow uncontrolled transactions between them could result in landlessness for some—the creation of the 'landless proletariat'—and the emergence of a rural bourgeoisie.

Underlying the labour and land laws was the idea that the 'native' was 'protected' by official action in his or her relation to colonial economy and society and hence there was no need for the 'native' to take action to protect his or her 'rights' outside the traditional sphere. Indeed the 'native' was considered conveniently incapable of taking any such action that would be in any way adequate. For example, the indentured labour law laid down extensive and detailed protective standards relating to conditions of work and to living conditions. These standards were to be enforced by colonial officials. They were, as we saw, often not complied with and were most inadequately enforced, but still the law presented a system that, at least formally, obviated any need for the colonized to take independent action outside the traditional context. The habit of such action could, of course, lead to political assertion and provoke class organization.

The extent of official 'protection' went well beyond labour and land laws. Protection was basic to those laws called native regulations, on which was based that whole system of so-called native administration, or native affairs, or, as it was revealingly put in the early days of colonization in Papua, native affairs and control (Nelson, 1975, p. 436). The native regulations were also premised on people's inability to care adequately for themselves in the traditional context as well. Under these regulations, the ability of officials to intervene in the lives of the colonized took such widespread and near comprehensive proportions as to be capable of use in containing any independent action (Wolfers, 1972, p. 73). The system has been well and extensively described by Wolfers (1975). Mair has observed that:

> The theoretical basis of the system was the idea that natives should do as they were told, and Murray's only concession to the principle of persuasion and consent was to exhort administrative officers (after the system had been in operation for over thirty years) to explain to the people that the orders given them were for their good. (Mair, 1970, p. 66)

The system conferred despotic control over what and where Papua New Guineans could build and grow (it was an offence not to plant or adequately tend sufficient subsistence crops), over the control of weeds and plant diseases, over what they could wear and over their health, over the safety and running of boats, over the disposal and inheritance of property, over movement outside of their 'tribal area', over recreation, over what traditional customs could or could not be followed, over what work had to be done in the maintenance of the village and of roads and briges as well as over numerous other matters.

A perhaps more subtle aspect of these laws in their relation to conservation and class containment is their part in preserving a certain 'native' identity. To quote again a little of Wolpe's incisive explanation:

> . . . it is in part the very attempt to conserve and *control* the non-capitalist societies in the face of the tendency of capitalist development to disintergrate them and thereby undermine the basis of exploitation, that accounts for political policies and ideologies which centre on cultural, ethnic, national and racial characteristics (Wolpe, 1975, p. 244)

It is in the insistence on these characteristics that laws of the petty apartheid type have their distinctive role, laws about what can be worn, about separate public facilities and the like. Thus with one native regulation "all employees, with the exception of certain categories such as clerks, were required to wear waistcloths and to be bare above the waist" and another regulation required permits for Papua New Guineans to wear (the European) shorts and shirt (Oram, 1976a, p. 71). Health reasons were usually advanced as a justification for such laws but it was also recognized that they served to keep the Papua New Guinean 'in his place', as the characteristic phrase has it (ibid., p. 71).

Examples could be multiplied but perhaps the most indicative law here is the White Women's Protection Ordinance. This Papuan law was passed in 1926. It required the mandatory death penalty for any person convicted of the rape or attempted rape of a European woman or girl. Severe penalties, including flogging, were provided for various lesser sexual offences against European females. Despite some deference to 'universal morality' in that a male of any race could be convicted, the law was aimed solely at Papuans (see Inglis, 1974, illustration facing p. 80). No European was ever charged under the law. At the time it was introduced there had been no known rape of a 'white woman' in Papua, though there had been a few assaults which provoked near-hysterical responses on the part of the community of colonists. It is clear that this law meant something very fundamental for the resident colonists. Various official debates and publications described it as the most significant law in the land and described assault on a 'white woman' as an incomparably heinous crime (ibid., pp. 75 – 76, 94, 103, 109). The 'white woman' was something 'sacred'—'God's greatest gift'—who would be 'defiled' by sexual contact with a Papuan (ibid., pp. 25, 95, 103). Measures for her protection had to be particularly severe because she was considered weak and irresponsible in sexual matters and the Papuan was seen as possessed of a base but potent sexual appeal, the standard notion of the 'Black Apollo'.

The revealing element of 'overkill' in this law is captured with grim humour in this Papuan view of it:

> If a Papuan smiled at a white woman he was gaoled; if he looked at
> her, he was gaoled; if he touched her, he was gaoled; if he touched her
> on the breast, he would be hanged. (ibid., p. 83)

It is usual in social formations based on hierarchical and ascribed status for women of the dominant ethnic group or caste to bear a heavy symbolical load and to be seen as central to the maintenance of that dominance (see for example, Cash, 1941, p. 103; Douglas, 1970, p. 130). That this law was basically concerned with the affirmation of general dominance and with keeping the Papuan 'in his place' becomes evident when the context of its passage is looked at more closely. The beginnings of a disturbing change were then becoming apparent. Some Papuans were breaking out of the colonial fixed order and assuming what can accurately and suggestively be called positions of responsibility (Hank Nelson, personal communication). Something of the colonist's response is captured by F.E. Williams, the noted anthropologist to the Papuan administration:

. . . let the native hold to a course of his own, and the white man (I am speaking of the British [that is, including the Australian—P.F.]) will tolerate and even admire him. But let him presume, or ape, or try to be "a white man with a black skin" and the average European in Papua will bristle with suspicion and resentment. (Quoted in Oram, 1976a, p. 59)

Moreover such an *évolué* was not only disliked by the colonist but also feared (Inglis, 1974, pp. 7, 8, 11, 57). A common view of the colonist was that "some of the natives, as they become partly educated and are granted privileges, are inclined to be insolent" (quoted in Oram, 1976a, p. 60). A small but very telling point noted by Oram is that "for many years Europeans discouraged Papua New Guineans from speaking English to them" (ibid., p. 200).

The Papuan new man could be looked on as transitional or, more optimistically, as an anomaly, but either state is apt to be viewed as a threat to the existing order (Douglas, 1970, pp. 53, 116). Add to this the structural centrality of 'white women' and the persisting and profound insecurity of the colonist, and it begins to appear that the White Women's Protection Ordinance was an appropriate affirmation of continuing colonial domination, the basis of which was seen as coming under threat. In this light it is not so remarkable that no rape and few assaults preceded the law. This interpretation is borne out in the colonists' assumption that, typically, the Papuan new man was responsible for supposed sexual attacks (Inglis, 1974, p. 11). A similar point emerges from a particular application of the labour laws in Papua when men from one area were restricted in being employed in the capital. This was because the colonist, without justification it seems, considered these people to be too much inclined towards sexually assaulting others. However, these people were too much inclined towards independence; Murray noted that one group of them were "the only natives of Papua who . . . ever looked as if they might be in any way dangerous to the Government" (Oram, 1976a, p. 48; Wolfers, 1975, pp. 38 – 39).

There were numerous other laws which more overtly sought to keep the Papua New Guinean 'in his place'. It has already been argued that the indentured labour law undermined class organization. This law would be adequate in this for plantations and mines but where, as in towns, large numbers of workers were concentrated there remained some residual potential for class action, as the Rabaul strike of 1929 illustrated. As well, controls on employment would not be adequate to check the build-up of a 'landless proletariat' in the form of the urban unemployed or dispossessed. So, there were numerous additional controls on mobility and on urban residence (for a general account see Jackson *et al.*, 1976). These may now seem, in sum, extremely excessive and may have to be explained, to a considerable degree, in terms of the colonist's great insecurity quite apart from their objective functions of conservation and containment. Outside the net of employment, movement and settlement apart from the sphere of the traditional were closely controlled. Various 'vagrancy' and 'native administration' laws had overlapping provisions which penalized people for having "insufficient lawful means of support" and for being "absent from his tribal area" and being unable to give a good account of "his means of support". As applied by the courts "means of support" was equated exclusively with being employed by a colonist. For good measure, it was illegal for a Papua New Guinean to remain in a town for more than four days unless employed or unless (s)he had official permission. In any of these cases the court had power to return a convicted person to his or her home area. As for regulating actual urban residence, workers had to stay in their quarters after a certain hour at night unless given permission by an official or by the employer, permission which could usually only be given in limited circumstances. Without the employer's permission, a Papua New Guinean worker could not have another Papua New Guinean in premises provided for the worker. In New Guinea towns, Papua New Guineans were only allowed to reside in premises provided by their employers or in special reserves. Recreation was often tightly controlled. In New Guinea towns, a Papua New Guinean could not attend certain large social gatherings without official approval. The playing of sports by Papua New Guineans in one large town was subject to prohibitively complex regulation which confined it to certain areas and made it dependent on the approval of officials and employers. Gambling and the consumption of alcohol were prohibited, perhaps for good intentions among others, but such activities, like sport, provided inducements for Papua New Guineans to associate together. Reed notes that, in New Guinea, the most frequent cases before "the numerous courts for native affairs" involved the charge of being absent from residential quarters at night (Reed, 1943, p. 177). Although this is somewhat of an exaggeration, a great deal of the work of these courts in towns entailed the enforcement of laws which sought to prevent Papua New Guineans associating together.

In rural areas overt legal restraints were more complex and varied somewhat from one colonial regime to another. In German New Guinea the extent of colonial settlement and the general level of exploitation did not measure up to metropolitan expectations. So, New Guineans were encouraged and even legally compelled to plant and maintain cash-crops. To promote their involvement in a money economy the use of traditional shell currency was prohibited (Power, 1974, p. 49). New Guineans could use the proceeds of cash-cropping to pay the German head tax and as this ability reduced the incentive to labour to earn cash, planters opposed the extension of cash-cropping to New Guineans (Willis, 1974, p. 45). The Australians in New Guinea, building on the German's economic base, maintained something of a settler colony. But the metropolitan interest was weaker and less concerned with an intense exploitation of the colony. On the issue of cash-cropping by New Guineans, the trend was for the settlers now to have their way. The settlers were not just concerned to prevent cash-cropping as a disincentive to labour. As the labour frontier expanded, it left areas where few people would serve under indenture in any case. Hence, on this score there was little or nothing to be gained in preventing cash-cropping by New Guineans in these areas. The settlers' other concern was with competition from New Guineans, particularly in the initial processing of crops (Lubett, 1977, p. 16). Cash-cropping by New Guineans was no longer compulsory and it was rarely encouraged. On the contrary, it was prohibited and restrained in various ways. As a result such cash-cropping stagnated and declined. This process was helped along, it seems, in the depression of the 1930s when the large plantation and trading enterprises "to keep control of a greater share of diminished total business . . . discouraged the buying of indigenous copra and other crops" (Brookfield, 1972, p. 79).

The most significant law here was one which required a trading licence for, among other things, the buying of copra. Such a licence could not be issued for the buying of copra within two miles of a plantation or buying facility, thus giving the plantation or other facility a monopoly within that area. In all, the law had the effect of restricting the buying of copra to Australian and German planters and traders. This monopoly enabled colonists to buy copra at prices which even colonial officials had to recognize were exploitative in the extreme (McCarthy, 1963, p. 80; Melrose Report, 1939, pp. 31 – 32).[1] In this way the law greatly inhibited the growing and harvesting of copra (McCarthy, 1963, p. 79). As Salisbury writes of the traditional area he studied, the law created a situation where "in effect, Vunamami had become a captive labour force for the plantation", since Vunamami was within two miles of the plantation and so could only sell its copra to this outlet (Salisbury, 1970, p. 124). Charitable academics have noted that the adverse effects this law had on New Guineans were 'unintended', that it operated "not from any desire to discriminate against natives" but to keep out Chinese buyers who were more competent than the Australians (Radi, 1971, p. 107; Salisbury, 1970, p. 124). But this and other laws were used quite deliberately to restrict New Guinean enterprise (see for example, Melrose Report, 1939). This law also served to nip in the bud a troublesome "susceptibility of . . . [New Guinean leaders] to any influence likely to stimulate trading possibilities" amongst themselves (Melrose Report, 1939, pp. 18, 20).

To the extent that the colonists found law insufficient in this, they relied on its repressive image. An idea was fostered by traders and officials that the initial processing (drying) of copra by New Guineans was illegal (McCarthy, 1963, p. 81; Melrose Report, 1939, p. 23; Salisbury, 1970, p. 243). Traders and officials created difficulties when New Guineans attempted to set up copra driers (Epstein, 1968, p. 45; Melrose Report, 1939, p. 27). A justification given for this was that copra dried by New Guineans was of an inferior grade (Lawrence, 1964, p. 60). To the extent, if any, that this was so, it was an extremely convenient argument, since it was the colonists who denied New Guineans the chance to set up adequate driers in the first place. Further, if widespread processing of copra by New Guineans took place, this would have made it easier to store and transport the product and thus facilitate its sale outside the two mile restriction on copra buying.

Other laws which professed to be exclusively for the protection of Papua New Guineans had a similar general effect. Some laws subjected contracts entered into by 'natives' to official approval if the price or value of the subject matter exceeded a certain level. Other laws required people who traded with 'natives' to be licensed by the colonial administration and enabled a court to set aside or vary the terms of contracts to which a 'native' was a party (Seddon, 1974, pp. 55 – 64). Taking each of these laws in turn, it seems to have been the case in New Guinea that official consent would not be given to a contract providing a New Guinean with loan capital for an enterprise that would compete with colonists (Epstein, 1964, pp. 60, 66; Melrose Report, 1939, pp. 27 – 30). The law requiring a licence to trade with 'natives' was used to prevent New Guineans setting up economic enterprises by restricting the issue of licences or by imposing conditions on their issue that New Guinean traders would find difficult or impossible to comply with (Melrose Report, 1939, p. 23 and see Chapter 7 later). As Wolfers has gently commented, "Papua New Guineans were so assiduously protected from exploitation and the disruptions that development might bring that they were sometimes denied opportunities to participate in . . . benefits that might follow from development" (Wolfers, 1975, p. 5). As for the law enabling a court to set aside or vary the terms of contracts, it must have proved too offensive to bourgeois legality for not one case mentioning the law could be found by a legal scholar who has worked extensively on it (Seddon, 1974, p. 62). This account of laws restrictive of cash-cropping and of crop processing has been largely confined to New Guinea because in Papua, as we shall see shortly, matters took a different course.

The indentured labour law was also based to an extent on the protection of 'natives' in their entering into contracts, because they were seen as not having adequate bargaining strength (Territory of New Guinea, 1958 – 59, p. 101). Hence the law laid down minimum protective standards. As we have already seen, these standards were low and the provisions poorly enforced, except to the extent that provisions making for the conservation of the traditional mode could be construed as protective. Controls on contracting also underlined the worker's dependence on the employer. There was a standard prohibition on the worker's entering into any other employment contract during the currency of the term of indenture. In Papua, the labour law of 1941 prohibited the worker from entering into any contract at all during this time.

A final set of legal restraints can be related to the capacity of Papua New Guineans for collective organization, a matter considered more fully in its traditional context in the next chapter. Here, one should distinguish between large-scale and small-scale organization. Small-scale organization typified enduring social structures: the basic Papua New Guinean social formation having from 50 to 800 members. Despite, and because of, this small-scale of organization and because of the famed 'looseness' or structural indeterminacy of Papua New Guinean social formations, large-scale organization manifests considerable flexibility and adaptability. Large-scale organization does coalesce in political structures of some enduring formality, structures most commonly described as tribes and whose membership can run into several thousands. The response of the colonist to collective organization by Papua New Guineans depended on whether it was small-scale or large-scale. Small-scale organization was the basis for conserving the traditional mode of production and, in the main, for limited indirect rule. It was also used directly as a basis for economic exploitation in Papua through laws setting up 'native plantations', as we shall now see. I shall then try to show how large-scale organization when it moved outside the traditional sphere, which its flexibility and adaptability made it prone to do, was prohibited or suppressed in various legal measures.

In Papua, there was no Germany to build a settler economy which Australia could latch onto. Like the Germans, the British had a law under which Papuans could be compelled to produce copra but, apart from plantings in a few small areas, not much came of it partly because of the expectation that colonial settlement would lead to sufficient production (Donaldson and Good, 1979b, p. 5; Power, 1974, pp. 49 – 50, 201 – 204). Despite efforts by an over-extended Britain and by Australia to attract settlers, the attempt was, as we saw, largely unsuccessful. Under Australian rule, the colonial authorities then discovered a commitment to 'native development' and sought to realize this through a scheme of compulsory production on 'native plantations'. As Murray observed "the only alternative to the European is the Papuan" (quoted in Power, 1974, p. 206). Under the British law, official direction and ease of official supervision had resulted in crops sometimes being grown on an organized basis resembling, in physical layout, plantation agriculture. The Australian administration built on this and, despite objections that native plantations would lead to a labour shortage, introduced in 1918 the Native Plantations Ordinance and, far from coincidentally, the Native Taxation Ordinance. Miles summarizes the thrust and content of the plantations law this way:

> It was to be partly educational, but it was to bring tangible economic benefits; it was to enable natives to pay the recently introduced taxes and to give them the means to raise their standard of living . . . . Briefly the Ordinance empowered the Lieutenant-Governor either to declare Crown lands native reserves for the purpose of establishing a plantation or with the consent of the owners to establish plantations on native land. The crop was to be shared between the cultivators and the government. The proceeds from the government's share were to be paid into the Native Education Fund while the natives' share was to be divided among them, usually according to the number of days worked. (Miles, 1956, p.324)

Under this law people could be compelled to set up and work on plantations. Under a related law, they were required to work at least 60 days a year. These laws were supplemented by a special 'native regulation' compelling people to carry crops over long distances to market them.

On the whole, these plantations were not profitable. The colonial administration had scant resources to devote to their development. They netted the administration annually on average "a sum amounting to something greater than ten per cent of total Government expenditure" but much of this came from the tax as well as from the administration's share of the profits (Power, 1974, p. 219). Likewise, what was left of profits for the Papuan participants was meagre in the extreme (ibid., pp. 215 – 217). This lack of economic incentive meant that legal coercion had to be relied on to make people work on plantations and such coercion further alienated people from the scheme. In all, the plantations were not a success commercially because of this lack of incentive and resulting coercion, because of the lack of resources devoted to them and because of the ineptness of colonial officials who lacked agricultural expertise, promoted unsuitable crops, selected unsuitable sites and held erroneous views about the commercial organization of traditional social formations thereby creating many disputes over land (ibid., pp. 214 – 218; 223 – 224, Crocombe, 1964). The plantations did succeed in generating revenue for the colonial administration. This revenue paid for the 'education' of Papuans, mainly through the subsidizing of missions, paid for the services of the government anthropologist and paid for officials involved in the scheme (Power, 1974, p. 219). In fact the scheme was intended to provide little more than tax and pin money for the Papuans. The administration anticipated that, since the traditional mode would continue to be the Papuans' support, they would be prepared to work for little on the plantations (ibid., pp. 221 – 222). In short, the plantations law provided a highly controlled outlet for Papuan economic activity and the activity provided an increment to the colonial exchequer without being disruptive of the traditional mode.

Another, but spontaneous, troublesome and often large-scale, form of group organization was the famed 'cargo-cult'. It is true that these organizations were often based on grandoise delusion, seeking wealth and power through ritualistic means that could not conceivably attain such ends (Burton-Bradley, 1975, p. 11), but it is also true that there were cults and cults and that in many the dominant ethos was pragmatic and realistic. Wolfers notes that a power to declare cults illegal in Papua was used indiscriminately to the effect that "movements that were the products of a tough and innovating, if sometimes misguided, indigenous leadership" were suppressed and "in short, leadership as a relationship between a capable Papuan of ambition and his followers was abolished" (Wolfers, 1972, p. 72). Anthropologists contributed to the indiscriminate labelling of new movements as irrational cults worthy only of correction and suppression (Valentine, 1973, p. 231). In contrast, Worsley in his noted study sees cults as incipient nationalist movements (Worsley, 1971). It certainly was the case that officials often considered the movements politically dangerous (Oram, 1976a, p. 91). Some movements, especially a few emerging shortly after the second world war, were quite massive in scale, uniting ethnically diverse groups:

> [They] . . . united masses of natives whose mother tongues were virtually unintelligible. The people have sunk their differences and come together, using pidgin-English or some other lingua franca for communication. The leaders, too, have shown powers of organization in handling thousands of followers and effectively preserving public order. (Hogbin, 1970, p. 228)

Rowley notes the "profound political implications" of one such movement in that it "brought together, in a common cause, so many villages formerly divided by suspicion and memories of warfare and sorcery" (Rowley, 1972, p. 176).

It was not only the 'rational' movement or the 'rational' aspect of movements that was threatening. The "irrational' had its exquisite potency. Many movements irrational in some ways were none the less motivated by a correct perception of economic inequality in the colonial situation and a consequent desire to put this right (Brookfield, 1972, p. 175; Burton-Bradley, 1975, p. 29). Marvin Harris thus acutely locates the source of irrationality (it being usually located of course in 'the native mind'):

> In the South Seas, as in other colonial areas, the Christian missions enjoyed a virtually unchallenged mandate to provide the natives with an education. These missions were not about to disseminate the intellectual tools of political analysis; they did not offer instruction in the theory of European capitalism, nor did they embark upon an analysis of colonial economic policy. Instead they taught about creation, prophets and prophecies, angels, a messiah, supernatural redemption, resurrection, and an eternal kingdom in which the dead and the living would be reunited in a land of milk and honey.
>
> Inevitably, these concepts—many rather precisely analogous to themes in the aboriginal belief system—had to become the idiom in which mass resistance to colonial exploitation was first expressed. "Mission Christianity" was the womb of rebellion. (Harris, 1977, p. 111)

McSwain's study of one movement serves to show that a literal adoption of the teachings of Jesus can constitute something like a revolutionary ideology (McSwain, 1977, p. 165). Even where, because of their irrational aspect, movements did not effectively challenge colonial political rule, they none the less could profoundly disturb the colonial economy. Many movements emphasized a new life with the destruction of existing produce and means of production thus disrupting the traditional mode. Great emphasis could be placed on equality including the breaking down of the master – servant relationship and laws against cults were enforced to maintain the supply of labour (ibid., p. 90).

More generally, it is hardly surprising that colonial law and state were much concerned with the suppression and containment of these movements and cults. Besides outright prohibition "cult leaders have been charged with breach of the law against 'spreading false reports' in case after case to the present day" and leaders were sometimes given severe sentences on charges not related to the movement so that, in all, "the impression on villagers must be that the government uses the law for its own purposes rather than administers even-handed justice" (Rowley, 1972, pp. 163, 179; and see also Lawrence, 1964, pp. 215 – 221; McCarthy, 1963, pp. 227 – 228). After the second world war, as we will see in more detail in the next chapter, the colonial strategy for dealing with large-scale movements was less to suppress directly and more to contain them in legal forms that were integrated into the colonial system of administrative control such as local government councils and co-operatives (see for example, Maher, 1961, pp. 57 – 77; P. Worsley, 1970, p. 199; cf. Rowley, 1972, p. 179, n. 26). Although this method was less significant in the pre-war years it did have a place. Thus one official report dealing with an association of New Guinean copra producers said that ". . . any such movement should be clearly examined and definitely forbidden, unless and until it could proceed under strict administrative guidance and control" (Melrose Report, 1939, p. 25). This particular association was a sober and eminently practical body formed to break the colonists' monopoly of the processing and buying of copra. The colonial administration used illegal means, for want of better, to suppress the association. It prohibited meetings of the association, directed that its copra driers be dismantled and directed that the association's members deal only with the two largest colonial trading enterprises, all without any warrant in law (ibid., p. 23). The administration then conceded an official form of 'village councils' in the area of the association's activity. These councils would be presided over by a colonial official and they would "examine any just complaints by the natives and any suggestions put forward by them for improvement in their lives" (ibid., p. 38). Councils with similar functions were also set up in pre-war Papua (Jinks, *et al.*, 1973, pp. 126 – 128; Oram, 1976a, p. 48).

There were several other laws which could have been used to restrict Papua New Guinean economic activity that sought to move out of the traditional context. As we saw in the last chapter, some New Guinean laws would not allow a company to undertake a wide range of activities unless a majority or, in another case, at least two-thirds of its shares were held by 'British subjects'. New Guineans were not British subjects. They could not legally have got around this simply by not operating as a company, because New Guinea's company law contained the standard prohibition on "an association or partnership consisting . . . of more than twenty persons which has for its object the acquisition of gain" unless it is registered as a company. Such registration was also out of the question for the people had no access to the legal and other skills needed to effect it and to comply with the continuing requirements of company law. These matters are not followed up here because they did not become relevant, so effectively were new forms of organization suppressed. It is only after the second world war when the economic and political assertiveness of Papua New Guineans becomes more effective that these further legal restraints are brought into play. I will now look at these and other aspects of law and state in the creation and containment of a peasantry in the period following the second world war.


## Notes

1. I am very grateful to Susan Gardner for referring me to this extremely valuable report.

# 5 The Peasantry[1]

In the post-war period, the 'undifferentiated mass' of the colonized starts to be differentiated. Emerging, indigenous class forces and increased capitalist penetration combine in the creation of a peasantry, a proletariat and elements of a national bourgeoisie. These elements, including the big peasantry, are seen by the colonist as a possibly acceptable 'ruling class' that must be fostered in the prospect of an 'independence' that must come, hopefully later rather than sooner. Initially, the economic basis for this ruling class can only be found in the rural areas where the traditional mode of production and cash-cropping for the market could be judiciously combined in the creation of a peasantry. Increased economic opportunity, state action promoting this ruling class and differentiation within traditional social formations, all interact to create a stratum of the big peasantry as opposed to the 'mass' of the peasantry. Law and state aid in the emergence of a big peasantry in two ways. First, they provide a supportive system of private property and impersonal obligation alternative to the collective and personalized relations of the traditional mode—a system that supports capital accumulation over distributive traditional obligation. Second, law and state play a more forceful part in laws that specifically create the conditions for the big peasants' emergence such as laws 'individualizing' traditional land tenure. Law and state continue in their function of class containment, basically through conservation of the traditional mode of production. The traditional mode supports the peasant household, maintains the wider peasant community and, in so doing, preserves ethnic division. Conservation contains the peasantry generally and, in particular, serves to counter the class consolidation of the big peasantry thus lessening its effectiveness in challenging the dominance of the metropolitan bourgeoisie. Organization by the peasantry outside the traditional sphere is not so much directly suppressed, as were the pre-war cults and other movements, as smothered in legal forms that integrate it into the state system.

Prior to the second world war there was, as we have just seen, little scope for a peasantry to emerge apart from the latter part of Germany's occupation of New Guinea during which time cash-cropping by New Guineans was extensively encouraged. This was done over the objections of the German settlers. The supply of plantation labour was a serious problem and settlers were concerned that cash-cropping would provide a preferred source of money to meet tax payments and to acquire introduced goods. However, the Imperial government, representing as it did a strong and burgeoning industrial power, was more interested in increasing the overall volume of raw materials produced by its colonies, than in deferring to its settlers. Australia, on the other hand, was in terms of industrialization, weak and backward and was basically a producer and exporter of raw materials itself. Hence it had little comparable interest in a more intensive exploitation of New Guinea and as a colonial power it deferred to its settlers on the issue of peasant production. As a result, the growing and processing of cash-crops by New Guineans were legally restricted or prohibited in various ways. In Papua the end result was the same but, as we have seen, the circumstances different. After the failure to attract settlers, 'native development' was resorted to by using the laws relating to 'native plantations'. Basically, this system was used to finance colonial rule in the supplementing of Australia's niggardly contribution to the colony's government. However, what was left of the profits of the scheme for Papuans was meagre in the extreme. This, combined with their resentment of compulsion and with official ineptitude, meant that the scheme was very far from successful, and provided more of a disincentive to produce for the market than any basis for an emergent peasantry.

The post-war world was such that the Australian colonist had to realize that independence would come. In this and in the changes in its colonial rule, Australia was following trends initiated elsewhere, especially by the British, trends in line with growing struggles for liberation and independence in the third world and in line with greatly increased capitalist penetration. Given this and its own economic burgeoning and increasing industrialization, Australia's involvement in Papua New Guinea after the second world war increased greatly and the colonist set about promoting neo-colonial structures and, it was hoped, compliant class elements. In so doing, it was responding in part to efforts at liberation on the part of the colonized, efforts usually located by scholars in the 'unrest' of the war period, 'the ferment' caused by its "disruptive impact and its demonstration of European technical achievement on a colossal scale" (Legge, 1956: 218). Such achievement, particularly in the immense presence of the United States war machine, must have rendered the colonists decidedly second-rate, as must have their rout by the Japanese. It was also the case that:

> The war had created new leaders among the Melanesians, sometimes directly encouraged by Government in the search for satraps who would facilitate the swift reimposition of control. Many people had learned new avenues of entrepreneurship, unfettered by the restrictive constraints of the commercial system . . . . There was a widespread disinclination to return to pre-war conditions of employment, and attempts to reimpose such conditions generated both covert and overt unrest. The pre-war colonial authorities were no longer seen as the only possible form of government, and new patterns of race relations [arising out of comparatively egalitarian contact with soldiers—P.F.], briefly glimpsed, were not forgotten. (Brookfield, 1972, p. 96)

In a somewhat similar view Oram describes how:

> Many [Papuans], as soldiers and carriers, had been in situations in which they felt themselves to be the equals or superiors of Europeans. Some had held positions of considerable responsibility. Many had developed skills as tradesmen, such as carpenters, clerks, supervisors and storemen . . . . A number of economic associations were formed and an increasing number of men turned to wage labour as a means of satisfying their wants. (Oram, 1976a, p. 83)

Allen has vividly described a similar situation in the area he studied in New Guinea, bringing out both the rebellious element generated by the war and how this element took the form of radically innovative economic activities (Allen, 1979, pp. 12 – 18). The accumulation of wages earned during the war and the receipt of war damage compensation gave Papua New Guineans capital resources which many were anxious to use.

The economic basis for promoting compliant class elements did not then exist in the towns which had been maintained strictly as enclaves of the colonist. Any attempt to create such a basis would confront the colonist's pervasive penetration of the urban economy, but a basis existed in rural areas where the traditional mode and cash-cropping could be combined in peasant production, and the post-war restlessness accommodated. True, for this purpose some expansionist settlers would have to be restrained, but overall economic domination by the colonist could be maintained by retaining a monopoly in the processing and marketing of cash-crops (see for example, McSwain, 1977, pp. 56 – 58). In this way a peasantry could emerge in co-operation rather than confrontation with the colonist.

Thus, after the second world war the colonist broadened agricultural extension activities to include Papua New Guineans and removed many legal restrictions on cash-cropping. But this, and Australia's greater involvement generally, did not mean that it suddenly changed into an intensely exploitative colonist. Unlike many other colonial situations, there was no introduction of coercive, large-scale and highly regulated schemes for agricultural production. This continuing lack of metropolitan pressure for more intensive exploitation left room, as it were, for the comparatively relaxed policy of 'gradual development' associated with the long reign, beginning in 1951, of Hasluck as the Australian Minister for Territories. An effective policy of restraining but not completely preventing further Australian settlement was implemented by Hasluck early in the piece (see for example, Finney, 1973, pp. 46 – 47). (In this he was opposed by the settlers and, sometimes, by the colonial administration.) The policy of gradual development was considered appropriate to Papua New Guineans, Hasluck foreseeing that the process would stretch "over a number of generations" (Hasluck, 1976, p. 69). The process would be lengthy also because it was, in terms of the policy, to be one of 'uniform development'; this was supposed to mean an egalitarian raising of the mass rather than a precipitate development of the few in advance of the many.

Although the policy of general development did not survive the end of Hasluck's reign at the end of 1963 and had been crumbling for some time before—"the steeper upward climb to achievement began about 1960 – 61" (ibid., p. 419)—it was far from a spitting into the wind. As with the pre-war colonial administrations, Hasluck and various official reports emphasized again and again that traditional society must be preserved (ibid., p. 159, for example). Papua New Guinean development was to be built "on the foundations of native society" or on "native social organisation" and the 'native' was to remain attached basically to his land and to his village (ibid., pp. 141, 161). The legal restrictions on dealing in 'native land' remained, and still remain, in force. In 1946 the Director of the Department of Agriculture anticipated that "the basic unit of the community will be the rural family securely settled on its small-holding, and producing food and other crops for its own and local consumption and export'', thus foreshadowing later state action explicitly aimed at this end (Stanner, 1947, p. 75). As late as 1962, Hasluck still envisaged a 'native peasantry' that would "not be a major employer of wage earning labour" (Donaldson and Good, 1979, p. 21). Thus, the Native Loans Board, a not exceedingly generous body, set up in 1955, showed "extreme reluctance to grant loans to permit employment of any labour" and the government authority charged with land allocation "with rare exceptions made available to indigenes only small [agricultural] blocks suitable as family units" (Crocombe, 1965, p. 35). To preserve the traditional mode against misjudgement by the colonial administration, the Australian law constituting Papua and New Guinea as one administrative unit, provided that colonial legislation could not be effective until approved by the metropolitan government if that legislation related "to the sale or other disposition of or dealing with land" or "to the employment of persons" (Leibowitz, 1976, p. 154). Controls on dealings in 'native land', similar to those already described, applied also in the post-war period.

Basically, then, the traditional mode was still to be conserved and the peasantry was to operate from within it. Hopefully the traditional mode would thus remain to subsidize and maintain the supply of labour for capitalist production on settlers' plantations and in the towns. However, and this is a new dimension, the traditional mode can now also serve to subsidize the peasants' production for the market. Within the traditional mode a peasant's subsistence, or much of it, will be provided for and functions of social security will be performed. This element of subsidy enables the peasant to endure the competition of more 'efficient' capitalist production and to endure widely fluctuating commodity prices. Further, if the peasantry can produce for the market within the traditional mode potentially disruptive class elements could continue to be contained: there would be no 'landless proletariat', as official reports so often put it, and the peasantry itself would have difficulty organizing across ethnic barriers. Official concern to conserve the traditional was so paramount, that it was even the case with early agricultural extension efforts by the colonist that communal production was emphasized, because it was thought this would fit the traditional mode of production (Finney, 1973, pp. 61 – 62; Mair, 1970, p. 130; Shand and Straatmans, 1974, p. 23). Such thinking, as we shall see, was somewhat wide of the mark. The effective emphasis on preserving the traditional mode is also illustrated by the fact that state action which would have, unwittingly or not, weakened the traditional mode was severely circumscribed in operation. Examples of this come up later but taking one from this early stage, there is Hasluck's repeated insistence on the need to formalize individual rights in land which, if it had been effected, would have upset the pivotal and sensitive balance between individual and group rights in the traditional mode. The Native Land Registration Ordinance of 1952 was intended as a first step in effecting Hasluck's purpose but it was hardly used to any practical purpose at all (Bredmeyer, 1973, pp. 1 – 2; Hasluck, 1976, pp. 117, 122).

Having used the policy of gradual and uniform development to justify the conventional foundation of an exploitable peasantry, the colonist then did little to ensure that 'development' was in fact uniform, even if simply by doing little he ensured that 'development' was indeed gradual. There were two potent aspects making for unequal development. The pattern of colonization in Papua New Guinea, as we have seen, had resulted in widely separate centres of plantation activity. Transport and marketing factors were oriented towards serving these centres; these factors could easily be extended to Papua New Guineans in the vicinity but not at all easily to others (see for example, Townsend, 1978, p. 50). The other source of inequality arises within traditional society itself. Basing production for the market "on the foundations of native society" means, because of the nature of that society, that some are in a better position than others to engage in and benefit from this production. This point is basic to the formation of the big peasantry and to understand it one must understand traditional social formations. Such an understanding is essential, also, in order to grasp the adaptive and supportive part the traditional mode of production plays in the formation of the peasantry generally.

To provide a summary account of traditional social formations is a daunting matter. Not only is there the famed variety of Papua New Guinean social formations—over 500 language groups—but there is also a great diversity of terminologies used by anthropologists in describing them. Much of the problem is that what is being described is found to be elusive. In contrast to, say, the (overdrawn) corporate solidity of African social formations, those of Papua New Guinea are said to exhibit great "structural looseness", which includes considerable fluidity and flexibility of group composition (Barnes, 1962; Sankoff, 1972, p. 556). As a result, anthropologists have 'despaired' of finding an "ordered social system" (Du Toit, 1962, p. 397). Although, as far as I am aware, the following account is adequate, it cannot help but be tentative and partial.[2]

Very generally, the Papua New Guinean traditional social formation is of the small group type usually known as stateless societies, possessed of an 'ordered anarchy' and lacking formal political authority. Production was largely a matter of shifting agriculture. Perhaps, as de Lepervanche argues, since this type of agriculture requires relatively large amounts of land "too many people [in a group], and thus too great a dispersal of gardens, would prevent convenient assembly for communal tasks and defence" (Lepervanche, 1973, p. 2). This still left room for considerable diversity in group size. Particular environmental circumstances, such as soil fertility and geographical blocks to sustained communication, and particular group histories of alliance and segmentation were all doubtless relevant in complex combinations. Whatever the reason or reasons, enduring groups were small in scale, ranging from 50 to 800 members. Communal tasks involved clearing of cultivated land, fencing, house building, canoe making and, on the coast, fishing. These were activities carried out by men. Defence of the group was primarily also a male function. Land was owned by the group collectively with the small family unit having access to it. Cultivation, harvesting and the maintenance of gardens were matters for the small family unit and were carried out mainly by wives on land allocated to husbands. Women did the bulk of child-rearing. Overall, the cast of groupness was male, and woman's role and her base in the group and its economy were disjointed or fragmented. This feature was accentuated in women usually being outsiders marrying into the group. Women were, in all, quite comprehensively subordinate.

As well as the accessibility of land, the simplicity of the technologies of production made them also widely accessible. Every male was a generalist and specialization, for example, as leader in canoe building or as the possessor of knowledge of ritual, was incidental. The available technologies did not allow of the preservation and accumulation of necessities except that there was some scope for such accumulation with pig-husbandry. Generally, however, and excepting the position of women, enduring relations of domination could not be grounded in production. Accumulation and domination were more marked in relations of exchange, but exchange itself, as will be now seen, did not provide a basis for institutionalized domination.

Much of what was produced was distributed within the group, exchanged in varying degrees of formality on the basis or in the idiom of kinship, and much was exchanged with other groups. Predominantly, a person relates to property through personal relations of reciprocal exchange. Exchange was the social cement which maintained the group as the ultimate provider and guarantor of social security. The group was basically self-sufficient. Wider exchange and trade, although sometimes significant, were usually marginal and with nearby groups, except for some great trading networks and some immense ceremonial prestations. Wider exchange and trade could only in exceptional cases be considered impersonal, purely economic exchange; fictive kin relationships were extended to trade partners and personal and spiritual elements permeated the economic. As well as through wider exchange and trade, groups were linked through marriage, military alliance and, somewhat perversely, through warfare attended with ritual restraint. They were linked sometimes by wider groupings such as the following of a 'big man' or the over-arching 'clans' of the Trobriands and Buka Islands.

Relations between and within groups left people with considerable leeway in establishing and maintaining their own relations. Within groups, kinship genealogies did not usually run far back in time and they could be vague and adaptive. This left room for maintaining relations in various group contexts and for criteria of group membership besides kinship such as residence location and participation in exchange and in group activities. For example, Andrew Strathern notes that group membership is a complex idea:

> For Hagen it is more appropriate to think of clan-group membership as defined by a number of factors, not all of which may be present to an equal extent in every case, and to recognize that in a small number of cases a man's affiliation may be uncertain, either in the sense that he keeps up a dual affiliation or that his allegiance to a group is weak. (A. Strathern, 1972a, pp. 97 – 98)

These factors include co-residence, demonstrating identity through participation in ceremonial exchange, land rights, and contributions to traditional payments (ibid., pp. 97 – 98, 213 – 215). Du Toit mentions one collection of groups where the feeling of community becomes more important than kinship, so that relatives who cease residing with a group often become of secondary importance whereas people residing together, even if some are only vaguely related, constitute the basic group (Du Toit, 1962, p. 398). With regard to land, the fundamental means of production, Crocombe and Hide see the major principles on which land holding groups were formed as descent, locality and participation in common activities (Crocombe and Hide, 1971, p. 301). There were many reasons why people would take advantage of this flexibility. Their own group may have been decimated in warfare, or they may have seen further or better opportunities for political and economic advance in another group or a big man may have wished to have his followers from other groups incorporated into his own. In any case, the big man manipulated this flexibility to advance politically and economically through relations of exchange within and outside of his group. But of course exchange did not just provide an abstract opportunity; it bound the parties and integrally involved the performance of obligations. Those who came out 'on top' economically and politically were those who maintained the element of opportunity in significant advance of the element of constraint.

This maintenance of significant advance in exchange relations basically indicates the achieved status of the big man, although skills in oratory, combat, sorcery and, as we will see, dispute-settlement were also relevant. Even in that minority of societies where ascribed, hereditary status was important, personal achievement was still necessary to attain operative leadership (Connell, 1979, pp. 8 – 9; Powell, 1967). Production, the control of land and labour, could also be important in this context particularly at the outset of the big man's climb: if a big man could produce more, or rather have others, especially wives, produce more for him, he had more to exchange and hence was better placed to put others in his debt and to support his followers. Exchange, however, including the exchange of women and bridewealth, was more determinatively significant and the more eminent the big man the more exchange provided the basis for his advance, the apogee probably being the vast ceremonial exchanges in the Highlands where immense amounts of wealth were manipulated with consumate skill. More generally, and usually more modestly, the big man will obtain much of his wealth through the organizing and funding of inter-group exchanges, especially exchanges of brides and bridewealth.

In this process the big man built up exchange partnerships with other big men and developed a following not confined to his group. We can call this following the big man cluster. Although it was the foundation of his exalted position, the big man was expected to distribute wealth among and in other ways assist members of the big man cluster. Distributive demands were bolstered by a strong ideology of equality which had a realistic basis in relations of production and by the possibility of sorcery directed against the big man—an instance of sorcery's well-recognized function as an ultimate legal sanction (T.S. Epstein, 1973, p. 85). Some see the big man as subject to quick removal if he acted arbitrarily whilst others, most notably Salisbury, see him as having despotic power (Hogbin, 1970, pp. 158 – 159; Salisbury, 1964). Perhaps in some few societies where ascribed status was very significant, strong powers were associated with leadership (see for example, Blackwood, 1935, pp. 48, 50). Given the material basis of the big man's position, Salisbury's seeming assertion of sustained despotic rule is most unlikely (see Strathern, 1966). Whatever the case, these distributive demands as well as the claims of his exchange partners and heirs all tend to the dissipation of the big man's empire on his death; its reality and coherence as an ongoing system focused and depended on him personally (Sahlins, 1966, p. 169). This casual and unstable nature of economic and political leadership militated against the formation of enduring systems of political rule and social stratification. There was a possible but seemingly never fully realized element of continuity in that sons of big men could sometimes use and take over their father's wealth even during his lifetime and so be in a stronger position than others to become big men themselves (Standish, 1978a; 1978c). Epstein notes that "in many societies the heir to a rich man was in a favoured position" (T.S. Epstein, 1973, p. 85). Andrew Strathern's precise study of the Melpa indicates that sons of big men had a much greater chance of becoming big men themselves and that the eldest son was particularly well placed in this (Strathern, 1971, pp. 210, 213). Even so it was probably the case that one could not become a big man on that basis alone but would have also to prove oneself independently.

This general account of traditional social formations takes only oblique account of two aspects that are central here, one being the extent of individual rights to land and the other the nature of traditional law and dispute settlement. These will now be elaborated on. Views on individual rights to land cover an illuminating diversity. Some say that there were simply no individual rights in land (for example, Herskovitz, 1960, p. 358), but it is clear that in a great many social formations individual rights were well developed and well defined (Lea, 1964, p. 72; Meggitt, 1965, p. 294; Shand and Straatmans, 1974, pp. 142 – 143). This is usually related to greater population density (Crocombe and Hide, 1971, p. 305; Howlett *et al.*, 1976; pp.100 – 101). The matter has recently been incisively investigated and analysed by Brown and Podolefsky (1976, pp. 217, 221). They find a greater practical definition of individual rights, more precisely a tendency towards individual inheritable rights to specific marked plots, with greater agricultural intensity but, naturally enough, there was also a high correlation between agricultural intensity and population density. Hence, to anticipate later argument, one could posit that intensive cash-cropping, even in areas of low population density, would lead to a development and greater definition of individual rights.

Traditional law and traditional dispute settlement are of course inter-related categories. As Unger notes, "for customary law, the issue of what in fact happens can never be kept clearly separate from the question of what ought to be done. There is a point at which deviations from the rule remake the rule itself" (Unger, 1976, p. 49). The maintenance of and deviations from the rule are most significantly tested in dispute settlement. More generally, traditional law is usually seen as indistinguishably integrated with the political and economic element of the social formation. The perceived lack of formal explicitness in traditional law has led anthro-pologists to focus on the functional aspect of dispute settlement. For that reason this focus will be used here, but with formal aspects being taken account of in so doing. Some points are stressed more because they are of particular relevance to the consideration later of dispute settlement within contemporary peasant communities.

To start with a crude summary of the account of traditional social formations, the relations of production were such that individuals, or at least adult males, were roughly equal. Although there was some collective organization of production, individuals or small family units stood largely in an independent relation to the means of production. The ties that comprehensively bind came from exchange—a transactional mode posited on equality. Apart from the sexual division of labour, there was no material basis for enduring ideological, political or legal domination. It follows that dispute settlement was basically a matter of agreement between the parties to the dispute, a matter of private negotiation. A dispute, especially one between close relatives, would most often be settled completely in that way. If not, it could very easily assume a public aspect; that is, it could become a concern of the group as a whole, since all members of the group were bound to each other in a set of ties that were intimate, complex and quite comprehensive. Typically, the moot or public meeting then came into play. It was informal and open to all, although there were restrictions on the participation of younger people, and of women. Because the public meeting is so important, both in the present context and as a contrast to much present-day dispute settlement, there follows an indicative and beautifully observed account of how the meetings of one group operate:

> A meeting is announced by beating on a bomb casing, or if many people are away in their gardens, by sounding a shell trumpet. Usually people assemble desultorily, often taking an hour or more to straggle in, and the procedure, which begins when the first speaker

stands, is informal. No one is barred from attending and usually most of the village is present, for the *lupunga* [public meeting] is a social occasion. Observers and potential participants sit on nearby verandahs and steps, on the ground and around small fires. There is an undercurrent of sound during a meeting: children talk and cry; inattentive people gossip or engage in side discussions: people come and go. . . . There is no order of speakers. People stand and speak where they are without regard to age, sex, or the relevance of their remarks to the preceding argument. Decorum and restraint are not part of the etiquette of *lupunga* debate, and spoken arguments are often accompanied by exaggerated pacing and gesticulation and an occasional dramatic advance into the centre of the gathering. The *lupunga* continues until all who wish to talk have had their say. Then, if unmediated, the gathering slowly breaks up as people drift away to their homes or sit smoking and talking about other matters. In the absence of a mediator, it was often difficult for us to determine whether agreement had been reached. We were told that we could know if things were settled only by watching the future behaviour of the "litigants". If conciliatory acts were made, then settlement had been reached: if not, then there was no one who compelled the disputants to make peace and further trouble could be expected. (Counts and Counts, 1974, pp. 119 – 120)

As this example illustrates, public involvement in the dispute was secondary to party agreement. Of course, public pressure would usually have been of enormous significance in bringing the parties to consensus. This element could override consensus and legality even though the outcome usually took still the form of a private settlement; people still 'agreed' even if some had to agree more than others. The elements of public and private as well as of the political and the legal are vividly and most explicitly illustrated in an exceptional type of dispute settlement on Goodenough Island—the "fighting with food" described by Young (1974). This process he describes summarily as "essentially a political activity: a contest in which the antagonists attempt to inflict humiliation upon each other by public potlatch of food wealth. A lost contest is a political defeat for the weaker party and his clan . . ." (ibid., p. 44). Despite his emphasis on the political, there is a strong element of legality since, in terms of marshalling support in this exchange process, there is involved also an uncommitted 'public' and it is this public which benefits most in material terms from the contest (ibid., pp. 46 – 47). This marshalling of support involves the "appeal to common moral attitudes and cultural values" (ibid., p. 41). It can happen that political aspects of the case predominate (ibid., pp. 47 – 48). However, and possibly, hence, there appears to remain a persistent rump of legality in that "occasional sorcerers are not condemned as evil, and those appealing to the sanction of resentful self-injury are deemed neither foolish nor childish" (ibid., p. 66).

There are three, in some ways, exceptional, aspects of dispute settlement that must be emphasized especially for their relevance to later radical change in processes of settlement. These aspects involve the place of rules in traditional dispute settlement, the role of mediators, arbitrators and adjudicators and, finally, the presence of other types of settlement besides party agreement.

As to the first aspect, the place of rules, it is of course, something like an anthropological truism that the legal reality in traditional society is not a separate or distinct reality with its own sustaining specialists. Law is popularly accessible. The legal is embedded indistinguishably in the totality of social relations. Legally relevant situations are thus so various that rules have to be flexible or even ambiguous and contradictory. Hence Epstein notes of moots on Matupit that ". . . each side relies on different, though equally valid, principles or rules" (Epstein, 1974b, p. 112). It is a fairly common view in this general context that rules are reducible to process; that is, rules are virtually non-existent or are thoroughly subordinated to the negotiated and political character of dispute settlement (see for example, Twining, 1964). The element of legality would, however, strongly suggest that, to resort again to Epstein's description of Matupit moots, ". . . for the most part the rules are certain and well known, and remain unaffected by the outcome of particular cases" (Epstein, 1974b, p. 111). Indeed Epstein would discern in "Melanesian societies" something of a *corpus juris*, a point that seems to be disputed by some (see Epstein, 1974a, p. 5 and Counts and Counts, 1974, p. 150). Much of the difference may be in the eyes of the beholders (cf., Bohannan, 1957, p. 57 and Gluckman, 1955, p. 229). Be that as it may, the case seems to have been that there was some explicitness, persistence and autonomy of rules.

The next somewhat exceptional aspect is the role of mediators, arbitrators and adjudicators. In the securing of a settlement to a dispute, especially in a public forum, mediators often played an important part. They would usually be big-men or lineage leaders. Skill at facilitating the settlement of disputes was a possible and advantageous attribute of the aspirant and the actual big man. Further, it did happen that parties would refer a dispute to a big man for arbitration. Neither mediation nor arbitration are inconsistent with settlement as actualized by the parties. Adjudication poses difficulties; Epstein has noted generally, but without examples, that it can happen that "disputes within the group will be brought before the big man for formal adjudication, and he will normally have a variety of sanctions at his command by which to enforce his judgment" (A.L. Epstein, 1973, p. 178). This imparts a degree of power and of its institutionalization that is quite inconsistent with the picture drawn earlier of traditional society. If this picture is correct, then in general a decision could not assuredly be imposed on the parties. But there were also situations where adjudication had a general and definite, if limited, part. These will be considered shortly.

Although the structure is getting complicated, it may be recalled that we are considering three aspects of dispute settlement that are somewhat exceptional to its character of party-agreement. The first involved the presence and part of rules and the second involved mediators, arbitrators and adjudicators. The third will now be elaborated on. It involves the operative presence of other methods of dispute settlement. Such methods become relevant in two situations. One is where, apart from the alternative of segmentation, the dispute is important for ongoing social cohesion or where the matter is considered to have serious public significance, such as homicide often is. In these cases, party-agreement may either be seen as irrelevant or it may be backed by a less contingent mode of settlement if it should fail. Adjudication or divination and revelation may thus be resorted to and certain fundamental rules relied on. The second situation in which alternative methods are relevant is where they are used in support of dispute settlement as party-agreement. Spiritual methods may thus be used to establish facts in dispute or to support outcomes agreed in the settlement of disputes. The latter is particularly significant. Outcomes based on agreement may not stick. As there is obvious social value in the final resolution of disputes and since there is no institutionalized authority to secure this, spiritual sanctions and spiritual affirmations of the rightness of results are common.

There are three broad ways in which traditional social formations respond to production for the market. First, traditional formations provides a basis for the big man to assume a position of advantage in production for the market. Second, traditional rights in land adapt to give the peasant greater individual rights. These two aspects can be seen as making for the undermining of the traditional mode of production. The third restores something of a balance for it is the general strengthening of traditional formations in their adapting to production for the market. Each of these aspects will now be looked at briefly and then related to the increased involvement of law and state in the period of 'accelerated development' in the 1960s and to the ensuing shape of the formation of the peasantry. This account of the peasantry formed, with its emphasis on the continuing conservation of the traditional mode, provides a basis for the analysis, in the following chapter, of law and state in the containment of the proletariat, and for an account in Chapter Eight of the emergence of new legal forms in the contemporary situation.

Even in its earliest phase the policy of gradual and uniform development was being undermined by the activities of big men. The big man cluster was an adaptive and sometimes extensible source of capital accumulation and labour (Epstein, 1964, 1968, p. 46; Finney, 1969, pp. 21, 28, 1973, pp. 100 – 102; Strathern, 1972c, p. 497; Uyassi, 1978, p. 50).[3] Academic observers have seen the big man as operating a system of 'primitive capitalism' or one 'preadapted to capitalism' (Epstein, 1968; Finney, 1973, pp. x – xi). These are one-sided exaggerations—traditional social formations would fit no rigorous definition of capitalism and in many respects they are just as 'preadapted' to socialism—but these assertions do underline that some big men became big peasants by using traditional relations. The point is susceptible of much refinement. Uyassi finds that in the area he studied there is a break between big men of the purely traditional type and the newer big men who engage in production for the market, although the newer men do rely, at least initially, on a traditional-type big man cluster (Uyassi, 1978, pp. 23, 36). Also it seems that in the modern context, with the more intense dissemination of shell currency by the colonist and the introduction of money, there are more, and more accessible, assets for use and manipulation by aspiring big men and hence wider opportunities for big men to emerge (Lepervanche, 1973, p. 25; Strathern, 1971, p. 207; Uyassi, 1978, p. 5). Whatever its beginnings, the big man's success does not always result from continuing to rely on the 'capitalism' of traditional society. Success for some entails a containing or even a rejecting of traditional distributive obligations (Epstein, 1968, pp. 52 – 53; Finney, 1973, p. 77; Gerritsen, 1975, pp. 6, 13; Sankoff, 1969, pp. 71 – 72). These obligations, it will be recalled, result from exchange relations on which the big man's position in traditional society is predominantly based. Such exchange relations are used by the big man in engaging in production for the market, including the provision of services. With the labour and 'pooled' money of his cluster group the big man operates initially in the growing of cash crops and the running of 'passenger trucks' and 'trade stores', the custom for such trucks and stores coming largely from his group. Whilst retaining a base in cash cropping, some big men move further afield into the buying and processing of cash crops, other agricultural as well as pastoral activity, and into various enterprises based in rural towns such as garages, bars, restaurants, transport and retail stores. Because production for the market, particularly in the initial phase, relies on traditional exchange obligations, exchange has some purchase on production for the market. Production with a nexus to the market really provides, however, a base for the big men alternative to traditional exchange—a base for an economic expansion potentially much more extensive than anything required to meet traditional obligations (see for example, Connell, 1979, p. 23). Production for the market breaks the tie that contains the big man's wealth within obligation-bearing relations of exchange. Wealth is no longer purely personalized but becomes capable of abstracted expansion.

The second way in which traditional society adapts to production for the market consists in its system of land tenure changing to provide land rights characteristic of a peasantry. With the extension of cash-cropping and, later, cattle-raising, there is a greater awareness of land as having a reified value and there is effective pressure for more clearly defined individual rights in land (see for example, Crocombe and Hogbin, 1963b, p. 75; Page, 1964, p. 17; Shand, 1969, p. 310; Strathern, 1972a, p. 34). Collective group production does exist but is exceptional, officially discouraged, as we see later, and often attended with severe organizational difficulties (see for example, Mitchell, 1976, pp. 88 – 90). Pressures for individual rights are doubtless contributed to by the actuality and the potentiality of land shortage in many cases (Barnett, 1976). The greater definition of land rights that results is vividly illustrated by the work of land demarcation committees under the Land Titles Commission Act of 1962, which were charged with the ascertaining and marking of land boundaries. In areas of extensive cash-cropping, the committee's work proceeded with much greater ease and rapidity than in other areas (Bredmeyer, 1973, p. 5; Crocombe and Hide, 1971, p. 317). There is evidence from many communities that a person must have strong rights in land before planting cash-crops and before establishing the more enduring individual-land relation involved in the long cycles of use typical of cash-crops in Papua New Guinea (Jackson, 1965; Shand and Straatmans, 1974, p. 145). Traditional devices enabling an outsider to use the land of a group or enabling a person to use land to which another has predominant rights appear not to have been extended to cash cropping. Thus among the Tolai, *totokom*, a type of lease extending usually to one cycle of use, can now only be used for subsistence crops (Epstein, 1969, p. 136; Smith and Salisbury, 1961, p. 7). As a further example, the custom of separating rights in land from rights in economic trees, so as to allow of property in the fruits without affecting rights to land, does not appear to extend to cash cropping (Page, 1964, p. 8; Panoff, 1969, p. 24). However, Crocombe and Hogbin have said that, for a group of the Orokaiva, cash cropping is "in harmony" with traditional rights to economic trees, yet they say also that there are no precedents on how to treat cash cropping (Crocombe and Hogbin, 1963b, pp. 72, 79).

As these various restraints on cash cropping indicate, the group appears to maintain considerable control over land despite the strengthening of individual rights. This can be seen as part of the third way in which traditional social formations respond to production for the market, a way which involves their strengthening or at least their adaptive survival. Overall group control of land use appears to persist (see for example, Epstein, 1969, p. 302). Cash-crops involve such a commitment of the land that it seems to be general that group permission must be obtained before their planting (Hogbin, 1965, p. 73; Morawetz, 1967, p. 13; Page, 1964, p. 13; Salisbury, 1970, p. 71; Smith and Salisbury, 1961, pp. 8, 13). It is often the case that the group refuses to allow the planting of cash crops (Harding, 1971, p. 196; Shand and Straatmans, 1974, p. 143). In one area where land was legally taken out of the traditional context and converted to individual tenure under the Land (Tenure Conversion) Act of 1963 (considered later) traditional authorities can still discipline and even dispossess land owners who do not cultivate their land properly (Dakeyne, 1966). There is evidence however that with the wider acceptance of cash-cropping, individuals try and sometimes succeed in asserting their rights to land independently of group control (Salisbury, 1970, p. 123; Shand and Straatmans, 1974, p. 144). Control of the disposition of land in some areas is said to be now more in the hands of the small-family group than with the extended traditional land group (Ward, 1977, p. 13). The extent and strength of this tendency, if it be such, seems doubtful. The extensive and recent investigation by the Commission of Enquiry into Land Matters (1973) led to the conclusion that group title to land would serve as the basis of a nation-wide formal tenure system (see also, Ward, 1977, p. 13). Even strong individual rights and powers over land do not, as yet anyway, seem to be inconsistent with the maintenance and continued relevance of wider group relations (Birmingham and Scoullar, 1977, pp. 8 – 9; Dakeyne, 1966; Gray, n.d., p. 7; cf., Meggitt, 1971, p. 208; Morawetz, 1967, pp. 36 – 37).

Such a general assessment hides important variations. The mass of the peasantry may well continue to rely on group relations as a necessary guarantor of social security, but a big peasant may seek to minimize the efficacy of these relations and to minimize group control over land. Traditional social formations themselves contribute to this in their assisting the big peasant's emergence with the provision of land, labour, and capital contributions from members of the big man cluster. Also, and as we saw in the last chapter, the extension of traditional exchange, as a result of colonization, strengthened the position of big men since they were the organizers of major exchange activities and, building on their position in traditional society, they took advantage of various opportunities presented by colonial penetration to bolster their position generally. The direction such advantage took them in was not invariably away from traditional relations, however. Such relations, as well as promoting the big peasant, also operate to restrain him in the interests of the collectivity: distributive demands continue to be made in the new context and continue to be backed by the use of sorcery as well as by threats of physical attack (Finney, 1973, p. 114; McSwain, 1977, p. 125; Narakobi, 1978, pp. 21 – 23; Uyassi, 1978, pp. 47, 63). Some big men aspire to break away and be of the pure bourgeoisie but, as we see later, most will use the new opportunities to improve their standing in the traditional context. The scope for a big man to do this can be vast, especially it seems within the exchange networks and inter-group alliances of the Highlands. This has resulted in 'combined' forms of economic venture, forms which combine investment in production for the market with elements of traditional distribution and organization, and in the emergence of relations of patronage and brokerage. Underlying this is the continued conservation of the traditional mode of production. This conservation, as we saw in the last chapter, is in part maintained because the effects of production for the market are largely contained within traditional social formations. To a great extent this is possible because of the limited penetration of production for the market and this point is taken in more detail later. Thus the influx of new goods and new currencies was largely absorbed in an expanded traditional exchange. The suppression of warfare and the introduction of simple, labour-saving technologies created time for increased exchange activity, and released labour for production for the market and as well as for work on the colonist's plantations and in towns. The traditional social formation continues also to set the context and content of the subordination of women and although some few women, through production for the market, surmount this situation, this is done on a small and far from disruptive scale.

In short, traditional legal rights of property are changing not, as is usually asserted, to individual rights but to a combination of more distinct individual rights and continuing group rights, changing, in other words, to a legal system characteristic of a peasantry.

I will move on now to the period of 'accelerated development' which is one of greatly increased involvement of law and state in the formation of the peasantry. This involvement builds on apt elements of traditional society in their conjunction with production for the market, but the involvement is not merely a response to these elements in this conjunction: its explicit orientation is towards the purposive creation of a bourgeoisie or at least of a big peasantry. The political aspect represented by the state acts in advance of the economic so far as the national bourgeoisie and the big peasantry are concerned; it is largely access to state benefits and state power that secures economic advance. This involvement of the state also has fundamentally contradictory characteristics which will have to be taken into account.

The period of accelerated development is usually dated from the early 1960s when a particularly persuasive combination of events impelled Australia to anticipate independence ''sooner, not later'', as Australian Prime Minister Menzies put it (Jinks et al., 1973, p. 373). There was the castigation of Menzies at the Commonwealth Prime Ministers' Conference in 1960 for Australia's 'reactionary' colonial policy; there was the pressure of the decolonization—or recolonization—of West Papua New Guinea; 1960 saw the adoption by the United Nations General Assembly of the declaration for the abolition of colonialism and this reflected numerous contemporary liberation struggles (thirty 'new states' emerged between 1960 and 1962); there was the report in 1962 on Papua New Guinea of a particularly influential visiting mission of the UN Trusteeship Council recommending accelerated political and economic development; and it seems also that the debacle in the Congo was particularly influential (Brookfield, 1972, p. 108; Hasluck, 1976, pp. 365 – 367; Hudson and Daven, 1971, pp. 158 – 159). It is difficult to locate the change in terms of general policy pronouncements and it seems probable that these events gave a push to the direction Australian involvement was taking anyway (Hasluck, 1976, p. 397). A considerable increase in agricultural extension was provided in a three-year plan commencing in 1959 and the individualization of land tenure was contemplated before 1960 (ibid., pp. 315, 319 – 322). As early as 1961, a new influx of Australian agricultural officers had agreed on the need to individualize land tenure and to "develop a small class of purposeful elite farmers" (McKillop, 1974a, p. 18). Overall acceleration was, none the less, highly significant. Established positions in the Department of Agriculture increased from 408 in 1963 to 1919 in 1968, and the number of Papua New Guinean state employees rose by over 40% between 1962 and 1974 compared with an increase of ¼ over the previous decade (Conyers, 1976, p. 5; Garnaut et al., 1977, p. 1). The main ideological impetus for and affirmation of acceleration came from the World Bank Report (International Bank for Reconstruction and Development, 1965). This, in line with what passed for general development theory of the day, recommended a building on the best, a concentration of effort where financial returns would be highest or, in the agricultural sphere, the promotion of the 'progressive farmer' in advance of his fellows—all this being in polar opposition to the idea of gradual and uniform development. Gradual development as a policy was undermined, however, well before this. Production concentrated itself around existing centres of plantation activity, as it was bound to do without massive infrastructural investment spreading opportunity more evenly. There was also the development from within traditional social formations of the big man as an incipient big peasant or as an incipient bourgeois. It is this development which has to be looked at more closely here, since it is the basis on which law and state promote the big peasantry and since it also helps explain constraints on the emergence of this class element.

Initially however, some qualifications are necessary. Most of the studies of big men in their relation to production for the market are set in areas of existing plantation activity where big men could rely on the existing infrastructure of such production and be seen plausibly as an emergent big peasantry. This position cannot be generalized for the whole country. There are also related effects of academic bias. Epstein's influential work on one group of the Tolai leads her to generalize that traditional relations are incompatible "with success in business ventures" whereas Salisbury, having studied another Tolai group, reaches a conclusion that seems quite opposite (Epstein, 1972, p. 56; Salisbury, 1970, p. 274). Finney's especially influential work on Gorokan society is oriented by a concern with individual "entrepreneurship" which leads him to disregard "mere examples of clan business or communal enterprise" (Finney, 1973, p. 107). Radical accounts show a similar bias in their implicit yet basic assumption that the emergence of the peasantry nationwide can be described adequately in terms of big men bursting into bourgeoisdom. (Gerritsen, 1975; Good, 1979). Almost in passing, it should be mentioned that some of these studies are of the Tolai or rely on the experience of the Tolai, who, being matrilineal, place particular importance on the wide extension of kinship ties and this factor, together with some preferring of sons over nephews which now takes place, would tend to emphasize the conflict involved in the big peasant's emergence (cf. Douglas, 1969).

In moving into production for the market the big man at first takes the big man cluster with him, and indeed uses the new economic activity to extend and sustain these group ties; within the context of traditional relations of exchange the big man cluster provides labour and capital contributions and the big man will rely usually on traditional access to land (see for example, Epstein, 1968; Finney, 1973; Freund, 1971; Oostermeyer and Gray, 1967, p. 31). Within this traditional context also, distributive demands on the big man continue to be made but there is some tendency for the big man to resist or to seek to minimize them in the interests of capital accumulation (Finney, 1969, p. 31; Gerritsen, 1975, p. 6; Sankoff, 1969; Uyassi, 1978, 41.–42, 59, 62). He will seek to control and allocate returns so that he obtains a disproportionate share (see for example, Fleckenstein, 1975). In this he can be assisted by the uncertainties and complexities that attend the extension of traditional relations into new activities—the nature and diversity of understandings and claims involved in contributions to a venture can be complex in the extreme (see for example, Crocombe and Hogbin, 1963a; Strathern, 1972b, p. 373). These understandings and claims are neither fixed nor formal. They are part of continuous, personalized, ever-changing, traditional-type relations. As such, they can be subject to convenient interpretation or manipulation. For example one group which I studied creatively called more formal legal categories in aid of their claims: they made contributions to different passenger truck enterprises; if an enterprise succeeded they claimed they were basically shareholders with a continuing stake in the enterprise and its profits and that they could not be bought out; if an enterprise failed, they would resort to the category of lender and claim repayment. But most manipulation of this complexity and uncertainty comes from the big peasant. He has more scope, for he has production with a nexus to the market as a base alternative to personalized, continuous exchange relations. Many big men seek to subordinate, transform or replace traditional relations in favour of relations typical of the new base. They will seek to assert the discontinuous nature of relations involved in the enterprise: labour and capital contributions rather than being part of a continuous, personal relationship give rise to obligations that the big man attempts to put into the contract form, to extinguish by reciprocal assistance or repayment (Crocombe, 1967, p. 9; Jackson, 1965, p. 13; Strathern, 1972c, p. 496). There is some propensity for the big peasant to employ outside paid labour instead of labour from within the traditional context, a point further illustrated later (Crocombe, 1969, p. 9; Howlett, 1977, p. 9; Morauta, 1974, pp. 31, 35). Big peasants take to living in a more splendid isolation outside of their area of traditional residence (Finney, 1969, p. 33; Oostermeyer and Gray, 1969, p. 33; Uyassi, 1978, p. 47). And it is being increasingly recognized that the loan from the government or from a finance company is a less troublesome alternative to capital contributions from the big man cluster (Oostermeyer and Gray, 1969, p. 33; Strathern, 1972b, p. 372; To Robert, 1967, p. 75). Thus with the large Hoskins Oil Palm Project, officials insisted that Papua New Guinean settlers rely on government loans; the officials feared that moneys put in by settlers might include contributions from relatives, thereby giving the relatives a basis for making demands on the venture (Anton Ploeg, personal communication). Despite these various moves, the big peasant will try to accommodate group pressures and to still group recrimination by making some distributions, by conferring patron-like favours, by emphasizing the community nature of the venture and by fostering an ideology that 'businessmen' deserve more (Finney, 1969, pp. 31 – 32; Sankoff, 1969; Standish, 1978a, pp. 21 – 22). Underlying this, as we noted already, is the fear of group reprisal through sorcery or physical attack.

The outcome of the conflict between these forces will be examined later, once the wider setting in which it operates is sketched. The immediate concern here is with the relation of these forces to law and state in the period of accelerated development, more particularly with the ways in which law and state promote a big peasantry. State action generally now takes two forms: a system of combined agricultural extension and government lending on the one hand, and, on the other, supportive and protective legal intervention. To deal with the first briefly, extension and lending cannot be looked on as something incidental to the big man's rise—as something like advice and ancillary assistance. A big peasant is not necessarily or even usually the vigorous 'entrepreneur' beloved of many development theorists: progress has to be thrust upon him. Agricultural extension officers will be closely and continuously involved in the management of the venture, often to a greater degree than its profitability could warrant (Fleckenstein, 1977, p. 41; McKillop, 1974a, p. 12). The Development Bank—the government lending agency—often gives big men loans of close to 100% of the capital needed for a venture, and indeed has to 'persuade' many 'applicants' to borrow at all (Gunton, 1974, p. 108; Standish, 1978a, pp. 21 – 22). The overall picture then may approximate less to ventures set up and run by big men assisted by the state, and more to ventures set up and run by the state assisted by big men, but with the state-subsidized profits going to the big men.

Despite the policy of gradual development, agricultural extension work after the second world war had from the start largely focused on the big man (Donaldson and Good, 1979, pp. 22 – 24; Epstein, 1972, p. 51; Finney, 1973, p. 63). This is partly explainable in terms of big men being, traditionally and as bolstered by colonization, in a favoured position to take advantage of any new opportunity. It is also partly explainable in organizational terms for, as McKillop's acute analysis has shown, it is easier to measure success and hence easier to evaluate promotion through the ranks of officialdom by focusing extension activity on a few farmers and pastoralists (McKillop, 1974b, 1975). It was with the period of accelerated development that this approach was given a more explicit emphasis and impetus. The end result was an almost exclusive attention to the ventures of a wealthy few (Curtain, 1978, p. 3; Howlett et al., 1976, pp. 247 – 250; McKillop, 1974a, p. 14; Potter, 1977, p. 15). To further assist the big peasantry the colonial administration's Department of Agriculture helped them form pressure groups and marketing bodies (Gerritsen, 1975; Nicholls, 1971, p. 1). Group ventures sometimes pushed their claims for agricultural extension assistance and for loans, but officials processing these claims took the view, with justification, as we shall see later, that only individuals or small partnerships should benefit because group ventures were illegal (Barry Shaw, personal communication).

Almost half of agricultural extension work is taken up by the administration of supervised credit (McKillop, 1974a, p. 14). After the small amount of lending undertaken by the Native Loans Board in the period of gradual development, the extent of government lending increased dramatically with the setting up, as recommended by the World Bank, of a state lending corporation with the Papua New Guinea Development Bank Act of 1965. In terms of the effect of lending, the activity of the Development Bank is crucial because loans by commercial banks to Papua New Guineans are close to insignificant. Only one finance company lends to Papua New Guineans to any great degree, and this is hire-purchase lending for acquiring passenger trucks. The Savings and Loans Societies Act of 1961 enabled popular credit associations to be formed but these have not played a great part in the provision of credit for economic enterprises. The Development Bank provides loans that are heavily subsidized in the charging of low interest rates and the acceptance of close to negligible security. The actual costs of lending are very many times the interest rate charged. The Bank shows a modest loss or profit for each year of its operation, but if the enormous costs involved in the processing and supervising of loans by officers of the Department of Agriculture or, as it is now called, of Primary Industry were included the Bank would be making huge losses. Characteristically, Development Bank lending has been to the few rather than the many, the wealthy rather than the poor, the individual rather than the group and, to a significant degree, to the literate and the formally educated (Keith Crellin, personal communication, Howlett *et al.*, 1976, pp. xliii – xliv; McKillop, 1974a; Moulik, 1970). It also helps to be a member of the national legislature (McKillop, 1974a, p. 16; Standish, 1978a, pp. 21 – 22). With agricultural extension and governmental credit, law performs a service function, a structuring, support part, in providing forms of loan transaction, especially for a variety of secured loans, and by providing organizational forms for pressure group activity. The loan form also acts as a 'cover', as we see shortly, for official efforts in the creation of individualized land tenure.

As for more purposive legal intervention, the most explicit case is the Land (Tenure Conversion) Act of 1963 which, in its 'long title', provided for "the Conversion of the Tenure of Native Land into Individualized Tenure" for reasons that are well enough stated in its preamble:

> . . . it is generally considered that a most efficacious method of promoting the agricultural development of a country and the economic well-being of its people and especially of its agricultural population lies in the provision of a method whereby guaranteed individual titles to land may be given to the owners thereof . . .

A person could apply for a conversion order and, subject to restrictions which are described later, such an order conferred absolute legal ownership of the land and, as the act says, the land would then ''cease in all respects to be subject to or regulated by native custom''. To ensure that conversion was basically in favour of individuals and as something of a counter to fragmentation, ownership of the converted land could not be vested in more than six owners. A conversion order was not to be made unless all persons with interests in the land agreed to the conversion. It was common for a big man wishing to convert land to secure consent by giving various undertakings on the side, as it were—undertakings that some traditional interests would continue to be recognized or that some benefit would be forthcoming for giving them up; but it was not unusual for a big man to ignore these undertakings once conversion was secured (see for example, Good and Donaldson, 1979, pp. 28 – 29; Ward, 1977, pp. 9 – 10). Legal provision was made for conversion to be subordinate to present and future need for land for subsistence cropping, but this restriction does not seem always to have been effective: the leading British exponent and proponent of individualization was moved to ''view with misgiving the carving of large personal holdings out of fully occupied tribal lands, as at Mt. Hagen'' (Simpson, 1971, p. 12). A tenure conversion in this area in favour of one person covered 265 hectares.

However, this law was, as we shall see later, of limited effect in practice and other methods of individualization were also used. Probably the most significant is the ''Clan Land Usage Agreement'' created and widely used by the Development Bank (see Gunton, 1974). The Bank often makes such an agreement the basis of a rural loan. In terms of the agreement, traditional land authorities representing group interest acknowledge and agree to the loan applicant's ''right under native law and custom for the whole of his lifetime to use the land''; the use is not confined to the period of indebtedness to the Bank. The making of the agreement is often attended with some pomp and a surplus of official presences and signatures, but the agreement is not considered enforceable in terms of the national legal system. Doubtless it is not basically these stratagems which account for the remarkable success of the Clan Land Usage Agreement—only one agreement had been disputed when the matter was checked in 1974 (Rodney Cole, personal communication). Rather, the agreement reflects and builds on the adaptation described of traditional legal rights to production for the market: there is a strengthening of individual rights in land but a retention of some overall group control.

People have also sought a secure legal title to land by entering claimed individual rights in informal or semi-official registers operated by several Local Government Councils and some government officers (Bredmeyer, 1973, p. 11; Crocombe and Hogbin, 1963b, pp. 39, 89 – 90; Ogan, 1972, pp. 82, 159 – 160; Ward, 1978, p. 19). For a considerable time the relatively wealthy Tolais have been buying land from the neighbouring Bainings and having the transactions recorded in the local office of the Government's Land Titles Commission even though the transactions are of very doubtful validity in terms of the national legel system (Bredmeyer, 1973, p. 11; Jim Fingleton, personal communication). Pressures to record individual rights will probably grow with what seems to be an increase in land dealings between different land-owning groups (Ward, 1977).

In a somewhat similar if more oblique vein, Epstein has described how a law requiring registration of cocoa growers as a disease control measure was used to bolster ownership claims among a Tolai group because they were said to believe that the 'licence' resulting from registration represented a legal title to ownership (Epstein, 1968, pp. 115, 129). Epstein has also noted how, in the competition between sons and nephews amongst the matrilineal Tolai (the rights of nephews and the matrilineal element can be taken here as a representation of the group interest), fathers would seek to favour sons in preference to the traditional rights of nephews by putting vehicles in a son's name under vehicle registration laws, by putting cocoa proceeds in bank accounts in sons' names and by buying land in their names (ibid., pp. 67, 112, 118; Epstein, 1964, p. 67).

The most effective legal avenue to individual ownership is the obtaining of a long term lease of government land. Some large areas have been leased to members of the big peasantry and the government lease can be an effective way of avoiding group claims based on land (Crocombe, 1967, p. 8; McKillop, 1974a, p. 15). Much government leasing has involved resettlement schemes, either to ease particular population pressures or to provide something of a captive labour force for foreign plantation companies in 'nucleus estates', that is, estates where the nucleus of the company's plantation and processing facility is surrounded by small blocks leased and worked by Papua New Guineans. Although these schemes usually involve smallholder blocks, members of the big peasantry sometimes operate them either directly or as absentee landlords (Anton Ploeg, personal communication).

Inheritance laws were changed in the period of accelerated development to facilitate the passing and accumulation of the new property created in production for the market. In one way traditional legal mechanisms of inheritance have already adapted to this situation. It is the case in many traditional social formations that a person can indicate who is to succeed to property on his or her death and this mechanism has been extended to the new property (see for example, Wanji, 1977, p. 7). A person can, it seems, also indicate this through some of the informal registration systems, and through some of the various ways of evidencing legal title to property that have just been described (Epstein, 1968, pp. 107 – 108; Ogan, 1972, pp. 159 – 160). The Wills Probate and Administration Acts of 1966 and 1970 enabled Papua New Guineans to will property except, broadly, land that had not officially been taken out of the traditional context and other property still dealt with in that context. This exception means that the great bulk of land, even if it is used in production for the market, cannot be passed by will but remains subject to traditional inheritance laws. This new law was seen officially as a needed response to "the growth of commerce and economic enterprise in the Territory" (see Kassam, 1974, p. 15). It is too early to gauge its effect. Many Papua New Guineans have shown that they want to depart from or restrict the range of traditional obligations of inheritance and to focus succession more on the nuclear family or on a favoured son (Commission of Enquiry into Land Matters, 1973; Jackson, 1965, p. 49; Morawetz, 1967, p. 26; Ogan, 1972, pp. 159 – 160; Rijswijck, 1966, p. 45; Ward, 1978, p. 22). This tendency could lead to an adaptive change in traditional inheritance laws. A small survey of state employees showed it to be a common view among them that people should be able to will new property and should make a will if they have a large amount of such property (Wanji and Jerewai, n.d.). Many blockholders on one resettlement project have made wills and the Development Bank provided them with 400 completed wills to help them in this (Bob Gunton, personal communication). But wills do not seem to be at all widely used nor is their use promoted by extension agencies or, normally, by the Development Bank. The significance of this shall be brought out shortly.

So, not without qualification or hints of qualification, the concern so far with the period of accelerated development has been to show how law and state encourage the emergence of a big peasantry and a rural bourgeoisie. This encouragement, together with the general legal protection and upholding of property rights and of contract, provide something like a system alternative to the traditional relations that the big peasant can opt into in whole or in part. The Native Customs (Recognition) Act of 1963 makes it explicit that traditional law is not effective when in conflict with the national legal system, that is, the system which the big peasant can use. People, Uyassi notes, perceive that laws work for those involved in production for the market (Uyassi, 1978, p. 5). In addition, law and state provide measures to counter challenges and competitive alternatives to the emergence of the big peasantry. Many of these measures serve as well in the class containment of the mass of the peasantry. These measures will now be considered.

Sorcery has already been seen as a traditional restraint on the dominance of the big man and as a restraint that continues to be relevant in the context of production for the market. In 1971 the Sorcery Act discerned a "widespread belief . . . that sorcerers have extra-ordinary powers which can be used for good purposes but more often for bad ones" and proceeded to strenghten prohibitions against sorcery, although sorcery had always been prohibited by the various Australian regimes. The 1971 Act can be seen as a measure protective of the big peasantry, whose parliamentary representatives certainly supported it strongly. As Uyassi notes of sorcery, big men expect "courts and the police" to protect them (ibid., p. 47). However, there have been, interestingly, few prosecutions for sorcery. Sorcery, as we saw earlier, is functional in preserving social order. It is commonplace that sorcery increases to deal with increased social strains and social conflict (see for example, Belshaw, 1955, p. 6; Glick, 1973, pp. 182–185). In this, sorcery is something of a safety valve releasing stressful pressures that could otherwise explode in physical violence and general social disruption. Hence sorcery has an important part to play in the maintenance of traditional social formations including the conservation of the traditional mode as well as an important part in the preservation of "law and order", an importance heightened in the weakness of the colonial (and post-colonial) state. Hence the protection of the big peasantry has to give way before weightier considerations and sorcery not be intensely prosecuted.

Where protection of the big peasantry corresponded with the general class containment of the mass of the peasantry, law and state were more unequivocal in operation. Various group ventures producing for the market or organizing such production were competitive with the emerging big peasantry. To some extent these ventures were contained and constrained within corporate legal forms—a matter taken up in more detail shortly. The types of restraint considered here involve pure legal prohibition. Prohibition was justified in such official and academic terms as the inherently unsatisfactory nature of these ventures because of their involving distributive demands (Andrews, 1975, p. 15; Crocombe, 1971a,

p. 383; Epstein, 1968, pp. 52 – 53). There were, as we saw in the last chapter, numerous prohibitions and restraints on group ventures which had a limited operation so far as Papua New Guinean enterprise was concerned. These now started to have a wider effect (see for example, Fairbairn, 1969, p. 37). To the extent that these restrictions were based explicitly on differences of racially ascribed status, most had, with many other such restrictions, been repealed by the mid-1960s, a matter treated in more detail in the next chapter. However, many restrictions discriminating in practice against Papua New Guinean group enterprise remained. This tended to encourage the individual enterprise by leaving it as the only alternative (Epstein, 1968, p. 72). Probably the most significant example was the provision in various Companies Acts, and standard in corporate laws derived from the British, prohibiting ''an association or partnership consisting . . . of more than twenty persons, which has for its object the acquisition of gain'' unless the body is incorporated as a company. The cost and complexity of incorporation and of continuing compliance with corporate law were such as to make this avenue impossible for almost all Papua New Guinean groups. By the end of the 1960s only a very few companies controlled by Papua New Guineans had been incorporated (O'Connor, 1970, p. 2). It was this prohibition which justified that view of extension officials, including those processing loan applications, that only individuals or small partnerships were 'legal' and worthy of the benefits they dispensed. A loan to a group operating in breach of the prohibition could not be legally recovered and this restrained the Development Bank in lending to groups (Barry Shaw, personal communication). In 1971, the senior legal official in the colonial administration advised the extension officers responsible for 'business development' that they could be committing the serious criminal offence of conspiracy if they assisted groups operating in breach of the prohibition (Lindsay Curtis, personal communication). It was probably in reference to this prohibition that the head of this department responsible for 'business development' warned an officer who assisted a large group enterprise that its operation ''may be considered illegal and that if a prosecution is made he cannot expect departmental support'' (Andrews, 1975, p. 148). When some larger scale groups attempted to incorporate in the early 1970s, they were met by official obstruction in a pedantic and sometimes erroneous insistence on points of law. On one occasion, such a group, after incorporation as a company, was prosecuted for failure to lodge the annual return required by company law. A search of the official records of various companies at about that time showed that some significant metropolitan-owned companies were likewise in breach of this requirement (Chris Gregory, personal communication). They were not prosecuted. As in the pre-war period, group enterprise was also subject to general official harassment (see for example, Crocombe, 1971b, p. 183; Lawrence, 1964, pp. 215 – 221).

There were, and are, other prohibitions not as significant but of some influence. For example, we have seen that tenure-converted land cannot be registered in the names of more than six holders. This provision applies as well to all registered, that is, non-traditional, land. The arcanum of the 'rule against perpetuities' has had some effect. This rule makes invalid any arrangement under which property does not 'vest' for a certain time. Hence, to take recent practical instances, shares in a company held by someone on behalf of a group would not 'vest', in terms of the rule, until the group is 'closed', that is, until its exact, final and unalterable composition is determined. Traditional groups can never be said to have a closed membership in this sense. This being so, the rule against perpetuities would make legally invalid an arrangement to hold shares on behalf of such a group. More generally, the rule obviates the use for a group of any legal device, such as the trust, under which property can be held by someone on behalf of others. The effect of this rule, as well as of those rules restricting the number of holders of registered land and prohibiting associations unless incorporated as companies, can be illustrated in the case of one group who wished to purchase two foreign-owned plantations. In 1957 the group members entered into a contract to buy the plantations and they paid the purchase price. Title to the plantations could not be legally transferred to an unincorporated group but a drawn-out shuttle of the matter between various government departments did not result in the discovery of a suitable legal form of incorporation. When the matter was last checked in 1971, the people still did not have title to the plantations (Public Solicitor's File L413, ''Tulu and Navalen Plantations'').

However, containment and restraint extend further and include the big peasantry. By promoting this class element and a national bourgeoisie, law and state begin to assume a more complex dimension. In encouraging the emergence of a resident 'ruling class', law and state are responding basically to the interests of the metropolitan bourgeoisie but the embryonic national bourgeoisie and big peasantry are, as part of this process, given some political power and use this power to further propel their own emergence. The more complex dimension now assumed by law and state involves mediating between the national bourgeoisie and the big peasantry on the one hand and the metropolitan bourgeoisie on the other. This does not necessarily mean that law and state are now in some way above these class elements; in the Papua New Guinea context, law and state continue largely to reflect the dominance of the metropolitan bourgeoisie. This is not the case of a dynamic and restless national bourgeoisie chafing at foreign constraint. Rather, the colonial state as an agent of the metropolitan bourgeoisie takes the leading role in promoting the national bourgeoisie as well as the big peasantry and in so doing it seeks to mould these class elements in a way conformable to the interests of the metropolitan bourgeoisie. On the whole, and not without qualification, the national bourgeoisie and the big peasantry emerge in a subordinate relation to the metropolitan bourgeoisie. The mass of the peasantry are similarly subordinate, and become in several ways subordinate also to the big peasantry and other elements of the national bourgeoisie.

The wide range of ways in which different agricultural products are marketed makes a generalized illustration of this argument difficult. Although detailed structures of surplus extraction differ from one product to another the general orientation is the same for each, so the idea here is to look at one product in some depth. Coffee has become far and away the major export crop and coffee provides perhaps the most dramatic example because much more than any other crop its cultivation is in the hands of nationals and predominantly so. The position described here is that prior to recent changes which will be accounted for shortly. The next stage after growing and harvesting the coffee bean is its sale either as unprocessed cherry or semi-processed parchment. This initial processing to the parchment stage will have involved the use of a coffee pulper and this will usually be under the control of a big peasant who will use it to take an initial slice of the surplus. The next stage—the sale of the cherry or parchment—was regulated under marketing legislation introduced in 1963. The Coffee Marketing Board, set up under the legislation, licensed buyers and, although it was not legally empowered to do so, it restricted the issue of licences. As far as Papua New Guineans were concerned, it could back up this abuse of power because there were standards in the legislation which it was difficult for them to comply with, such as a requirement that each buyer should have an expensive type of storage shed. If a buyer tried to work outside the licensing system without such a shed he could be prosecuted out of a buying existence. The Board issued most of the buying licences to resident colonist and foreign coffee processors who farmed out many of these licences to roadside coffee buyers. The buyers were usually nationals and often emerging as big peasants. In this way, and sometimes in conjunction with tied loans providing capital for buyers, the buyers were bound to the particular processor who held in the licences. The binding of buyers helped also to minimize the risk involved in the fulfilling of forward contracts entered into by processors and exporters. Further sale to exporters was the next stage in the process. Almost all coffee is exported by foreign companies and the dominant company here also has substantial interests in processing. The matter should then be taken into the realm of international marketing and of the international coffee agreement but will not be. In all, the extent of the colonist's and foreign involvement increases in each step, from cultivation, to selling of the unprocessed or semi-processed bean, to processing and to export and international marketing.

Recent changes in this situation help to take the argument further and introduce something of a qualification. Due to the intense efforts of a national Minister for Agriculture and despite strong opposition from his own Department and from the Coffee Marketing Board, which was in law subject to the Minister, the Coffee Dealing (Control) Act of 1974 was enacted, under which the roadside buying of coffee was limited to nationals and related tied loans and other tied arrangements were denied legal effect. The pressure for this tended to come from younger emerging big peasants. It was opposed by more established big peasants who sided with Australian settlers, such settlers often being their mentors and having assisted these big peasants in their emergence (Finney, 1973, p. 55; McSwain, 1977, p. 57). It may well have been the case also that established big peasants gained from the established system, and would stand to lose with the greater competition that was expected to flow from this change. As it turned out, the change did provide openings for a wider range of emergent big peasants. However, there was a not unexpected continuation of tied arrangements; many buyers were still bound effectively if not legally because of their need for working capital. Also there were some, but seemingly not many, 'fronts' which gave the appearance of exclusive national ownership but which were set up in such a way as to allow of foreign control. The same Minister who effected this change also used legal controls to forbid the buying of coffee in the unprocessed cherry form. He argued this was to discourage the theft of cherry from coffee trees and to encourage Papua New Guinean processing at least to the parchment stage. His opponents claimed that the measure was to help big peasants whose coffee was being stolen and who controlled the coffee pulpers needed to process cherry to the parchment stage. It was certainly the case that some small-scale growers objected on this latter ground. However, more influential objection came from the mainly foreign processors who found it more profitable to take their processing from the cherry rather than the parchment state. The opposition of foreign processors and of small-scale growers was effective in having the prohibition on buying cherry lifted.[4]

As this account shows, the alignments and influences of different class elements in concrete situations can be more complex than the attribution of their overall and respective strengths would allow. What particularly appears here is that general domination by the metropolitan bourgeoisie is not incompatible with effective self-assertion by the national bourgeoisie and the big peasantry, at least in the lower reaches of the economy, and that this is so even if it involves defeat of elements of the metropolitan bourgeoisie, particularly, yet again, defeat of the resident colonist.

It is in this perspective that changes at the political and constitutional-legal level can also be explained. No longer is it the pure colonial case of law and state acting on the 'undifferentiated mass' of the colonized. The national bourgeoisie and the big peasantry are not merely acted on; they, or their representatives, act within the state system. To be in a position to do so, they are buttressed and promoted through law and state but their advance is contained within a particular structure of power. By hastening and helping the emergence of the national bourgeoisie and big peasantry, law and state may well be helping create some opposition to the metropolitan bourgeoisie but there is a counterveiling element in that this allows law and state, and the state generally, to take part in the shaping of these class elements. These elements come 'into their own' in the context of a state system on which they depend, a state system that is temporarily in advance of their emergence politically as well as economically. Thus with and from the Papua and New Guinea Act of 1963, pre-packaged, British-type, constitutional forms are introduced and the participation of the colonized in these gradually extended (Leibowitz, 1976, pp. 147–173). In this way power is conferred yet contained. It is close to a mere continuation of this process for the national bourgeoisie and big peasantry to act in their own advance from within the state system. Thus a study of one large ethnic group, in summarizing recent developments, sees that political "power at the local and national levels is increasingly used to reinforce economic status, leading to the emergence of a rural elite as well as an urban elite . . .," and "certain government agencies" are seen as "the main stimulus'' in this process (Howlett *et al.*, 1976, p. 6).

Even in earlier periods of colonization big men used appointed positions of colonial rule to increase their wealth. Such positions were used to obtain labour, to erect some independence from demands of followers and generally to obtain a preponderant share of the valuables introduced with colonization (Finney, 1973, p. 91; Meggitt, 1974, p. 84). When local government councils and co-operatives were introduced after the Second World War new positions of power were used to acquire wealth, to obtain access to government lending and extension services, and to step outside the checks of traditional social formations (Brown, 1963, pp. 11 – 13; Good and Donaldson, 1979, pp. 40 – 42; Howlett *et al.*, 1976, p. 185; Salisbury, 1964, pp. 231, 235). In more recent times there may be a tendency for some of the big peasantry to desert councils and to aim for the richer rewards associated with election to the national legislature (Finney, 1973, pp. 117-118; Uyassi, 1978, pp. 23, 36). The contemporary introduction of provincial government, a tier intermediate between councils and national government, was in part a response to pressure from the big peasantry who are heavily represented in provincial governments (Barnett, in press). Electoral politics seem generally to be viewed as an avenue to wealth and a great number of candidates compete at national elections and spend a great deal of money in the process (Standish, n.d., p. 6; Stone, 1976, p. 530). Another political avenue to wealth is seen in the phenomenon of senior state operatives acquiring plantations and other rural property. These people, although they occupy a contradictory class location, must be seen as having some identity of interest with the national bourgeoisie and big peasantry.

In addition to emerging within the confines of a particular structure of power, the big peasantry is contained through the maintenance of traditional social formations. The ultimate logic of 'letting the Kulaks run' is the breaking down of the traditional mode of production and the comprehensive substitution of capitalist relations. But in terms of the interests of the metropolitan bourgeoisie, the traditional mode must remain to subsidize capitalist production and to counter challenging class consolidations. Hence the Kulak must only run so far. The traditional social formation, as we saw, assists by continuing to assert demands incompatible with capitalist development, it does not lightly let go of its own. It has some purchase on the big peasant because he retains an operative commitment to the traditional mode.

The checks and hesitations of the Land (Tenure Conversion) Act of 1963 and in its implementation provide perhaps the most dramatic example here. Even in its terms, the Act's expressed commitment to the individualization of land tenure was hedged about almost to the point of extinction. The Act imposed drastic restrictions on dealing with converted land. Section 26 provides that:

(i)   the land may be transferred or leased [only] to the Administration or to a Native. . . .;

(ii)  the land may be mortgaged or charged but . . . the mortgagee or chargee is not entitled to remain in possession for longer than three years or to foreclose the right of the mortgagor or chargor to redeem the mortgaged or charged land; and

(iii) the land shall not be taken under a writ of execution or under or in consequence of a bankruptcy or insolvency, or in any similar or analogous manner.

However, an official body within the colonial administration could direct that the restrictions would no longer apply in specific cases. The liberal use of this power of exemption provoked a change in the Act subjecting each sale of converted land to the consent of the Australian Minister for Territories and tightening up drastically on other dealings beside sale. More particularly, the idea behind the exemption power was:

> . . . that the new unsophisticated title-holder needed protection in the early days of registered ownership but that the restrictions could be lifted when they were no longer required. But the . . . [relevant colonial official] adopted the practice of lifting the restrictions whenever he made a conversion order with the result that the Ordinance was amended in 1968 so that every sale required the consent of the Minister for External Territories, every lease or mortgage required the consent of the Administrator's Executive Council (that is, the Cabinet) and the restrictions on the mortgagee's powers were mandatory in every case (Bredmeyer, 1973, p. 9)

Further, the colonial administration in 1965, that is very soon after the Act was actually brought into operation, gave a direction that conversions be limited and the main body charged with making conversions "had inadequate staff or funds to carry out the whole process" (ibid., p. 9). The upshot was that tenure conversions were few and a great deal of the few were for urban house sites (ibid., p. 10; Howlett *et al.*, 1976, pp. 98 – 100; Simpson, 1971, p. 7). In a much studied area where there were many rural conversions, traditional obligations relating to land and some group control over it continue (Birmingham and Scoullar, 1974; Dakenye, 1966; Gray, n.d.; Morawetz, 1967). Some people accept that traditional inheritance rights will continue to apply to their converted land (Morawetz, 1967, p. 25; Wanji, 1977, p. 25).

Inheritance can be seen in this context as something of a testing point—a test of the ability of emerging dominant class elements to reproduce and consolidate their positions. As we saw, legal changes in the period of accelerated development enabled Papua New Guineans to will 'new' property, that is, unregistered or unconverted land, remains to be dealt with within the traditional mode, a situation confirmed by the continued application to inheritance of certain colonial 'native regulations'. This land includes most of the land used by nationals in production for the market. In describing traditional social formations it was seen that a big man's empire dissolved on his death. It was built and held together as a set of personal relationships focused on him. In a similar vein, Finney has recounted how the venture of a modern 'business leader' was dissipated on his death in a multitude of claims resulting from his exchange relationships (Finney, 1973, pp. 100 – 104). Although its effects have not been studied in detail, the death of a political leader and big peasant, Kondom Agaundo, seems to have had a similar result although his venture had been somewhat dissipated in his lifetime (Vincent Kondom, personal communication). A recent case involved the death of one of the wealthiest national cattlemen, Doa Minch (or Mints). Although his 265 hectares of land was tenure converted he had not made a will and the court decided that his estate should be dealt with under traditional law (Kassam, 1974, pp. 25 – 27). The final outcome is as yet unclear: as a continuing entity, his venture has all but disappeared. The Development Bank had much of the estate sold up to repay its loan to Doa Minch and also to repay two loans he had guaranteed (John Oates, personal communication), thus revealing the limited nature of its commitment to the maintenance of the big peasantry. The land is now leased to what are largely foreign interests. Doa Minch's clansmen claim they helped in the creation of his wealth and are entitled to a share in his estate. He strongly resisted similar claims in his lifetime and was constantly in fear of his life (Bob Gunton, personal communication). In the same vein, people discuss sorcery as a possible cause of all these deaths. There seems to have been only one instance so far of a large venture surviving and this was due to an exceptional conjunction of circumstances. This was the case of a transport and earthmoving partnership of two brothers, partly based in their rural village and partly in the nearby national capital. One of the partners was murdered, it has never been discovered by whom. The venture was started mainly with a government loan and hence kin had little direct claim on it. Even so a wide-ranging and enormously complex collection of kin-demands was made on the estate and there can be little doubt that the venture would have dissipated without the surviving partner to hold it together (Joe Shaw, personal communication, and see also, Andrews, 1975, pp. 82 – 83). That there appear to be only a few cases to go on is probably due to the latter day emergence of the national bourgeoisie and big peasantry. Epstein foresees numerous disputes breaking out among the Tolai when the present generation of big peasants begins to die (Epstein, 1972, pp. 56 – 57). However, traditional inheritance law may well be changing to favour more the smaller-family unit and it seems to be part of this tendency for holdings to remain intact (Ward, 1978, p. 22). Also, in the traditional context there was some scope for sons of big men to build on a privileged position and perhaps this factor applies to production for the market, although many such sons are now more oriented to the opportunities opened up through formal education especially in government employment. As far as law and state are concerned, however, and despite their promotion of a big peasantry, the examples of tenure conversion and inheritance strongly suggest that in matters of ultimate right as between the big peasant and the conservation of the traditional mode it is conservation that is preferred.

In the containment of the mass of the peasantry, law and state provide forms that are also used in the bounded advance of the big peasantry—the local government council and the co-operative. Hasluck once homilized that "the wisdom of government is to anticipate and avoid the building up of a destructive flood, and ensure that the energy of people flows along quieter and happier channels" (Jinks et al., 1973, p. 361).

The idea of the co-operative was borrowed from British colonies in Africa. The first operative law was the Co-operative Societies Ordinance of 1950. It followed the British model closely. However, only a few co-operatives were ever registered under this law. Until 1967 the hundreds of others were registered under the Native Economic Development Ordinance of 1951. This was a simple law which provided for corporate registration of 'native' enterprises, almost all such enterprises actually registered being in the co-operative form. It gave officials enormous power over these co-operatives. Even Hasluck objected to it for the "wide powers" it gave officials "to take charge of native activities in an extreme form of economic paternalism" (Hasluck, 1976, 153). These powers were, however, fundamental to the law's function. The co-operative form was introduced as a response to an upsurge of group economic and political organization after the Second World War (Jackman, 1972, p. 213; Oram, 1976a, p. 83). These group organizations or associations were usually founded financially on wages accumulated whilst working for the military administration and war damage compensation. They often transcended ethnic divisions; their membership sometimes numbered in the thousands and they were, understandably, felt by many colonial officials to be politically dangerous (Hogbin, 1970, p. 228; Oram, 1976a, p. 91). "Tactically the Administration's assistance [with co-operatives] was designed to guide potential forces of resistance into proper channels" (Legge, 1956, p. 218; see also Committee of Enquiry, 1972, pp. 58, 125). "The Administration [also] tried to guide the members of different movements towards the formation of co-operative societies" and restricted the growth of the larger movements (Oram, 1976a, p. 91 and see for example, Maher, 1961, pp. 71 – 74). Early colonial officers involved with co-operatives were imbued with a great enthusiasm for them, thinking them, as did the British in Africa, somehow natural for 'communal' societies and "a simple panacea for the slowness of indigenous development" and often imposing them on people (Good and Donaldson, 1979, pp. 17 – 18; Lubett, 1977, p. 21; Salisbury, 1970, p. 218). Officers held out great and often unreal inducement for people to form and join co-operatives. Among the more sedate, officials told people that only by forming co-operatives could they get legal recognition and government loans (Bill Barclay, personal communication). An officer promoting the Chimbu Coffee Co-operative told people that if they showed their membership cards they would be able to have free rides in co-operative trucks and aeroplanes (Vincent Kondom and several members of the co-operative, personal communication). (This is ascribed by officials to "inflated expectations" generated within the native mentality. I will leave it to the reader to decide, after the account following of local government councils, as to the source of the inflation.)

Containment took the operative form of the most comprehensive control, but before considering control in detail, one has to consider briefly the later legislation, which was the relevant law from 1967 until very recently, the Co-operative Societies Act of 1965. The old Native Economic Development Ordinance had to go in the (fairly) general repeal of laws based on differences of racially ascribed status, since its operation was confined to 'natives'. The new law was officially described as being a decisive move away from the control-orientation of the old: it was "to encourage self-help among co-operatives and to ensure that Administration control and direct participation [was] only exercised where unavoidably necessary'' said the senior legal official in introducing the law to the legislature (Territory of Papua New Guinea, 1965, p. 1051). This statement of legislative intent, like others about this time, is helpful for one has merely to take the opposite of what is being said in order to discern the true purpose: see for example, the trade union laws discussed in the next chapter. The new act, although more like a fully-fledged if sloppy co-operatives law of the British brand, still gave a Registrar of Co-operative Societies enormous power. Quantitatively, the act gave the Registrar close on 50 distinct and, often, broad discretionary powers. Qualitatively, they gave the Registrar control over a co-operative's investments, lending, borrowing and distributions and gave him power to dismiss a director, officer or employee of a co-operative. But the Registrar's formal powers, broad and narrow, were, in an important way, irrelevant or subsidiary. Under both the old and new laws, registration as a co-operative entailed becoming closely involved with and subordinated to the requirements of a government extension agency for co-operatives headed by the same official who was Registrar. These requirements were ostensibly aimed at ensuring the economic success of co-operatives and to this end justified the continuous and comprehensively dominating involvement of administration officers (see Committee of Inquiry, 1972, pp. 8 and 162). There is one official for every 2·3 co-operatives operating (Division of Co-operative Development, 1974, pp. 4, 24). The Division ''in effect makes most major business decisions for Co-operative Societies'' and does much of the more routine work for them (Committee of Enquiry, 1972, pp. 8, 168). Officials have to do this because the people cannot (yet) do it themselves. Without official control co-operatives would fail (ibid., p. 205). The need to control still defines the inferiority of the people.

Generally, and in official theory, such control was necessary to ensure profitability but was to be temporary, awaiting the advance of Papua New Guineans to appropriate skills. The control argument, in this light, could be dented by showing that official intervention did lead to profitability and/or that Papua New Guineans were being provided with the appropriate skills. The official commitment to education in these skills has, however, been slight and recent (ibid., pp. 65, 178, 191; Singh, 1974, pp. 182 – 190). Co-operatives have generally failed in terms of profitability (Committee of Enquiry, 1972, p. 22 and annex 6; Division of Co-operative Development, 1974, pp. 26 – 33). This is not to say there was some deep plot to undermine co-operatives, although there are instances in which they were kept out of areas where the colonist objected to them as competitors (McSwain, 1977, p. 54; Reay, 1969, p. 66). Rather, the hardy incompetence of Australian officials running the co-operatives was more than adequate to obviate any risk of profitability (Committee of Enquiry, 1972, pp. 65, 191). For example, an analysis of the Registrar's power over loans made by co-operatives, as it has been used since August 1966, shows that it has been used to get co-operatives to make loans:

> . . . to support schemes initiated by the Division without reasonable feasibility studies, plans or projections, and which were either in financial difficulties at the time or were subsequently in financial difficulties. The . . . loans were all unsecured and the applications were unsupported by any analysis of the projects they were financing. (ibid., p. 224)

In this and other ways officials foisted numerous dubious ventures onto co-operatives which resulted in great losses for the people (ibid., pp. 38 – 57). Not that these were aberrations no matter how massive, for the whole official orientation was not one aimed at profitability. Thus the law required that accounts be audited each year and for almost all co-operatives this was to be done by officials. The Registrar was not vigilant in enforcing this law, which was in effect against himself, and few audits have actually been carried out (ibid., pp. 237 – 238). Although officials present profitability as fundamental, when it fails to materialize they assert that the main goal has all the time been to provide a service (ibid., pp. 7, 32, 125 – 126). Reeling from our obtuseness in failing to see this all along, any vestigial illusion is then shattered in the attribution to the co-operative of the ultimate service of self-destruction, for the co-operative "fosters a state of confidence and self reliance not hitherto apparent in the individual person" whence it becomes "redundant" and leaves the field to those who can "go it alone" (Division of Co-operative Development, 1974, p. 14—co-operative development indeed! See also Department of Business Development, 1974, p. 6). Such success has to be seen in the context of the wider success involved in providing an organizational form that diverted the larger scale groupings and types of collective organization that were emerging after the second world war and at various times following. This form fitted the structure of peasant society. With very few exceptions, co-operatives were officially promoted as having marketing and/or consumer-supply functions, production being left to the peasant household. McSwain notes of the area she studied that "traditional elements in the social system suffered little change through the introduction of co-operatives" (McSwain, 1977, p. 103). They were also promoted on the basis of existing ethnic divisions. A survey of co-operatives which I conducted in 1970 showed that out of a total of 332, 286 had a membership of less than 500.[5] Other figures reinforce the point. Of this total 301 had less than 700 members, and 314 less than 1000; only five had more than 2000 members and only two more than 4000.

As to the failure of co-operatives, something of an alternative view perhaps deserves a mention. The official view of this is that traditional relations which lead to misappropriation of the co-operative' goods and funds by members as well as their general incompetence are what causes failure. The first national Registrar of Co-operative Societies has stated that co-operatives have not failed, "it has been just some people who have failed" and "there are ways and means of changing and correcting these weaknesses" (*Post-Courier*, 29th October, 1973). There is no shortage of academic support for this position (see for example, McSwain, 1970; Singh, 1974). Enough has been said, I hope, to show that this view is nonsense. Nothing happened to change traditional relations and next to nothing to provide an appropriate competence. On the contrary the traditional is to be conserved and a smothering official control left no room for the development of this competence. Moreover, official control, and its disasterous effects, resulted understandably in the disillusionment of the people and their alienation from co-operatives (see for example, Allen, 1975, pp. 24 – 25; Committee of Enquiry, 1972, pp. 57, 193).

The story of local government councils is similar. The idea was again borrowed from British colonies in Africa. Under the Native Village Councils Ordinance, introduced in 1949, such councils, soon after called "native local government councils", were set up. As with co-operatives, this legislation contained a most comprehensive set of controls (Simpson, 1978, p. 32). Officially, the councils were seen as legitimizing direct rule. They were not meant, despite some contrary rhetoric, to be effective instruments of self-government (ibid.; Brookfield, 1972, p. 115). Again like the co-operative, the council had the function of channelling dissent and of containing enterprising political leaders (Simpson, 1978, pp. 26 – 27, 34, 37; and see for example, Worsley, 1971, p. 199; cf. Rowley, 1972, p. 179, n. 26). Councils were "sold" by officials as a means to economic development (Simpson, 1978, p. 37). Hasluck's account of how councils were set up appears facetious but of course is not:

> The approach was simple. The initiative came from the Australian officer. With variations suited to circumstances he said in effect to the people, "Don't you think it would be a good idea if you had a council just like the people over at _____ ?" (He named some neighbouring group whom they envied.) When curiousity had been stimulated, he told them in effect, with local variations, that when they got a council, they would be able to do such things as build a council house, get a lighting plant, start a rice-mill, have a saw-bench, buy a vehicle or do something else which they coveted but which was beyond their means as individuals in a village. (Hasluck, 1976, p. 1976, p. 242)

People were often coerced to form or to join councils (Simpson, 1978; Uyassi, 1978, p. 7).

Containment took operative form, again, as the most comprehensive control. But, like co-operatives also, there was, in the period of accelerated development, supposedly redeeming legislation in the form of the Local Government Act of 1963. This act was more like British or Australian local government legislation. The act was, in Hasluck's view, to initiate the transformation of councils into effectively governing bodies (Hasluck, 1976, pp. 399 – 400). The Commissioner in charge of councils has wide powers over them. Councils must seek his approval on numerous matters. He can dismiss a councillor, disallow council rules and control a council's borrowing. As Conyers comments:

> On the one hand they [councils] were to act as an administrative arm of the colonial administration as their predessors, the village officials, had done; on the other, they were supposed to provide the basis for the establishment of democratic self-government. In practice, the emphasis in most councils has been on the first function and a large part of their efforts have been devoted to ensuring that national regulations and instructions are obeyed, carrying out minor functions on behalf of the central government departments and providing information on local affairs. As effective local governing bodies, they have been, in most parts of the country, relatively ineffective. (Conyers, 1976, p. 7)

As with co-operatives, yet again, it was considered that an absence of official control could lead to failure (Simpson, 1978, p. 25). Hence:

> The effectiveness of Councils came to depend on the supervising officer, while the development of a meaningful participation by the Councillors was stifled, due to the controls vested in the District

Officer over the legal, financial and administrative functions of the Councils. (ibid., p. 36)

Little wonder that, for example, "Chimbu councils have not been success-ful organizations politically, economically or socially. Disenchantment with the councils is frequently expressed and is also reflected in the tax collection rate, which has fallen spectacularly in the last few years, and by the low voting rate in elections" (Howlett *et al.*, 1976, p. 183). These points can be fairly widely generalized, but there remains that kind of success in containing the peasantry which such as assessment leaves out. Councils, like co-operatives, served to contain political and economic movements. They were officially envisaged as being based on and as main-taining traditional relations (Jinks *et al.*, 1973, pp. 343 – 344; Simpson, 1978, p. 28). Although councils covered several traditional groups, coun-cillors in practice represented such groups. Councils also involved a ward committee system based on these groups.

It now remains to assess the impact of these various forces on the forma-tion of the peasantry. Of special importance for its relevance to later chapters is the extent to which the traditional mode of production is opera-tive and the extent and effect of differentiation within the peasantry. The degree of operative commitment which people have to the different modes of production is not something susceptible of precise definition and arbitrary division. At one extreme some people will operate almost wholly within the traditional mode and have only a small degree of commitment to the capitalist. Cash from production for the market is desired because the ability to buy introduced foods, clothing, fuel and simple tools is universally prized. This supplements and aids production for use and for traditional exchange and the traditional mode remains a comprehensively accessible retreat. At the other extreme would be a big peasant producing for the market, aspiring to join the bourgeoisie and systematically attempting to reject obligations grounded in the traditional mode. He, presumably, would not find this mode easily accessible. Some peasants will, in varying degrees, be dependent on both types of production. The conditions of production for the market may, in some cases, be so extremely constrained that the peasant can be seen as approximating to a proletarian selling his labour, and a blockholder on one of the nucleus estates could be an example of this.

Starting with the big peasant, it seems to be common for him to start his climb by relying on traditional relations, though this reliance may be lessening with the increased role of governmental lending, and then to move partly in the direction of ownership and control on an individual basis or in partnership with other big peasants (see for example, Epstein, 1968, pp. 52 – 53; Finney, 1973, p. 77; Gerritsen, 1975, pp. 13, 16 – 17; To Robert, 1967, p. 75). In many areas there is a great differentiation in terms of property and monetary income between the big peasants and the mass of the peasantry (see references in Epstein, 1970, pp. 50 – 51 and also Conroy and Skeldon eds., 1977, pp. 109, 127, 145, 165; Crocombe, 1967, p. 17; Finney, 1973, p. 85; Good and Donaldson, 1979, pp. 31 – 34; McKillop, 1974a, p. 15; Morauta 1974, pp. 72, 74; Strathern, 1972b, pp. 373 – 374). Structural supports for the maintenance of the big peasantry as a distinct class element emerge: various mechanisms develop for easing property out of the domain of the traditional mode; 'new' property can be willed; education serves as a point of preference in the allocation of governmental resources; the big peasantry form pressure group organizations transcending ethnic boundaries and develop something of a corporate identity (Gerritsen, 1975; Moulik, 1970; Ploeg, 1973, p. 38; Uyassi, 1978, pp. 47 – 49).

The metropolitan bourgeoisie remains dominant, however, and in the interests of that class element the traditional mode is conserved. The emergence of the big peasantry tends to be bounded by this. There result certain combined forms of economic organization, forms that combine production for the market with a continuing significant relation to the traditional mode. One form is that of the 'development corporation', a phenomenon treated in more detail in Chapter Eight. Typically, it involves a large ethnic grouping and sometimes relies on, or on an extension of, traditional exchange networks. Component smaller groups and individuals within the grouping invest in the corporation as shareholders. The corporation engages in economic activities in its own right and sometimes invests in other ventures. The big peasant plays a dominant role in the organization of corporations, and the ventures in which a corporation invests will sometimes include his. These ventures will often include also those of the metropolitan bourgeoisie and there will be other types of intimate linkages with this class element. Some development corporations have, or had, something of a nationalist, radical inclination. Gerritsen would distinguish these from certain organizations explicitly dominated by the big peasant, but Uyassi seems to be correct in saying they are basically no different (Gerritsen, 1975; Uyassi, 1978, p. 1). The radical corporations are often just as implicated with the metropolitan bourgeoisie, or have tried to be, and the lifestyle of their leaders, formally executives of the corporation, strongly suggests an appropriation of surplus entirely comparable to the efforts of more conventional big peasants. At the political level, and in a context where turnover in membership of the national legislature is very high, the big peasant operating with a development corporation or with some other type of large, ethnically-based formal organization appears more likely to be re-elected (see for example, Donaldson and Good, 1978, p. 23; Skeldon, 1977, p. 23). More generally, observers have recently noted the emergence of brokerage and patron–client relations—classic forms tying the mass of the peasantry in relations of dependence on the big peasantry, and forms which have obvious antecedents in traditional society (Howlett et al., 1976, p. 207; Salisbury, 1964, p. 238; Standish, 1978a, p. 24, 1978b). These forms are politically structured in elected politicians' being typically reliant on a particular ethnically defined, block vote (Oram, 1976b, p. 525; Stone, 1976, pp. 534–536). Overall, it appears that the big peasant does not break away decisively from traditional social formations (see for example, Connell, 1979, p. 23; Strathern, 1972b, p. 378). There are also combined forms of economic organization not involving the big peasantry. These are movements and organizations based on traditional groupings which engage in marketing or production for the market but whose leaders operate in a less economically dominant and more egalitarian frame and although these are probably widespread they are of those group enterprises that have been discriminated against or surpressed by the state and they tend to be organizationally unstable (Barnett, in press; Fitzpatrick and Southwood, 1976).

As for the mass of the peasantry, their involvement in production for the market is quite small (Howlett et al., 1976, pp. 211, 220; McKillop, 1977b, p. 8; Shand and Straatmans, 1974, p. 185). Even in those areas where general production for the market is intense, it tends to be concentrated in the hands of the big peasantry and of the metropolitan bourgeoisie. As far as nationals are concerned, law and state and supportive state action generally have been largely dedicated to the big peasantry. Production for the market has been imported and encouraged neither comprehensively nor intensively. Most peasants engage in production for the market as something incidental to production for use and for traditional exchange. Dependence on production for the market is probably quite strong with many settlers on nucleus estates and on government resettlement schemes but these settlers are a very small minority. In some areas cash crops may have been planted to the point that land for subsistence production is becoming inadequate (Howlett *et al.*, 1976, p. 225; Lambert, 1979; Mitchell, 1976, pp. 140 – 143). This does not seem to be a general trend. Nor is the commitment of land to production for the market irreversible: in several areas cash crop land has been returned to subsistence production in the face of population pressures. Doubtless the rapid increase in population will increasingly test the adequacy of available land. Also of relevance here are those communities—peri-urban and further afield—which operate to an overwhelming degree in the maintenance of an urban workforce and which depend to a considerable degree on remitted wages (see for example, Harding, 1971). More direct challenges to the integrity of the traditional mode come from changing relations to the means of production. Individual control over land in some areas seems to have developed almost to the point of the exclusion of group interests and some land is now treated as a commodity (Howlett *et al.*, 1976, pp. 41 – 42; Morauta, 1974, p. 68; Salisbury, 1970, p. 123; Shand and Straatmans, 1974, p. 144; Simpson, 1971, p. 10). The provision of labour for the big peasantry on a proletarian basis is becoming increasingly common (see references in Howlett, 1977, pp. 8 – 9 and also Crocombe, 1967, p. 9; Epstein, 1968, p. 104; Finney, 1969, p. 33; Gerritsen, 1975, p. 46; Good and Donaldson, 1979, pp. 25 – 26; Morauta, 1974, pp. 31, 55; Philipp, 1971; Salisbury, 1970, pp. 8 – 9). Also, some wider exchange networks have contracted or broken down (Collins, 1979, p. 23; Hogbin, 1970, p. 202; Ploeg, 1979, p. 10). Despite all this, the tendency remains towards the conservation of the traditional mode. The following recent description of one large group can, subject to pockets of exception, be generalized, and this group is comparatively intensely involved in production for the market and is subject to great population pressures:

> Chimbu socioeconomy has never been challenged by an innovation so successful, never been subject to an external force so drastic, that any irrevocable structural modification has occurred in it. The traditional culture *has* changed . . . but its essential elements have survived. (Howlett *et al.*, 1976, p. 5)

All this is not to suggest that in the class containment of the peasantry law and state have been invariably successful and that this is a quiescent class element. Indeed the instruments of containment provided by law and state have suffered recurrent and often fatal crises of legitimation. With the conservation of the traditional mode, there remains much still of popular and independent access to the means of production and of approximate equality. This forms and sharpens a persistent critical edge to the people's relation with authority. Increases in sorcery, coffee stealing and 'tribal fighting' have strong elements of popular rebellion although strenuous official efforts are made to confine them to categories of criminal offence and to deal with them as such (Good and Donaldson, 1979, p. 54; Strathern, 1977). Peasants are acutely aware of inequalities. 'Cargo' movements oriented against them persist, disadvantaged peasants have supported radical political movements, and "a correlation is apparent . . . between the areas of most intense political unrest and those where informal smallholder cash cropping was most concentrated" (Collins, 1979, p. 38). Law and state are not unresponsive to these pressures. Given the continued limitation on coercive responses, because of the inherent structural weakness of the state, new legal forms of containment have to be and are devised. The rest of this chapter and much of Chapter Eight are devoted to considering these.

The form of containment considered here involves an adaptation of traditional dispute settlement, joined with the emergence of dominant class elements in the rural areas. In summary, dispute settlement in traditional social formations was largely based on agreement. Such 'agreement' could, however, contain political elements that were coercive of parties to the dispute. Disputes not readily resolved by the immediate parties could be settled in the heavily-persuasive context of the public meeting. This was informal in its proceeding and all could participate. As well as the element of the political there was a significant element of legality. This included the operative presence of legal rules even though these tended often to be very flexible or were even sometimes inconsistent. Big men often played significant parts in dispute settlement as mediators or arbitrators. Dispute settlement as party-agreement could be supplanted or supplemented by other methods of resolution such as adjudication or divination in the limited circumstances described earlier. In the colonial period, as we saw, a system of petty 'indirect rule' operated in practice. The theory was different in that traditional dispute settlement was not incorporated as a formally legitimate part of colonial rule. The reason advanced for this was that the colonist could find no elements in traditional society capable of applying 'law', meaning bourgeois legality (Simpson, 1978, p. 30). Of course, as far as the colonized were concerned, the colonist used a comprehensively authoritarian legal system. As part of this, the colonist did appoint various 'native' officials within the village. These were often people having traditional authority but this was not always the case. Sometimes officials would act as agents of traditional leaders. Colonial field officers encouraged these 'native' officials to hold courts modelled on the officers' own Courts of Native Affairs. The 'native' officials had considerable responsibility for the enforcement of colonial legal rules. Although the officials used their connection with the colonial regime to bolster their authority and sometimes adjudicated disputes, in their role of dispute settler they acted predominantly as mediators in the traditional manner. When local government councils displaced the system of appointed officials, matters remained much the same. Councillors now heard and mediated or, sometimes, adjudicated disputes, they were effectively encouraged by the colonial administration to do so and they relied on their links with that administration to bolster their power (see for example, Epstein, 1974b, pp. 19 – 20, 30 – 31; Reay, 1974, pp. 212 – 213).

Such activities were, at best, outside of the (colonial) law. The pretence that bourgeois legality should or would be exclusive was maintained. This position was reaffirmed recently and most influentially in the Derham Report (see Bayne, 1975, pp. 12 – 20). This report provided a court structure for the last stage of the colonist's rule and it saw the future of dispute settlement solely in terms of the extension of the courts of bourgeois legality. It ruled out any legitimate role for the traditional mode in dispute settlement. Overall, the structure of dispute settlement in the colonial situation has been well summarized by Marilyn Strathern:

> [For dispute settlement] Hageners visualise a hierarchy of officials: at the bottom are *komiti* [ward committeemen of the local government councils] who handle minor issues; troublesome cases are referred to councillors, who in turn take matters too large for them to settle to the police, *kiap* [colonial field officer] or LCM [Local Court Magistrate]; these may themselves transfer cases to higher officials, including Supreme Court judges. ("If the matter does not go straight, then the *kiap* takes it to the big judge.") It is a continuum of process (the transfer of cases from one body to another) and also of authority, so that in this context councillors are seen as the immediate subordinates of *kiap* . . . . The hierarchical model envisages a chain of personnel down which strength is passed, so that the power and authority of *kiap* can be tapped. (Strathern, 1972, pp. 119 – 120, 137)

Of course, the Hagener's perception was more accurate than the official view of dispute settlement but both were to be disturbed by the rumblings of a changing reality.

There have been recent and growing strains on the efficacy of traditional dispute settlement or on the variants of it just described. The emergence of capitalist relations of production, as well as provoking a great number of disputes to be settled, also tends to undermine the basis of traditional dispute settlement. Other and related strains are by now commonplaces of recent academic accounts: growing pressure on land in many areas because of population increase and cash-cropping; the undermining of moral constraints based on religion through the destructive activity of missions; the disappearance, to a considerable degree, of colonial authoritarian controls without comparable replacement and, related to this, the colonial administration's failure adequately to extend the coverage of conventional courts as recommended in Derham. In this situation the traditional types of dispute settlement continue and somewhat adaptively fill this gap (Reay, 1974, pp. 239; Strathern, 1977, pp. 139 – 140). They are qualified or inhibited in their operation by two related factors: first with the tendency for relations of production to become more individualized and separable from traditional formations, group controls are weakened; the second factor is the emergence of new dominant class elements having an economic and political basis for their power which is to a degree independent of the traditional social formation. Traditional control may be weakened but this class element presents something of a replacement. However, the subsequent development of dispute settlement, now to be outlined, is not simply a matter of resolving the contradiction between old types of settlement and the use of new forms of power. The traditional is conserved and there is, in significant degree, a blend of the old and the new. Rules, leaders and adjudication all had parts in traditional dispute settlement as we saw. Their significance is heightened in the colonial period. They are then drawn on and magnified in a new and remarkable type of dispute settlement, the 'village court'.

With the advent of self-government, a report in 1971 by the senior colonial legal official in Papua New Guinea and by the senior legal official in the Australian government concerned with Papua New Guinea expressed great concern both with the 'gap' left by the declining system of colonial control and with the persistence of traditional dispute settlement. The authors saw the prospect this way:

> We think it very likely that some system of village courts would be established as soon as local political control over the legal system is established. If it is established now, it could be fitted into the existing courts system. This would have the virtue not only of eliminating or controlling major abuses which are likely to occur if dispute settlement

> continues unofficially but by a process of education secure the
> adoption of certain basic procedures. (cited in MacTeine and
> Paliwala, 1978, p. 4)

Bourgeois legality, having for so long served as a justification for not recognizing traditional dispute settlement, was now used to bring it in from the cold but in an appropriate garb. Another immediate impetus for village courts came from an influential Commission of Enquiry into Tribal Fighting in the Highlands (1973). It was concerned with the gap in authority also and with what was perceived as a resulting lawlessness. It recommended the setting up of village courts and of village peace officers—a lay rural police—attached to the courts. Explicit demands at the local level were emerging. The best study of these is provided by Uyassi in his account of informal, local government type councils in the Eastern Highlands (Uyassi, 1978). Here leaders of the councils were seen by people as 'using' the councils for their own political and economic advance. As a result, the people were becoming disaffected with councils and were refusing to co-operate with them. Leaders pressed the national government for village courts to enforce their decisions. One leader saw it vividly as a case of "without village courts the . . . [councils] would be like a dog with no teeth" (Uyassi, 1978, p. 32). Reay has remarked on a dissatisfaction throughout the Western Highlands on the part of local government councillors and committeemen that they could not impose gaol sentences as part of their dispute settling activities (Reay, 1974, p. 226). Also various councils and regional development movements had set up tribunals of some formality (Reay, 1974, p. 214; Silikara, 1978, p. 133).

The response enacted by the first national government was a remarkable piece of legislation, the Village Courts Act of 1973. It provided for a system of courts at, broadly speaking, village level and for a supporting system of 'peace officers'. The Village court magistrate is a lay person. He, or, exceptionally, she is appointed by the government although there is an element of popular election of possible appointees. The court is given broad powers: it has jurisdiction over most civil matters likely to involve nationals. There are a few exceptions to this jurisdiction. The most significant is that land disputes are excluded. Land being the basic means of production is too important to be left to the control of dominant class elements at the local level. Provision does exist in the Land Disputes Settlement Act of 1975 for local leaders to be appointed land mediators but adjudication is left to specialist courts of the national legal system. Criminal jurisdiction is also very broad: it includes most offences likely to arise in a village context except some considered particularly serious. The court can enforce rules of local government councils, a significant power, as we shall see. Reminiscent of pure colonial rule, the court can penalize a failure to obey directions as to cleanliness and hygiene in the village. The court can impose fines up to what is a considerable amount, given low cash incomes. In civil cases, the court can, as well as awarding compensation, order the performance of up to one month's work for the benefit of a wronged party. In criminal cases it can order the performance of community work for up to one month. The court can order imprisonment for failure to follow its decisions or for disturbing court proceedings. There is, in the Act, a remarkable legitimation of legal duality: a court can define and direct compliance with 'customary' obligations; generally, it is to apply the 'custom' of its area; section 30 says the court "is not bound by any law other than this Act that is not expressly applied to it" but "shall. . . decide any matter before it in accordance with substantial justice". Given the predominance of adjudication as the mode of courts' decision-making (a matter taken up shortly), there will be a strong tendency for custom and customary obligation or traditional law to be reduced to formal rules. The court's decisions can only be appealed against for lack of compliance with the Act or for lack or procedural natural justice, that is for failure to give notice of proceedings to a party or failure to allow him or her to be heard.

As for process, the Act in section 19 envisaged that "the primary function of the Village Court is to ensure peace and harmony, by mediating in and endeavouring to obtain just and amicable settlement of disputes". Technical rules of evidence are not to apply, and professional legal representation is not allowed. The governmental body responsible for setting up particular village courts asserts that they are popular courts (MacTeine and Paliwala, 1978, p. 41). The first national Minister for Justice saw the Act as attempting "to place the law back in the hands of the people" and "village communities will be able to continue to mediate and to decide disputes. . ." (Kaputin, 1975, pp. 11 – 12). The reality is rather contrary: the courts are self afflicted with an excessive formality, and adjudication is very much the predominant mode of resolution. Many magistrates express the wish to learn and apply more 'government law' and some assert, wrongly, that they have to apply such law (Paliwala, 1979, p. 20). In appearance the proceedings are the opposite of traditional dispute settlement. Magistrates and peace officers ensure a hushed respect for the court-at-work. The magistrates tend to take a dominating part, and most of the interested populace are left outside the courtroom. As one magistrate told an audience at a village court:

> This is not the good old times when every person, whether he is a party to a dispute or not could crowd around to hear and talk about the disputes. The village court is a completely different institution running under a new law. We must all respect the village courts. It is only those people who are concerned that can come to the village court to settle their disputes. Everybody else must go home and involve themselves in coffee gardening, business and their families. (MacTeine and Paliwala, 1978, p. 21)

Hearings usually take place in a special courthouse in or near the government buildings. The interior design of formal higher courts is emulated. A court can be many miles from a village over which it has jurisdiction; several traditional groups will be included in such jurisdiction and so the court can have a basis independent of any one group. This element of independence is emphasized when magistrates, several of whom will be appointed for each court, sit together rather than singly as they feel this gives them more power and places some distance between them and their particular groups (Awesa, 1975; MacTeine and Paliwala, 1978, pp. 19 – 20, 41 – 43; Paliwala, 1976, p. 4; Uyassi, 1978, p. 33). The legislation encourages this requiring that three magistrates are required for adjudication. (For mediation, one is enough.)

All of which does not look like popular justice. On the contrary, and as MacTeine and Paliwala note of one area:

> The village people see the village courts as another one in a line of governmental and semi-governmental instrumentalities meant to control the village. They saw the Luluais and Tultuls [the local-level, "native" officials in the colonial period], the co-operatives and the local government councils in this light. They do not readily accept the courts as being merely specialist dispute settlement institutions. Neither do the magistrates. (MacTeine and Paliwala, 1978, p. 47)

The magistrates tend to be actual or aspirant community leaders (Bayne, 1975, p. 6; MacTeine and Paliwala, 1978, p. 13; Paliwala, 1976, p. 4; Uyassi, 1978, p. 33). The position of magistrates is used as a new route to general power; magistrates, for example, use the court to make people obey their orders to work on or contribute money to a particular 'development' project—a project from which they will often stand to gain substantially (MacTeine and Paliwala, 1978, p. 48; Mogu and Bwaleto, 1978;

p. 91; Uyassi, 1978, p. 34). Generally and understandably, the magistrates appear to be ardent and even oppressive in the use of their power (MacTeine and Paliwala, 1978, pp. 40, 44 – 46; Paliwala, 1976, p. 5; Uyassi, 1978, pp. 33 – 34). The state supports village courts but exercises little supervisory control. However there are indications that control is increasing (Paliwala, 1979, p. 12).

Given the analysis so far and the close links between leadership and wealth in Papua New Guinea societies, it could be expected that magistrates would have a distinct economic basis for their power, a basis identifiable in terms of an actual or aspirant big peasantry previously described. This is usually the case (Paliwala, 1979, p. 15). However, the point is disputed by some. Warren, for example, says of a significant area of the Eastern Highlands that magistrates and other leaders are different from other people in political terms only and not in economic (Warren, 1978, pp. 114 – 115). However, the most detailed and acute study of this issue so far is provided by Uyassi (1978) and it is set in the same area. He identifies a distinct stratum of 'middle peasants', wealthier than the mass but not as wealthy as big peasants. They are concerned to advance economically and politically through using local-level political positions. It is from this stratum that magistrates tend to come. Generally and in terms of constitutional legal structures, the overall tendency is quite clear. Village courts will be closely tied to local-level government, whether formal local government councils or the widely emerging system of community councils (Conyers, 1978). Magistrates and various kinds of councillors are often all part of the local power elite with membership of the magistracy and of councils sometimes overlapping. It is local government councils which most often put forward candidates for the magistracy. Enforcement of council rules and directives is becoming a major part of village court work and a great deal of revenue for councils now comes from fines levied by village courts.

Most of the points made about village courts can only be tentative. The first courts were set up in 1974 and then only a few of them; a great number were set up in 1976. They now cover almost half the population (Paliwala, 1979, appendix). Nowhere could they have displaced traditional dispute settlement. Like co-operatives and local government councils, village courts were introduced to deal with a threat to the existing order, this time seen as ''a deteriorating law and order situation with problems such as coffee theft and tribal fighting'' (Paliwala, 1979, p. 13). Like co-operatives and local government councils, this was done when existing forms of containment were losing their efficacy. Like co-operatives and local government councils, the benefits of village courts had often to be somewhat thrust upon the people (Paliwala, 1979, p. 13). Like 'native' officials of the colonial period and local government councils, village courts provide a means for law and state to penetrate traditional social formations, since magistrates are keen to apply 'government law' and obviously base much of their power on the fact that they are apparently doing this. Like 'native' officials, co-operatives and local government councils, people, already, are rejecting village courts. Hence people in one large area are turning away from village courts especially in their being dominated by these new class elements; they are coming to see the village court as another variant in the succession of governmental organisations of coercion and control (A. Strathern, personal communication). In this they are at one with the people so sensitively studied by MacTeine and Paliwala (1978, p. 47). This litany should be enough to show the essential continuity. The point will be developed further in Chapter 8.

## Notes

1. A large part of this chapter has appeared in a somewhat different form in Fitzpatrick (1980). I am grateful to E.L. Wheelwright and Ken Buckley for being able to draw on this piece.
2. For example, this account when used in a seminar was criticized by some anthropologists as being too reflective of social formations in the Highlands, particularly in its description of leadership. The account could reflect rather the concerns of more recent ethnography. In either case, I would argue that my description has a general accuracy but it would be disproportionate in the present work to pursue this point and other such.
3. I much appreciate Pamela Denoon's referring me to Uyassi's excellent work.
4. This paragraph is based on personal observation and on personal communications with Bob Densley, Barry Holloway, Fred Leahy, Iambakey Okuk and Barry Shaw.
5. This total figure excludes 'secondary' co-operatives whose members are not individuals but are collections of co-operatives since to include them would unfairly bias the result in favour of the point being made. The total also excludes one co-operative for which figures could not be obtained.

# 6 The Working Class

With the working class the basic ingredients of the legal mix are much the same as those used with the peasantry. Indeed, I hope to show that in terms of class containment the legal regulation of the working class and the formation of the peasantry are closely connected. Unlike the case of 'pure' colonial regulation, the part which law and state play after the second world war in the limited creation and the containment of the workforce is no longer primary. Law and state now fasten upon and strengthen social and economic forces that are already in play within the national social formation. Explicit, colonial-type coercion recedes but does not disappear; part of it stays to serve as some insurance when other measures are not adequate. In another respect there is continuity between the 'pure' colonial and the new situation in that laws protective of the worker remain poorly enforced.

Prior to the second world war the consolidation of a working class was next to impossible. A system of comprehensive legal control over the conditions on which labour was supplied and over urban residence ensured that wage labour was basically an occasional experience for people who remained integrated into their disparate traditional social formations. This system explicitly legislated and implicitly fostered such an utter dependence of workers on their 'masters' as to make workers' class organization almost inconceivable. In the face of all this, such events as the Rabaul strike and the large number of 'desertions' indicated a significant disaffection and a potentiality for class action.

However, this system of indentured labour was compatible only with a demand for unskilled labour and skilled national workers were rare in the pre-war period. That is, the investment in the development of skills would be wasted or lost if the skilled worker were compulsorily repatriated. So the system was not compatible with the post-war demand for skilled labour. Even with unskilled labour, critical demands were being placed on the system. By 1940 recruitment of indentured labour was close to saturation point (Legge, 1971, p. 48; Radi, 1971, p. 132). The labour demands during the war of the Australian military administration had greatly aggravated the situation (Roe, 1971, p. 143). This did not only involve a stretching of supply; the unparalelled severity of the military administration in labour matters probably had an inhibiting effect on the post-war supply. People were, after the war, dissatisfied with the pre-war indenture system and attempts to reimpose it generated unrest (Brookfield, 1972, p. 96). Although a modified system was introduced it could not, in short, meet demand (Skeldon, 1978a, p. 17). In African colonies the genesis of the working class outside indenture systems is usually located in the depression of the 1930s when cutbacks in rural production drove people into towns in search of employment (Kay, 1975, p. 106). In Papua New Guinea there were also cutbacks in rural production but the development of gold mining in New Guinea appears to have maintained overall demand for indentured labour (Chris Gregory, personal communication). Also, and perhaps to a greater general extent than in Africa, for the Papua New Guinean worker traditional social formations remained an accessible retreat.

The demand for significant numbers of skilled workers also originated out of the war period when nationals were trained in various skills to meet the demands of war (Oram, 1976a, pp. 58, 63). The increased involvement of Australia after the war sustained and expanded the demand for skilled workers mainly for secondary industry (largely concerned with production for the local market) and, especially, for the expansion of the colonial administration. The change, however, was certainly not dramatic. The non-indentured workforce did grow fairly rapidly and by 1950, it has been asserted, a 'free' labour force had emerged ''forced to rely on the European for existence'' (an official assessment described in Gregory, 1975, p. 2). In 1951, one of Hasluck's first policy pronouncements considered ''the Territory will have to think more purposively in terms of greater mechanization and the raising of the skills of the individual workman'' (Hasluck, 1976, p. 47). Yet during the 1950s, the period of so-called gradual development, there was only a gradual modification of the concern to prevent 'detribalization' and the emergence of a 'landless proletariat', as official reports continued to put it. This gradual modification was possible because pressure of demand was relieved by the Highlands

Labour Scheme, described later. Pressure increased enormously with the so-called accelerated development of the 1960s. In 1950 the officially "enumerated workforce" totalled 50 817 of which 67% were 'free' workers operating outside of the indenture system. (The indenture system was supposedly abolished about this time and replaced by something called the agreement system. I will continue to call it the indenture system for reasons that come up soon.) By 1960 this workforce totalled 72 938 of which 57% were free workers. So, at the outset of the period of accelerated development the indenture system remained of great significance. However, the number under indenture reached a post-war peak in 1960 and by 1968 of a total enumerated workforce of 115 517, 81% were free workers (Territory of Papua New Guinea, 1970, p. 33). This total figure does not take account of all in wage labour and this would be put at about 145 000 of which the indentured workforce would be under 16% (figures adapted from Brookfield with Hart, 1971, p. 264). Of the enumerated total the rural workforce comprises about 30%. In all, for a population of close to three million, we are dealing here with a small working class.

Both in terms of state action and as the largest employer, the state plays a most significant part in the emergence of the working class. Its involvement in education was particularly important and revealing. Before the second world war the colonial administration was little concerned with education, it being considered that the most education Papua New Guineans needed would be in some basic technical skills (Jinks et al., 1973, p. 91; Rowley, 1971, p. 71). However, the missions considered it part of their work to provide some very rudimentary academic education and the colonial administration did support them in this. It may possibly have been the case that, as with Africa, "religious education was emphasised because it was considered an excellent vehicle for indoctrinating the colonized into a cult of subservience" (Ake, 1976, p. 201). Apart from fuelling 'cargo' movements, mission education posed few risks, for its standard was nowhere much better than abysmal. The post-war period of gradual development was supposedly to be one of uniform development. There was to be no precipitate raising of an elite in advance of the mass. Hence universal, or near-universal, primary education was supposedly to be achieved before secondary education was promoted. As a result secondary education was close to non-existent. Hasluck did say in 1956 that "for practical reasons—and by this I meant both the need that existed [for skilled labour—P.F.] and the interest of the native people themselves in getting a good job—the next priority was in training for employment"

(Hasluck, 1976, p. 221). However, very little was done about it. An Apprenticeship Ordinance in 1952 provided for 'natives' to be trained as apprentices but the Native Apprenticeship Board set up under this law applied Australian practice in laying down a ratio of one apprentice to one master and there were few masters to begin with. The accelerated development of the 1960s brought dramatic changes. Hasluck announced towards the end of 1961 that there would be a greater emphasis on secondary and technical education and in 1962 he initiated an enquiry into setting up a university (ibid., pp. 387 – 389). Secondary and tertiary education did mushroom in the 1960s, but despite this it has not been widely accessible and has been oriented towards the creation of an elite element in the working class.

The period of accelerated development also saw a more active involvement of the state as an employer of nationals. The number of Papua New Guinean state employees rose by over 40% between 1962 and 1964 compared with an increase of one quarter during the decade previous (Garnaut *et al.*, 1977, p. 1). This was part of a general expansion of state operations and it was not, with some few exceptions, a matter of nationals taking over from foreign employees. In the result, by the end of the 1960s Papua New Guinea had a large state bureaucracy which included some 7 000 foreign operatives. In 1972, the first national government announced dramatic and effective 'localization' measures under which the bulk of these positions came to be rapidly filled by nationals. The continued expansion of the state bureaucracy has so far provided sufficient opportunities for the products of 'higher' education. In both the state sphere and 'private' enterprise the occupations open to foreigners were progressively limited under the Employment (Training and Regulation) Act of 1971. This law has been greatly influential in localizing the 'lower' levels of the workforce but it has not been applied to upper administrative or executive levels. These upper reaches in private enterprise remain largely the preserve of foreigners.

Law and state also influenced the formation of the working class through modifying and lifting various colonial restrictions and by yet retaining some controls and erecting substitute types of control. The indentured labour law did allow of very limited exceptions to its coverage where this was compatible with continued reliance on the traditional mode of production. These were exceptions for employment near a worker's home area and for very short periods of employment. These exceptions were somewhat broadened in the 1950s. The indentured labour system and laws limiting the contractual capacity of 'natives' were modified to permit labour contracts for specific tasks and, in limited ways, "to give an opportunity of free engagement for employment to those native workers who were able to fend for themselves in urban areas" (Hasluck, 1976, p. 227). But restraints comparable to labour under indenture applied to those new or part-free workers. Perhaps most significantly, their collective organization was prohibited and there remained controls on their residence in urban areas. Somewhat in contrast, and more dramatically, the indenture system was purportedly abolished at the end of 1950 as a consequence of the 'new deal' promised by the Australian social democratic government after the second world war. As we have just seen, it was suggested officially about that time that a free labour force had emerged. However, the connection is too simple. Of the total workforce, 33% was under indenture at the time the system was purportedly abolished (Territory of Papua and New Guinea, 1970, p. 33). Predominant and general emphasis in "the control and regulation of native labour" continued to be placed on "measures that maintain village life and the attachment of the native to his land" (Hasluck, 1976, p. 226). That formula is repeated constantly in official reports of the period. Hasluck strongly reaffirmed this "historical foundation of the native labour policy" especially, and this should be stressed, in its application to "low-skilled and unsophisticated native workers" (ibid., pp. 228–230). Hasluck produced in 1956 "a basic document in the development of labour policy" which said in part:

> For half a century, successive Governments have been carefully regulating the employment of natives away from their homes for the express purpose of ensuring that village life is not disrupted, the village food supplies are not diminished, and the village cycle of marriages and births not interrupted by reason of the prolonged absence of the young and able-bodied men. Care has been taken, hitherto with a fair measure of success, to see that the native social order is not changed too rapidly by the breaking up of the chief social unit—the village—or by destroying those elements that give coherence to native society. Careful measures have been taken against the displacement and dispossession of the native people. During my own term of office, reminders of the fundamental importance of these considerations have been given by me on several occasions whenever the subjects of lands policy and casual labour have been under notice. The special concern of the [Australian] Government over the risk of building up a "landless proletariat" and over the congregation of "foreign" natives on the outskirts of the larger towns, has been made

> clear on several occasions and action has been taken to try to reduce
> both risks. (ibid., pp. 228 – 229)

This was an admonition to the colonial Administrator who wished to
hasten the emergence of a free workforce. Quite apart from the restrictions
on the new or free workers, the indenture system continued, by and large,
under another name. What the alleged abolition of the system involved
specifically was the abolition of penal sanctions against workers. But under
the new law an 'agreement system' was set up structured similarly to the
indenture system. In particular the new system still contained provision for
repatriating workers to their home areas on the expiration of agreements.
As for coercing the workers, officials relied on law's image and sustained
the system through 'bluff' (Oram, 1976a, p. 168; Rowley, 1972, p. 102).
A senior Australian official provides some details:

> After 1950 sanctions did not really go out. The system survived by
> bluff. I would act in the interests of both the employers and the
> employees. I would tell employees who left to go back to work and
> they would. Sepiks [workers coming from the Sepik area—P.F.]
> coming to Rabaul were using the trip [paid for by the employer—
> P.F.] just to get to Rabaul and they would leave as soon as the plane
> landed. Companies lost many thousands of pounds over this. I would
> send local [that is, national—P.F.] police to meet the plane. The
> police would not say that the men must go to work but they would
> look them over very carefully and the idea was got across that they
> could be recognised in future if they did not go to work. (personal
> communication[1])

Further, an alternative type of sanction was introduced with the new law.
This involved a simple type of court action whereby, on certain grounds,
an employer (and, on other grounds, a worker) could apply to the court to
have the employment contract terminated and to have 'damages' paid out
of the worker's deferred pay. The new law still provided that much of the
worker's pay must be accumulated for payment at the end of his term of
employment. This itself must have been a considerable disincentive to
leaving before that time. The grounds for bringing a court action included
such as being absent from work for more than seven days and ''exerting a
bad influence on his fellow workers''. Taking the New Guinea figures
referred to in Chapter Three, the average number of court orders of this
type made annually in favour of employers was 549 (the average number a
year in favour of workers was five). This figure was quite on a par with the
level of convictions of workers under the penal provisions of the

indentured labour system. Such convictions averaged 652 a year, but the annual number of people under indenture for most of the pre-war period exceeded the annual number post-war, including the agreement system in this. However, it has not been possible to take account of pre-war civil actions against workers for damages and this should be done for a valid comparison. It is most unlikely that such actions were significant.

Any immediate risk in 'abolishing' the indenture system was more than off-set by the opening up after the war of the Highlands, the greatest labour frontier of them all. That the rugged Highlands area was heavily populated was only discovered by the colonists in the early 1930s. Because of the Highlanders' susceptibility to diseases in the coastal plantations, the indentured labour laws had laid down health standards which had prevented the recruitment of labour from the Highlands. Because of the shortage in the post-war supply of indentured labour and responding to pressures from the planters, the colonial administration relaxed these health standards and introduced the Highlands Labour Scheme (Collins, n.d., p. 1; Department of Labour, Research and Planning Division, 1969, p. 1). This operated under the indentured labour laws and was a massive scheme of labour recruitment and migration run by the colonial administration. Although the scheme did not formally come into operation until the end of 1951, it had, effectively, been operating on a trial basis for two years before that (Department of Labour, Research and Planning Division, 1969, p. 1). By the time the indenture system was purportedly abolished at the end of 1950, 14% of the indentured workforce had been supplied through the Highlands Labour Scheme; within a further 15 years more than half the indentured workforce was supplied through the Scheme (Territory of Papua and New Guinea, 1969, p. 33). As elsewhere, people from the Highlands tended not to re-engage in indentured labour (see for example, Hatanaka, 1972, p. 35). As we have seen, the indenture system generally declines in significance.

With accelerated development and the greatly increased demand for labour the comprehensive legal control of the workforce becomes impossible short of a massive, all-pervasive bureaucracy of the South African type, which was beyond consideration since Papua New Guinea's economy could not sustain it and the Australian government thought itself excessively generous in doing as much as it did. On 28th March 1963 all restrictions in the native labour laws controlling workers outside of the indenture system were removed. On the same day alternative methods of controlling labour came into effect, the trade union and industrial relations legislation—legislation presented by the colonist as having a positive and beneficial effect on the organization of the working class.

The first Papua New Guinean trade union was an organization of workers based in the capital and founded in 1960. It emerged out of an ethnic association set up in 1958 (Kiki, 1968, pp. 97 – 98). These bodies had political as well as 'industrial' aims and they strongly (for the times) asserted both (Kiki, 1970, p. 616). Hasluck was quick to provide assistance for the union in pressing its industrial claims and suggested that it put a case for increased wages to the relevant official body (Kiki, 1968, p. 98). As a result, the union was instrumental in obtaining, in 1960 and 1961, a doubling of the minimum wage in some urban areas. In 1960 a union based in another urban area was formed, also arising out of a prior ethnic association (Stevenson, 1968, p. 114). Soon after several other unions were formed in large towns (Territory of New Guinea, 1961 – 62, p. 118). Of these first two unions the colonial administration said that ''special attention is being given to such organizations to ensure that they are founded on sound principles and develop along constructive lines'' (Territory of New Guinea, 1960 – 61, p. 118). Until these unions were formed, it was ostensibly thought by the colonial administration that the time was not ripe for trade unions, basically because the people would not be able to organize them and so the colonial administration's 'protection' of the worker would have to continue—a protection that of course involved continuing control of the workforce (Territory of New Guinea, 1958 – 59, p. 101).

On 15th August 1961, Hasluck announced a major change in approach. He said that ''new labour measures'' would be introduced; these would be of particular ''interest'' to an emerging group of ''urban workers'' who were not greatly in need of protection (Commonwealth of Australia, 1961, pp. 11 – 12). These changes quite explicitly anticipated the accelerated 'development' that Australia would promote in the sixties:

> I suggest that we will see the situation more clearly if we recognize the present measures as indicating the direction of changes which are just beginning and which will gather pace in the next ten years. What we do now is less for to-day than for the decade ahead of us. (ibid., p. 12)

Hasluck then announced the formation within the colonial administration of a Department of Labour and indicated that:

> It will be one of the functions of the new Department of Labour to

assist groups of workers in the formation of trade unions. I admit to having had some hesitation about committing this function to a government department. It will be difficult in practice for a conscientious officer to distinguish between the moment when he is assisting workers to form a union and when he is telling them what to do; between the moment when he is guiding and informing them, and the moment when he is deciding what should be done.

Yet the Territory Administration has had some success in a similar task in respect of the formation of co-operative societies to help the economic progress of the people. When a group indicates that it wishes to form a co-operative society, an officer is on hand to tell them how to go about it, to arrange for the training of their clerks and storemen, to explain the customary rules of such bodies, to explain how to raise capital and how to open a bank account and to give friendly guidance in the early stages. A similar success has followed the Administration's efforts in encouraging the establishment of Native Local Government Councils. In the same way I think we can rely on the officers of the Public Service to give impartial and disinterested counsel and guidance to those wishing to form a trade union, and to arrange for the training on accepted lines of their union officers. (ibid., p. 15)

Enough has been said earlier about co-operatives and local government councils to indicate a further if implicit aptness in the comparison. In providing these new measures, Hasluck went on:

At this stage our purpose has been to provide the minimum necessary for the legal existence, recognition and proper functioning of industrial organizations and for the conduct of industrial relations, and to leave as much room as possible for development and adjustment so that the people of the Territory may work our for themselves the form of organization and the industrial system best suited to local needs and their own wishes.

We have tried to refrain from imposing on the Territory too many of our own ideas or methods. (ibid., p. 15)

Dr. Gunther, the then Deputy Administrator, in introducing the new measures to the colonial legislature in 1961 was even more disarming:

Quite simply the purpose of this ["industrial organizations"] Bill is to recognize the existence of such formal organizations, and to regulate their existence so that they will best serve the purpose for which their members came together . . . . It can be said that the ["industrial relations"] Bill generally is a fairly standard piece of industrial legislation providing for the prevention and settlement of disputes. (Territory of Papua and New Guinea, 1961, pp. 229, 232)

He did add that registration as an "industrial organization" would be compulsory because of the "relatively great degree of supervision and perhaps assistance" trade unions would need and because without this compulsion there would be "a strong likelihood" of unions being used "for purposes which were basically non-industrial, perhaps subversive" (ibid., p. 230).

It was quite clear by 1960 that the rapid growth of trade unions in the third world after the second world war was due more to the growing demand of colonized peoples for freedom than to 'industrial unrest' narrowly conceived (see, noting date of publication, Knowles, 1960, p. 311). Perhaps partly hence we find that this "fairly standard piece of industrial legislation" was fairly standard for a repressive colonial situation (see for example, Davies, 1966, pp. 40, 42, 76). Even a "fairly standard" borrowing from Australian industrial relations law would be, comparatively, very restrictive. Under the Papua New Guinea legislation political affiliation by trade unions is obliquely but effectively prohibited. In giving guidance in 1960 on the changes in labour policy, Hasluck said:

> My own view is that the political advancement of the people will be better served if their political organization is based on broader questions than employment. We have to think of the self-governing state of the future, in which the membership of any political party will be composed largely of native people, and I would doubt whether there would be much profit to them in dividing themselves into a party of native wage-earners opposed to a party of native self-employed persons or native employers. I would foresee great damage to the country if self-government were to start with a division between an urban proletariat and country-dwelling occupiers of land. Furthermore, in the period before self-government comes, any political organization based on employment would necessarily put most of the Europeans on one side and most of the indigenes on the other and that racial division in politics is one of the dangers we have to work to avoid. (Hasluck, 1976, p. 235)

Returning to the legislation, strikes by organized workers are in effect prohibited. The industrial relations law prohibits the organizing of a strike when an award applies as one would to most urban workers. Almost all other organized urban workers would be prohibited from striking by specific legislation covering their occupation such as the Public Service Act. Except for some recent and not very extensive efforts, rural workers remain unorganized. The "industrial organizations" law makes it an offence for any person to manage or act for an unregistered trade union. The Registrar of Industrial Organizations has wide powers of supervision and control over registered trade unions. In their internal ordering, trade unions are subjected to a system of complex and detailed legal rules. For various and numerous infractions, individual unions can be de-registered by the Registrar and thus it would become an offence then to manage or act for them.

The actual operation of these new laws followed and refined their general orientation. Under the guise of the new policy "to facilitate the growth of industrial organizations" officials became closely involved in the affairs of trade unions sometimes going to great lengths to sustain trade union organization (Territory of New Guinea, 1960 – 61; Worsley, 1966, p. 41). One student of the system concluded, "it is my contention that many workers' associations in the Territory would cease to function were it not for the time and energy spent by these officers and others from the Department [of Labour] who supplement their services" (Worsley, 1966, p. 40). Trade unions were clearly meant to and did integrate workers into a controlled system of 'industrial relations' not just in the cause of class containment but also to help provide some organization and discipline where this was needed for the efficient operation of the new economy (Paterson, 1969, p. 28; Worsley, 1966, pp. 60 – 61). Officials also typically claim that were it not for their involvement unions would not exist at all. A former head of the Department of Labour has said that the colonial administration could not wait for trade unions to develop "entirely from below" because opposing political views could otherwise gain a foothold (Worsley, 1966, p. 43). Moderate observers find the system under the new measures repressive and restrictive; they see the legislation and its enforcement as smothering and hindering rather than helping union activity (Martin, 1969, pp. 159 – 161; Seddon, 1975, p. 103).

In short the increased involvement of metropolitan capital and of the colonial administration created a demand for labour that, both in quantity and quality, could not be met by the indenture system. At the same time law and state could in the 1950s, continue directly to act in conservation of the traditional mode because demand was not great. From the period of accelerated development direct legal regulation has to decline but law and state continue to play a significant if more indirect regulatory role in the trade union and industrial relations laws and in, as we shall see shortly, numerous other laws as well. But first, to pursue law and state in its function of containing the working class in the current situation, it is necessary to attempt an overview of the contemporary formation of the working class related to the forces that brought it about.

Two related concerns are central here. One is the continuing relation between the traditional and capitalist modes of production in its effect on the formation of the working class. The other is the division or some contradictory class location within the working class itself. A subordinate distinction is that between the urban and the rural workforce bearing in mind Marx's indicative equation of action by a subordinate class with urbanization (Dunning, 1972, p. 417). The position of the rural workforce is a convenient starting point. True to type, this workforce is almost completely lacking in unionization or in any other class organization. It is unskilled and poorly paid and its relation to the capitalist mode has not changed structurally since the days of the dominance of the indenture system. Indeed, the indenture, or agreement, system, including the Highlands Labour Scheme, modified slightly and redubbed the Rural Employment Programme, continues to supply much of rural labour on a migratory basis helping to ensure that workers are reintegrated into the traditional mode and, now, into peasant production. Many rural workers outside the indenture system work near their home areas and in this way the traditional mode remains accessible. There is, however, and as we saw in the last chapter, a tendency for big peasants to engage wage labour and, it can now be added, this labour is often obtained from far-off areas so as to obviate the effect of traditional obligations—such obligations involving demands for an equivalent return for labour (Crocombe, 1967, p. 9; Finney, 1969, pp. 36 – 37; Howlett, 1977, p. 9; Morauta, 1974, pp. 31, 55; Philipp, 1971; Salisbury, 1970, p. 101). Big peasants would seem to be niggardly employers (Donaldson and Good, 1979, p. 56; Epstein, 1968, p. 104; Finney, 1969, p. 38; Morauta, 1974, p. 55). Some people seem driven, nonetheless, to seek such employment because of the poverty of their home areas or because of the increasing shortage of land in particular parts (Curtain, 1977, p. 35; Howlett, 1977, pp. 8 – 9; Morauta, 1974, p. 55).

The rural situation provides an extreme picture of elements that remain present in the urban setting. Although urban labour no longer operates under the indenture system, traditional social formations remain an accessible alternative to the great majority of urban workers, circular migration remains the norm, most workers have a low degree of 'urban commitment' and there is a great volume of exchange transactions between town and village (Garnaut *et al.*, 1977, p. 185; Levine and Levine, 1979, pp. 28, 33; Skeldon, 1977b; Strathern, 1975, pp. 401–403; Wright, 1975, pp. 12, 23; Wright *et al.*, 1975, pp. 2–3, 47). To return to Meillassoux's description of the third world generally, "through low wages and precarious employment the labourer is periodically expelled from the capitalist sector and sent back to the rural areas", so conservation of traditional (or some other alternative) social formation remains an "absolute requirement" for these labourers (Meillassoux, 1973, p. 89). Curtain's incisive analysis of the Papua New Guinea situations concludes that:

> . . . the lack of married accommodation provided by employers, the single man's wages [that is, wages based on the needs of the single man –P.F.], urban accommodation tied to employment, the disputes with local land owners over squatting rights, the precariousness of unskilled employment all did not help to greatly change the labour migrants' initial views of the towns as basically hostile places to to be endured for a limited period and then to return home. (Curtain, 1977, p. 17)

Elsewhere and more generally he summarizes the situation this way:

> The degree of proletarianization has been minimal in Papua New Guinea. Rather than speaking of a growing proletariat, it is better to see wage employment as mostly peasant adaptations to the growth of the introduced economic system, in which a wage job is seen as an alternative to cash cropping for a short period for those with adequate rural holdings, or for a longer period for those from the poorer regions. (Curtain, in press).

Except for the capital there is no national labour market and, to a large extent, workers migrate to a town from its surrounding district (Wright, *et al.*, 1975, pp. 1, 7). This further emphasizes the operative integration of the traditional and capitalist modes and the maintenance of ethnic divisions within the working class. A related and interesting factor is introduced by the overall pattern of Papua New Guinean urban development. In Chapter Three I mentioned how capitalist penetration took the form of a wide spread of discrete economic centres. As a result there is now a large number of widely dispersed, small urban centres. According to the last census in

1971, there were only three towns with a population of over 20 000 and there were 46 towns with at least 500 inhabitants (Garnaut *et al.*, 1977, pp. 5 – 6). Reflecting this, many trade unions are based on urban or regiónal groupings. This dispersal of the working class is further underlined by the small size of work places, less than 5% of which contain more than 100 workers (Peter Williamson, personal communication).

Elements of the traditional mode of production, although not probably any integral traditional mode itself, operate in urban areas. Intra-urban and peri-urban villages are usually much dependent on wages but they do provide housing and some food for the workforce (see for example, Belshaw, 1957). Apart from these traditional villages about half the people in urban areas cluster into 'migrant' or 'squatter' settlements formed on ethnic bases and within these settlements traditional-type supports are sustained (Levine and Levine, 1979, pp. 18, 41 – 42). In a similar vein, 'voluntary associations' formed on ethnic lines, although understandably not as evident as in other third world towns, help with life crises and with integration into the urban scene (Oram, 1976a, pp. 139, 142 – 143; Skeldon, 1977a). Much food is provided in urban subsistence production, as is most of the construction and maintenance of housing (Garnaut *et al.*, 1977, pp. 121 – 122; Housing Commission, 1975, pp. 2 – 3; Thaman, 1977). Each household typically has one or more persons employed within the capitalist mode and this tends to provide a nucleus for maintaining other residents of the household (Garnaut, *et al.*, 1977, pp. 121 – 122; Levine and Levine, 1979, p. 42). The urban household and the wider ethnic-based community serve as supports when formal employment in the capitalist mode is unavailable, unstable or occasional. Apart from housing and urban agriculture there is little popular production, that is, there are few urban-based petty commodity producers. Compared to other third world social formations, urban unemployment is not high mainly because of the continued accessibility of and resort to rural areas (Conroy, 1977, p. 8; Garnaut *et al.*, 1977, p. 185). Nevertheless, it has often been predicted that the urban population and urban unemployment would soon swell (see for example, Manpower Planning Unit, 1975). This prediction now looks very questionable with the quite dramatic slowing down of urban population growth, with the possible exception of the capital (Skeldon, 1978b).

This general account covers a great variety. A recent survey has shown that male 'absenteeism' from many rural villages is very high (Clunies

Ross, 1977a, pp. 41, 45). This underlines the fact that many 'migrants' to town are becoming long-term or permanent ones and that several villages are heavily dependent on the capitalist mode in remitted wages (see for example, Harding, 1971, p. 199; Levine and Levine, 1979, p. 33). In the period of accelerated development up to the early 1970s urban populations grew rapidly, not just because of the increased demand for labour but also because of the attraction of considerable wage increases. At first the growth was largely attributable to the influx or working-age males. Then between the 1966 census and that of 1971 the urban population grew from a little less than 5% of the country's total population to almost 10% and about a half of this remarkable increase can be accounted for as dependents of those in wage employment, so much so that the sex and age balance of the urban population now approximates the composition of the overall national population (Garnaut *et al.*, 1977, pp. 3, 7, 185). This strongly indicates a much more widespread 'urban commitment'. It would appear, in significant part, that "the system of circular migration is changing towards more permanent movements" (Skeldon, 1978b, p. 13; *cf.* Levine and Levine, 1979, p. 28). Something of an equilibrium having been reached in the composition of the urban population and the demand for urban labour having been stagnant since 1973 – 74, the rate of increase in the urban population starts to taper off (Garnaut *et al.*, 1977, p. 187; Skeldon, 1978b). However, as we saw earlier, the capital appears to be an exception with the rate of increase being maintained, thus suggesting that there may be some potential for larger-scale working class action here.

This change in the composition of the urban population can be seen as related to a key difference within the working class. It is divided into two quite distinct segments. One is called for convenience the unskilled. It is unskilled or low-skilled from the perspective of the capitalist mode. In that perspective, it is without formal education or has little of it. It is largely migratory and retains integral, operative links with the traditional mode. The members of this segment are often low-paid in occasional and unpermanent employment and often unemployed. They depend on the support of kin in the urban area and on urban agriculture. Their housing is low-cost, produced and located in ethnically based settlements. Alternatively, they obtain some food as well as housing and kin support by remaining in traditional intra-urban and peri-urban villages. Some members of what can be called the skilled segment also live in these villages. This segment is, in the perspective of the capitalist mode, skilled and formally educated. It is largely committed to urban life and its links to the traditional mode tend to be incidental. Its members are comparatively highly paid and in permanent and stable employment. They live in high-standard housing, usually provided and often subsidized by the state, in ethnically diverse suburbs. The great majority in the skilled segment are state operatives, policemen, military personnel and teachers—people traditionally and integrally involved in maintaining the dominant order and who are given some special status in reward. This division into unskilled and skilled segments may be a little overdrawn and it does disregard some penumbral blending of characteristics from each. It is also a division that is little studied but its existence is quite conspicuous (Garnaut *et al.*, 1977, pp. 43 – 44, 123, 130; Levine and Levine, 1979, pp. 20 – 21, 40 – 41, 86, 96; Whiteman, 1973). By and large each segment is separately unionized. With the unskilled, there is a very low degree of unionization; ethnicity serves as an effective bar to collective action and to the very perception by workers of its feasibility. Divisions and hierarchies are seen in ethnic terms and the wage – labour relationship is viewed as basically personalized (Levine and Levine, 1979, pp. 86, 92 – 94). The unions of the unskilled segment are beset with immense financial and organizational problems and are prone to ethnic division. In some exceptional cases, such as with the Port Moresby Waterside Workers, ethnic solidarity within a union can make for effective action against employers but this solidarity involves keeping members of other ethnic groups out of the occupation on which the union is based, so wider class cohesion is still further undermined. The unions of the skilled segment tend to be much more stable and effective and this segment is very highly unionized. The country's largest union, the Public Service Association, a union of state operatives, provides an interesting exception to the separate organization of the unskilled and the skilled segments. Although in numbers and in action it is dominated by the skilled segment, it does contain members of both segments. In hearings before the official wage-fixing body in 1972, this union advocated the same cash increase for all its members regardless of their status or wage. Solidarity has since been tested to breaking point with the government's effecting wage restraint which has meant that the upper echelons among state operatives have suffered a decline in real income (Uwe Lilje, personal communication). Generally, unions of both the unskilled and the skilled share the characteristic of a lack of effective militancy, with occasional and limited exceptions.

Despite unions securing considerable increases in urban wages in the 1960s and early 1970s, the state seems to have an effective dominance over them. This is achieved, broadly, in two ways. One is the system of trade union and industrial relations laws which I have just dealt with. The other, and related, way is through the involvement of unions and their leaders and members in the state system. The great majority of total trade union membership is employed within the state system. The members of the Public Service Association, the Teachers' Association and the Police Association comprise some 70% of total trade union membership. Most people belonging to these unions are legally enjoined not to strike. Many members of the various national governments began their political careers in trade union leadership. Once in government they are adept at finding a 'national interest' that is incompatible with working class assertiveness. The Public Service Association has recently relied on the brokerage of the then major political party in the government to secure a large overseas loan for the building of offices. Several unions rely heavily on the state's Bureau of Industrial Organizations for organizational assistance. The latter part of this account of the contemporary formation of the working class is somewhat miscellaneous, but I hope the account provides some basis for looking now at law and state in the containment of the working class.

At first sight law and state retreat in the contemporary situation from the class containment of labour. Such a retreat is partly a necessary giving way in the face of contrary pressures making for the formation of a working class and partly a conscious and controlled allowing of the emergence and limited organization of the working class. Thus I have already instanced the purported abolition of the indenture system, then the use of more adaptable legal controls in the gradual emergence of the urban working class in the 1950s and, finally, the introduction of trade union and industrial relations laws, not just for class containment but also to ensure a degree of organization necessary for the stable participation of 'free' labour in a more complex economy. The retreat has wider ramifications, being part of the general change from the explicit, racially based regulation of the colonial situation to more indirect controls structured around class relations. For labour, the more immediate aspect of the change was the abolition of the legal regulation of migration to and residence within towns. This was done gradually: at first more draconic controls were introduced in Papua in the early 1950s to bring it more in line with New Guinea. But in the later 1950s and extending up to 1969, legal controls on migration and urban residence were repealed. This was part of a general scheme initiated by Hasluck to remove all laws based on racial discrimination: to have "only one law for both black and white" (Hasluck, 1976, p. 346). His efforts in this, although for the most part successful ultimately, were met with a protracted and devious obduracy on the part of the colonial administration (ibid., pp. 334, 346 – 355). The colonial official correctly saw these laws as central to explicit colonial control. The change to bourgeois legality marked the passing of a certain order. Hasluck was one to see the matter with analytical clarity:

> We should work towards a single body of law and a single system of justice, equally accessible to all and even in its incidence . . . . [W]hen self-government and independence come, there should be a soundly based and universally recognized rule of law, administered by independent courts on high standards of probity, to ensure the protection of the individual against the state. The courts should be freed from Administration influence so that in future years they could not become the instrument of any government. (ibid., p. 182)

To give some affirmative support to bourgeois legality a Discriminatory Practices Act was introduced in 1963. It prohibited certain discriminatory behaviour based "only [on] . . . race or colour". Although fairly bold in prescription, and that in itself had great symbolical importance, it was delicately cautious in its enforcement since any prosecution required the consent of the senior legal official in the colonial administration. There do not appear to have been any prosecutions under the Act.

Central to this general change was the eradication of discimination in the administration of the legal system itself. In 1959 Hasluck commissioned a report by an Australian legal academic of note which conveniently recommended a uniform "administration of justice" (ibid., 349 – 350; Bayne, 1975). As a result a single court system for Papua New Guineans and others was introduced in 1963. *De facto* discrimination was to a large extent maintained because the rules conferring and limiting the jurisdiction of various courts, although racially neutral, still resulted in nationals being dealt with in the main in one court and colonists being dealt with in others (Paliwala *et al.*, 1978). Also several discriminatory laws persisted until quite recently, and a few of great significance persist yet. Adultery between Papua New Guineans is a criminal offence but it is not so between foreigners. The administration of the estates of decreased 'natives' is still controlled under the remnants of the native regulations. Dealings in traditional land remain restricted. All these persisting laws relate indicatively to the conservation of the traditional mode of production. Laws relating to inheritance and land were mentioned in the last two chapters. Adultery is of significance because it disturbs marriage exchanges between, and sometimes within, groups, and these exchanges are important for the cohesion of traditional social formations. Generally, the greater presence of bourgeois legality has to be related also to the increased involvement and the emergence internally of the bourgeoisie, something broached in the last chapter and developed further in the next two.

Despite the passing of the explicitly discriminatory and comprehensive regulation of labour and the advance of universalism and formal equality with bourgeois legality, law and state continue to operate in discriminatory ways in the containment of the working class. Their role is now more supplementary to social and economic forces but this role can be prominent when these forces are inadequate or in conflict. There are conflicts aplenty here. The most fundamental are the conflict between the conservation of the traditional mode and the need for an urban workforce, and the conflict between this need and the disruptive or revolutionary impact that an urban workforce could have. The two conflicts are closely related, since one way of diffusing the impact of the urban working class is through the maintenance of ethnic division in the conservation of the traditional mode and of its urban semblances. Underlying both conflicts is the division between the unskilled and the skilled segments of the working class. The skilled segment cannot be conveniently re-integrated into the traditional mode, as its members have a strong commitment to urban life, they have great organizing abilities, their work tends to provide organizational foci facilitating unionization and they are highly unionized and, indeed, comprise the great bulk of trade unionists. This skilled segment obviously needs special attention. By and large its members are, putting the matter crudely, bought off in high wages, subsidized housing and in varieties of social status. In the upper reaches of this segment, the bureaucratic bourgeoisie stands in a contradictory class location having some affinity with the bourgeoisie in its control over the considerable resources of the state and, increasingly, in the establishment by its members of economic enterprises and of considerable investments, and this often with the aid of governmental loans and grants. Law and state do have some part in the containment of this skilled segment. Thus trade union and industrial relations laws and legal prohibitions on striking predominantly affect this skilled segment. Also, through these laws, including wage-fixing laws, the trade unions of this segment become involved within the processes of an ostensibly pluralist state system. But law and state have probably a more significant part in the containment of the unskilled segment, which we now consider.

An ostensibly standard legal regulation of the urban environment, through such as housing and town planning laws, comes to serve functions formerly performed by the direct and explicitly discriminatory controls on migration and urban residence. The colonial administration did little to provide for the growing urban labour force after the second world war. Its own laws obliged employers to house their employees but this was not enforced and it was the chief offender. Such housing as was provided was for 'single men'. All of this led to the emergence of 'squatter' settlements, usually on the perimeters of towns and usually involving illegal occupation of land. Such purposive neglect resulted in "the creation by colonial authority of what it saw as a *cordon insanitaire*" (Jackson, 1976a, p. 54). Generally, it resulted in the discouragement of permanent settlement by town migrants (Wolfers, 1972, p. 78). Building and town planning laws laid down such unattainable standards as to prevent migrants integrating into the urban environment on a legitimate and stable basis. The most knowledgeable observer of such matters saw the position in the capital this way:

> The existence of unrealistic building regulations has had a harmful effect on the development of Port Moresby. The Administration regarded the majority of houses built by Papua New Guineans as illegal and, in consequence, discouraged any action by government agencies, for example, the Public Health Department, or by the settlers themselves, to improve living conditions in the settlements. A study of the relationship between health and housing conditions in Gorobe settlement showed that overcrowding and sub-nutrition were basic health problems in the settlement and that overcrowding was directly caused by such discouragement. . . . Improvements which have taken place in the settlements have been in spite of government policy.
>
> While government officials considered that the migrant settlements were illegal, little was done to prevent their growth. (Oram, 1976a, p. 196)

"Then, in the late fifties," said Hasluck, "we were hit between the eyes by the facts of urban residence and by the inadequacy of the policy that natives should be sent back to their villages" but, Hasluck proceeded to caution, "in providing for the town dwellers we have to avoid adding unduly to the attractions of the town" (Hasluck, 1976, pp. 336 – 337).

So, although restrictive legal standards were retained, a start was made in the early 1960s in providing urban accommodation and a state housing authority was set up for this purpose. This authority became in 1968, the highly significant Housing Commission, following the Housing Commission Act of 1967. Its main task, and in considerable part its achievement, was to provide low-cost accommodation for Papua New Guinean urban residents. The Housing Commission has also been the best analyst of its actions. In a National Housing Plan published in 1975, it pointed out that "only forty per cent of the urban population can afford the cheapest Housing Commission conventional house" and:

> Present urban housing need is approximately 7,000 dwellings per annum, to accommodate population increase. The total number of conventional dwellings constructed annually together with allotments provided in resettlement and settlement improvement schemes is approximately 3,000 making an annual shortfall of 4,000 dwellings when compared with urban housing need. (Housing Commission, 1975, pp. 2 – 3)

In terms of the 1971 census the breakdown of the workforce in major urban areas was "6·5 per cent professional and managerial, 35 per cent skilled, 20 per cent semi-skilled, and 40 per cent unskilled" (Levine and Levine, 1979, pp. 75 – 76, with no explanation of why the total slightly exceeds 100%). The implication of putting these figures together seems clear. The overall housing situation is that the skilled segment of the workforce is housed on a stable and comparatively comfortable basis, mainly by the Housing Commission. The Commission allocates its housing in an ethnic mix so as to encourage the formation of a supra-ethnic urban identity and thus to promote 'urban commitment'. The unskilled segment continues to be housed in 'self-help' housing in squatter settlements grouped on an ethnic basis or in traditional villages (Jackson, 1976a, p. 63).

The legal minimum wage from its inception in 1960 until 1972 was related to the needs of a 'single man' only (Department of Labour and Industry, 1974, pp. 2, 3, 5). A limited allowance has since been made in the minimum wage in some urban areas for a worker's wife and, in others, for a wife and one child, and there has been a small loading added to the single man basis of the rural minimum wage (National Minimum Wages Board, 1976, p. 15). In short, for numerous workers a significant, necessary dependence on the traditional mode (and related urban systems of support) remains. The current Building Act of 1971 and the regulations made under it are lengthy and impose complex and exacting standards, the application of which depends on their being mediated in the involvement of professionally recognized architects, engineers and builders. The Act gives the widest powers to the official building authority. Any proposed building or alteration must, in terms of the law, have "plans and specifications" which must be submitted to the authority for approval. This approval may be granted "subject to such conditions . . . as to the . . . [authority] seem fit". This system has been used to maintain standards that make the housing aspect of urban residence of the unskilled segment illegal and hence such residence is made to a degree provisional. Not that it is the case, of course, that official efforts to enforce these standards and dispossess settlers are always successful or strenuous (Oram, 1976a, pp. 196 – 197). The unskilled segment does have its place and it has to have housing, but the maintenance of some precariousness in this is functional. In 1973 the building law was amended to allow of less exacting standards in designated areas. These standards are still too stringent to affect the situation greatly (Housing Commission, 1975, p. 2; Oram, 1976a, p. 197). They allow probably for the relatively secure housing of elements of the higher paid 'semi-skilled' workers needed to occupy positions with some stability. In any case, these relaxed standards still involve the submission of 'plans and specifications' and the seeking of the building authority's approval, thus still entailing implication in the system of official control.

Official control also entails, as we have seen in previous chapters, a prohibition on dealing in 'native land' except with the government or except 'in accordance with native custom'. This prevents urban migrants acquiring legally valid or secure interests in land except through the government, and in this the government has done next to nothing for the inhabitants of squatter settlements. Other laws make illegal the setting up of many appropriate economic ventures in settlements and thus also militate against their becoming viable and settled communities. For example, Jackson notes that "the strong hold held on many urban [local government] councils by white business interests has frequently resulted in continuing campaigns of prosecution of 'illegal' trade store owners in the settlements" (Jackson, 1976, pp. 54 – 55). These restrictive laws are considered in the next chapter. Jackson also provides a sensitive and apt assessment of the overall situation:

> The battery of legislation available to urban administrative authorities is therefore large . . . . The size of this "battery" is depressing, for two reasons. First because it is exceedingly difficult for any ordinary person (and often as difficult for well-educated persons) to make head or tail of them or to know how to set about tackling the

problem of getting a roof over his head in a "legal" manner. In this case, it is remarkable that the one major group of people who are confronted by this legislation is possibly the least equipped to even comprehend what they face—because they are the only major urban group that is expected to provide and build its own housing. This leads to a second reason for pessimism: urban planning laws have shown themselves to be reasonably adequate as implements of restriction and social and ethnic segregation but they have yet to prove their worth as positive stimuli to the search for solutions to the new problems which towns in an independent Papua New Guinea are facing. (in Jackson *et al.*, 1976, pp. 78 – 79)

To the extent that indirect legal regulation and other forces are inadequate in the containment of the working class, direct controls retain a supplementary function. We have already seen that the indenture system and alternative direct controls continued to operate in the gradual transition of the 1950s and that a modified indenture system still covers much of the rural workforce. In the urban areas direct controls now go under such heads as public order, vagrancy laws and wage-determination.

Repression under the public order head in other third world contexts is associated with the unrest caused by high levels of urban unemployment (Kay, 1975, p. 187). Perhaps then, since urban unemployment is a problem of comparative insignificance in Papua New Guinea, resort to public order measures has not been extensive. Public order laws do exist, however, conferring wide discretionary powers on the government. The colonial administration introduced comprehensive and, in terms of British-type law, standard public order controls in the Public Order Act of 1970—a response to nationalist assertions by the Tolai and to claims they were forcibly making to 'alienated' plantation land. The dominant party in the first two national governments strongly opposed these measures. The independence Constitution of 1975 contains human rights provisions overriding some aspects of the public order law. Nevertheless, one such national government in August 1976 introduced into parliament a bill containing substantially the same public order law, so as to negative these constitutional modifications. In the face of protests by trade unions, students and the parliamentary opposition the government withdrew the bill for 'reconsideration', and it has not as yet been reintroduced. An earlier indication of the same government's response to public order problems arose out of rioting in the capital in 1973 after a football match between the Papuan and the New Guinean teams in which the Papuan won. As Oram comments on this:

The riots were largely instigated by Chimbus and Eastern Highlanders [large New Guinean groupings—P.F.], who were members
of the poorest and most insecure groups living in the town, although
other New Guineans joined in. They resented the greater wealth of
many Papuans and they were alarmed at the threats to their continued
residence made by supporters of the Papua Besena movement [a
Papuan separatist movement—P.F.]. The stoning of the cars of
Papuans, Europeans and even New Guineans by the rioters, suggests
a growing hostility towards the ''haves'' on the part of the ''have-
nots''. (Oram, 1976a, p. 144)

After this event the government issued a draft bill aimed at amending the
Public Order Act. With this proposed bill, a person could have been
removed from a ''proclaimed area'' if (s)he were officially considered a
potential threat to public order or if his or her conduct were such that it
was considered that (s)he ought not remain in the area. A person in such an
area and ''not in regular employment'' could have been required to enter
into a recognizance to keep the peace and be of good behaviour. There was
stringent provision requiring sureties to back the recognizance in all cases.
''Pending the entering into of the recognizance'' the person was to be held
in custody and there was nothing in the Bill which assuredly would have
got him or her out of custody if the amount of the recognizance and sufficient sureties were not obtained. The draft was not proceeded with but its
draconic provisions provide some indication of the government's thinking
and likely response in such situations. Although the draft was hatched by
some colonial remnants, calls by politicians for measures of a comparable
and of an even more drastic kind are frequent and increasing in their frequency. The independence Constitution makes provision for very broad
'emergency powers' involving the suspension of many legal safeguards but
which are attended with considerable formal safeguards. Such powers have
very recently been used to deal with 'tribal fighting' in the Highlands. It
is, however, indicative of the influence of progressive elements in trade
unions, parliament and the main university that the proposed new public
order law has been shelved. This, in turn, is indicative of some continuing
vitality of the consensus politics and political liberalism that have so far
characterized self-governing Papua New Guinea. Given the experience of
other third world social formations, the maintenance of this situation end
the holding back of draconic public order laws may well depend on continuing to rein in unemployment. If so, the absorption of unemployment
within traditional social formations will be a significant aspect of the

conservation of the traditional mode in the cause of maintaining order.

Some indication of the likely orientation of law and state here is given by the Bougainville miners strike in 1975. The large copper mine on Bougainville had then recently come into production and become the provider of most of the country's foreign exchange and of a large part of its revenue. Accounts of the strike vary but, in neutral terms, there was a large-scale confrontation between the workers and the police, mass arrests and the trial—and acquittal—on public order charges of five 'ringleaders', as the media dubbed them. The circumstances of the strike make it abundantly clear that the mining company was seeking a structurally defining event in relation to its labour. Part of its aim was to impose ethnically and residentially divided worker representation—a type of company unionization—on the relatively very militant mine workers union (Cunningham, 1975). The company's flexible and co-operative approach to labour during the construction phase of the mine and its initial operation gave way to refusal to negotiate or even communicate with the miners union and to the adoption of a rigid stand over the immediate issue involved, one of wage differentials for skill. The company did not refer the dispute for authoritative determination under the industrial relations laws as it could have done, nor did the government as it could have done. The police gave persuasive indications of acting not just in close collaboration with the company but in subordination to it (ibid.). Various official voices were vigorous and close to unanimous in their condemnation of the mine workers. Government ministers with trade union backgrounds, including the Prime Minister, were strident in their denunciation of the mine workers. In 1976 the mine workers organized a conference at which the Premier of the province where the mine is located warned them "against striking and other forms of protest of a trivial nature" which were "against the national interest". Shortly after the formation of the first national government, the Prime Minister had set such a tone in addressing the Teachers' Association. He cautioned that "unionism could undermine efforts to make Papua New Guinea a nation" and he described the idea of a union as a body "prepared to take militant action to ensure its members' rights" as "as unfortunate inheritance from Australia".

Vagrancy laws, although they have a long history in British-type legal systems, serve as a form of control comparable to the colonial native regulations in their ordering of urban migration. These regulations persisted until quite recently. For example, the regulation making it an offence for a 'native' to be in town for more than four days "without lawful and reasonable excuse, the burden of proof of which is on him" was not repealed until 1969. It was not until 1976 that there was a repeal of the native regulations which made it an offence for a Papua New Guinean to be "absent from his tribal area" and unable to give a good account of his means of support. Such regulations controlled, and the vagrancy laws still do control, not people in stable employment but people unemployed or occasionally employed. The colonial vagrancy law penalized people for having "insufficient lawful means of support". The courts applied this as meaning anyone not in wage employment. As a result of efforts to liberalize or abolish the vagrancy laws, a new Vagrancy Act was passed in 1977, but it effected no substantial change. Under the new law the basic offence of being "without lawful means of support" remains and, further, a court can order a person to stay out of the province in which the offence is committed for a period of up to six months. Vagrancy laws are not always enforced by the police with consistent emphasis, enforcement often being in occasional bursts of intense activity. So, even in periods when the vagrancy laws are not being strongly enforced they remain as a threatening element making for instability in urban life. A senior police officer at a meeting in the capital on public order in 1973 gave the following account and justification of the operation of the vagrancy law:

> A suspected vagrant is a person who looks like one and who is on the streets after 9 p.m. [interestingly, the old colonial curfew hour when a 'native' could not be outside his or her urban quarters—P.F.]. If such a person could not give an adequate explanation of himself, the police might go and search his house and in that way we might be able to recover stolen property.

Given such an ethos, it is understable that police have been found to abuse their powers in operating the vagrancy laws (Commission of Enquiry, 1971). Instead of preventing crime it may be that the vagrancy law by tainting urban existence outside employment with criminality fosters the growth of a 'sub-culture' of crime.[2] In this perspective the vagrancy law could lend some substance as well as suggestion to the largely unjustified official view that people in squatter settlements are parasites and criminals (Oram, 1976a, p. 170). Such a view is obviously functional in maintaining instability in the urban existence of people in the settlements.

A final type of control is the legal determination of wages which is done by an official board under the industrial relations law. Langmore notes that "legal regulation of minimum wages for both unskilled and skilled employees has been the principal influence on wage levels'' (Langmore, 1972, p. 2), and although the observation is overdrawn it does reflect the great significance law has in determining wage levels. The state has also, being by far the largest employer, successfully applied a policy of wage restraint through holding down wage levels of state employees. 'Equity' and other arguments used by economists now serve to legitimize the holding down of urban wages by comparing them to the actual and notional incomes of the rural dweller (National Minimum Wages Board, 1976, pp. 7 – 13, 51 – 54). Wage restraint has also undermined solidarity between the skilled and unskilled segments within the Public Service Association because it has operated to erode differentials for skills and made the skilled segment resentful of what they see as too great a decline in their advantage (Uwe Lilje, personal communication). Wage determination by legal fiat is, as a control, mainly relevant to the skilled and the organized—largely corresponding categories. For the unskilled, who are mostly not organized, the determination of a minimum wage is presented as a protective measure. As such it serves to legitimize low wage levels—levels that, as we have seen, are not sufficient even in terms of official determinations to maintain and reproduce the unskilled segment of the workforce.

Further, enforcement of these and other legal measures protective of labour is scant. For offences against all provisions protective of labour, from 1961 to 1970 inclusive, there were only four convictions of employers. There were only three employers convicted between December 1969 and March 1976 inclusive. Fines of employers have increased recently much over the derisory amounts of the earlier colonial period, but they are still not very significant. The average fine per conviction from December 1969 to May 1976 inclusive, was Australian $53·00.[3] Officially recorded complaints by workers that could, on the face of them, warrant prosecution have run into the hundreds and sometimes the thousands each year but prosecutions of employers are few. For example in New Guinea for one particular year there were 2286 such complaints and seven prosecutions (Territory of New Guinea, 1959 – 60, pp. 237 – 238). Breaches of minimum wage provisions have in recent times been common in the Highlands (Brookfield, 1961, p. 306; Isaac, 1970, p. 24). For rural areas generally figures submitted by employers to the Department of Labour strongly suggest widespread breaches of the minimum wage laws in rural areas (Public Service Association, n.d., p. 5). Although one cannot be categorical about these figures, because the classifications used in collecting the information are too crude, this conclusion is close to inescapable even on this basis of figures submitted by employers themselves. Similar difficulties attend the urban figures, but these also strongly suggest a considerable evasion of minimum wage laws (Garnaut *et al.*, 1977, pp. 128 – 130). Papua New Guinean employers of labour have often been found not complying with these laws (Donaldson and Good, 1979, p. 56; Epstein, 1968, p. 104; Finney, 1969, p. 38; Morauta, 1974, p. 55). Indeed, in order to encourage such 'entrepreneurs' the Department of Labour has a policy of not prosecuting them for breaches of legislation protective of workers. The policy was slightly departed from with some recent prosecutions, which themselves had trouble getting through the system, of some Papua New Guinean and foreign employers for failure to lodge information returns with the Department, and it was also departed from with a prosecution of a radical development corporation for failure to insure its workers. Price control laws appear to have a very limited effect. Few officials are allocated to their enforcement and fines on conviction are derisory (Clunies Ross and Lam, 1979, pp. 13 – 14, 50).

There is no need to go in detail over the 'lessons' of this chapter—they have perhaps been underlined too much. What is emphasized is the more supplementary, less structurally central role of law and state with the more 'natural' integration of the economy and the increasing efficacy of economic determinants located within the capitalist mode of production. Yet still the conservation of the traditional mode is fundamental to the subsidizing of labour provided by the unskilled segment of the working class and to its containment and law and state retain a highly significant part here. The skilled segment has a greater involvement and identification with the dominant order and its members are basically contained in this way. Here law and state play a distinctly supplementary part. There are controls in reserve, as it were, which can be extended to this segment or tightened in their application to it, such as the public order and trade union laws. The wider emergence of the working class and of capitalist relations of production provide more of a basis for bourgeois legality. However, colonial-type controls persist, partly because bourgeois legality cannot be effective in countering fundamental challenges to itself. The ability of the working class greatly to affect law and state is blunted in its domination by the state and in its division and diffuseness.

## Notes

1. Embarassingly, I do not have the name of the official on my interview sheet.
2. I am indebted to Loraine Blaxter for this point.
3. The preceding figures in this paragraph come from a survey of files of the Department of Labour. It is possible but unlikely that all of the relevant files were not found.

# 7 The Bourgeoisie

In the rural areas the national bourgeoisie tends to exist in the enduringly incipient form of the big peasantry. The colonist promoted a rural bourgeoisie, but then sought to contain this class element and to limit its emergence mainly in the conservation of the traditional mode of production. The resulting demi-bourgeois remains tied to this mode in the continuance of traditional exchange relations, in the newer combined forms of the development corporation and other group enterprise and in links of the patron–client type. Although this class element provides something of a basis for a resident 'ruling class', it does not widely consolidate in class terms and so is unable to challenge the metropolitan bourgeoisie effectively. This analysis would extend to national enterprises within the smaller towns in that these towns are thoroughly integrated into rural life and such enterprises are increasingly owned by big peasants, sometimes jointly with members of the metropolitan bourgeoisie (see for example, Good and Donaldson, 1979, pp. 34 – 37).

In the larger towns the position could potentially be different. A national bourgeoisie here could more easily break from the confines of the traditional mode. The larger urban environment should facilitate class consolidation and make for a more effective challenge to the metropolitan bourgeoisie. Thus different methods of containment may be called for in the larger urban areas. Such methods can be derived from the plethora of laws that impose ostensibly neutral controls and standards on economic enterprises. These pitch capitalist production well beyond the resources of almost all nationals. Such laws are ostensibly contradicted by others which aim to promote a national bourgeoisie. These laws create artificial monopolies that favour aspirant members of this class element both as against other nationals and as against the metropolitan bourgeoisie. In this, law and state in part meet and defuse nationalist aspiration. Despite their nationalist cast such laws end up integrating the national bourgeoisie in a subordinate relation to the metropolitan. Law and state here serve to mediate between elements of the bourgeoisie who may not always see eye to eye. The national legal system can be seen as moving more towards bourgeois legality which itself has a distinct mediating function—one that is brought out more in the next chapter. This move to bourgeois legality is a response to the increased involvement of the metropolitan bourgeoisie and a response to the emergence of a national bourgeoisie. But, for the national bourgeoisie, bourgeois legality is less supportive and more a factor tying and subordinating it to the metropolitan bourgeoisie.

In this chapter I will look firstly at the increased penetration of the metropolitan bourgeoisie during the period of accelerated development. Towards the end of this period the state moved weakly to promote a national bourgeoisie in towns and this move is next considered. The part that law and state play in effecting and responding to these changes is then elaborated on. Following this, the emergence and shape of the national bourgeoisie is sketched in. Then there is a general analysis of why the national bourgeoisie and the class element of urban-based petty commodity producers have emerged but weakly. A detailed account of how law and state contain these two class elements ends the chapter.

In the period of accelerated development the state encouraged the inflow of metropolitan capital—Australian capital and, increasingly, capital from other sources. This was, in the developmental rhetoric of the day, done to promote economic growth, the benefits of which would trickle down to the mass of Papua New Guineans (International Bank for Reconstruction and Development, 1965). This metropolitan capital was allowed unrestricted access except for limits on the further expansion of plantation activity. Papua New Guineans were at a hopeless competitive disadvantage. There was no extensive indigenous tradition of commodity production and commodity exchange to build on. Nationals had been excluded from towns except as employees of the colonist. It was not until 1969 (that is, towards the end of the period of accelerated development) that those native regulations were repealed which made it unlawful for a national to stay in town more than four days without official permission—and this permission was not given merely for making one's way in the world. In short, Papua New Guineans remained excluded from the capitalist mode of production except as employees or as peasants. During the period of accelerated development the capitalist economy certainly grew, and grew rapidly, but the relative share of Papua New Guineans in the income it generated decreased (Shand and Treadgold, 1971). In terms of the ownership of capital, the participation of nationals was very small (Garnaut et al., 1977, p. 5; O'Connor, 1970, p. 2; Oram, 1976a, p. 118). It remains small today (Ministry of Labour, 1976, p. 10; National Investment and Development Authority, 1977).

In the result, the metropolitan domination of capitalist production is deep and comprehensive. Even those small scale, labour intensive economic activities that are the preserve of nationals in many third world social formations are in Papua New Guinea dominated by metropolitan capital. Thus under a law requiring the licensing of pedlars, 95% of the licences issued in the capital in 1973 were held by foreigners, often employing nationals, of course (Fitzpatrick and Blaxter, 1975, p. 44). Even so, metropolitan investment was and is not large, except in a few types of natural resource extraction, by far the most important being copper mining. However, natural resource extraction is capital intensive in operation and relies overwhelmingly on imported inputs. It leads to few 'linkages' or 'multiplier effects' within the national economy. There is little investment in secondary industry. Papua New Guinea offers only a small internal market and, so far, few comparative advantages in industrial production. Papua New Guinea's exports are almost wholly confined to agricultural production and natural resources extracted with close to minimal local processing or manufacturing. The rest of the capitalist economy is largely involved in servicing-type activities—wholesale and retail trade, transport, maintenance and repair (Baxter, 1976, p. 87). Apart from agriculture, what small national involvement there is in the capitalist economy has been in areas where low capital requirements and labour intensity have given resident factors of production a very strong comparative advantage, areas such as road haulage, taxis, building and some services. This short list can, of course, be relevantly run off for many other third world social formations (Arrighi, 1970, p. 242).

Towards the end of the period of accelerated development the state, having advanced the big peasantry, turned unenthusiastically to the promotion of an urban bourgeoisie. In 1971 a previously minute governmental division was expanded somewhat into a Department of Business Development. As a department this has, however, remained starved of funds and of competence, a matter of small budgets and small minds (Andrews, 1975, pp. 15, 17, 156–157). In 1971 also, the outgoing colonial administration decided that some vague preference should be given to Papua New Guineans in the allocation of land for commercial purposes and where land was allocated to foreigners conditions could be imposed requiring some future involvement of nationals in the ownership of the enterprise (Department of Lands, Surveys and Mines, 1971). This has had no great effect. Of a little more significance was the Housing Commission's adopting, soon after this, a policy of awarding house-building contracts to 'suitable' national builders. Probably of yet more importance, but still only minor in impact, has been the decision, in 1973, of some of the bodies concerned in allocating government contracts, to allow in tendering small margins of preference to enterprises wholly or partly owned by nationals. The Development Bank has been the most resourceful promoter of an urban bourgeoisie. After spending its early years mainly in financing metropolitan owned enterprises, the Bank turned more determinedly in the early 1970s to promoting national 'entrepreneurs'. This was done mainly in the provision of loans on very favourable terms. More unconventionally the Bank, because it found the Department of Business Development quite ineffectual, set up its own comprehensive extension service, the operation of which the Bank described this way:

> A considerable problem which many Papua New Guineans face in setting up a business is their lack of experience in management. Where considerable management and technical assistance is necessary the Bank's Projects Department has set up the business, trained the entrepreneur in management and commercial techniques, and closely supervised the business. Over this period, the business is under the ownership of the Bank which in this way takes the business risk. When the manager's experience has increased to the point where he can take control, the business is handed over to him and the Bank's equity is converted to a loan to the new owner. (Development Bank, 1974, p. 7)

No, or very little, thought was given to why such largesse should be conferred on the fortunate 'manager' rather than, say, on the workers involved in the enterprise (Bob Gunton, personal communication). There is another and equally dramatic type of generosity practiced by the bank. For many new urban commercial sites, the Development Bank takes a long term lease from the government and assigns the lease to a Papua New Guinean making a loan to him or her for the purchase of the lease. The loan is usually for ninety per cent. of the purchase price but it is sometimes for even more. The loan is secured on the lease. The Papua New Guinean then typically sub-leases to a foreigner. The rental on the sub-lease is used to pay off the loan. Having done this, the Papua New Guinean 'businessman' has obtained a valuable long term lease for next to nothing.

So far in this chapter, law and state can only be seen as playing a facilitative and merely responsive part in the emergence of a national bourgeoisie. Government contracts, loan contracts, contracts and conveyances giving security and the lease are all convenient and adaptive forms. The company, as we will see later, is another such. But law and state also play a more positive or leading part. The Discriminatory Practices Act of 1963 although not, it would appear, enforced, signalled that nationals should not be manifestly discriminated against. The Land (Tenure Conversion) Act of 1963 was, as we saw in Chapter 5, of little operative significance, but it evidenced some commitment by the state to the development of a national bourgeoisie. Following the Wills, Probate and Administration Acts of 1966 and 1970, nationals could will some types of property and thereby seek to keep it out of the traditional sphere and reproduce a class position.

Probably the enactment which has so far had the most practical impact is the Passenger Transport Control Board Act of 1968. Much of the following account of it is derived from Fitzpatrick and Blaxter (1973). In terms of the act, "the [Passenger Transport Control] Board shall exercise general supervision over the licensing of public motor transport in Papua New Guinea in the interests of the public, with a view to its greater integration, safety, efficiency and economy". The Board also has particular functions which oblige it "continuously to examine procedures in the licensing of vehicles carrying passengers for hire or reward . . . and to assess the relationship between the supply of, and demand for, the services of such vehicles". In its early life the Board's main function was to protect foreign-owned bus companies. These were beleaguered by the low-capital operation of passenger trucks by nationals. However, the bus companies were not a significant force economically. Although some remained protected to a degree, the Board became increasingly responsive to the interests of national enterprises. The Board sees these as "operators owning one or two vehicles". The passenger road transport industry should, in the Board's view, "provide adequate returns to the operators while still offering the public a system that is efficient, safe and relatively cheap". To achieve adequate returns, the Board operates a method of "controlled licensing": it favours, at least in urban areas, individual operators and a selection of them at that. The Board gives predominant recognition to the category of individual "operators owning one or two vehicles" and operating them on a purely economic basis. But the great majority of trucks are owned by communities. These community trucks carry for "hire or reward" or they are officially presumed to—the assumption has not been legally tested—and hence they are caught by the Act. They are, however, not merely objects of economic investment. They are also objects of consumption—"the poor man's collective equivalent of the rich man's private car" as one development advisory group described them (Overseas Development Group, 1973, p. 89). Hence communities are often denied the provision of their own transport so that the demand can be met by the aspirant bourgeois. The Board reinforces the reality of its own restrictive labelling in two ways. First, it requires applicants for licenses, at least in the capital, to be checked for suitability by the Department of Business Development. Second, for its own guidance, it has encouraged the setting up of "advisory committees" on which existing licence holders are heavily represented. The Department of Business Development has also helped in the formation and organization of pressure groups of licence holders. One senior official of this Department, at a meeting of local government councils about transport licensing, succinctly advocated that "operators should come together to set up an association to control everything" (Lesley Andrews, field notes, unpublished). But, it may just be recalled, the Board must in law consider the "interests of the public". This injunction is, however, clearly subordinated to the central concern with promoting the emergence of the national bourgeoisie. Thus in 1973, in a survey which one of its innovative operatives conducted, the Board found that to meet public demand in and around the capital there would have to be something like twice as many passenger trucks as it had licensed.

Potentially a more significant law in the promotion of the national bourgeoisie is the Business Licences Act of 1971. It would cover most retail and mobile trading and some other specific areas. Its promoting officials saw it as protecting national 'businessmen' from the perils of 'over-competition' from other Papua New Guineans. Licences would be issued restrictively so as to ensure a 'reasonable profit' and 'efficiency'. No thought seems to have been given as to what is a reasonable profit nor to how it could be ascertained in all or any cases (Fitzpatrick and Blaxter, 1979, pp. 119 – 120). As with the issue of transport licences, the central concern is with promoting the national bourgeoisie through restriction pure and fairly simple. This licensing power would probably go to provincial governments which are particularly susceptible of capture by national bourgeois interests. However despite being passed in 1971, and amended in 1974, the Act has yet to be brought into operation—a point returned to later. We will also see later that various licensing powers of local government councils have been used in a highly restrictive way. Other laws promoting the national bourgeoisie less directly are considered then as well.

During the period of accelerated development legal measures were taken to attract and accommodate the metropolitan bourgeoisie. Several manufacturers of import substitutes were afforded tariff protection. The Industrial Development (Incentives to Pioneer Industries) Act of 1965 gave a tax holiday to "pioneer industries". Tax on corporate profits was low. In the tax legislation, closely modelled on that of Australia, in computing taxable income generous allowance was made for depreciation of assets and for carrying forward losses and, as well, liberal deductions were allowed for expenses incurred in agricultural and pastoral production and in natural resource extraction. The legislature in 1966 passed a "declaration" seeking to give metropolitan investors a most comprehensive and most favourable set of guarantees which, in terms of the declaration, could not be abrogated without the approval of a majority of the electors. Constitutionally this was not effective to bind future legislatures and as we will see in the next chapter legislation has since been passed in disregard of the declaration. But the declaration shows that a legislature with a considerable national membership, which supported the declaration, was prepared to go even further than the colonial administration in accommodating metropolitan capital. The Fisheries (Licensing) Act of 1966 and the Mining (Bougainville Copper Agreement) Act of 1967 provided for the exploitation of the resources mentioned in their titles. The former has assumed considerable importance with tuna fishing. The latter relates to what was by far the most economically significant intervention of metropolitan capital. It gave legislative status to an agreement between the colonial administration and a company controlled ultimately by Rio-Tinto Zinc Corporation Limited of Britain. This agreement related to the exploitation of a large deposit of copper on Bougainville Island. That one mine (a further large one is currently being developed in another part of the country) has been sufficient to make Papua New Guinea a major producer of copper in the third world. Until the recent slump in prices, copper production had come to dominate the Papua New Guinean economy. The export value of copper in 1972 – 73, for example, was 55% of the value of total exports. It would be disproportionate to go into the detailed terms of the agreement here and this has been done often elsewhere (see for example, Paliwala, 1974). Generally, in comparison with the terms on which copper was extracted in other third world settings, the agreement was quite unfavourable to Papua

New Guinea (Overseas Development Group, 1973, pp. 68 – 69). So much was this so that the mining company could offer only token resistance when the government insisted on the agreement's renegotiation soon after self-government—a matter considered in the next chapter. In the original agreement the company was given a special legal status: it performed some governmental functions itself, and it was given a three year tax holiday, which was effectively longer because of depreciation provisions. The state was prohibited from fundamentally affecting the company's property rights and its freedom to choose its employees.

Several legal measures of a general kind were taken to make Papua New Guinea a land fit for metropolitan investors and a national bourgeoisie. These measures involved the modernization of the legal system and the formal strengthening of bourgeois legality. The underlying operative assumption was that Australian-type laws should now be introduced in a comprehensive and systematic way so as to create a familiar or hospitable environment for a bourgeoisie (Kerr, 1968; Paliwala et al., 1978). An acute 'elite' of national lawyers would be trained as apt operatives (James, 1975, p. 208; Kerr, 1968, p. 20). Thus the period of accelerated development saw a huge amount of legislation covering the modernization of many aspects of commercial law, the prohibition of 'racially discriminatory prac-tices', the regulation of industrial relations, covering industrial safety, infrastructural development and the creation of special state corporations to deal with this. It also covered legal structures for international borrow-ing and for the making of agreements between the government and metro-politan investors, and finally, the organization of the state bureaucracy and of the police.

In terms of bourgeois legality, the most significant change was in the court system following on the Derham report of 1960 (Bayne, 1975, pp. 15 – 22). What Hasluck saw as "a pre-war tradition of the subordina-tion of justice to administration" gave way to a system approved by "lawyers bred in the British and Australian traditions of the rule of law" (Hasluck, 1976, pp. 344 – 355). Derham saw the unreformed situation this way:

> In the history of the two Territories there was a natural and under-
> standable tendency for governmental development to be heavily
> weighed on the executive side. This, together with an under-
> standable though all pervasive paternal attitude towards the native
> population, prevented the development of a complete judicial system
> which was genuinely independent of the Executive Government and

which could operate according to law rather than according to the policies and wishes of the Executive from time to time . . . only those cases came to the Supreme Courts which, with some exceptions, it was convenient for the executive side of government to permit to reach them. (as quoted in Bayne, 1975, pp. 15 – 16)

A new system of courts was to administer a unified legal system—"One system of courts meant one body of law. One body of law meant one system of courts" (Hasluck, 1976, p. 347). The colonial administration introduced a Local Court supposedly to be run by specialist magistrates with jurisdiction over Papua New Guineans and foreigners. Its jurisdiction covered minor criminal matters and civil matters of small monetary value. At the other end of the hierarchy there remained the Supreme Court with jurisdiction over major crimes and civil matters of considerable financial substance. This court was also the ultimate appeal court within the colony but with appeals being allowed from it to the High Court of Australia. The calibre of judges on the Supreme Court improved considerably and they acted much more in accord with the tenets of bourgeois legality. Colonial officials often now expressed exasperation with the judges' concern with 'technicalities' in criminal trials of Papua New Guineans. In between these two courts was the District Court. This was run by specialist magistrates, more highly trained than those proposed for the Local Court. They had concurrent jurisdiction with the Local Court but, in addition, could handle a wider range of criminal matters as well as civil matters involving a more substantial value. A defendant in a criminal case in the Local Court could opt to be tried in the, as it were, higher grade District Court—an option availed of by foreigners. In practice, Local Courts continued to be run for a long time by generalist field officers of the administration. They are mainly concerned with petty criminal offences (cf., Quinlivan, 1975). Basically they would appear to be a continuation of the old courts of 'native affairs'. To a very large degree, the District Court and the Supreme Court remained in civil matters the preserve of foreigners (Paliwala et al., 1978). In short, despite a formal unity in the court system, an operative duality persisted. In terms of shoring up bourgeois legality, it should be mentioned that the colonial administration set up a public solicitor's office. This provided legal aid to indigent Papua New Guineans. But its efforts rarely extended beyond defending people in serious criminal trials.

So far, this legal modernization of the 1960s could be seen as a response to the greater involvement of the metropolitan bourgeoisie and to the emergence of the national bourgeoisie. The interests of the two are not always harmonious and coincident, however. In a more complex vein now, law and state come to serve in mediating between the two branches of the bourgeoisie and in maintaining the dominance of the metropolitan. The new-found universalism of bourgeois legality assists in this. There is now no discrimination: law applied equally to all, with a few exceptions such as the continuing protection of 'native land' on one side, and the special status of the Bougainville copper mining company on the other. The fact that some people find it easier to comply with legal standards is not relevant. The legal standards apply to all and are necessary: they are instruments of modernization. People have to change so as to meet the standards. This control function of bourgeois legality is copiously illustrated shortly, but to lend some concreteness to the discussion an initial example may help. It is a rather vivid example because it deals with company law which is supposed to be basically facilitative.

We have seen in Chapter 4 that company law in New Guinea discriminated on the basis of ascribed status to the effect that New Guineans were unable to form companies for most purposes. Such discrimination was incompatible with bourgeois legality and was eventually removed in 1961. In 1963 a complex company law almost indistinguishable from the Australian was enacted. It was a facilitative measure making the company form available to all. However it, like its predecessors, contained a potent discrimination against Papua New Guineans. To counter avoidance of the protective standards applying to companies the act prohibits "an association or partnership consisting . . . of more than twenty persons, which has for its object the acquisition of gain" unless it is incorporated as a company. (There were other legitimate corporate alternatives: the co-operative, the credit society and the non-profit association, but these only covered narrowly specific enterprises.) We have already seen how this law was instrumental in the shaping of the peasantry. Here the concern is more general: very few Papua New Guineans had access to the skills needed to incorporate a company nor the money to pay for them. The continuing requirements of company law were also prohibitively onerous, especially if the company was a 'public' one, broadly, one whose membership exceeded 50. One knowledgeable official in the Companies Registry estimated that the accountant's fee for the preparation of annual accounts and other annual returns required by the Companies Act would exceed the net annual profits of almost any Papua New Guinean enterprise (Tony O'Connor, personal communication). Efforts at reforming this situation (the outcome of which is described in the next chapter) were met with two persistent responses from key officials. First, the company law provided a familiar and protective system for the metropolitan investor and hence encouraged investment, which was the engine for development. Second, this law was needed to protect resident investors in companies. On both grounds, the law could not be altered. The fact that the frequent and manifest breaches of the law were rarely prosecuted was not allowed to sully the purity of these assertions. When Papua New Guineans commenced registering a few companies, often through the agency of the Department of Business Development, they were met with an obstructively pedantic insistence on the minutiae of the law by officials of the Companies Registry. The ultimate bind was put by one such senior official in the apt proposition that if people cannot come up to the standards of company law they should not be in business anyway.[1]

In order to depict more generally this discriminatory, control function of bourgeois legality and the wider function of law and state in mediating between the metropolitan and national branches of the bourgeoisie, it is necessary to describe first something of settled formation of the national bourgeoisie and of its relation to the metropolitan. This has already been done for the big peasant as an emergent, or an ever-emergent, bourgeois. As with the rural situation, the urban bourgeoisie seems to advance, at least at first, in some reliance on the traditional social formation and in some continuing relation to it. Members of this class element occupy an in-between po: .ion, remaining in urban or peri-urban villages and combining traditional and capitalist relations in their enterprises (Andrews, 1975; Langmore, 1967; Uyassi, 1978, p. 44). However, Andrews' study of businessmen in the capital identifies a distinct break between such "village businessmen" and the "young moderns" (Andrews, 1975). These latter seek to operate and, it seems, usually succeed in operating wholly within the capitalist mode. In this they are assisted somewhat by the extension and lending activities of the Department of Business Development and the Development Bank. But these activities have not been of great significance in the urban areas. In that context the national bourgeoisie has not emerged as an organized class element that is either distinct or significant. Andrews, in a most thorough study, could not discern any "business culture" or any cohesive grouping of national businessmen in the capital (Andrews, 1975, p. 67). Almost all of their enterprises are very small scale. This issue of scale and the continuing links with the traditional social formation suggest that many 'businessmen' could be more accurately seen as petty commodity producers. Their small enterprises are owned by individuals or small partnerships. Labour is often supplied informally by family members. Where people are employed as wage-labour they are few in number and this relation of wage-labour is often considerably modified by traditional relations.[2]

There will often be cause for conflict between the 'upper' reaches of the national bourgeoisie and such 'petty' elements in that the latter stand fair to be too effective as competitors, especially the smaller scale market and street traders. Law and state regulate and subordinate petty commodity producers in the interests of the bourgeoisie, both national and metropolitan. To ascribe this function to law and state is not to say they exclusively or invariably efficiently perform it. Law and state latch on to and support other social forces tending in that direction. For example, much of the reason why law and state can so effectively, even so easily, regulate and subordinate petty commodity producers is because the grander bourgeoisie has little interest in their increase and has some significant interest in their not increasing. In many other social formations of the third world, petty commodity producers are functional to capitalist production. Such production will often entail subcontracting or putting-out work involving petty commodity producers. It will also serve in the provision of cheap necessities for wage labourers. The part of petty commodity producers will be enhanced where there is a strong indigenous tradition of petty commodity production and where alternative means of livelihood in rural production are limited or unattractive. The situation in Papua New Guinea is quite markedly contrary on all these counts. Manufacturing contributes approximately 7% of the total wage-labour force, a labour force that is, in any case, very small (Utrecht, 1977, p. 69). Natural resource extraction is far more significant economically but it is capital intensive and relies almost wholly on imported inputs. Thus there can be little call for petty commodity producers in either subcontracting or in providing for a low-paid proletariat. The rural option remains largely open to people, as we have seen (Conroy, 1977, p. 9). Nor was there in Papua New Guinea a strong indigenous tradition of petty commodity production—one that could withstand significantly the competition of imported consumer goods. As a result metropolitan investment occupied areas usually the preserve of petty commodity producers and established vested interests which it would call on the state to protect when challenged. Despite all these inhibiting factors, a small class element of petty commodity producers has emerged and, as we will see, presented some challenge to the metropolitan bourgeoisie (Garnant *et al.*, 1977, pp. 8, 126 – 127). Selling in markets by peri-urban and other agriculturalists is a significant activity. Papua New Guineans have constantly tried with less success to engage in other kinds of retailing in urban areas. Subsistence production within urban areas in significant (Housing Commission, 1975 pp. 2 – 3; Jackson, 1976b, pp. 487 – 488; Thaman, 1977). Thus, this subsistence production and peri-urban and other agriculture for market selling develop largely unhindered by law and state, except that only officially run markets tend to be allowed. These activities of course remain based in the traditional mode of production or in an urban variant of it. Hence these petty commodity producers remain embedded in, and as a class element contained by, traditional relations much like the rural peasantry. Where petty commodity producers set up enterprises importing a potential for them to consolidate as a class element law and state move to contain them. This point will be developed shortly.

The national bourgeoisie emerges often in close co-operation with elements of the metropolitan bourgeoisie. Resident colonists will sometimes, we have seen, act as mentors to big peasants. The most academically traceable form of this co-operation, because of the accessibility of public records, is the so-called inter-racial joint venture company. Of recent times examples have increased greatly. This is, in part, a paradoxical result of those laws and other state action aimed at preferring enterprises wholly or partly owned by nationals. Also, with the advent of political independence, joint ventures are used to legitimate the continued presence of smaller scale enterprises of the metropolitan bourgeoisie. The flexibility of company law has enabled metropolitan domination of joint ventures to be disguised. A study carried out by Narakobi, Wanji and myself provided some concrete detail (Narakobi and Wanji, 1976). This was a study of a fair sample of joint venture companies several of which had obtained preference in tendering for government contracts on the basis that they were controlled by nationals. In determining whether to give preference, the relevant government agencies looked merely at who held the majority of shares. They had neither the time nor the expertise to check the company's constitution or operations so as to identify the source of real power, which in some cases was foreign. Of the sample of joint venture companies, 62% had a majority national shareholding and 63% of these latter were effectively controlled by foreigners through either or, usually, both of two stratagems. One was simply to have a majority of foreigners on the board of directors and the company's constitution, in standard terms, gave all power legally possible (which is almost all power over a company's affairs) to the board. The other stratagem, used with half the companies that had a majority national shareholding, was to provide in the company's constitution for a special class of shares having artificially restricted or no voting rights which shares, it should be added for completeness' sake, were held by nationals.

The joint venture is an explicit indication of wider, characteristic connections between the metropolitan and the national bourgeoisie. A clear pointer to the overall dominance of the metropolitan bourgeoisie is that areas into which the national bourgeoisie has entered are those where purely resident operations have an overwhelming comparative advantage. The national bourgeoisie has not had the political strength to counter significantly this economic dominance of the metropolitan bourgeoisie in such as a programme of import substitution. The Business Licences Act of 1971 provides an illustration of the ultimate hierarchy involved:

> When the law was being prepared, the Australian government expressed concern that the proposed administering authorities (local government councils) could, in granting licences, prefer nationals over the few large foreign investors that dominate the country's retail and wholesale trade. The then colonial administration, in response, explained that an appeal procedure was to be provided in the proposed law to counter such an eventuality; the appeal could, in terms of the law, be argued on the grounds that the granting of a license [to a foreign investor—P.F.] was in the national interest. (Fitzpatrick and Blaxter, 1979, p. 120)

Underlining the gravity of the matter, the appeal was to go to Cabinet. With a national government being formed in 1972 this appeal procedure may no longer be completely reassuring. Perhaps it is for this reason that the law has not yet been brought into operation. At least, the Act's dormancy indicates the weakness of the national bourgeoisie. The Act accommodated increasing nationalist assertiveness in the economic area but this has not been sustained or effective enough to carry the act's potentially great advantage through.

Further, most enterprises of the national bourgeoisie are dependent on the metropolitan bourgeoisie for their existence. Cash crops are largely processed and marketed by the metropolitan bourgeoisie. What manufacturing there is by nationals is heavily reliant on imported inputs. To a very great extent, wholesaling remains controlled by the metropolitan bourgeoisie. The considerable growth in national enterprises on Bougainville results largely from their being promoted by the mine company as a legitimating measure. They are considerably dependent on the mine's operation and, wider multiplier effects being far from conspicuous, when the mine is exhausted so too will be the enterprises.

A legal linkage that provides something of an ultimate legitimation for the domination of the metropolitan bourgeoisie was set up by the Investment Corporation Act of 1971. Under this Act a state corporation invests in the resident subsidiaries of selected metropolitan enterprises or, to a lesser extent, in enterprises owned by resident colonists. Such investment is usually for 20% of the shares in the enterprise, sometimes for 25 or 26%, occasionally for more but only in one small enterprise has it been for more than 50%. In this way the state has a direct 'stake' in these enterprises. Perhaps prompted by this involvement the government has extended tariff protection and other benefits to some of these enterprises. But the involving effect of the corporation's investments is spread much wider. Following the Investment Corporation (Unit Trusts) Act of 1973, nationals and national institutions are able, through the remarkable legal form of the unit trust, to share in all the corporation's investments. These unit trusts have proved very profitable to those fortunate enough to be able to afford them. In this ingenious way, metropolitan capital assumes a widespread, palpably beneficial and, hence, legitimating presence.

It now remains to elaborate on law and state in regulating conflicting interests of the metropolitan bourgeoisie, the national bourgeoisie and petty commodity producers. Of course each of the three and their interests are not always distinct. The national bourgeoisie and petty commodity producers merge in something of a continuum. Some petty members of the metropolitan bourgeoisie will often have more in common with the national bourgeoisie than with the grander element of the metropolitan. It is usually the enterprises of this petty element that are acquired, in whole or in part as a joint venture, by the national bourgeoisie with the advent of self-government and independence. However these and other possible complications, do not, I think, detract from the general validity here of this three-way division into class elements.[3]

The amount of law relevant here is truly massive. The detail of health regulations, for example, may seem a small thing worthy of little attention in an account of something so grand-sounding as law and state. Such laws may be thought of as something which an enterprise, by taking thought and a little care, could comply with easily. But the presence and enforcement of such laws can be crucial to the viability of many petty enterprises.

Those who cannot comply with enforced standards cannot attain a legitimate existence as an economic enterprise. There are, as well, more direct controls. Discretionary licensing laws give the state power over entry to many economic areas. Licensing in the ostensible official view is needed, variously and in several combinations, to ensure an adequate public service, to promote economic efficiency and economic stability, to promote social welfare, to protect governmental revenue and to protect professional standards. Such justifications are, as we will see, usually and at least suspect, and subordinate to class interests. It may seem that these discretionary licensing laws—entailing restrictive control on even commencing an economic activity—would cover areas in some way more significant than areas covered by legal standards applicable to the ongoing operation of an enterprise. The point offers little guidance because what is of significance is the cumulative or combined effect on the enterprise of a large mass of law, an effect that is part of a wider system of state containment based on securing some official involvement in or hold on the enterprise. Thus, even laws that merely impose legal standards often require contact with an official to get a 'licence' which is obtainable if the standards are complied with. These standards often import broad, official discretions as to whether they have been complied with. More pertinently, any contact brings into play a whole range of positive and negative sanctions available to officials and which are used to shape the enterprise to fit the official mould or to ensure its failure if it does not fit. I will now look in more detail at restrictive laws and then at their combined effect.

Several directly restrictive licensing laws have already been described. The business licences law was meant to operate in preferring select members of the national bourgeoisie mainly from the competition of petty commodity producers but with the hidden proviso that it was not to detract from the dominance of the metropolitan bourgeoisie. The law was officially justified as needed to ensure economic efficiency, stability and reasonable profits to enterprises. No provision was made or planned for making these aims operational. The law was to be a simple instrument of class advance. Much the same could be said of the law relating to the licensing of passenger motor transport. As we saw, the licensing board is directed in the law to "exercise general supervision over the licensing of public motor transport . . . in the interests of the public, with a view to its greater integration, safety, efficiency and economy". Very little has been done to make these aims operational and to check on whether or how the board's activity meets these aims. The law licensing coffee buyers analysed in Chapter 5 was justified as preventing the 'chaos' that would result from too much competition and as ensuring buyers' profitability. The system was basically protective of metropolitan interests in the coffee industry.

A measure also rather singlemindedly protective of metropolitan capital is the Liquor (Licensing) Act of 1963. This law repealed the prohibition on Papua New Guineans' being allowed access to alcoholic drink. In structuring a suitable way for Papua New Guineans now to have this access, the law is oriented towards the licensing of large bars centrally located in urban areas. The licensing body's policy follows this orientation. The official reason for this was that such bars would help ease relations between nationals and foreigners and between different ethnic groupings of nationals. All would gather in convivial harmony. It was incidental that only metropolitan capital could command the resources involved in setting up and maintaining such large establishments. The social reasons for having these large bars have been manifestly undercut by events. An official Commission of Enquiry, reporting in 1971, found that the Act had been little short of disastrous in its social consequences (Commission of Enquiry into Alcoholic Drink, 1971). The large, centrally located bars had exacerbated antagonisms between groups and, generally, created considerable problems of public order. The Commission recommended the siting of smaller bars on the outskirts of urban areas. Neither the law nor the policy have changed to effect this. There are specific cases illustrating the contingent nature of the social factor. In the early 1970s a national applied for a licence to run a small tavern adjoining a moderately busy street in the capital. He was refused because of the risk of accidents. Soon after a large metropolitan investor, with the support of the Department of Trade, was given a licence for a bar on one of the busiest intersections in the capital. A great number of accidents have resulted. This same bar was located near a site for which a licence had a short time before been refused to an aspirant member of the national bourgeoisie who wanted to set up a small bar. For three years he had vigorously and efficiently worked his way through the numerous legal and other official requirements involved. He had saved a considerable amount. The Development Bank had agreed to a loan. He had undertaken training, and numerous other preparatory steps could be detailed. Relevant government departments had designated the site as one for a bar. But at the end of the day the licensing body rejected his application on the ground that the site was unsuitable.

The most ironic rationale for licensing is that behind the Licences Act of 1923 (of New Guinea) and the Trading with Natives Act of 1946. The licensing involved with these acts was originally and ostensibly aimed at protecting Papua New Guineans from unscrupulous foreign traders. It is now used to protect unscrupulous foreign traders from Papua New Guineans. Willis and Adams provide the following example of the use of licensing under the Licences Act of 1923. It concerns the local government council of a large urban area where the predominantly foreign Independent faction were in conflict with national council members of the Pangu party:

> The council's Executive Finance Committee, which controls the issuing of licences, in August 1972 decided to refuse all future applications for pedlars' licences. The reason was that there were "problems associated with pedlars in town unfairly competing with store keepers whose overheads are much higher than the pedlars'". The Pangu councillors realised, too late, that in letting the control of licences pass to the Independent dominated Executive Finance Committee they had allowed the expatriate businessmen on the council to prevent an important form of . . . [Papua New Guinean] entrepreneurial activity from emerging. Peddling artifacts, soft drinks and hot dogs, or mowing lawns, repairing shoes and cutting hair from wayside stalls require little overhead and are therefore enterprises in which Niuginians could easily participate. (Willis and Adams, 1973, p. 14)

Both these laws enable councils to impose restrictive conditions on licences. One such condition imposed in the capital on mobile traders was that "a licencee or his agent shall not trade within 800 yards of any fixed premises retailing items similar to those retailed by the licencee". Some councils have laid down very high fees for the annual issue of a licence to pedlars. There are several other licensing laws which are restrictive in their imposition of artificially high fees.

Numerous councils have rules requiring pedlars and street-sellers to be licensed. Many of them then refuse to grant any licences at all. When several councils were asked why they did this the main reason given was the protection of that revenue derived from fees paid by sellers at council markets. But there can be little doubt that the amount of revenue possibly lost and more could be made up from licence fees. Another reason commonly given was that street sellers cause obstruction. In most Papua New Guinean urban conditions the point is absurd. Specific laws relating to the obstruction of roads and foot paths have been used to harass street-sellers.

Even if the hazards of discretionary licensing are overcome or inapplicable, there remains a daunting collection of standards that have been highly restrictive in effect. Standards in the areas of health and town planning have proved in practice to be the most significant. Others dealing with quality control, packaging and labelling, causing a public nuisance, industrial safety and the protection of professional monopolies, although of some effect, have not yet been greatly significant and will not be considered here.

With health, a few examples of legal standards should suffice so long as it is remembered that there are many of them. Under the Pure Food Regulations a seller of meals, including for example a street-seller, would need to have a dish-washing machine or double bowl sink and hot running water. Such standards are tacitly posited on a certain type and a certain minimum scale of operation. They are impossible for small scale enterprises to comply with. So, a health-type condition attached by the council in the capital to the granting of a mobile trader's licence, under the Trading with Natives Act of 1946, requires for the selling of meals "portable water from a reservoir tank of at least ten gallons capacity which shall be fitted within the body of the vehicle" with "an approved pumping apparatus". So a "vehicle" is obliquely required and it would have to be substantial to accommodate the more direct requirements. Similarly the Sale of Meat Act of 1951 prohibits the sale of uncooked meat within or close to towns unless a licence is obtained and to obtain one the "premises" involved must meet exacting standards. Hence premises are obliquely prescribed. Crude scale is not the only restrictive aspect here. Other examples would be ethnocentric requirements in the Pure Foods Regulations for handwashing with soap or for a store retailing foodstuffs to have walls of a "rigid, smooth-faced washable material". These have the effect of prohibiting inexpensive, traditional methods of hygiene and of building accessible to the mass of nationals.

It is probably laws shaping the urban environment that have been the most significant here. The Town Planning Act of 1952 is very plain and of a limited significance. It provides for simple land use zoning schemes based on almost mutually exclusive, prescribed zones such as "residential", "commercial" and "light industrial" zones. In this way it rules out "mixed-uses" characteristic of many third world cities, that is, for example, a combination of residential and commercial uses on a piece of land. There is some popular demand for such uses. The Department of Labour has done a survey of a large suburb in the capital which showed that many residents had taken leases in the hope of conducting businesses from the houses only to find this was prohibited. A great many urban residences are owned by the Housing Commission which prohibits mixed uses in its leases, with a few experimental exceptions.

A more significant law shaping the urban environment is the Building Act of 1971 and the building regulations made under it, which regulations impose complex and exacting standards. No building can be erected without the consent of the relevant authority. Before obtaining this consent "plans and specifications" must be submitted. Simpler standards, but still with the procedure for consent and plans, have recently been enacted. These have been made applicable so far only to a few small areas. At first they applied only to housing but then they were extended to all buildings. The standards themselves, however, remain suitable only for housing and still do not make legitimate building popularly accessible in the urban areas (Housing Commission, 1975, p. 2; Oram, 1976a, p. 197).

To get land in towns to commence all economic enterprise it is usually necessary to obtain a lease from the state. The complexities involved in obtaining such a lease and the conditions characteristically attached to it are for most people prohibitive in the extreme. Oram has noted, as of 1967, that "few people could obtain land because of the strict conditions attached . . . and procedures for obtaining leases and land were complex, requiring, according to one official, seventeen forms to be filled" (Oram, 1970, p. 54). The Lands Board, which is charged with allocating leases, insists that applicants be eminently credit-worthy, competent in the conduct of capitalist enterprise, have the capital to meet covenants to invest a substantial sum in the site and not intend to engage in mixed-uses. In addition particular restrictive conditions are attached to leases for particular uses. An applicant for land who wishes to set up a petrol selling facility has to prove there will be a demand for at least 20 000 gallons a month. This is well beyond the scope of a small-scale enterprise. What has to be proved and how it is proved is dictated, here as elsewhere, by metropolitan competition and this adds further barriers. For instance, in applying for land in 1972, British Petroleum used a complex, transport flow analysis based on computer calculations to prove the requisite demand for petrol.

So much for restrictive laws in their own diffuse categories. What has now to be emphasized is their combined effect. This effect is daunting for the petty operator. Even the aspirant national bourgeois could rarely comply with these laws without government assistance—which is often ineffective—or without linking-up in a joint-venture with metropolitan capital and its attendant access to skills and influence. (Looking inversely at the point, these laws thus serve to align the national bourgeoisie with the metropolitan.) Law and state here seem designed to maximize contact with officials. Very many economic activities are subject to obtaining a licence. Some legal standards are attached to the issuing of a "licence" that the official has no discretion to refuse. In setting up almost any economic enterprise in towns, numerous and varying official approvals are necessary. Such contact enables people to be processed to see if they fit or can be made to fit the officially shaped mould. Quite apart from compulsory contact, applicants for licences or leases of land are often screened by government officials to see if they could be 'good businessmen', that is, to see if they could reach the ragged ranks of the national bourgeoisie. Government assistance may be forthcoming to help the promising. Such assistance may, along with the restrictive laws, prove an apt means of weeding-out the unfit and the unworthy. Thus, in 1973, four women from a nearby village wished, with the help of kin, to set up an enterprise selling meals in the capital from a mobile bar. The requirement mentioned earlier for a ten gallon water tank and pumping apparatus in a vehicle meant they had to have a substantial vehicle with this apparatus if they were to get a mobile trader's licence. The application for the licence served to ensure that the expensive fittings required by health laws were also taken into account. These and other requirements would have involved the women in expenditure well beyond their plans and means. They therefore obtained a loan from the Development Bank. To meet the loan repayments the Bank envisaged that the enterprise would have to be run in a highly organized way and on a fairly large scale. To help the women do this, the Bank referred them to the Department of Business Development. The involvement of this Department was, somewhat true to form, disastrous. It imposed operating requirements that proved impossible to comply with and the enterprise failed. The reason which officials of the Department gave for this failure was that the women lacked "management skills". The failure was also contributed to by the condition attached to a mobile trader's licence prohibiting trading "within 800 yards of any fixed premises retailing items similar to those retailed by the licencee".

It is not only the defining density of the actual laws which is relevant when looking at their effect. The way in which official processes actually work in applying the laws can have a functional inefficiency and inflexibility. Hence the aspirant bourgeois who applied for a liquor licence found that although relevant government departments had designated the land he held as a tavern site, the licensing body rejected this designation. An apparently substantial metropolitan investor, with the Department of Trade smoothing the way, obtained with facility a licence for a nearby site. Another suggestive, recent example involves a somewhat isolated peri-urban settlement of about 800 people near the capital. It had no shops. Foreign operated mobile trading had commenced in the settlement, but the people resented this. At their request the Housing Commission drew up plans for the building of a shop. The plans envisaged that the shop would be the focus of the settlement with market stalls around it. The scheme could not proceed because the Lands Board would not modify the standard but onerous conditions attached to a lease of land for a retail shop nor would it extend the site by the small amount necessary for it to operate as a community focus.

Process includes enforcement and something has to be said about that. Many of the laws in this area are not always or consistently enforced. If they were, one official put it, "the people could not move". But Papua New Guinea's public bureaucracy is quite sizeable and in this area at least quite efficient. Even inconsistent or indifferent enforcement can create an unstable environment for economic enterprises. In Rabaul a health inspector stopped a thriving, illegal street trade ('cleared the streets') which his tolerant predecessor had allowed to grow up. When officials do not enforce laws, metropolitan enterprises have often successfully brought pressure to bear to have this rectified. Further, the range of prohibitions and controls is so great and they are so replicated that if one law is not adequately enforced another can have the repressive effect. It is probably no accident that what would seem to be the most effective and the most draconic legal restrictions are attached to the grant by the state of leases of land. This is self-enforcing, in that with most of the conditions a failure to meet them means that the lease is not granted, and there is rarely any other legally valid way of getting land for commencing an enterprise. Land is not needed for all enterprises but, again, it is probably no accident that the widest range and the greatest replication of restrictions are applicable to mobile trading.

There are some subjective and ideological aspects that deserve brief mention. Instances have already been referred to at the beginning of Chapter 4 of the defeatist attitude people had developed perceptively to the point where any economic innovation was looked on as illegal. This attitude persists in relation to such laws as we are now considering with people refusing to start or continue in enterprises because of law's generalized, inhibiting effect (Fitzpatrick and Blaxter, 1979). The related effects of bourgeois legality and of purported modernization can now be seen as underlying and reinforcing these attitudes. 'High' legal standards rooted in metropolitan factors of production (and usually brought into operation by officials in unthinking emulation of that context) are maintained in the name of modernization—a good repeatedly asserted by officials in the face of recent efforts at reform by 'lowering' many of these standards. Bourgeois legality would then have the standards equally applicable to all. Given this new universalism people unable to comply with the standards must simply overcome this inherent deficiency if they are to enter the economic kingdom. In other words, failure in economic enterprises because of the oppressiveness of standards is simply not perceived by officials. The cause is the inability of the people. Reducing standards is quite specifically perceived by officials as a betrayal of the civilizing mission, a mission that is felt most keenly in those areas emphasized here, namely, health laws and laws shaping the urban environment. This ideology of the civilizing mission is certainly not just a thing of colonialism. It and its variant of modernization are a felt support of a post-colonial bureaucratic bourgeoisie and can be seen as justifying its continued arrogation of the extensive official powers that characterized the colonial situation. For members of the bureaucratic bourgeoisie, the lowering of standards is often seen as a demeaning acceptance of something that is second-best or as an admission that they cannot maintain standards characteristic of the metropolitan power. These are matters which for officials seem to run deep. When proposed reforms for lower standards were presented to one senior official he said vehemently and repeatedly that they would be ''the end of everything''. A common official response to these reforms was that they would lead to a loss of necessary control. People are such that they need to be controlled. One senior official in extolling new health laws restrictive of street-selling said that they ''will keep people off the streets where they are a great problem, difficult to check on, leave rubbish and have no toilets''. Yet again the need to control imports the inferiority or inadequacy of these people who have to be controlled. Of course, apart from serving class domination, civilizing and modernizing standards do some small good in such as protecting health and this serves in their legitimation.

The next chapter on contemporary law and state is in many ways a continuation of this one and so any concluding comments here about the position and internal relations of the bourgeoisie would be premature. More has to be said also about the so-called bureaucratic bourgeoisie and this is done in the next chapter.

## Notes

1. This paragraph is derived from personal observation and from numerous interviews. I am particularly indebted to Colin Healy, Harry Jackman, Tony O'Connor, Greg Shechan and Ian Wiseman.
2. As well as her published work referred to here, for this paragraph I have gratefully relied on Lesley Andrews' field notes as well as on numerous discussions with her and on interviews with Gau Pako, David Parker and Joe Shaw.
3. With characteristic generosity, Loraine Blaxter has allowed me to draw here on our work on petty commodity producers in Papua New Guinea. For an overview of much of that work see Fitzpatrick and Blaxter (1979).

# 8 Contemporary Law and State

Changes in the post-colonial situation are ostensibly dramatic. The state discovers and asserts the virtues of 'Papua New Guinea ways', a kind of specific socialism. This is attended with state action promoting economic enterprise, based on traditional groupings, and with state action aimed at greater national control of the economy. The Bougainville copper agreement is renegotiated securing much more favourable terms for the state. Strong measures are introduced to control foreign investment generally. This chapter describes and tries to explain these and other significant changes in conjunction with the central part that law and state play in them.[1]

Explanation is found in two related perspectives. One is the continuation of the colonial economy in a markedly different political setting. The other involves the greater need in the post-colonial situation for law and state to mediate between the national bourgeoisie and what is now that "great absent member", the metropolitan bourgeoisie. As to the first perspective, these changes and the part of law and state are seen as stemming from a continuation of the economic forces of the colonial era in a situation where there is no longer the support of colonial rule and its legitimating ideologies. Internal class formation is too weak to provide a basis for a comprehensive new order and for a new legitimacy. In the result, the colonial concern with conserving resident social formations is still greatly emphasized even if often in new ways. This concern now takes such forms as nationalism and the assertion of a decolonizing identity and authenticity. Just as in the colonial era when law and state played a central part in this—protecting the traditional mode of production against the ravages of the capitalist mode—so it is still given strong emphasis in the same cause, only now there is less reliance on law and state as directly coercive control.

The post-colonial state is a recent, rapid and fragile creation lacking any strong, nationwide basis of support. It is often confronted by ethnic groupings strengthened and enlarged in the colonial period. It is not in a position to control much coercively. Instead there is more reliance on law and state as facilitative. Law and state are used to enable people to maintain or set up ethnic-based communities, economic enterprises and institutions of political rule and legal control. These bodies are then contained mainly through involvement in the state system. Ethnic identity and ethnic division thus tend to be reinforced. To a considerable degree this reliance on law and state as facilitative tends to blend with the continued emergence of the big peasantry. Law and state create new economic, political and legal frames for action which combine elements of community with the advance of the big peasant. Incorporating these elements of community helps legitimize that advance.

The second explanatory perspective involves the greater but still limited consolidation of the national bourgeoisie and its relation to the metropolitan bourgeoisie. Law and state come to play, in the post-colonial situation, a more significant part in mediating between these class elements. This more significant part leads to some change of emphasis in the form of law. Law here tends somewhat to take the form of broad, discretionary official controls whereas in the colonial period relations within the bourgeoisie were almost wholly a matter of bourgeois legality. The attainment of the political kingdom gives the national bourgeoisie a greater class identity. The rapid 'localization' of the public bureaucracy by the first national government created a bureaucratic bourgeoisie of considerable coherence. These class elements became more cohesively concerned with appropriating a fitting share of surplus value. There will be a tendency for them to establish economic bases, including a fiscally plump state system, often at the expense of the previously all-pervasive metropolitan bourgeoisie. Broad, discretionary legal controls are introduced and, to a limited extent, used for this purpose. These controls are also important for the legitimacy of the post-colonial state. In them the decolonizing state opposes itself to certain of the economic forces manifestly served by colonialism and asserts some power to control the economy in the cause of development. Controls or their semblance also help legitimize the continuing presence of the metropolitan bourgeoisie. This presence can be acceptable if it is seen as controlled. Broad, discretionary controls, because they are often ineffective and because they involve no specific criteria of accountability, serve to disguise a relation of close mutual interest and co-operation between the national (including the bureaucratic) bourgeoisie and the metropolitan bourgeoisie. Predominantly, however, law as it affects the metropolitan bourgeoisie remains a matter of bourgeois legality with its emphasis on stability, predictability and the constraint of state action. As well, its emphasis on formal equality continues to mask inequalities of substance to the benefit of the metropolitan bourgeoisie. In all, the metropolitan bourgeoisie remains the dominant cohesive and supportive force behind the state, and law, in its form and ultimate effect, reflects this.

The chapter will proceed something in this way. After a brief account of recent changes in economy an overview of changes in law and in other state action is presented. This presentation is largely in terms of officially attributed purposes and explanations and these are then analysed in relation to the nature of the present state system. Such an analysis shows the implausibility of these official attributions and points to the aptness of the explanatory perspectives just summarized here. The perspectives are then supported in a detailed account of the main areas of change in law and state. These involve the constitution, group enterprise, land, metropolitan investment as well as the whole remarkable effort at law reform.

The accelerated development of the 1960s involved a rapid growth in the capitalist economy. Although returns to nationals increased in absolute terms with this growth, in relative terms these returns declined progressively throughout the period to the extent that "the share of monetary sector output accruing to expatriates was estimated at over eighty per cent. in 1973" (Lubett, 1977, p. 12; see also Leibowitz, 1976, p. 168 and Shand and Treadgold, 1971). Following the Mining (Bougainville Copper Agreement) Act of 1967, the construction of the mine between 1969 and 1972 created a boom in the national economy. The mine came into production in early 1972 and for the next two years this production accounted for more than half of Papua New Guinea's exports. Then world copper prices slumped causing a recession in the national economy but one considerably mitigated by the rise in coffee prices. The Bougainville mine remains enormously significant, a giant of investment among the diminutive Australian investments in services and secondary industry. It is something much more significant than the recent, large Japanese, British and United States investments in agriculture, timber extraction and tuna fishing, even though investment in tuna fishing is very substantial by world standards. Steps are being taken to bring a mine of comparable size in the Star Mountains into production. There are also extensive oil explorations and plans for the large-scale generation of hydro-electric energy for export to northern Australia and for consumption by locally sited secondary industry. Apart from this last and uncertain prospect of some secondary industry developing, the overall picture is one of close to overwhelming domination by metropolitan capital engaged in natural resource extraction. More generally, I have suggested certain 'indicators of dependence' showing the Papua New Guinea economy to be an extremely dependant one (see Apthorpe, 1977, pp. 50 – 51). As in other post-colonial situations, Papua New Guinea has a more diverse dependency than in the colonial period in that there are a wider range of metropoles on which it depends. Since Australian 'aid' provides over 40% of the state budget, the Australian influence must remain enormous but it probably becomes increasingly an influence exercised as proxy for the wider, world capitalist system.

The preponderant involvement of capital tied to natural resource extraction would appear not to call for any great change in the overall Papua New Guinea social formation. Such involvement is capital intensive and relies greatly on imported inputs. Heightened or extensive class division within Papua New Guinea would not be functional for such capital since it only requires a small, skilled proletariat and it does not require extensive internal production for the market. Hence a stable 'backwardness' and ethnic division in the conservation of the traditional mode of production would conform more to the interests of such capital than generalized, capitalist production and class consolidation. As a source of surplus for dominant internal class elements, natural resource extraction can itself assist indirectly in the conservation of the traditional mode of production. In many social formations of the third world these dominant internal class elements rely on the peasantry to provide surplus value. If this reliance were stronger in Papua New Guinea there would be pressure to increase peasant production for the market which can result in an undermining of the traditional mode of production. So the generation of surplus through natural resource extraction buffers the traditional mode. The continued high levels of Australian 'aid' have also had this effect.

The government which took Papua New Guinea into independence was the first to mark a political break with the colonial past. It was the first effectively controlled by nationals. It was formed in early 1972; internal self-government followed in late 1973 and full independence came in 1975. This government started its life with a strong concern about the declining share of nationals in the national economy and with a vaguer concern about the country's considerable dependence. These concerns were crystallized and elaborated through the visit and report in 1972 – 73 of an advisory team on development strategy sponsored by an agency of the United Nations (Overseas Development Group, 1973). The report conformed to the then current fashion in advice about development (see for example, ILO, 1972; McNamara, 1973). But it struck specifically responsive chords in the Papua New Guinea context and provided something of a charter for change. The report had it that economic growth (as characterized by the period of accelerated development) was not sufficient for development and in some ways it was something detrimental. It created inequality, was inimical to participation by nationals in the economy and fostered economic dependence. Although economic growth was still to be encouraged, it had to be tempered, even restrained, in the cause of greater self-reliance and a more egalitarian distribution. Probably the main practical strategy recommended in the report was the promotion of petty commodity producers or, in its terms, the promotion of an informal sector based on popularly accessible resources and involving reliance on elements of the traditional mode of production. The informal sector was also seen as including the mass of the peasantry and, like so many recent 'development plans' in the third world, great emphasis was given to the promotion of agriculture. The report also proposed that the Bougainville copper agreement be renegotiated.

It was a package with something for (almost) everyone. It required no substantial denials of the capitalist mode, yet somehow it offered the prospect of being able to reverse or drastically modify the effects of accelerated development—effects of growing inequality, growing dependence and the constricting of participation by nationals in the capitalist economy. In suggesting that greater Papua New Guinea participation in the economy could be based on elements of the traditional mode, the report encouraged the emergence of a populist ideology. This was an ideology of, to use one of its slogans, Papua New Guinea ways. This anodyne would serve to legitimize the rule of new people whilst diverting any confrontation of the growing class inequalities among nationals. Apart from the vague mention of relying on the traditional mode and apart from appealing to the hesitant assertiveness of the national bourgeoisie, the report was not grounded in any operative dynamic at all. It was a series of prescriptive, disparate reactions to economic growth or to capitalist development. Like the new leaders, the report was against some of the effects of capitalism but it was not for any coherent alternative of relevance much less of plausible effectiveness.

The report very directly provided the basis for the government's "eight aims", the avowed bedrock of all future state action. These were widely publicized, acquired something of a scriptural quality and were constantly used as an ostensible touchstone for policy. There is, then, no avoiding quoting them in full:

1. a rapid increase in the proportion of the economy under the control of Papua New Guinean individuals and groups and in the proportion of personal and property income that goes to Papua New Guineans;
2. more equal distribution of economic benefits, including movement toward equalization of incomes among people and toward equalization of services among different areas of the country;
3. decentralization of economic activity, planning, and government spending, with an emphasis on agricultural development, village industry, better internal trade, and more spending channelled through local and area bodies;
4. an emphasis on small-scale artisan, service, and business activity, relying where possible on typically Papua New Guinean forms of organization;
5. a more self-reliant economy, less dependent for its needs on imported goods and services, and better able to meet the requirements of its people through local production;
6. an increasing capacity for meeting government spending needs from locally raised revenue;
7. a rapid increase in the active and equal participation of women in all types of economic and social activity; and
8. government control and involvement in those sectors of the economy where control is necessary to assure the desired kind of development.

At this level another influence came from the report of the Constitutional Planning Committee and the subsequent Constitution of 1975 (Constitutional Planning Committee, 1974). The national goals drawn up by the Committee and incorporated in the Constitution are broadly similar to the eight aims. With the goals there is a more explicit espousal of personal liberation and of Papua New Guinea ways as the basis for development—one goal being "to achieve development primarily through the use of Papua New Guinean forms of social, political and economic organization". The Committee put these additional perspectives powerfully and repeatedly:

The process of colonization has been like a huge tidal wave. It has covered our land, submerging the natural life of our people. It leaves much dirt and some useful soil, as it subsides. The time of independence is our time of freedom and liberation. We must rebuild our society, not on the scattered good soil the tidal wave of colonization has deposited, but on the solid foundations of our ancestral land. We must take the opportunity of digging up that which has been buried. We must not be afraid to rediscover our art, our culture and our political and social organizations. Wherever possible, we must make full use of our ways to achieve our national goals. We insist on this, despite the popular belief that the only viable means of dealing with the challenges of lack of economic development is through the efficiency of Western techniques and institutions. (ibid., p. 2/13)

The people for whom the constitution was being written:

. . . . can proudly claim that though in languages and in external forms of cultural practices we are diverse, we are, in essence, one people . . . . The fundamental premise is that we are a people. We are a race. We are a nation. It is through our ways that we should grow. (ibid., p. 2/14)

The constitution also contains numerous 'directive principles' for the fulfilment of the national goals. As well as the topics covered in the eight aims, these particularly stress the pertinence of Papua New Guinea ways. The principles call for "political structures . . . to provide for substantial decentralization of all forms of government activity . . . in view of the rich cultural and ethnic diversity of our people". There should be "a fundamental reorientation of our attitudes and the institutions of government, commerce, education and religion towards Papua New Guinean forms of participation, consultation and consensus" and a "recognition that the cultural, commercial and ethnic diversity of our people is a positive strength". Hence, there must also be a "fostering of a respect for and appreciation of, traditional ways of life and culture, including language, in all their richness and variety". Perhaps most significantly, the constitution calls for "traditional villages and communities to remain as viable units of Papua New Guinean society, and for active steps to be taken to improve their cultural, economic and ethical quality". The main architect and leading ideologue of the constitution has put this in a way that echoes colonial statements of policy, the irony being that his intended thrust here and with the constitution is strongly anti-colonial:

In Papua New Guinea, most of us already have a good idea of the kind of values and the kind of society we want to build. We want to preserve our traditional family ties. We want to preserve the sense of group solidarity that exists in most of our societies. We want to preserve people's attachment to their land. . . . We want the chance to improve ourselves, to learn new ways of doing things—but within the framework of our traditional values. (Momis, 1973, p. 1)

The constitution directs that all persons and bodies are to be guided by the national goals and directive principles. But no provision is made for enforcing this, except that the Ombudsman Commission can inquire into a government policy that may be contrary to the goals and principles.

Before looking at particularly significant aspects of law and state in the post-colonial situation, it will help direct analysis to indicate that the aims and goals, to the extent that they call for fundamental change, remain unfulfilled. The most obvious explanation for this is that there is no reason why they should be fulfilled. The manifestly established thesis of neo-colonialism shows that elsewhere the attainment of the political kingdom and the espousal of populist notions are not enough to bring about fundamental change. The point should hardly need to be made were it not for the constant operative assertion that change is about politics and populism. Even in their inspiring terms, the aims and goals have proved conveniently vague and ambiguous on fundamental issues. Shortly after the aims were announced, the Prime Minister, in reassuring vein, could see "foreign investment" expanding none the less (*Post-Courier* 16 December, 1972). Little account was ever taken in government of the conflict between this stance and the aims of rapidly increasing the proportion of the economy under the control of nationals, of equality and of self-reliance. As for this last, arguably most basic aim of self-reliance, the conflict has been resolved in something close to absurdity in that ". . . the government now accepts that self-reliance means the achievement of fiscal self-reliance through the controlled inflow of foreign capital and through foreign aid" (Lepani, 1976, p. 11). Berry has considered the aim of increasing both the proportion of the economy under national control and the proportion of income going to nationals, as well as the aim of a more equal distribution of economic benefits (Berry, 1977). There are difficulties in evaluating these aims because of the dearth of relevant statistics. This is remarkable even by third world standards and is surely indicative of the lack of importance attached in practice to these aims. Berry does, however, gather cogent evidence strongly suggesting these aims are not being met. There are something like exceptions. With the rapid and dramatic 'localization' of the state bureaucracy from late 1972 onwards, there has doubtless been some increase in the proportion of income going to nationals. The government also reserves certain economic activities for nationals and this probably has an effect here. This has not been of great significance, however. As amongst nationals there has probably been an increase in economic inequality (ibid., p. 154). Berry also considers the aim of self-reliance and although there is a statistical scarcity here also it seems quite evident there has been no advance in achieving this aim. Further, it would appear from recent policy pronouncements that the government has abandoned even an aspiration to attain self-reliance (ibid., pp. 157 – 158). Rarely have the aims or goals in any aspect been reduced to concrete commitments the achievement of which could be readily assessed. Various subsequent plans, programmes, strategies, all so-called and like most such in the third world, avoid clear targets of performance. Concreteness and clarity of targets here would tend to confront the underlying exploitation that the aims and goals serve to obscure. For reasons already suggested, the aims and goals focused on the conservation of traditional social formations have been the subject of much explicit and purposive state action, as we shall see shortly. The aims' concern with the greater participation of women in economic and social activity is largely replicated in the constitution. Except for a very small and exceptionally talented presence in the upper regions of the state system, there would seem to be no change in the position of women and little is being done for such change through state action.

Briefly and crudely, the dominant internal class elements were interested basically in some purchase on an existing system that sustains them. They were not interested in radically changing it. The head of the National Planning Office finds there is a lack of "political will" for significant change and he remarks that "at the political level, most leaders are involved in business ventures whether as individual entrepreneurs and/or partnerships, (often with foreign investors) or as the 'managers' of rural groups based on village or clan affiliations" (Lepani, 1976, pp. 23 – 25). Intimate ties with the metropolitan bourgeoisie are formed in financial support for political parties, in some but as yet little bribery and in a variety of joint-venture enterprises with nationals including joint-ventures with the state and with members of the government and of the legislature. The state system is seen basically as an arena of economic advance within an existing and unquestioned structure of economy (see for example, Standish, n.d., p. 6; Stone, 1976, p. 530). Earlier mass mobilizations in political movements have all but disappeared. Anti-colonial and nationalist aspiration has found consumation in recent and very limited political and economic gains by elements of the national bourgeoisie. Former divisions between political parties have been erased. These divisions were, basically, between the more nationalistic who wanted some change and early self-government and, on the other hand, the more conservative who wanted neither. Now, splits and coalitions within and between political parties occur with a frequency and regard to convenience that ignores former differences. These differences were largely a matter of politicians and state operatives from the longer-colonized and educationally 'advanced' areas wanting self-government and people from recently colonized regions less further along in the educational stakes wanting the colonial era to persist so they could catch up and get a more proportionate share of representatives in the state system. When self-government and independence came, this difference was somewhat undercut and more fundamental similarities of interest came to the fore. It is only a slight exaggeration to say that political parties now have no policies, no programmes and close to no existence as political parties. Later waves of potential radicals, largely emerging through the main university, have been absorbed and contained in the rapid 'localization' of the public bureaucracy and in its further expansion by 20% between September 1972 and September 1976 (Ballard, 1976, p. 15). This and a massive state funding of cultural activity have served to blunt the once distinct making of a critical national intelligentsia. Like the national bourgeoisie generally, many senior state operatives are closely involved in business enterprises and large investments. There has so far been enough on offer to satisfy these senior state operatives and the small national bourgeoisie. There has not as yet been any strong conflict between these two—a conflict which in many other third world social formations has led to an expansion of state control of the economy.

The pervasive ideology shared by much of the bureaucratic bourgeoisie and the national bourgeoisie generally is that of 'bisnis'. The concept is somewhat complex (Ploeg, 1971; Sankoff, 1969). Basically, it is given content in its reflection of the economic activities of the immediate colonial oppressor, the petty element of the metropolitan bourgeoisie, the small-scale Australian or Chinese retailer, coffee buyer, planter and so on. Attitudes functional to the reproduction of the colonial structures have been readily borrowed from the former rulers. For example the first Papua New Guinea Minister for National Development, and a trade union leader as well, was quick to defend the quasi-indenture Highlands Labour Scheme saying that it had operated in favour of the workers and that it had protected many "unsophisticated workers from exploitation" (*Post-Courier*, 8 August, 1973). The first national Registrar of Co-operative Societies, in terms that distil the views of his colonial mentors, has taken the line, as we saw in Chapter 5, that co-operatives have not failed, rather "it has been just some people who have failed" and "there are ways and means of changing and correcting these weaknesses" (*Post-Courier*, 29 October 1973). Examples could be multiplied (see Oram, 1976a, pp. 170, 250). Allen has noted of the area he studied that national officials view the people in such colonial stereotypical terms as ignorant, backward, stubborn, unco-operative, lazy and so on and that the people find these officials just as arrogant and difficult to approach as their colonial counterparts were (Allen, 1979, pp. 59 – 60).

However, the state system is not simply taken over and maintained unchanged. Significant effects come from the influence of the traditional mode of production. With colonial rule, elements of or related to the traditional mode have only a small, thoroughly subordinated part and Papua New Guineans have no positions of significant political power. Now, parliamentarians and senior state operatives often represent traditional groupings in various ways. A parliamentarian will usually owe his or her election to the support of a particular, quite small ethnic grouping (Stone, 1976, pp. 534 – 536). Many parliamentarians and several senior state operatives head or are closely involved in ethnically based, 'development' groups whose interests they represent within the state system. Ethnically based relations of the patron – client type mentioned in Chapter 5 thus find a niche in the state system and serve as a base in the competition for benefits distributed by the state. There are now indications that ethnicity is an influential factor in the advance of officials within the public bureaucracy (see for example, Howlett *et al.*, 1976, p. 208).

This overview of contemporary political economy has been no more than an outline sketch. It will be filled in when describing and assessing major contemporary changes involving law and state, something to which we now turn. Constitutional change is first considered, then the changes concerned with metropolitan investment and next there are the changes dealing with land and with group enterprise. Before concluding the chapter, there is an account and evaluation of a wide variety of actual and proposed changes in law and state.

The independence Constitution of 1975 can unfortunately be dealt with rather briefly. It is more significant for what it does not contain than for what it does. The emphases, already described, on Papua New Guinea ways, personal liberation and decolonization combine in the ideological assertion of a distinctive identity and of self-respect—a not uncommon but none the less exciting phenomenon in the history of many third world social formations. In line with this assertion, the main debate in the drawing up of the constitution was over its citizenship provisions—crudely, over the extent to which former colonists should be allowed citizenship. The debate was prolonged, intense and even bitter, carrying, as it did, a heavy symbolical load. It had only a transitory significance, however, and, in retrospect, cannot be seen as anything but diversionary in effect. For example, the Constitutional Planning Committee showed an acute awareness of the impact of foreign investment and produced a well-worked basis for its control to be included in the constitution. This was rejected by the government with hardly any debate ensuing. One reason for this rejection was indicative, the reason being that such matters are not appropriate in constitutions. Perhaps the main point to make about the constitution and about the bulk of the proposals of the Constitutional Planning Committee is that they are just so unsurprisingly appropriate and ordinary, despite repeated claims of novelty and the intense debates that constitution-making engendered. Great emphasis was placed on the constitution's being 'home-grown' (Constitutional Planning Committee, 1974, p. 15/1). It was to be a beginning to that "fundamental re-orientation of our attitudes and the institutions of government . . . . towards Papua New Guinean forms" which the constitution itself called for. Yet the Constitutional Planning Committee also recognized that no amount of superstructural fiddling about would be relevant if "processes of true mass involvement are not undertaken by our people" and in this leaders must point the way (ibid., p. 2/14). But no institutions pertinent to this process are identified, with the dubious exception of provincial government, which is considered shortly and discounted on this score. To take an example of persistent ordinariness, the Constitutional Planning Committee, bolstered by expert consultants, recognized that Papua New Guinea has been exceptionally "dominated by its [public] bureaucracy" (ibid., p. 10/1). Yet the Committee's proposals for this body and the constitution's provisions are quite unremarkable. As another example, what the Committee and the constitution say about the armed forces and the police is also quite unremarkable, yet the attitudes and aspirations of members of the armed forces are disturbingly similar to those of their coup-loving counterparts in other areas of the third world, and the police force has on occasions acted in defiance of the government (Colebatch, 1974 and see for example, Sundhausen, 1973, p. 36). More generally, the constitution is no more than the culmination of a considerable period of colonial 'political development', in which the 'Westminster system' was implanted and in which the colonial administration shifted easily into the mould of a constitutionally powerful public bureaucracy of the Australian type (Bayne and Colebatch, 1973; Leibowitz, 1976). The constitution enshrines the Westminster system without any change, except for a small degree of entrenchment which requires a variety of special majorities in the legislature for constitutional change, and except also for having a part dealing with human rights. (The former type of exception is, however, quite common in British colonial legislatures and the latter is quite common in the independence constitutions of former British colonies.)

There were features of the constitution and its making seen by its creators as specifically unusual especially in their often being grounded in Papua New Guinea ways. These ways were to be directly incorporated by giving 'custom' a more potent role in the national legal system (something considered later) or incorporated indirectly by using standard constitutional forms somehow in conformity with these ways. Unusual features of this latter, indirect type shared a convincing element, that is, the mistrust of political power. The Constitutional Planning Committee was dominated by members who were suspicious in some ways of the government and also more radical and nationalistic than the government. Some of the Committee's proposals for diluting the government's power would have empowered positions that certain members of the Committee could reasonably anticipate filling. The Australian influence on the government was exerted in favour of a strong central government partly because of fears that the country was prone to ethnic fragmentation. It is probable the government did not need this influence as its own opposition to the proposals was spontaneous enough. Generally the government and the Australian influence won out. So, the Constitutional Planning Committee envisaged a constitution in which political power was, in line with Papua New Guinea ways, diffused and constrained. It proposed a system of very powerful parliamentary committees. It proposed that important constitutional and executive decisions normally made by a prime minister or head of state were to be spread among several political offices and often made jointly by several holders of such offices. It proposed that there be no head of state. None of these innovations found any significant part in the constitution. In a similar vein but more conventionally an Ombudsman Commission was proposed and included in the constitution. Other proposals relevant here, for a leadership code and for a system of provincial government, proved more enduringly controversial and deserve a more detailed account.

The less important can be considered briefly. The Constitutional Planning Committee proposed a leadership code heavily inspired by those of Tanzania and Zambia. It was to cover a wide range of elected leaders, state operatives and public office holders. The Committee was concerned with the problem of corruption and, more generally, with ensuring that the private interest was not put before the public. The Committee also felt, quite reasonably, that the national goals would be jeopardized by leaders' "accumulating personal wealth, by collaborating with foreign or national businessmen or by accepting bribes" (Constitutional Planning Committee, 1974, p. 3/2). The Committee proposed restricting leaders' financial interests to a narrow range of investments, proposed a broad disclosure requirement and, for certain leaders, a superannuation scheme. In their general thrust these proposals were clearly at odds with the structure and ethos of post-colonial political power just briefly described. They proved controversial from the outset. It was not until 1978 that the government introduced a bill which, broadly, incorporated these proposals. A minority in government were by then becoming alarmed at growing corruption and the effects of leaders' involvement in business. Concern was expressed about the country becoming "a second Kenya". The immediate pressure for the bill came from certain senior state operatives whose investment activities the Prime Minister had already and informally curtailed. Apparently in an effort to gather support for the bill, the Prime Minister staked his premiership on its not being rejected by the legislature. Then the bill was withdrawn as a result of uncertainties over what type of parliamentary majority the atrociously drafted constitution required for its enactment and over the extent of parliamentary support it would command in any case.

The story of provincial government is a longer and even more illuminating one. The Constitutional Planning Committee's views and proposals provide a penetrating account of the issues involved. This blend of the idealistic and the practical proposed 19 or 20 elected provincial legislatures and executive governments as "opportunities . . . for our people to participate meaningfully in those aspects of government that directly concern them" for "power must be returned to the people . . . power must be decentralized'' (ibid., p. 10/1). In a more practical vein, the Committee noted that there was strong support and strong pressures for some form of provincial government but it also considered ''that the present fragile form of unity in our country'' must not be endangered—''nation-building'' and ''the maintenance of a unitary-state'' were prerequisite (ibid., pp. 10/2 – 3). Hence it rejected proposals for federalism and for a few, large, subordinate governments, saying:

> We are basically doubtful of any theory that fails to take full account of the diversity of our country at the local level. We distrust any attempt to employ a limited unity to divide us. The experience of a number of recently independent states, including Nigeria, should serve as a warning of the dangers attendant upon the establishment of a small number of large, politically powerful regions, in which ethnic sentiments serve as a basis for regional unity and deep national division. (ibid., p. 10/3)

and:

> The diversity of our country is one of its greatest strengths. We are fortunate that Papua New Guinea does not have large ethnic groups competing for power at the national level, and that our cultural heritage is nonetheless so rich and varied. We must ensure that our Constitution recognizes the value of our diverse national heritage, and fosters its development. We must not allow a dull uniformity to be imposed upon our people in the name of unity. (ibid., p. 10/4)

Provincial governments were to be small, subordinate to central government and have limited powers. They were to be founded on the colonial division of the country into small districts:

> The people of an increasing number of districts are becoming ever more conscious of the interests and problems that they share. The district is more than a simple administrative unit. It is, in fact, an important political unit with much of the administrative infrastructure necessary for further political development. It is also a known quantity: it poses no new problems of identity. (ibid., p. 10/4)

The ironic aptness of these views and proposals for the continuing maintenance of ethnic diversity need not, I hope, be elaborated on by now.

In the post-colonial situation there is certainly considerable impetus for some type of decentralized government and a heightened need to deal with ''the present fragile form of unity in our country''. Right from the start of its life in 1972, the first national government was confronted with an inherited political crisis on the Gazelle Peninsula—the area of the longest and perhaps the most intense capitalist penetration. This entailed strong demands for some autonomy and led, in the Gazelle Peninsula Affairs (Temporary Provisions) Act of 1973, to constitutional-type measures giving some recognition and formal powers to the large groupings involved. Several movements emerged subsequently in various parts of the country proposing or demanding varying degrees of political autonomy. By far the most influential was a disorganized but vigorously assertive and popularly supported secessionist movement in the Bougainville district—the site of the large copper mine referred to earlier. This movement was placated with a form of financially well-endowed provincial government in 1976. About this time, and as an agreed part of the Bougainville settlement, the government was preparing the constitutional framework under which provincial government throughout the country was shortly to be set up. This was much in line with the Constitutional Planning Committee's proposals despite the initial rejection by the government of provincial government on the ground that it would be too costly. Indeed, members of the government were, throughout, most reluctant to countenance provincial government, and it only emerged potently as a compromise advocated by a few more moderate members in the face of most members' wish for strong measures to quell the Bougainville secession. Once provided for, however, provincial government made rapid headway and there are now several fully-fledged governments and the setting up of the others is in train. The division of powers between the provinces and the centre is complex but the provinces, although having little actual power, do have great potential power if they choose to use it by legislating in certain areas. This potential power is held concurrently with the centre so in this way the balance between the centre and the provinces is yet to be fought out in detail. Also, the provinces do have considerable and entrenched financial autonomy.

Barnett sees three groups interested in the promotion of provincial government (Barnett, in press). One comprises the remaining colonial settlers who wish to establish protective links with conservative, local-level leaders and attenuate the influence of central government. Of more significance is the second group, one of big peasants seeking to further their interests in access to the political power and material largesse provided by provincial government. The third group comprise relatively young and formally highly-educated people who, either from choice or a lack of acceptable openings in the public bureaucracy, live in their rural home areas. These often take a leading part in 'development' movements of various kinds. Barnett sees this group as likely to come into conflict with the big peasants. However these younger people are often themselves in line for traditional positions of power and often work closely with big peasants. From this one would not readily conclude that provincial government was providing "opportunities . . for our people to participate meaningfully in those aspects of government that directly concern them" nor that power is being "returned to the people" (Constitutional Planning Committee, 1974, p. 10/1). Standish sees the ideal of popular participation as not being met. On the contrary, the early indications as he sees them show that provincial government is dominated by big men and big peasants responsive only to their own small ethnic groupings and promoting nepotism in recruitment on the executive side (Standish, 1978b). Barnett notes that provincial government is providing a "secure political expression" for "the economic base . . . [of] the rural business class" (Barnett, in press). Ghai considers it "a high probability . . . that power at the provincial level may be seized by a coalition of an emerging petty-bourgeoisie [meaning a bureaucratic bourgeoisie, probably—P.F.] and a petty kulak class" (Ghai, in press). He argues that innovations and the "political momentum of decentralization" have been contained in part in the uncertainties and complexities created by the legal and legalistic structuring of provincial government (ibid.). Generally then, it seems clear that provincial government is a legal/constitutional form which incorporates traditional and variant patron–client structures within the state system. I will return to that theme looking at laws relating to land and to group enterprise.

The law on metropolitan investment raises another central theme, that of the relation between the state together with those national class elements closely tied to it and the metropolitan bourgeoisie. Firstly, I would like to recap the internal presence of metropolitan capital and describe the laws seeking to regulate it. I will then provide an evaluation of those laws in operation. Although these laws present an assertive, restraining response to metropolitan investment, an examination of the laws in operation shows this response to be weak and little more than a matter of appearance. Explanations for this contradiction are then offered.

The most significant area of metropolitan investment now is in natural resource extraction, mainly in copper but with considerable investment in timber and tuna fishing. There are prospects for oil extraction and there is a proposed large project for the export as well as local use of hydro-electric power. The metropolitan presence in export agriculture remains dominant over the national. Generally, the Papua New Guinea economy remains subordinately complementary to the needs of the metropolitan economies. By and large other areas of capitalist enterprise in Papua New Guinea supplement natural resource extraction and export agriculture. Metropolitan capital is dominant in these areas, as in commerce and the provision of services. Secondary industry has a small presence only. In producing for export such industry involves only the initial processing of natural resources or cash crops or involves simple manufactures based on these. Production for the small local market is confined largely to the most basic assembly of imported parts and to some small-scale manufacturing of food-stuffs and building materials. Overall, the National Investment and Development Authority considers that "foreign investment constitutes an estimated eighty per cent or more of the private sector" (as quoted in Donaldson and Turner, 1978, p. 8; see also National Investment and Development Authority, 1977).

In the key areas of mining, timber extraction and fishing, the first national government inherited legislation giving it broad discretionary control over the conditions on which these resources can be extracted. Similar legislation dealing with petroleum exploration and extraction has been enacted more recently. The government also inherited broad, discretionary legal powers over exchange control, export prices and tax evasion. The first national government introduced standard regulatory regimes covering banking and insurance. It also suspended the operation of the legislation giving "incentives to pioneer industries", in the face of strong evidence that similar incentives were not effective in attracting foreign investment in other third world countries. The most significant legal change came with the renegotiation of the Bougainville copper agreement in 1976. The report of an influential advisory mission considered the first agreement to be overwhelmingly in favour of the company (Overseas Development Group, 1973, pp. 68 – 69). With the boom in copper prices the company had made enormously provocative profits in 1973. It is probable that the Australian government was willing to see more of this surplus going to the Papua New Guinea state as this would help ease the former's heavy aid commitment. The company initially postured in terms of 'a deal is a deal' (Post-Courier, 6 February, 1974), but the renegotiation was smooth and amicable. The basis of the new terms was that returns to the state would be increased through higher rates of tax on 'windfall' profits. The government did not seek a greater share in the ownership of the venture beyond its 20% holding, this aspect of the new terms being in opposition to strong nationalist pressures for a majority holding by the government in the mining company and "in any major mining venture" (see Momis, 1973, p. 6). In the year of the renegotiation returns to the state increased almost threefold. In the following year this gain was eliminated with the slump in copper prices. This approach based on increasing returns to the state as revenue has been generalized as policy for future mining and petroleum agreements. The metropolitan enterprise is "entitled to a fair rate of return" but through taxation the state is to get "the lion's share of windfall gains" (Lepani, 1976, p. 12). The government's resolve here was dramatically demonstrated in 1975, when Kennecott's licence under the mining legislation to develop the large Ok Tedi copper deposit in the Star Mountains was not renewed, mainly because Kennecott insisted on a rate of return beyond what the government's new policy would accommodate. In 1976 the government entered into a more acceptable agreement with a consortium in place of Kennecott. There is some further evidence of the government's general resolve in its termination in 1976 of an agreement with the subsidiary of a Japanese corporation for the development of large palm oil estates after the subsidiary had repeatedly broken the agreement (Utrecht, 1977, pp. 40 – 41, 66 – 67).

With the National Investment and Development Act of 1974, the state obtained broad, discretionary controls in the regulation of metropolitan investment generally. The Act was, in an immediate sense, the response to radical elements within the state system who wanted a restrictive and highly controlled approach to foreign investment. The influence of these elements became most explicit in the Constitutional Planning Committee's proposals for an investment code in the constitution which the government rejected. Nevertheless, something of this restrictive approach found its way into the directive principles of the constitution where they call for national domination of the economy, the strict control of foreign investment and the rejection of any such investment that imperils self-reliance. The radical sentiments sprang from a mixture of nationalist idealism and a hard-headed desire to create space for greater national involvement in the capitalist economy. The National Investment and Development Act was a compromise between these pressures and the more conservative elements within the state system, who tended unreservedly to look on metropolitan investment as a boon to be encouraged and appreciated. I will look at the making of the legislation in a little more detail later. Generally, the legislation reflected this underlying conflict directly in that its explicit purposes included the promotion as well as the control of foreign investment. A National Investment and Development Authority (NIDA) was set up to perform both these tasks. Under the act no 'foreign enterprise' (broadly defined) can carry on business in Papua New Guinea without registering with NIDA. Such registration can entail the imposition of terms and restrictions on the enterprise's operations in Papua New Guinea. A "National Investment Priorities Schedule" is, in terms of the Act, to be drawn up and then revised every year by the government. This schedule marks out certain areas, including natural resource extraction, where metropolitan investment will be encouraged; others where it is neutrally permitted; and others where it is restricted or not allowed. In drawing up this priorities schedule and in the administration of the Act generally regard is to be had to an extensive list of 'investment guidelines' laid down in Schedule 1 to the Act. These entail, mainly, the promotion of various internal linkages in the use of local resources and processing, the encouragement of related enterprises controlled by nationals, the employment of nationals and the formation of joint-ventures with them. The guidelines also include a strong emphasis on the acquisition of shares in resident metropolitan enterprises by the state and by nationals. With enterprises of natural resource extraction, this involvement "should normally be as great as practicable". Further and generally, "provision should normally be made for control of foreign enterprises to be transferred to Papua New Guinean hands". On the other hand, the Act, like many laws in the third world aimed at promoting metropolitan investment, does contain "investment guarantees" in Schedule 5, but the guarantees are hardly of the abject type usually found in these laws. Such laws were products of times when foreign investment was looked on as a pure good. The Papua New Guinean legislation came at a time when dependency theory and the view that foreign investment had some ill-effects were commonplace. A similar general influence came from more recent and more stringent laws such as the Andean Foreign Investment Code. So, the guarantee against nationalization or expropriation is weak in that it does not apply when there is "payment of compensation as defined by law" meaning such compensation as determined by law at any time or for any case. There is a 'right' to remit profits and payments of loan principal and interest as well as to repatriate capital, but all this is "subject to any laws relating to taxation and exchange control" and so the effectiveness of the 'guarantee' is again quite undercut.

In all, the state is endowed with a comprehensive and potent set of broad legal controls over metropolitan investment. The operation of these will now be evaluated, both generally, and by looking at examples of particular types of enterprise and particular laws. The evaluation ends with a partly descriptive and partly interpretative account of the persistence of bourgeois legality in despite of and in the midst of the form of broad, discretionary legal control.

The nationalist pressure for a stringent approach to metropolitan investment and the resulting and, in ways, remarkable legal responses found some general acceptance because of illusions of comparative plenty. With enterprises of natural resource extraction yielding considerable revenue, with the boom resulting from the construction phase of the Bougainville mine, and with continuing, high levels of 'aid' from Australia, many within the state system no longer perceived further metropolitan investment as an overwhelming necessity. As copper and timber prices dropped so did the resistance to unimpeded metropolitan investment. This resistance had no substantial basis, since further metropolitan investment did not affect the small national bourgeoisie in any immediately adverse way. Plenty of room continued to be found to accommodate the national bourgeoisie in the state-assisted acquisition of the enterprises of departing colonists, in joint ventures with the metropolitan bourgeoisie and in continuing promotion through state grants, loans and extension services. There was never a sustained or fundamental questioning of the desirability or necessity of metropolitan investment. Occasionally, prominent nationalists called for a rejection of capitalism and the working out of an alternative economy (see for example, Kaputin and Momis, 1974, p. 2). Such calls must now appear close to perfunctory in that nationalists continued to operate intimately within the capitalist economy. Papua New Guinea ways were advocated but without facing the conflicts and compatibilities between them and capitalism. These ways provided a transcendent path, a unique solution that seemed to make such issues irrelevant or subordinate.

It is hardly any surprise that law and state in their actual operation reflected the continued dominance of metropolitan capital. The legal measures to check and control it were there. The purpose and direction of the controls were clearly indicated in law, but the operative means were and are close to absent. Since the policy on natural resource extraction emphasizes returns to the state through revenue (and since only a small fraction of this revenue takes the form of royalties) taxation law provides a crucial example to begin with. This is the Income Tax Act of 1959—there is no tax on capital gains. This law is very close to its Australian counter-part, which is notorious for the breadth of the power it confers on officials to counter tax evasion. Yet the anti-avoidance measure relating to "businesses controlled abroad" has been used only once. An interview in 1972 with the chief official in charge of taxation (an Australian) indicated why this is so. In the context of discussing transfer pricing, which is the pricing of transfers of goods and services between related enterprises often as part of the evasion of tax and other laws, the official said that transfer pricing was no problem since the corporate tax rate in Papua New Guinea was so low that the metropolitan investors would not use such pricing to evade tax. This argument depends on the operation of tax law, and tax credits in particular, in the countries to which profits were remitted, a matter on which the official was ignorant except for the Australian situa-tion. The high tax rates on certain 'windfall profits' would now undercut this argument even in its own terms. Quite apart from these points, however, there are many other reasons besides tax evasion for using transfer pricing, and a use for any of these reasons could lead incidentally but just as effectively to tax evasion. In recent years the corporate tax rate has increased to more substantial if not onerous levels and with the law providing "incentives to pioneer industries" no longer being applied, tax holidays for metropolitan investors no longer operate. Although this appears to represent a more stringent approach to metropolitan investors, tax law leaves them with many consolations especially in a generous range of allowances against income for depreciation, past losses and certain capital expenditure. Donaldson and Turner find that "of the total number of registered companies in 1972/3 [few of which would be controlled by nationals—P.F.], only 1,125, that is 30·5 per cent of them, actually pay tax" (Donaldson and Turner, 1978, p. 24). Exchange control law is a simpler matter. It contains wide powers but they are rarely exercised mainly because of the government's policy of free trade and an avowedly 'liberal' approach to exchange control. The outcome of one attempt at direct control of metropolitan interests is perhaps instructive. A forceful Minister had, in 1974, set up a Commission of Enquiry into the Standard-ization of Selected Imports. An important part of its work was the devising of schemes of import rationalization and import substitution. In early 1976 the government affirmed the policy of free trade and rejected the Commission's extensive proposals because implementing them would harm Papua New Guinea's "traditional trading partners", that is, Australia in particular.

Turning to the legal regulation of particular types of enterprises provides no relief. Copper is something of an exception it seems, not because the state uses its wide powers very effectively, but because significant evasion is probably difficult given the fixed location of the mine and the presence of an open world market. There are several other ways of evading the legal controls which are not caught by these points, but I have not studied the matter and of course it is difficult to do so. More certain points can be made about tuna fishing, where the law's broad controls are almost an irrelevance. In 1971 the outgoing colonial administration entered into a series of agreements with Japanese and United States companies that were soon to make the waters around Papua New Guinea the world's third largest source of skipjack tuna. In 1972, after the election of the first national government, the parliamentary opposition objected to the agreements. One objection is only of passing interest: the opposition was against entering into agreements with the Japanese because of the xenophobia of its Australian mentors. The other objection was more substantial. The opposition pointed out that at about the same time as these agreements were concluded, the British had negotiated a comparable but more beneficial agreement for their nearby British Solomon Islands colony. The government rushed to the defence of the agreements but in doing so took the trouble to compare them with the Solomon agreement. It proved to be a different type of agreement, one that required little direct checking-on or enforcement, as befitted the weak capacity of the small Solomon Islands. The government could and did argue that the Papua New Guinea agreements were more favourable if they were adequately enforced. That settled the immediate matter, but the agreements were indeed heavily dependent on extensive supervision and enforcement. Papua New Guinea was and remains grossly deficient in the means of adequate enforcement, not least in the ships and planes needed. Despite occasional avowals by Ministers that enforcement is about to improve, it is notorious that the fishing corporations have to tolerate very little official hinderance. The government has also had considerable, if not as great, difficulty in controlling timber operations. The example of timber can be used to illustrate another significant problem. Timber agreements are largely founded on a market price, yet the market has a tendency to be closed and the price to be subject to manipulation by the timber corporations. The government has been quick to appreciate these difficulties but it fetters its response to them in the search for some comparable 'free' market price; a fetter which will be elaborated on more generally.

The explicit boldness of the National Investment and Development Act of 1974 provides a sharp contrast to its operation. Conflicts in the making of the legislation in 1973 provided strong pointers to its ultimate effect. Proposals from more radical politicians and state operatives for the legislation to contain stricter controls were partly rejected and partly diverted into the scheduled guidelines that metropolitan investors should, ideally, be made to comply with. One reason why there are so many guidelines is that they were greatly expanded in the making of the Act to accommodate the pressures of various radical elements. Concerning enforcement of the Act, there were two significant incidents in its creation. The Minister of Justice objected to the National Investment and Development Authority (NIDA) having the functions both of enforcing the controls in the Act and of promoting metropolitan investment. He suggested there was a risk of the agency's becoming a 'captive' of the interests it was to promote. To this the Minister in charge of the bill replied indignantly saying that the probity of state operatives could be relied on to obviate this difficulty. The other incident was the ready defeat of proposals that, because of the enormous problems in checking on and controlling metropolitan investors, the information-gathering and enforcement functions of the many government departments involved in this should be consolidated and given to NIDA. Operatives in these departments felt they were performing these functions adequately and that the proposals were irrelevant. Within less than two years after its birth NIDA adopted the view that its "regulatory phase" was now over and that it would concentrate mainly on the promotion of metropolitan investment. This change followed on the slump in the copper and timber prices which led, in terms of perceptions fostered within government, to a desperate need for more metropolitan investment so as to achieve "fiscal self-reliance". The "regulatory phase" itself consisted of little more than the collection of largely unprocessed information provided by metropolitan investors, as the Act required. Consistently enough, the investment priorities schedule has been timorous in the extreme in reserving economic activities for nationals.

Even on its face, this National Investment and Development Act in critical instances treats metropolitan investors with great delicacy or fails to provide adequately for its own enforcement. Hence, in terms of the Act, the investment guidelines are to be applied only "as and when appropriate". The Act says also, "for the avoidance of doubt", that the investment priorities schedule itself involves no element of "compulsion". These guidelines and the priorities schedule can, but need not, be used as a basis for imposing conditions on the registration of metropolitan enter-prises. Failure to comply with the conditions means that NIDA can report on this to the responsible Minister who refers that matter to Cabinet for a decision as to whether registration should be cancelled. In a similar vein, certain agreements involving payment in foreign exchange must be approved by the Minister or, if he so wishes, by Cabinet. These referrals to Cabinet indicate, of course, that disapprovals of such agreements or the cancellations of registrations are to be quite exceptional.

Underlying and informing these various deficiencies in the legal response to metropolitan investment is a subtle and pervasive view of law and state—a view grounded in bourgeois legality. Law does take more interventionist, discretionary, controlling forms in mediating between the metropolitan bourgeoisie and the national. We have just seen some examples. Bourgeois legality continues, however, as with the colonial period, to typify legal relations between and affecting the bourgeoisie. The significance of this in the dominance of the metropolitan bourgeoisie has already been illustrated in that part of Chapter Seven which deals with legal standards affecting production. A few, perhaps less obvious, themes from the present context can be briefly developed to support the link betwen bourgeois legality and the dominance of the metropolitan bourgeoisie. So, in the example of timber just mentioned, as well as with numerous others, price is determined by reference to a market price. Even with these laws giving officials broad, discretionary power to determine price in a trans-action, they tend to fall back on such narrower standards as ''arm's length price'' or ''market value'', standards not only more conformable to bourgeois legality but also tied to its basis of commodity exchange. In other words, even when their power is in broad, discretionary form, officials often relate their decisions to the market rather than to, say, the best price that could be determined in the interests of Papua New Guinea. That is, with these formulas and approaches the general and underlying assumption is that price in most cases will be determined by the market and law need only intervene to correct the occasional deviant case by reference to the market price: law supplements the market. Yet for many exchanges between affiliated enterprises there will be no comparable market price. In this situation 'price' becomes very much a dependent and manipulable element in the international voyages of surplus value. Quite apart from this, there remains the question of price 'distortions' in the market which can be reflected immediately in the formulas. Indeed, it may be argued that the predominant dynamic of the world economic system is increasingly monopolistic in its effect so that, in relying on a price determined within that system, the state will often be directly subordinating its interests to the monopoly power of metropolitan enterprises. Somewhat more particularly, it can be argued that the world economic system inherently discriminates against third world countries and that this discrimination will be reflected in 'price' even in a 'free' market. Further, bourgeois legality sees the state and law as being 'above' the legal subject. The legal subject or 'the individual' must even be protected by law from the powerful state. For bourgeois legality, the metropolitan enterprise is a legal subject 'equal' with any other. But bourgeois legality cannot reflect agglomerations of corporate power. More specifically, it is a truism that many metropolitan enterprises are more powerful economically than many third world countries. Indeed, some have been not unfairly called 'branch countries', so dependent are they on metropolitan enterprises for their very existence and identity. At the very least metropolitan enterprises, as legal subjects, are qualitatively different from domestic legal actors, in that they have considerable room to manoeuvre in the international arena, and so pose great and often insuperable problems for a third world state that seeks to control them. Faced with an often 'overmighty subject' in the metropolitan enterprise, the Papua New Guinea state, like many in the third world, limits its response not only in legal formulas of the 'market' variety but also in legal presumptions often meant to protect the weak legal subject against state power. So the state usually has the 'burden of proof' in any prosecution or other legal case it initiates against a metropolitan enterprise. Courts will 'read down' or 'strictly construe' laws under which the state 'interferes' with the 'rights' of the legal subject, such as tax laws. This approach also influences official behaviour in applying the law since the courts will usually be its ultimate interpreters. A related point is that in treating the metropolitan enterprise like any other legal subject, the state weakens its capacity in organizational fragmentation among such disparate legal-administrative categories as the regulation of natural resource extraction, company law, taxation law and exchange control. Faced with a powerful metropolitan enterprise mere efficiency would dictate that the state concentrate its technical enforcement and bargaining strengths and knowledge and not have them scattered, as now, over such legal-administrative categories. The need for 'co-ordination' in this is frequently stressed and invariably ignored. We have seen that proposals for this concentration of the state's capacity in NIDA were rejected by the departments already having these diffused powers.

What is perhaps even more important in the influence of bourgeois legality is that law is given the job of finally determining disputed issues yet only some issues are recognized as being so determinable. The point is obvious but I feel it is worth illustrating here. With bourgeois legality a worker, for example, is considered a legal subject equal to the metropolitan enterprise which employs him. The 'free' contract between them is definitive of their relation. It cannot legally be 'reopened' even if the employer derives a windfall surplus or it is discovered the employer has been maintaining an appearance of low or no profitability through transfer pricing and this appearance has been used to justify depressing wages. 'A deal is a deal'. The same applies to relations between the metropolitan bourgeoisie and the national. Thus in the post-colonial period, joint ventures combining these elements of the bourgeoisie become common. Frequently the metropolitan shareholder in the joint venture corporation contributes as share capital the assets of an existing enterprise and/or other non-monetary inputs. Overpricing such share contributions discriminates against the national shareholders who have given (more) adequate value for their shares, since the metropolitan shareholder will be draining off capital related profits at their expense. Legally, however, the price for the capital contribution is determined by the contract to supply it—a contract between the metropolitan shareholder and the joint-venture corporation, the latter often being effectively controlled by the metropolitan shareholder. Since, in line with the bourgeois legality, the law has no concern with the substantive fairness of contractual terms, courts will normally not disturb this price. As protection for the national shareholder there is an easily avoided and marginally relevant provision of the Companies Act, and some tenuous common law protection (Gower, 1969, pp. 106 – 107, this description of English law being applicable to the Papua New Guinea situation). National shareholders will not usually, in terms of the law, even have access to information about their joint venture partners. In company law the most that is required is that accounts of the locally incorporated subsidiary, but not of the metropolitan parent enterprise, are subject to disclosure and to company law standards about the content and accuracy of accounts. There is a patent inconsistency here in that company law requires a locally registered parent and subsidiary to file a form of group accounts because such disclosure is considered necessary to give an adequate picture of the operations of any corporation within a group. On putting this inconsistency to officials of the Companies Registry the unadventurous but sound response was that the scale and structure of metropolitan enterprise is usually such as to take any comprehensive accounting and disclosure requirements well beyond their administrative capacity. All of this may be to overlabour the point. Bourgeois legality obviously leaves the capitalist with power to dispose of the surplus, some capitalists will have more power in this than others and it should not be surprising that in countering this situation the law should be absent or inadequate.

In ending this section there does remain something of a conundrum: why does the law relating to the regulation of foreign investment, although so understandably ineffectual in operation, assume such a potent appearance? I would suggest three explanations. First, in the process of decolonization nationalist opposition is sometimes directed against metropolitan investment. Since this opposition is superficial, forms of control can serve to placate it. For example, the incorporation of radical proposals in the investment guidelines in the National Investment and Development Act helped meet many nationalist objections to metropolitan investment. Another explanation concerns legitimizing the place of new national class elements especially in their clustering around the state. The dominant national class elements, especially the bureaucratic bourgeoisie, find legitimation in related ideologies of development, of planning and of authenticity in such as the purported reliance on 'Papua New Guinea ways'. For development and planning, the new state must give an appearance of being grasped or even in charge of the overall situation, including the presence of the metropolitan bourgeoisie. Similarly, authenticity requires the assertion that metropolitan penetration can be controlled and subsumed to a distinct national or ethnic identity. To continue with the investment guidelines as the example, these are absolutely premised on the ability of the state to control metropolitan investment. As for authenticity, the guidelines require that "every effort should be made to conserve the environment", that "the essential relation between the spiritual integrity of the people and their physical surroundings should be scrupulously respected" and "foreign enterprises should not endanger Papua New Guinea's national sovereignty". In this the guidelines take up themes more fully developed in the constitution. A final and a somewhat perverse explanation is that laws seeming to regulate metropolitan investment serve to justify the ways of the metropolitan bourgeoisie in the post-colonial situation. The point, simply, is that if the metropolitan bourgeoisie is seen to be controlled and subordinated to the needs of development and so on, their presence is made acceptable. As a general concluding point, the ineffectualness of the broad, discretionary form of control leaves bourgeois legality predominant in regulating the relations of the bourgeoisie and predominant in its facility of favouring those already most favoured, the metropolitan bourgeoisie

The next area of major change or proposed change in law and state, that relating to land, can be dealt with much more briefly. The land issue provided what was, at the national level, the first great signal for revolt. In 1971 the colonial administration introduced a comprehensive set of land bills into the legislature. These were heavily influenced by the Kenyan experience (Bredmeyer, 1973, pp. 12 – 15). They sought to facilitate the registration of land, lessen controls on dealings in land and give control to local-level land boards, which would have been eminently susceptible of capture by the big peasantry. The bills, if enacted, would have strongly tended to the more effective individualization of land tenure and to the making of a commodity of land. The bills were withdrawn after considerable criticism both within and without the legislature, one of the main strands to the criticism being the detrimental effect the bills would have on the integrity of traditional social formations (Ward, 1972).

As the result a Commission of Enquiry on the land question was set up in 1973 by the first national government. The Commission's fascinating report seemed to reflect closely popular opinion gathered at hundreds of interviews and meetings all over the country (Commission of Enquiry into Land Matters, 1973). The Commission saw its proposed legal regime as a "building on a customary base". The "basic social structure of the people" was to be maintained and the Commission was concerned not to recommend "either collective or individualistic extremes". This approach was specifically pitted against the creation of landlessness and of the class divisions characteristic of capitalism (ibid., pp. 12 – 13). Hence the Commission was against simple individualization and in line with this the government suspended the operation of the limping Land (Tenure Conversion) Act. But the Commission also rightly considered that with cash cropping there is a greater tendency towards the creation of individual rights in customary land. It also considered that "customary groups are not very successful commercially"—the word "commercially" never being elaborated on, but meaning that capitalist criteria were aptly imported to dismiss collective production from consideration (ibid., p. 18). 'Extremes' were avoided in a fitting compromise, the fundamental aspect of which was that:

> Customary land should not be registered as full freeholds. The basic
> pattern of registration should be to register group titles, and make

provision for the registered group to grant rights of use in the form of
registered occupation rights, leases and other subsidiary rights to
individuals or sub-groups wishing to use land. (ibid., p. 27)

Individuals were envisaged as by far the main holders of occupation rights
and leases. These could be inheritable. Disposal of rights to people outside
the group would rarely be allowable. Dealing in land generally was to be
subject to restrictive and complex legal regulation. The Commission's
recommendations on the settlement of land disputes led to the Land
Disputes Settlement Act of 1975 under which land mediators, who would
usually be local-level leaders, attempt to mediate a settlement. Failing this
the dispute is referred to a specialist land court. To allow adjudicative
settlement through local leaders would give too much power to the big
peasantry over the basic means of production. Hence the village court does
not have jurisdiction over land matters. A matter to which the Commission gave particular emphasis was the return of "alienated land", an
issue that had generated much protest against the colonist. As a result of
the Commission's recommendations, the government has had enacted the
Lands Acquisition Act of 1974, under which, broadly, the government
could on payment of compensation take over land owned by foreigners.
This was part of a "plantations acquisition scheme" under which the
government in various ways assists traditional groupings to acquire
foreign owned plantations. There was much popular support for such a
scheme (ibid., p. 13). Conveniently, there were many plantation owners
wishing to sell. The scheme and the Act have not, however, led to the
large scale return of alienated land. A long hope that the Australian
government would make up for colonial depradation in grants for compensation on the acquisition of plantations did not materialize. To the extent
that foreign-owned plantations have been acquired, the people have got at
best dubious bargains (Gordon, 1976).

There is little that need be said by way of a more general evaluation of
these changes, proposed and performed. The Commission's recommendations appeared in an immediate way as a nationalist blow against colonial
designs and as a practical affirmation of Papua New Guinea ways. But the
earlier description of the peasantry in Chapter Five throws a different light
on the matter. For the mass of the peasantry the changes can be seen
basically as bringing law into line with economy, with the combination of
group and individual elements in the peasant's relation to land. For most of
the country, the Commission recognizes, the new system of registration
will not be needed, or not as yet, for traditional regulation remains

adequate (ibid., p. 22). However, the defining effect of registration and specified means of dispute settlement are now needed to regulate peasant tenure in some few areas where cash cropping and generally greater agricultural intensity place strains on traditional regulation. The changes are also consistent with more vintage colonial land policy and practice, aimed at the conservation of the traditional mode of production. With the postcolonial period the relations of production remain the same and at the political level a fragile state finds itself in just as weak a position as the colonial state. These factors and continued economic stresses on the integrity of the traditional mode mean that law and state still play a central part in its conservation. One source of such stresses is the emergence of a big peasantry and aspirant rural bourgeoisie. They provide some pressures for greater individualization of land tenure and for an effective tenure conversion system (Donaldson and Good, 1978, p. 11). These pressures have led to the occasional use of the Land Disputes Settlement Act to secure something like a tenure conversion. A fictitious dispute is created and the parties agree to a settlement of it which settlement can then, as provided in the Act, be recorded and given the effect of a court order (Ward, 1978, p. 19). The Commission of Enquiry is itself not very clear on the specifics of containing the big peasantry, except for a general and quite unrealistic recommendation restricting the amount of land that can be held by any one person (Commission of Enquiry into Land Matters, 1973, p. 42). The Commission does not seem to take account of the big peasants' power within the 'customary' setting. The big peasant could well dominate decision making in the operation of group titles, and obtain a large amount of land under a strong derivative title. The conflicting aspects of the relation between the big peasant and the conversation of the traditional mode remain, therefore, unresolved in the Commission's scheme of things. This absence reflects a division between the commissioners, most of whom were sympathetic to the big peasants, but an effective minority put predominant emphasis on the conservation of the traditional mode. General legislation broadly giving effect to the Commission's recommendations has only recently been introduced into parliament for consideration and its final form was not settled at the time of my last enquiry in early 1979 but it seemed the legislation may give more scope to individual rights than the Commission recommended.

The conflicts and the compatibilities between the big peasantry and the conservation of the traditional mode are basic to post-colonial law and state affecting group economic enterprise. Bohannan has presented a brief rhapsody to the legal form of the joint-stock company in its ability to combine the community element of groups of North American Indians with their profitable involvement in the wider capitalist economy (Bohannan, 1967, p. 58). Papua New Guinea now presents this type of combination in symphonic dimensions. As well as a creative use by traditional groups of the company form, the first national government introduced several measures in support of traditional group organization. Company law was changed to facilitate the formation and operation of large group corporations. Other laws provided for the incorporation of smaller 'customary' groups as economic enterprises. A five-year tax holiday was introduced for companies and incorporated groups composed of nationals. Development grants were provided for groups. Groups were to be entitled to interest-free loans in purchasing foreign owned plantations. It was announced that groups would have preference over individuals in government lending. Some shift in agricultural extension in favour of 'community involvement' has been reported (Potter, 1977). As we have seen, the operation of the existing tenure conversion law has been suspended. The governmental Law Reform Commission has recently proposed that traditional group 'custom' should be the basis of inheritance (Law Reform Commission, 1978). The changes and proposed change were backed by specific affirmations of policy. For small scale economic enterprise the eight aims call for reliance "where possible on typically Papua New Guinean forms of organization". In addition to its affirmation of 'Papua New Guinean ways', the constitution called for "active steps to be taken to facilitate the organization and legal recognition of all groups engaging in development activities". The Prime Minister, in a more penetrating credo, said:

> The extent to which we should move towards equalization of incomes and limit the possibilities of an individual accumulating personal wealth from his own endeavours has been raised again and again as a fundamental issue. It is difficult for national leaders to resolve this, for many of our societies place high value on both individualistic entrepreneurial activity and communalistic sharing. As Chief Minister, I have constantly directed that institutions promoting Papua New Guinean business activities should concentrate their efforts on supporting representative communal groups rather than individuals. (Somare, 1975b, p. 110)

There were two main legal innovations. One dealt with larger scale organizations and the other with small scale 'customary' groups. The law dealing with larger scale organizations arose out of difficulties which they had had with company law. They often had a large number of members with small holdings. This and the absence of a public market in shares raised numerous and immense administrative difficulties. This was partly remedied in the Companies (Amendment) Act of 1974. As a result, for a company whose membership is, broadly, restricted to nationals, the Registrar of Companies can make certain modifications to the general company law. The most important of these modifications concern simplified prospectus provisions to facilitate the raising of capital from numerous small shareholders, less onerous requirements for filing particulars of shareholders with the Registrar and allowing the company to buy its own shares, but this last is subject to prohibitively stringent restrictions.

The legal changes relating to small scale groups were perhaps more significant. In apparent contrast to the restrictive colonial approach, the Business Groups Incorporation Act of 1974 provides a simple and accessible legal regime for the incorporation and regulation of 'customary groups'. Once incorporated such a group has power "to conduct business enterprises, to borrow money and to acquire, hold, dispose of and manage land" so long as the land is not 'customary' or 'native' land. The Act is based on the assumption that the group's internal affairs will be regulated by 'custom', although its constitution can specifically abrogate or modify any custom. Provision is made for the settlement of disputes internal to the group, the aim expressed in the Act being "the self-resolution of disputes within . . . groups without requiring recourse to non-traditional courts". The Registrar of Business Groups has extensive powers under the Act. He has a broad discretion to refuse incorporation of a group and once incorporated he has a broad discretion to wind it up. Apart from certain minimal matters anything further in the group's constitution is subject to the approval of the Registrar as is any change in the constitution. The Registrar also has very wide powers to enquire into the affairs of an incorporated group. He can direct that such accounts and records 'as he thinks proper' be kept. He can inspect these and require that they be filed with him. He may at any time require a meeting of the group to be held. The purport of these controls will be touched on shortly. A broadly similar law is the Land Groups Act of 1974, the preamble to which describes it as "an Act to recognize the corporate nature of customary groups and to allow them to hold, manage and deal with land" including 'customary' or 'native' land. It was introduced as part of the plantations acquisition scheme but can be used as a legal basis for any group land holding.

As well as these new pieces of general legislation, creative use has also recently been made of company law to create particular legal regimes in the form of what have become known in Papua New Guinea as development corporations. These are an innovative adaptation of the capitalist mode, and of the capitalist company form, to Papua New Guinea ways or to the persistence of traditional social formations. These development corporations often have broad, developmental aims but almost invariably they engage only in their own enterprises and in conventional investment activities. They often have a large membership derived from a wide ethnic grouping. With the permissive or facilitative element of company law people can, within broad limits, create in the constitution of the corporation a legal regime that is binding on the membership. Looking at several of these constitutions one finds that many development corporations restrict membership to nationals or to people belonging to a particular ethnic group. This practice is encouraged now by the changes in company law just described which allow concessions to companies whose membership is restricted to nationals and, more significantly, by recent changes in tax law allowing a tax holiday to such companies. The constitutions of many corporations, reflecting perhaps traditional egalitarian values, provide that each member should have one vote only, no matter what the member's capital contribution. In a similar vein, one constitution limits the number of shares that can be held by a member. Shares can usually be held by an individual or by a leader on behalf of a traditional grouping, sometimes incorporated under the business groups law. It is this representative type of holding which permits one of the most striking features of the legal structure of many corporations (see for example, Fitzpatrick, 1975, pp. 186 – 187; Good and Donaldson, 1979, p. 57). The representative holders are expected to act as intermediaries between the management and the wider or represented membership. Sometimes constitutions provide for a formal body of these representative holders to stand between, in terms of normal company structures, the board of directors and the members' general meeting. Some corporations use representative holdings in a particularly interesting way. It arises out of the legal position under company law, whereby small companies called proprietary companies have less onerous obligations than larger companies called public companies. Generally, to qualify as a proprietary company there must be not more than 50 members. So, to take the case of a particular corporation, several, but less than 50, sub-clan leaders hold shares on behalf of many thousands of people who are looked on as the members of the corporation, even though they are not formally such. Of course if they were formally members, the company would be a public one with more onerous legal obligations. Constitutions sometimes involve the use of traditional roles in giving titles and functions to different standard and unconventional offices in the corporation. Thus with one corporation, the constitution provides for a person "to enquire into and report on any aspect of the affairs of the . . . [corporation] on behalf of the members". Such a person is called a *tson kahete*. For this grouping a *tson kahete* traditionally was a protector, a person who ensured the security of a group, for example a group of women going to the garden who may be attacked. Traditional meanings are sometimes invested also in the choice of a corporation's name and symbol and of specified guiding principles incorporated in the constitution. For example, the name of one corporation, the *Tuki ni Buka*—the *tuki* belonging to the Buka people—neatly contains much of the idea of capitalist investment in a more attractive cover:

> On Buka Island the *tuki* ritual is only conducted occasionally nowadays. It is organized by a lineage leader. It involves the making of a small, fenced-in area. Everyone in the lineage puts ordinary goods inside this area—inside the *tuki*. Then a feast is held and after that the *tuki* is cut open and the food inside it distributed. The ritual symbolises and guarantees the fertility and productivity of the land.
> (Fitzpatrick, 1975, p. 183)

Tradition sometimes makes its appearance in the conventional 'objects clauses' of the constitution. For example, Malinowski would indeed be surprised to find that now a development corporation on the Trobriand Islands has as one of its objects the provision of "facilities, services and other matters to cater for all types of *Kula* exchange". Political and broad developmental objects sometimes appear but the narrowly economic objects predominate in the constitutions and, as we shall now see, in operation.

The conservation in its integral vitality of the traditional mode of production under colonialism and the economic opportunities presented by capitalist penetration meant that traditional groupings persistently sought to engage in new economic enterprises. These efforts usually failed for various reasons, not the least of them involving colonial repression, as we saw in Chapter Four. In particular, large scale groupings with economic and/or political aspirations were purposively suppressed under colonialism. Dramatic changes now occur with this type of organization.

In the last days of colonialism with the weakening of colonial rule various large political and economic associations emerged which would not be put down. They tended to be run by the young and the formally educated, although older leaders often played effective if less conspicuous parts. They were politically assertive, anti-colonial and in this sense nationalist, yet they were basically tied in activity and aspiration to their constituent ethnic groupings. The reliance on traditional forms of organization, on traditional values and symbols was usually emphasized. These associations were often assertive economically as well. The first to be incorporated as a company, in so doing and in the effective publicising of its struggles, popularized the idea and the name of the development corporation.

With the exception of the Hahalis Welfare Society, none of these associations was radical in the proper sense. Their demands were, effectively, for state recognition and accommodation, including an end to colonial discriminations. These demands were fitfully resisted by the weakened colonial state. Such demands were added to when, in the post-colonial situation, the idea of the development corporation was adopted by more conservative but potent organizations. These newer development corporations also usually have a large membership based in a broad ethnic grouping, but they tend to be more narrowly investment corporations with the members' contributions being invested in local-level enterprises including those of the big peasants who tend to dominate these corporations. Such corporations also serve as a political power base for their leaders and as a structure for patron–client relations between the leaders and members. Donaldson and Good observe of the area they studied that "the developmentalism and populism expressed by the Development Corporations . . . had a real meaning and obtained an effective response from the people" but that the corporations "were formed and are controlled by the rich rural classes, usually in collaboration with expatriate businessmen and managers and members of the educated petty bourgeoisie [meaning the bureaucratic bourgeoisie, it seems—P.F.]" (Donaldson and Good, 1978, p. 16). The earlier corporations have tended to become more sedate. Most have settled down in being contained by the new legal recognition, tax holiday and other new benefits provided by the state. Erstwhile radicals developed a type of group capitalism which somehow managed to favour them in particular. Development corporations, generally, found themselves "being assisted [by the state] to a degree out of all proportion to their numbers, widening the gap between the privileged minority and the rest, as well as creating greater regional inequalities" (Howlett, 1977,

p. 7). Such corporations do, however, magnanimously employ their less fortunate fellow nationals on low wages. They have invested heavily in such developmentally dynamic concerns as luxury urban flats, luxury tourist hotels, plantations and supermarkets. Where they do not establish joint ventures or other close linkages with metropolitan capital it is usually not for the want of desperately trying to do so. Despite its early tinge of radicalism, the development corporation seeks in the end to take over small bits and pieces of the capitalist economy. It becomes a political base for its leaders and a structure for patron – client relations which serve to contain large and sometimes restive ethnic groupings within the state system. It integrates large numbers of people into the capitalist economy in a way that gives them a small investment stake in that economy but that does not disrupt their traditional base.

If the legal changes created by and around the development corporation serve in a new type of containment, the Business Groups Incorporation Act presents a more familiar reflection of the continuing efficacy of colonial social forces. It and its operation present little more than a refurbished version of earlier legislation analysed in Chapter 5 from which it has largely taken over, namely the Co-operative Societies Act of 1965 and its predecessor the Native Economic Development Ordinance of 1951. It uses the 'customary' as a basis for controlled economic organization and it contains comprehensive powers of official control. It is being vigorously and successfully promoted by its sponsoring department, the Department of Business Development, a department until this conversion vehemently opposed to group enterprise (except co-operatives) which it saw as a distributive drain on the accumulating tendencies of the entrepreneurial few. In contrast, the department, in promoting the incorporated business group, now emphasizes that the group must be bound together by custom, an emphasis that ignores a group's ability under the Act to replace all or part of custom in its constitution. Exclusive emphasis is placed on the settling of disputes in accordance with custom whereas the Act says that the dispute-settling body "shall endeavour to do substantial justice between all persons interested, in accordance with this Act, the constitution and any relevant custom". Instructions to officials in the field require scrupulous checks on whether the group is 'customary', whether that particular grouping is the best for the purpose and whether provision for dispute settlement is likely to be adequate. There is a large backlog of groups awaiting registration and even at this early stage the containment function of the incorporated business group is evident. Ghai notes:

The legislation has brought the communities securely within the ambit of the state. Now whenever a community or group of individuals want to co-operate on a project, they are advised (whether by public servants or the educated members of the community) to form a group under the legislation. The pressure to form the group is high if the group wants a loan, and indeed that is an important reason to incorporate; almost all groups have some sort of state loan. Officials have been posted to all the provinces to help people who want to form groups. Officials decide whether the business group is the most suitable form. . . . Although the legislation intended to provide a simple procedure for the establishment of the group, the process has become highly bureaucratic and various forms have to be completed. There can be long delays in getting registered; sometimes as much as one year. As one lawyer who has helped various groups to incorporate has said "What was supposed to have been an easy method of registering customary type corporations, is now as complex as company or co-operative society formation." Once a group is registered, official involvement in its operations continues. (Ghai, in press)

All this must seem by now like a repetition of an old story but there is one distinct underlying feature to the Act, a feature which, in concluding this part on group enterprise, serves to raise in this context the relation between the maintenance of the group or of the traditional social formation and the 'individualizing' effect of capitalist penetration, especially in the emergence of the big peasantry. In the drafting of the Act the view taken of the typical group was one where a core of managing big men was surrounded by a cluster of capital contributors. This aspect was reflected in the Act's conferring limited liability on an ordinary member—"liability limited to the amount of his interest in the property of the group [as a corporation]"—whereas a member of the managing committee of a group is liable without restriction for its debts. The Act's premise here is not universally accurate. There were available when the Act was drafted several studies of groups that did not fit it (some are described in Fitzpatrick and Southwood, 1976). Ghai observes of the contemporary situation and of groups registered under the act:

In some of these the members are fairly passive, the initiative left to one or more members of the committee. Others are based on collective participation in production, and these tend also to be run on the basis of collective decision-making. (Ghai, in press)

A report of a recent debate involving both academics and officials illustrates the terms in which the broader issue is perceived:

> Some people pointed out that groups are now better treated by several government instrumentalities and indeed are often given preference over individuals. It was suggested that, compared to the colonial period, this showed a dramatic turnaround on the part of Government. But, and somewhat in opposition, other people argued that these groups were often "fronts", as it were, for big men and, increasingly, for members of the "èlite" who give their ventures a group appearance in order to meet formal government requirements for preferring groups. In a somewhat similar vein one commentator said that, even where group ventures start out as "genuine", the forces making for capitalist individualism are such that the group element is manipulated and destroyed through prominent members using it for their personal advancement. (Fitzpatrick and Southwood, 1976, p. 1)

It certainly is the case, although the matter has not been studied in detail, that many big peasants have set up group ventures in which they have a large interest but which have enough 'groupness' to qualify for government benefits. Such a structure is of some popularity with politicians in which instance it can serve as a conduit in the allocation of government benefits to supporters and also promote patron-client relationships. The continuing and effective influence of 'individualization', and of the big peasantry, is also illustrated in the changes in coffee marketing described in Chapter Five, which gave the big peasant a foothold on the lower rungs of the system. Despite policy statements to the contrary mentioned earlier in the present chapter, there does not in fact appear to be any significant shift in government extension and lending towards group enterprise. Many of the 'groups' to whom the Development Bank lends are partnerships of two to four members. The contradiction between the conservation of the traditional mode and 'individualizing' local-level effects of capitalist penetration result in combined forms of organization—the development corporation and smaller, less spectacular examples. To a significant degree it is not a matter of the individual *or* the group but of both.

Finally there are numerous and more diverse efforts at law reform. Such reform was given high rhetorical priority in the early post-colonial phase, it being often combined with populist sentiments. Ghai makes the interesting observation that:

> Law had played such a visible role in the colonial period, as an

instrument of suppression of the indigenous population and for the stifling of their initiatives for self-improvement, that it was not surprising that the law came to be perceived as a powerful instrument of social change. Because of this view of the potency and instrumentalism of the law, and because of the lack of popular mobilization and thus of politicization, the discussion of the policies that the Papua New Guinea leaders favoured were also heavily couched in terms of the law and its reform. (Ghai, in press)

In 1973, the Prime Minister called for a legal system which

. . . must respond to our own needs and values. We do not want to create an imitation of the Australian, English, or American legal systems. We want to build a framework of laws and procedures that the people of Papua New Guinea can recognise as their own—not something imposed on them by outsiders. There is great scope for imagination and creativity in making the law responsive to the needs of the people and I put this challenge to all of you who are concerned about the future of our nation: how can we build a legal system that will truly serve the people's needs. (Somare, 1975b, p. 14)

Shortly after, in announcing legislation setting up a Law Reform Commission, the Prime Minister envisaged it as undertaking a review of the laws ''to get rid of those which are not suitable to our people, and to reform or replace other laws and make new laws so that our legal system assists in achieving our national goals''. The Constitutional Planning Committee saw the Law Reform Commission as ''a body to review all existing legislation and policies with a view to bringing them into line with the National Goals and Directive Principles'' (Constitutional Planning Committee, 1974, p. 2/16). The goals include, of course the prime reliance on Papua New Guinea ways. The constitution itself envisaged the development of ''a truly indigenous jurisprudence'' and saw the Law Reform Commission as playing a key part in this. Bayne has noted that ''the sentiment that the legal system imposed by the Australian government was opposed to the values of Papua New Guinea communities was articulated by politicians whenever legal issues were discussed'' in the legislature (Bayne, 1978, p. 11). The Law Reform Commission itself was composed of influential commissioners and had an imaginative, dynamic staff. All this may be to labour the point, but it is perhaps important to emphasize that in terms of policy and political intention, radical law reform had much going for it. Its general failure is hence the more stark and illuminating. The basic argument here is that the failures, as well as the

successes, of law reform can be explained in terms of the social forces continuing on from the colonial situation. Perhaps most significant is what
simply has not been done. The existing legal system has continued with
incidental adaptation. To rely again on Ghai's acute observations:

> The legal system in Papua New Guinea is a permanent carrier of
> foreign ideas and culture, since it is tied to the English and Australian
> legal systems, the latest decisions of which are in practice binding on
> Papua New Guinean courts. The basic rules of interpretation and the
> presumptions of the law find their source in an alien system, whose
> hold continues even after independence. The crises of legal doctrine in
> England are all too readily assumed to be the crises of law in Papua
> New Guinea, and the latest law reforms in England and Australia are
> seen by many as setting the pace for Papua New Guinea. The develop-
> ment of the law based on indigenous concepts and contemporary
> problems is stultified because of the force of foreign imitation.
> Foreign decisions are cited and applied as if they had some intrinsic
> merit and foreign textbooks are consulted as if they represented the
> authoritative law of the land. (Ghai, 1978)

Such 'home-grown' adaptations as there have been arise out of the need,
outlined earlier in this chapter, to give fuller recognition to elements of
traditional social formations so as to incorporate and contain them more
integrally within the state system.

It may help organize an apparently diffuse collection of reforms and
attempted reforms by looking at them in relation to the various class categories already discussed. Taking first the metropolitan bourgeoisie and its
interest in bourgeois legality, one would expect reforms based on Papua
New Guinea ways to conflict in fundamental instances with such legality.
With the dominance of the metropolitan bourgeoisie, the conflict should
spell the end of reform in these instances. Such seems to be the case. Thus in
a working paper on "fairness of transactions", later presented as a report
to the legislature, the Law Reform Commission considered that "the
English common law of contract is often harsh and we are not convinced
that it suits the needs of our country. It assumes that people enter contracts
on equal terms" (Law Reform Commission, 1976, p. 1). Accordingly, it
recommended that:

> The courts should have the power to re-write the conditions of con-
> tracts where one person enters the contract on unequal terms and
> accepts conditions which place the greater part of the burden of the
> contract on him. The contract should be re-written so that its terms
> and conditions are fair to both parties. (ibid., p. 2)

In so doing mediation was to play an important part. This was a clear and courageous attempt to incorporate Papua New Guinean legal elements of substantial justice. In this it obviously struck at the heart of bourgeois legality. Not surprisingly, as Bayne discovered, "spokesmen for the local expatriate business community have objected to the key recommendations of this paper and have claimed that the principles of English law are a protection to their business activities" (Bayne, 1978, p. 27). As of the Commission's annual report published in 1979, the proposed reform had not been implemented (Law Reform Commission, 1979, p. 3).

The outcome has so far been the same for a perhaps even more adventurous proposed reform. This is the Law Reform Commission's proposals relating to the "underlying law" (Law Reform Commission, 1977b, pp. 6 – 7). At present the constitution has a close to standard reception provision which adopted as law "the principles and rules that formed, immediately before Independence Day, the principles and rules of common law and equity in England". However 'custom' is also, with uncertain qualifications, adopted but, in all, it appears that English law is to be applied primarily and generally except that its application may be qualified by custom when it is applicable. In the making of the constitution this provision for the underlying law was recognized as temporary and specific legislation dealing with this subject was anticipated. The Law Reform Commission has now prepared draft legislation which would make 'customary law' the underlying law, regard being had to English law only where this customary law was not applicable (ibid., pp. 13-27). This qualification is not to be a huge one for the Commission envisages that "English common law should only apply in exceptional cases" (Law Reform Commission, 1977a, p. 11).

Even if such a spectacular measure were enacted, it would rely heavily on the higher judiciary for its implementation. This would also be the case for the 'fairness in transactions' law, particularly in its effect on the metropolitan bourgeoisie. The constitution does specifically recognize that the higher judiciary has a responsibility creatively to develop "a truly indigenous jurisprudence"—one that takes account of custom and the national goals. That all this involves an excessive optimism has been borne out by the performance of the higher judiciary. O'Neill concludes a study of this judiciary's treatment of the constitution by saying that:

> In the first year since Independence, the judges have shown themselves reluctant to accept the challenge laid down by the Constitution

to develop Papua New Guinea's underlying law in a way that suits the conditions of the country. . . . The judges, with the exception of the Deputy Chief Justice, have avoided the steps for the development of the underlying law set down in the Constitution. There is little evidence that members of the profession have taken pains to assist the judges in their law development task. But perhaps most importantly of all, both the bench and the members of the profession have been trained to believe that, despite the wealth of evidence of the contrary, judges do not make the law, they only interpret it. (O'Neill, 1976, p. 258)

Of course formalism does have its virtue. A recent report by the official in charge of the state's legal aid, in referring to "the intention of the government to continue encouragement of outside investment", emphasized that "any future outside investors . . . may well look very critically at the standard and composition of the ultimate court in the land in order to ascertain whether they could expect any dispute they had with the Government, or an individual, to to be resolved by a completely impartial and competent mind" (as quoted in Bayne, 1978, p. 17).

In late 1979, bourgeois legality was tested in a dramatic if inconclusive way. The government made a deportation order against a foreign academic who was an adviser both to the leader of the parliamentary opposition and to the government's Minister for Primary Industry. The academic applied to the National Court to have the order set aside. The court suspended the operation of the order whilst it was considering the matter. The Minister of Justice—a vigorous, reforming minister and a critic of the then exclusively foreign composition of the higher judiciary—then wrote to the Chief Justice saying that the judiciary could not and should not intervene in deportation matters. The Chief Justice objected and made the letter public. Largely prompted by the leader of the parliamentary opposition, contempt proceedings were brought against the Minister. After a hearing before the highest judicial body, she was sentenced to eight months imprisonment. The Prime Minister then assumed the Justice portfolio. As the new Minister of Justice he, as he was legally entitled to do, then ordered the release of the former Minister after she had served a day of the sentence, the release being one pending a hearing by the normal legal body that considers pardons. Four judges of the National Court then resigned in protest, timing their resignations to facilitate the appointment of replacements. A more sensitive judge had already resigned before the hearing of the contempt case. This left three judges of the National Court—the only who were once colonial officials. The Prime Minister's action also provoked widespread protest by opposition parties, unions and students.

We saw earlier that the rule of law often gives way in the face of political conflict within third world social formations. However, the present instance was not only an internal political conflict as it affected the independence of the higher judiciary, a matter basic to bourgeois legality and of concern to the metropolitan bourgeoisie. Indeed, some senior state operatives expressed concern over the effect the incident may have on foreign investment. But in some ways the incident can be seen as not greatly significant for the interests of the metropolitan bourgeoisie. Firstly, much professional legal opinion in the country and much media comment there and abroad (for example *The Age* of 12 September, 1979 and *The Australian Financial Review* of 24 September) considered the judges' reactions throughout to be excessive and the sentence to be draconic. In other words, the Prime Minister could be seen to have acted reasonably and he certainly did not act illegally. Secondly, shortly after releasing the former Minister, the Prime Minister issued a lengthy statement affirming the government's commitment to the rule of law. Thirdly, and perhaps most reassuringly, another Minister has, without repercussion, since been sentenced by the National Court to ten days imprisonment with hard labour for failure to obey a court's order to have a company of which he is a director lodge certain returns required by corporate law.[2]

Law reform aimed at encouraging a national bourgeoisie in the urban areas and petty commodity producers has been no more successful. The report of the Overseas Development Group, which formed the basis for much of the ideology and policy of the first national government—placed predominant emphasis on the development of an ''informal sector'' (Overseas Development Group, 1973). This is very much a term of art (see for example, Fitzpatrick and Blaxter, 1975). To avoid the large amount of scholarship now expended on the subject, it should be enough to say that it is a supposed sector of small scale enterprises, such as craft, market and bazaar-type enterprises, that uses popularly available skills, resources and technologies. Fashion in development consultancy current at the time of the report saw the promotion of this sector as a basis for development and as a way of creating employment (see for example ILO, 1972). The Overseas Development Group saw it likewise and recommended that laws restraining it be reformed (Overseas Development Group, 1973, p. 26). In line with this the Prime Minister announced as government policy in 1973 that:

We will expand small-scale commercial activity. We will cut down the restrictions that prevent people from earning money by selling goods, supplying services, or engaging in small-scale business. In particular, we will conduct a thorough review of current legal restrictions. We will begin to create a truly Papua New Guinea form of economy. Our current licensing regulations are borrowed from a Western style of economy. They may have no meaning in an independent Papua New Guinea. This review should make it easier for Papua New Guineans to engage in food and drink processing and distribution, craft industries, joinery and construction, tailoring, transport, personal services, retail trade, and other businesses.

Following this, the cabinet approved wide-ranging modifications of these legal restrictions in their restraining effect on elements of the national bourgeoisie and on petty commodity producers. The further implementation of these reforms was taken up with considerable enthusiasm by the Law Reform Commission and the National Planning Office. The reforms have stalled because, in part, numerous officials oppose them on the grounds that they involve a weakening or an abolition of necessary standards. Examples of such standards and of the attitudes underlying this opposition have already been given in Chapter 7. In line with the analysis there, the reforms can be seen as stalled, because some elements of the bourgeoisie have interests placed in the maintenance of these restrictive laws.

Continuing this narrative of negatives, the working class and related class elements of the 'unemployed' and the 'dispossessed' have gained nothing from law reform. The Law Reform Commission did give some consideration to proposals extending the exemption of trade unions from civil liability for action connected with an industrial dispute. Nothing seems to have been done about this. Maintaining its record for sensitive intentions, a report of the Law Reform Commission recommended the abolition of the offence of vagrancy, but there was also a minority report recommending its retention (Law Reform Commission, 1977a, p. 10). This minority report formed the basis for the arguably more draconic Vagrancy Act of 1977. But on this more repressive side it has to be said that the Law Reform Commission has had some modest success. It improved the system of minor offences—the 'police offences'—in work that resulted in the Summary Offences Act of 1977, and in the amendment of the Act in the following year to add further offences concerning public order. Following the withdrawal of the Public Order Bill in 1976, the Commission has worked with other governmental bodies on a new bill. It has also devoted much of its time to improving the system of criminal law in such particular areas as committal proceedings, juvenile offenders and the trying of more offences in lower courts.

Law reform of particular effect on the peasantry is something more complex. Contemporary disorder in the rural areas is now much commented on, taking such forms as 'tribal fighting', coffee stealing, destruction of government property and theft from state operatives (Allen, 1979, p. 61; Good and Donaldson, 1979, p. 54; Howlett *et al.*, 1976, pp. 21 – 25). At the time of writing in September 1979, a state of emergency is in force for the Highlands area because of 'tribal fighting'. Andrew Strathern's incisive description of popular perceptions of legality among a large group of Highlanders provides an apt focus here:

> First, it is clear that the colonial administration stopped warfare, and asserted further surveillance over all acts of inter-personal violence. Second, by introducing new laws, administrative officers implied—and indeed stated—that the old ways were bad and to be rejected. Third, the notions of individual punishment and jail were substituted for ideas of collective responsibility, vengeance, and compensation [as between groups], although the people never regarded this as a valid substitution, but rather held that while the administration had to carry out its rituals they also had to carry out their own; and so a dualistic view of "law" and "custom" was created. Once such a dualistic view was established, the effects of control over violence and the introduction of new laws seen as "good" were partly nullified. The people continued to define themselves as partly "bad", i.e. still partly adhering to custom. On the other hand, the power of the administration was an obvious fact, and by comparison the people defined themselves also as "powerless". Their overall reactions to a situation in which the image of the powerful administration subsequently crumbled [with decolonization—P.F.] and administrative officers themselves told the people that they must exercise responsible power at the local level, settle their disputes for themselves, and assume self-government, are therefore explicable: "If you want us to do that, we shall have to do it in our way, by fighting and paying compensation". Of course, such an outright view is rather too simplistic. Many Hagen leaders continuously exhort their people to follow the "new way", listen to the missions and the government, understand law and so on. The difficulty, however, inheres in the basic dualistic scheme of ideas. (Strathern, 1977, pp. 8 – 9)

The state has attempted to overcome the effect of this duality through, in part, various combined legal forms. State authority provides the ultimate frame of rights and obligations but it is combined with supporting legal and other elements in traditional social formations. Besides the examples of development corporations and incorporated business groups, the most notable example of this combined legal form is the village court already considered in detail in Chapter Five. This form is statutorily constituted and combines traditional knowledge and traditional legal controls with the backing of state power which will ultimately enforce the courts' orders through imprisonment. The lynch-pin is provided by dominant class elements who act as lay magistrates. The state is influential in the selection of magistrates, actively promotes courts and supervises their activities. Paliwala notes of magistrates that:

> The most significant qualification appears to be links with insti-
> tutions that have their base outside the village. Thus magistrates are,
> or have been, councillors, policemen, "luluai", "tultul" [local-
> level, lay colonial officials—P.F.], medical orderlies, co-operative
> officers or church officials. That is village courts are clearly identified
> as part of the state machinery and court officials see themselves as
> links between the State and the village. (Paliwala, 1979, p. 15)

Although the courts were heralded as vehicles of popular justice relying on Papua New Guinea ways, and although they rely on elements of traditional social formations, they have come to be, in terms of both procedure and function, means of control by the state and by dominant class elements. Despite already considerable popular disenchantment with the courts, they seem so far to be significantly effective. Paliwala, in a general yet graphic description of the courts, says that:

> The picture of an effective village court is one which attempts to
> achieve stability by punishing fighting, bad language, drunkeness
> and gambling and being tough with young offenders. It protects pro-
> perty by punishing theft and trespass. It facilitates traditional and
> modern transactions by enforcing contracts and debt. It keeps
> women under control by ensuring that they do not obtain divorce too
> easily, and by punishing unorthodox behaviour. Finally it acts as a
> judicial arm of the [Local Government] Council. (ibid., pp. 20 – 21)

Indeed, the village court, in conjunction with councils or with the widely emerging types of community government, is becoming the focus of legal and political power at the local level.

There are several other examples of proposed or actual combined forms.

Recent legislation has recruited local-level leaders in the process of settling 'tribal fighting' and, as we saw earlier, in mediating land disputes. The Law Reform Commission has recommended that 'customary law' be taken more into account in assessing responsibility and deciding on punishment in the operation of the criminal law (Law Reform Commission, 1977b, p. 45). It is also working on a system of civil compensation enforced by the state but grounded considerably in the ways of 'custom' (Law Reform Commission, 1977a, pp. 17 – 18). The Commission's most fundamental proposals in this area concern succession to property on death. They are contained in a recent working paper and draft bill (Law Reform Commission, 1978). These would make "custom the most important factor in the distribution process" after death and even a "will shall only have effect insofar as . . . it is not inconsistent with custom" (ibid., p. 8). In this the proposals can be seen as conforming to the tendency to conserve the traditional mode of production. It is partly in the maintenance of traditional principles of succession that this tendency has proved detrimental to the reproduction of the big peasantry and to its class consolidation independently of the traditional mode. However the proposals in their detail contain aspects favourable to the big peasantry. Thus the control of an individual over the disposition on death of his or her property would be greatly facilitated through the admission of a variety of 'wills'—"a person may make a will in any form he chooses, orally, in writing or by any other means", which provokes wild speculation about other means, and even more greatly facilitated by allowing all property to be disposed of in this way (ibid., p. 4 of the draft bill). Also a will "shall be presumed to comply with custom until the contrary is proved. When there is dispute, a court shall decide" (ibid., p. 11). In the case of a significant estate of a big peasant the relevant court would be the 'highest' one and it would be inaccessible to almost any potential objector seeking to assert custom. As well, although the Commission considers that "the welfare of the immediate dependants of the deceased will normally be assured under customary law" it also "feels these [i.e. their] rights should be entrenched by statute, and should not be extinguished by the operation of any custom or any statement of testamentary intentions" (ibid., p. 13). One of the factors to be taken into account in deciding how much goes to the immediate family is "the value and composition of the property of the deceased" (ibid., p. 6 of the draft bill). In short, these proposals, if implemented, should have a considerable impact on class formation in the rural areas.

The rash attempt in this chapter to take matters into the contemporary situation has degenerated into something of a miscellany. But underlying the diffuseness there are a few integrating themes. The overall domination of the metropolitan bourgeoisie is not being significantly countered. Papua New Guinea shares in the greatly increased, contemporary metropolitan investment in the third world but, as with other comparable social formations founded on natural resource extraction, this investment reinforces existing tendencies. The traditional mode of production continues to subsidize the operation of the capitalist mode in the support of peasant and plantation labour and of unskilled and semi-skilled urban labour. The conservation of the traditional mode still serves also in class containment, a function heightened with the weakness of the post-colonial state. Law and state continue here to check the destructive effects of the capitalist mode on the traditional and to function in the containment of dominated classes. At the same time, compliant but weak national class elements still need to be fostered and law and state play a part in this. The main change is that in the post-colonial situation a resident 'ruling class' is needed and explicitly metropolitan domination politically now lacks legitimacy. Law and state serve in legitimating new political rule at the national level and not least in the presentation of central aspects of law and state as being now opposed to colonial structures. Somewhat paradoxically, law and state serve also to legitimize the continuing presence of the metropolitan bourgeoisie and to mediate between this class element and the national bourgeoisie. This mediation is not a neutral or 'autonomous' function but one that reflects and helps secure the ultimate domination of the metropolitan bourgeoisie.

## Notes

1. Obvious difficulties with this chapter are that the near contemporary situation is being dealt with and that the ground is not well worked academically. Where specific references are not given, the information comes from people closely concerned in the events described and from personal involvement and observation.
2. This account of the incident is derived from a wide variety of newspaper sources. I am grateful to Tony Fitzpatrick for providing most of these.

# 9 Conclusion

I would like to attempt a concluding overview of what the book has been saying. I will look first at theory then at the specific Papua New Guinea case. The theory rarely transcends a limited history or a static functionalism. The shaping context of theory has been the 'internal aspect' of those social formations of the third world called colonies, nations or countries. The theory sought to encompass both the external forces operating on these social formations and their internal collection of resident or traditional social formations. With the extensive colonization of the later nineteenth century, capitalism's penetration of the third world did not fundamentally transform resident social formations. Such social formations were of course, in many varying ways, profoundly affected in this. But to an extent that is central, resident social formations were conserved. Indeed, the social formation, as colony or nation, is grounded in an operative combination of the capitalist mode of production and what I have hesitantly called the traditional mode of production, with the capitalist mode occupying a dominant integrative position. The traditional mode subsidizes the provision of labour used in capitalist production. It also helps create surplus, in such as peasant production, which is extracted and retained within the capitalist mode. The conservation of the traditional mode functions as well in class containment through, for example, the maintenance of ethnic division. This function is of special significance given the weakness of the colonial and post-colonial state.

Law and state, as creatures of the capitalist mode of production, function distinctively in the conservation of the traditional mode. In the colonial period, the limited penetration of capitalist economic forces meant that law and state were fundamentally constitutive of the colonial social formation. They had to integrate the two modes of production yet protect the traditional mode from the solvent effects of the capitalist mode. In this way the development of integrative economic forces was inhibited thus confirming the reliance on law and state. An authoritarian system of legal administration was required, one extending to the most comprehensive and arbitrary control. Law and state forced the colonized to provide labour and surplus for the capitalist mode, yet law and state also had to restrain the colonized lest in this they ceased to be tied to the traditional mode. Colonial rule created a discriminatory legal system of 'native administration', which served not only in the control of the colonized but in the maintenance of their traditional, ethnic identities. As well, the conservation of the traditional mode enabled the weak colonial state to be bolstered in various systems of 'indirect rule', including the reliance on traditional legal organization. In contrast, law and state also provided a legal system largely attuned to bourgeois legality which served the resident colonist and the metropolitan bourgeoisie. Law and state also played distinctly ideological parts. As an aspect of the 'civilizing mission' law not only helped effect but also justified changes in the traditional mode of production where these were needed. But in its operative relation to ideologies of 'trusteeship' and 'protection', law helped justify its own part in the conservation of the traditional mode.

Despite related efforts at conservation and class containment, the penetration of the capitalist mode of production led to some emergence and some effectiveness of class elements characteristic of that mode—class elements that often built as well on aspects of the traditional mode. The economic crises of the period between the two 'world' wars prompted the political assertion of these class elements. They were given even greater operative definition in the period after the second world war with capitalism's more intense involvement in the third world. In this situation, the predominant response of a still weakly-embedded capitalism was the promotion and recruitment of compliant resident class elements whilst maintaining and extending the containment of potentially antagonistic elements. The 'undifferentiated mass' of the colonized can now be seen as giving way to a complexity of class positions. To a degree, the complexity can be resolved by viewing some of these positions as a 'contradictory location' between the classic positions of the capitalist mode, the bourgeois and the proletarian. Thus the so-called bureaucratic bourgeoisie in the third world can, like senior state operatives elsewhere, be considered as occupying a contradictory location between the bourgeoisie and the proletariat. Complexity can be further resolved if some class positions are seen as located in both the capitalist and the traditional mode of production. The peasantry and the class element of urban-based petty commodity producers typify this double location. If to these are added the classic capitalist positions of the bourgeoisie and the proletariat, one has the main, if not always distinct, lines of class division in the third world. The bourgeoisie has to be seen as internally divided between a metropolitan and a national bourgeoisie.

In this more complex setting the part of law and state also becomes more complex if somewhat less central. As the emerging class elements indicate, capitalist economic determinants are more operative in maintaining the colonial or national social formation. A related point is that the combination of the capitalist and traditional modes comes to rely more on particular economic determinants. For example, legal measures to protect the traditional mode are not so much required when the outrageous instabilities of commodity production repeatedly confirm for the peasant the necessity for conservation. Still, capitalism does not have a comprehensively transforming effect. The basic combination of the capitalist and traditional modes persists and continues to be effected significantly by law and state. (Further, the need for law and state to conserve the traditional mode of production is heightened in the stronger emergence of class elements that tend to undermine it.) For example, much of the proletariat remains integrally tied to the traditional mode through legal controls on urban migration and urban residence as well as through property and housing laws, making urban life precarious and provisional. Some class elements develop a potential for transcending containment based on the conservation of the traditional mode, so law and state come to provide new variants. Thus laws regulating trade unions as well as public order laws serve to contain the proletariat. Instances could be multiplied but particular attention has to be given to the most paradoxically placed class element, the national bourgeoisie.

Law and state promote yet constrain the national bourgeoisie. With the advent of political independence, some laws purposively promote national bourgeois elements as a resident 'ruling class'. Further, the system of law as bourgeois legality that served the colonist now provides a frame of property and contractual relations that the incipient bourgeois can use to negative obligations grounded in traditional relations. Yet the national bourgeoisie is also severely constrained by law and state. In the rural areas the aspirant bourgeois operates in structures of patronage, and is checked through the conservation of the traditional mode with its attendant redistributive obligations. The national bourgeoisie in the urban areas is subordinated and tied to the metropolitan by laws that sustain metropolitan standards of production, which standards the national bourgeois finds difficult or impossible to meet alone. Bourgeois legality reinforces this subordination since these laws apply 'equally' to all.

Law and state extend, however, to the control of the metropolitan bourgeoisie in such as investment codes and natural resource regulation. This extension can reflect some significant assertiveness on the part of national bourgeois elements but predominantly law and state are of very limited potency in actually controlling the metropolitan bourgeoisie. Indeed, law and state here serve to legitimate the continuing presence of the metropolitan bourgeoisie: if this class element is apparently controlled, its presence is rendered more acceptable. The new bureaucratic bourgeoisie has a necessary place in the exercise of this apparent control and so it finds some legitimacy here also. In usually taking the form of broad, discretionary powers, this control conveniently imports no specific criteria of accountability and masks a fundamentally co-operative relationship between the state, the national bourgeoisie and the metropolitan bourgeoisie. More generally, law and state now serve to mediate between different elements within the bourgeoisie. This mediation is all the more effective because of the dependence that national bourgeois elements have on the state—a dependence created in such forms as the erection of artificial monopolies through licensing laws and the high salaries of senior state operatives. In all, the national bourgeois elements are economically stunted and dependent on the metropolitan bourgeoisie, unable to change the very basis on which they so largely depend. In this mediating function, then, law and state are predominantly responsive to the metropolitan bourgeoisie.

The colonial forms of law persist. The broad discretionary form with its authoritarian cast continues in the service of functions of conservation and class containment. This form also serves in mediating between different elements of the bourgeoisie. Bourgeois legality is strengthened in the greater presence of the bourgeoisie and it provides some security for capitalist relations of production. Its general effectiveness is inhibited, however, in the conservation of the traditional mode. It is not only the case that conservation calls for discretionary forms and authoritarian state action; conservation also inhibits the development of social practice supportive of bourgeois legality. To the extent that people operate within the traditional mode of production, bourgeois legality is for them an irrelevance. Generally, there is little basis for generating popular consensus and involvement in support of law and state, although efforts are often made at calling such forth. (Indicatively, these efforts often appeal to the people's traditions.) Hence law and state are hard put to it to hold down their territory. This, as well as the economic weakness of national bourgeois elements and the present inability of the metropolitan bourgeoisie to rule directly, all make for great political instability and a persisting insecurity in the post-colonial state. A partial resolution has been found in the state's relating integrally to the traditional mode of production, for instance through the distribution of resources on the basis of patronage networks and through the state's incorporating elements of traditional political and legal organization. The use of 'customary law' in national legal systems provides an example of this. But the traditional mode can only operate in limited and subordinated ways at the level of the national social formation, given the dominance there of the capitalist mode of production.

Papua New Guinea was colonized in the later nineteenth century, in the midst of the second imperialism. There were fitful efforts at an intense exploitation of its resources, but Papua New Guinea provided predominantly a case of weak capitalist penetration and of minimal colonization—a situation confirmed in the particular economic debility of its main colonizer, Australia. Law and state structured the colonial social formation. They effected the combination of the capitalist and traditional modes of production and operated in conservation of the traditional mode. They secured land and labour for the colonists' plantations and mines yet restrained exploitation of land and labour so as not fundamentally to disrupt the traditional mode. Law as both protective and 'civilizing' in content served also to legitimate colonial rule. Yet such legal measures were most inadequately enforced except where they were of benefit to the colonist or except where they secured the integrity of the traditional mode or otherwise operated in controlling the colonized. Law itself, as bourgeois legality, was presented as a legitimating element of colonial rule. Yet in its effect on the colonized, law was a matter of being subordinated to broad, arbitrary and comprehensive powers and subordinated to pervasive discrimination. A distinct legal system of 'native administration', relying in part on a type of petty indirect rule, was used to 'keep the native in his place'. Despite this system and conservation-type laws, capitalist economic forces sometimes enabled the colonized to transcend 'place' and to assume potentialities for class action and on occasion these were tellingly realized.

The objectively weak, resident colonist erected a draconic set of laws to counter these eventualities in such as minute controls on associating together in urban areas, controls on rural commodity production and the suppression of rural organization that was not both small-scale and traditionally based.

With the appearance of efforts at liberation on the part of the colonized and the more intense metropolitan involvement after the second world war, the colonial situation began to change rapidly. Various class elements emerge among the colonized. In the reluctant anticipation of eventual political independence, the colonist aimed first at the promotion of an innocuous peasantry of petty producers—one that would remain thoroughly integrated into the traditional mode but which could somehow emerge gradually as a compliant 'ruling class'. International pressures on the metropole and the growth of differentiation within the peasantry soon rendered this scenario obselete. The colonial state then turned to the rapid promotion of a big peasantry building largely on structural inequalities within the traditional mode. The big peasantry and the peasantry generally are founded in a combination of the traditional and capitalist modes, one made operative in various similarly combined forms of, for example, land tenure, corporate organization and dispute settlement.

The part of law and state in all this is a mix of promotion and containment. Many legal measures, including the extension of bourgeois legality to the colonized, serve in the state's promotion and the self-advancement of the big peasantry. These measures are, however, usually muted in their effect or their implementation. For example, a law for the conversion of traditional land holding to 'individual tenure' is trumpeted but then severely constricted in its operation. The 'kulak' cannot be allowed to run too far lest the traditional mode be irreparably undermined. Group political and economic organization is no longer so peremptorily suppressed, but containing legal forms of the co-operative and local government council help ensure that the ethnic diffusion of the peasantry and the family basis of its production are maintained. Generally, law and state serve still in the conservation of the traditional mode and this conservation operates in the containment of the peasantry, including the big peasantry which is thus rendered less effective in challenging the dominance of the metropolitan bourgeoisie.

Post-war demand for labour was incompatible with the detailed legal control of the workforce and this control was gradually eased. Law and state adapt to this emergence of 'free' labour in indicative ways. Official supervision of organized labour and drastic restraints on its engaging in industrial or political action are erected in laws for the control of trade unions and for a system of dealing with industrial disputes. These laws serve in the containment of what can be called the skilled segment of the proletariat—predominantly state operatives. The unskilled segment is mostly unorganized and is contained in ways distinctly neo-colonial. Vagrancy laws serve as a continuing control on urban residence. Housing, urban planning and property laws confirm the prevalent insecurity of the unskilled segment in the urban areas, encouraging 'circular migration' between town and country and encouraging the maintenance of prime and integral ties with the traditional mode of production. Structures tying the rural worker to the traditional mode persist. Minimum wage laws are based on the traditional mode continuing to subsidize the provision of unskilled labour for the capitalist mode. In contrast, the state's provision and regulation of housing encourages 'urban commitment' and the development of a supra-ethnic identity among the skilled segment. For both segments of the proletariat, broad legal powers of the public order type serve as a backstop of control.

The national bourgeoisie and urban based petty commodity producers occupy subordinated and dependent class positions. There is little that tends to their burgeoning. The metropolitan presence provides few economic opportunities for them and it dominates urban economic activity, even of a small-scale kind. The option of returning to the traditional social formation remains almost wholly open to urban residents, and it will usually be easier for the unemployed to do this than to attempt to engage in urban petty commodity production. Licensing and other legal measures ostensibly aimed at the promotion of a national bourgeoisie are implemented desultorily or not at all. A plethora of laws, most significantly those relating to public health and those shaping the urban environment, reinforce metropolitan standards of production. In this way such laws serve either to exclude national class elements or to tie them in subordinate relationships with the metropolitan bourgeoisie. On the other hand, law and state respond in supportive ways to increased involvement of the metropolitan bourgeoisie.

The contemporary, post-colonial situation brings, ostensibly, dramatic changes in law and state. Constitutional forms are introduced in terms of their being fundamentally innovatory. There is the legal recognition of traditionally based groupings and their promotion by the state in supposed preference to favouring the big peasantry. Apparently strong legal controls on the presence of the metropolitan bourgeoisie are introduced. Moves are afoot to put the legal system on a 'customary' basis. The list could go on. However, an analysis of these changes, actual and proposed, reveals certain broad, underlying consistencies. Where the changes are basically neo-colonial they are successful. Forces operative in the colonial situation continue even if in different forms. Fundamental changes, especially those countering the metropolitan bourgeoisie, are either not enacted or assume an anaemic existence at the level of enforcement. The changes accommodate and legitimate new political rule within a persisting economic situation.

It is difficult to see that national class elements can effect any fundamental change in the immediate future. Because of the necessary conservation of the traditional mode, and the pervasive economic dominance of the metropolitan bourgeoisie, dominant national class elements are weakly based economically, disunited and organizationally unstable. Law and state thus have still to build up and bolster these class elements whilst serving the very forces that undermine them. This weakness of resident class elements could make for considerable future changeability at the political level but these will merely be changes of personnel. There is no imminent, radically different political alternative. Neither the working class nor the mass of the peasantry currently exhibit any potentiality for this. The peasantry and the unskilled segment of the proletariat remain diffusely tied to the traditional mode of production. The skilled segment of the proletariat is located in seductive approximation to the dominant class elements. The present political leadership makes ineffectual, *ad hoc* calls for greater industrialization, not so much to develop internal class forces and generate integrated development, but to help meet problems seen in terms of 'unemployment' and 'fiscal self-reliance'. In terms of a recent statement of "post-independence national development strategy", "government policy will give the highest priority to development of farming systems which sustain subsistence production per head" and there will as well be a "continued expansion of export crop production", thus keeping the mix as before with the mass of the peasantry (Central Planning Office, 1975, p. 25). Given the persistence of these various tendencies law and state continue to provide a frame for the presence and dominance of the metropolitan bourgeoisie, taking their form from bourgeois legality. But law and state also adopt the form of broad discretionary control in performing both the function of mediating between the metropolitan bourgeoisie and the national, and the function of containing the dominated class elements.

In shaping and reflecting the compatibilities and conflicts between the emergence of capitalist relations and the conservation of the traditional mode, law and state tend increasingly to take combined forms, forms incorporating state authority and elements of traditional social formations.

# References

Aharoni, Y. (1966). *The Foreign Investment Decision Process*. Harvard University, Boston.

Ake, C. (1976). The Congruence of Political Economies and Ideologies in Africa. In *The Political Economy of Contemporary Africa* (P.C.W. Gutkind and I. Wallerstein, eds). Sage, Beverly Hills and London.

Allen, B. (1979). "The Road Was Blocked, So We Tried Another Road": Attempts by the People of the Dreikikir Area of the East Sepik Province to Gain Access to Government Services (History of Agriculture Working Paper No. 15). University of Papua New Guinea and Department of Primary Industry.

Amin, S. (1974). *Accumulation on a World Scale: A Critique of the Theory of Underdevelopment*. Monthly Review Press, New York.

Anderson, P. (1974). *Lineages of the Absolutist State*. New Left Books, London.

Andrews, C.L. (1975). *Business and Bureaucracy: A Study of Papua New Guinean Businessmen and the Policies of Business Development in Port Moresby* (New Guinea Research Bulletin No. 59). New Guinea Research Unit, The Australian National University, Port Moresby and Canberra.

Apthorpe, R. (1977). *Social Indicators and Social Reporting in Papua New Guinea*. United Nations Research Institute for Social Development, The Hague.

Arrighi, G. (1970). International Corporations, Labor Aristocracies and Economic Development in Tropical Africa. In *Imperialism and Underdevelopment: A Reader* (R.I. Rhodes, ed.). Monthly Review Press, New York and London.

Arrighi, G. and Saul, J.S. (1973). *Essays on the Political Economy of Africa*. Monthly Review Press, New York and London.

Arthur, C. (1978). Editor's Introduction. In *Law and Marxism: A General Theory* (E.B. Pashukanis). Ink Links, London.

Awesa, F. (1975). Report on the Operation of Village Courts in Mendi. Law Faculty, University of Papua New Guinea.

Bairoch, P. (1975). *The Economic Development of The Third World Since 1900*. Methuen, London.

Balandier, G. (1965). Traditional Economic Structures and Economic Change. In *Africa: Social Problems of Change and Conflict* (P.L. van den Berghe, ed.). Chandler Publishing, San Francisco.

Balandier, G. (1970a). *The Sociology of Black Africa: Social Dynamics in Central Africa.* Praeger, New York.

Balandier, G. (1970b). *Political Anthropology.* Allen Lane, London.

Ballard, J. (1976). Wantoks and Administration. University Printer, University of Papua New Guinea.

Banaji, J. (1973). Backward Capitalism, Primitive Accumulation and Modes of Production. *Journal of Contemporary Asia* 3, 393 – 413.

Banaji, J. (1977). Modes of Production in a Materialist Conception of History. *Capital and Class* 1977, No. 3, 1 – 44.

Baran, P. (1969). *The Longer View: Essays Toward a Critique of Political Economy.* Monthly Review Press, New York and London.

Barnes, J.A. (1962). African Models in the New Guinea Highlands. *Man* 62, 5 – 9.

Barnet, R.J. and Muller, R.E. (1974). *Global Reach: The Power of Multinational Corporations.* Simon and Schuster, New York.

Barnett, T. (1976). Land and People in Papua New Guinea. *Yagl-Ambu* 3, No. 4, 203 – 213.

Barnett, T. (in press). Politics and Planning Rhetoric in Papua New Guinea. *Economic Development and Cultural Change.*

Barratt Brown, M. (1972). A Critique of Marxist Theories of Imperialism. In *Studies in the Theory of Imperialism* (R. Owen and B. Sutcliffe, eds) Longman, London.

Barratt Brown, M. (1974). *The Economics of Imperialism.* Penguin, Harmondsworth.

Baxter, P.F. (1976). *An Input-Output Matrix for Papua New Guinea 1972 – 73* (Monograph No. 5). Institute of Applied Social and Economic Research, Boroko.

Bayne, P. (1975). Legal Development in Papua New Guinea: The Place of the Common Law. *Melanesian Law Journal* III, No. 9, 9 – 39.

Bayne, P. (1978). Legal Policy Making in Papua New Guinea: 1972 – 1977. Paper delivered at the conference *Policy Making in Papua New Guinea, 1972 – 1977*, The Australian National University, January, 1978.

Bayne, P.J. and Colebatch, H.K. (1973). *Constitutional Development in Papua New Guinea, 1968 – 1973: The Transfer of Executive Power* (New Guinea Research Bulletin No. 51). New Guinea Research Unit, The Australian National University, Port Moresby and Canberra.

Beckford, G.L. (1972). *Persistent Poverty: Underdevelopment in Plantation Economies of the Third World.* Oxford University Press, New York.

Belshaw, C.S. (1955). *In Search of Wealth: A Study of the Emergence of Commercial Operations in Melanesian Society of Southwestern Papua* (American Anthropological

Memoir No. 80). *American Anthropologist* **5**, No. 1, Part II.

Belshaw, C.S. (1957). *The Great Village: The Economic and Social Welfare of Hanuabada, an Urban Community in Papua*. Routledge and Kegan Paul, London.

Berry, R. (1977). Some Observations on the Political Economy of Development in Papua New Guinea: Recent Performance and Future Prospects. *Yagl-Ambu* **4**, No. 3, 147 – 161.

Bettelheim, C. (1972). Appendix 1: Theoretical Comments by Charles Bettelheim. In *Unequal Exchange: A Study of the Imperialism of Trade* (A. Emmanuel). Monthly Review Press, New York and London.

Birmingham, D. and Scoullar, B. (1974). *The Ombisusu – Tara Village Rubber Project of the Northern District* (Extension Bulletin No. 7). Department of Agriculture, Stock and Fisheries, Port Moresby.

Black, D. (n.d.). The Mobilization of Law (Working Paper No. 15). The Program in Law and Modernization, Yale Law School.

Blackwood, B. (1935). *Both Sides of Buka Passage*. Clarendon Press, Oxford.

Boehringer, G.H. (1976). Imperialism, "Development" and the Underdevelopment of Criminology. *Melanesian Law Journal* **4**, No. 2, 211 – 241.

Bohannan, P. (1957). *Justice and Judgment among the Tiv*. Oxford University Press, London.

Bohannan, P. (1967). Africa's Land. In *Tribal and Peasant Economies: Readings in Economic Anthropology* (G. Dalton, ed.). The Natural History Press, New York.

Braibanti, R. (1968). *The Role of Law in Political Development*. Center for Commonwealth Studies, Duke University.

Bredmeyer, Theo (1973). The Registration of Customary Land in Papua New Guinea. Paper delivered at *Seventh Waigani Seminar, Law and Development in Melanesia*, University of Papua New Guinea, April, 1973. Now in *Melanesian Law Journal* **3**, No. 2, 267 – 287.

Brenner, R. (1977). The Origins of Capitalist Development: a Critique of Neo-Smithian Marxism. *New Left Review* **104**, 25 – 92.

Brookfield, H.C. (1961). Native Employment in the New Guinea Highlands. *Journal of the Polynesian Society* **70**, No. 3, 300 – 313.

Brookfield, H.C. (1972). *Colonialism, Development and Independence: The Case of the Melanesian Islands in the South Pacific*. Cambridge University Press, London.

Brookfield, H.C. with Hart, D. (1971). *Melanesia: A Geographical Interpretation of an Island World*. Methuen, London.

Brown, P. (1963). From Anarchy to Satraphy. *American Anthropologist* **65**, No. 1, 1 – 15.

Brown, P. (1972). *The Chimbu: A Study of Change in the New Guinea Highlands*. Schenkman, Cambridge Mass.

Brown, P. and Podolefsky, A. (1976). Population Density, Agricultural Intensity, and Group Size in the New Guinea Highlands. *Ethnology* **15**, No. 3, 211 – 238.

Burman, S.B. (n.d.). Use and Abuse of the "Modern" versus "Traditional"

Law Dichotomy in South Africa. Centre for Socio-Legal Studies, Oxford.

Burton-Bradley, B.G. (1975). *Stone Age Crisis: A Psychiatric Appraisal.* Vanderbilt University Press, Nashville.

Cain, M. (1974). The Main Themes of Marx' and Engels' Sociology of Law. *British Journal of Law and Society* **1**, No. 2, 136 – 148.

Cain, M. and Hunt, A. (1979). *Marx and Engels on Law.* Academic Press, London and New York.

Cash, W.J. (1941). *The Mind of the South.* Knopf, New York.

Central Planning Office (1975). *Post-Independence National Development Strategy.* Central Planning Office, Port Moresby.

Central Planning Office (1976). *Programmes and Performance, 1976 – 77.* Central Planning Office, Port Moresby.

Chalmers, D.R.C. and Paliwala, A.H. (1977). *An Introduction to the Law in Papua New Guinea.* Law Book Company, Sydney.

Clark, D. (1975). Australia: Victim or Partner of British Imperialism? In *Essays in the Political Economy of Australian Capitalism*, Vol. 1 (E.L. Wheelwright and Ken Buckley, eds). Australia and New Zealand Book Company, Sydney.

Clinard, M.B. and Abbott, D.J. (1973). *Crime in Developing Countries: A Comparative Perspective.* Wiley, New York.

Clunies Ross, A. (1977a). Village Migration Patterns: Notes Towards a Classification. In *The Rural Survey 1975* (Yagl-Ambu Special Issue) (J. Conroy and G. Skeldon, eds). Papua New Guinea Institute of Applied Social and Economic Research, Boroko.

Clunies Ross, A. (1977b). Motives for Migration. In *The Rural Survey 1975* (Yagl-Ambu Special Issue) (J. Conroy and G. Skeldon, eds). Papua New Guinea Institute of Applied Social and Economic Research, Boroko.

Clunies Ross, A. and Lam, N.V. (1979). Stabilization Policy in Papua New Guinea (IASER Discussion Paper No. 23). Institute of Applied Social and Economic Research, Boroko.

Cohen, R. and Michael, D. The Revolutionary Potential of the African Lumpenproletariat: A Sceptical View. *Bulletin, Institute of Development Studies* **5**, No. 2/3, 31 – 42.

Colebatch, P. (1974). *To Find a Path: The Army in Papua New Guinea.* Ph.D. thesis, University of Sussex.

Collins, G.D. (n.d.). *An Appraisal of the Highlands Labour Scheme.* Department of Labour, Port Moresby.

Commission of Enquiry (1971). *Report of Commission—J. Aisa.* Roneo, Port Moresby.

Commission of Enquiry into Alcoholic Drink (1971). *Report.* Government Printer, Port Moresby.

Commission of Enquiry into Land Matters (1973). *Report.* Port Moresby.

Commission of Enquiry into Tribal Fighting in the Highlands (1973). *Report.* Port Moresby.

Committee of Enquiry (1972). *Report of Committee of Enquiry into Co-operatives in Papua New Guinea*. Acting Government Printer, Port Moresby.

Commonwealth of Australia (1961). *Parliamentary Debates, House of Representatives*. 23rd Parliament, 3rd Session, 15 August 1961.

Connell, J. (1979). The Emergence of a Peasantry in Papua New Guinea (History of Agriculture Working Paper No. 27). University of Papua New Guinea and Department of Primary Industry.

Conroy, J.D. (1977). Urban Growth and Unemployment in Papua New Guinea (IASER Discussion Paper No. 16). Institute of Applied Social and Economic Research, Boroko.

Conroy, J. and Skeldon, G., eds (1973). *The Rural Survey 1975* (Yagl-Ambu Special Issue). Papua New Guinea Institute of Applied Social and Economic Research.

Constitutional Planning Committee (1974). *Report, Part 1*. n.p.

Conyers, D. (1976). *The Provincial Government Debate: Central Control versus Local Participation in Papua New Guinea* (Monograph No. 2). Institute of Applied Social and Economic Research, Boroko.

Conyers, D. (1978). Introduction: The Future of Local Government in Papua New Guinea. *Yagl-Ambu* 1, No. 5, 8 – 19.

Costa, J. (1969). Penal Policy and Under-Development in French Africa. In *African Penal Systems* (A. Milner, ed.). Routledge and Kegan Paul, London.

Cotran, E. (1966). The Place and Future of Customary Law in East Africa. In *East African Law Today* (The British Institute of International and Comparative Law). The British Institute of International and Comparative Law, London.

Cotran, E. (1969). Tribal Factors in the Establishment of East African Legal Systems. In *Tradition and Transition in East Africa: Studies of the Tribal Element in the Modern Era* (P.H. Gulliver, ed.). Routledge and Kegan Paul, London.

Counts, D. and Counts, D. (1974). The Kaliai Lupunga: Disputing in the Public Forum. In *Contention and Dispute: Aspects of Law and Social Control in Melanesia* (A.L. Epstein, ed.). Australian National University Press, Canberra.

Crocombe, R.G. (1964). *Communal Cash Cropping Among the Orokaiva* (New Guinea Research Bulletin No. 4). New Guinea Research Unit, The Australian National University, Port Moresby and Canberra.

Crocombe, R.G. (1965). *The M'Buke Cooperative Plantation* (New Guinea Research Bulletin No. 7). New Guinea Research Unit, The Australian National University, Port Moresby and Canberra.

Crocombe, R.G. (1967). Four Orokaiva Cash Croppers. In *Papuan Entrepreneurs* (New Guinea Research Bulletin No. 16). New Guinea Research Unit, The Australian National University, Port Moresby and Canberra.

Crocombe, R. (1971a). Land Reform: Prospects for Prosperity. In *Land Tenure in the Pacific* (R. Crocombe, ed.). Oxford University Press, Melbourne.

Crocombe, R.G. (1971b). Social Aspects of Co-operative and Other Corporate Land Holding in the Pacific Islands. In *Two Blades of Grass: Rural Co-operatives in*

*Agricultural Modernization* (P. Worsley, ed.). Manchester University Press, Manchester.

Crocombe, R.G. and Hide R. (1971). New Guinea. In *Land Tenure in the Pacific* (R. Crocombe, ed.). Oxford University Press, Melbourne.

Crocombe, R.G. and Hogbin, G.R. (1963a). *The Erap Mechanical Farming Project* (New Guinea Research Bulletin No. 1). New Guinea Research Unit, The Australian National University, Port Moresby and Canberra.

Crocombe, R.G. and Hogbin, G.R. (1963b). *Land, Work and Productivity at Inonda* (New Guinea Research Bulletin No. 2). New Guinea Research Unit, The Australian National University, Port Moresby and Canberra.

Cunningham, A. (1975). Law and Order v. Rule of Law: The Challenge of the Bougainville Incident. *Melanesian Law Journal* **3**, No. 2, 346 – 352.

Curtain, R. (1977). The Patterns of Labour Migration in Papua New Guinea with Particular Reference to the Sepik Area. Draft chapter, Ph.D. thesis, The Australian National University.

Curtain, R. (1978). Introduction. In Accounts of the History of Cash Crops in the Yangoru Area, Maprik District (History of Agriculture Discussion Paper No. 19). University of Papua New Guinea and Department of Primary Industry.

Curtain, R. (in press). The Structure of Internal Migration in Papua New Guinea. *Pacific Viewpoint*.

Dakeyne, R.B. (1966). Changes in Land Use and Settlement among the Yenga. In *Orokaiva Papers: Miscellaneous Papers on the Orokaiva of North East Papua* (New Guinea Research Bulletin No. 13). New Guinea Research Unit, The Australian National University, Port Moresby and Canberra.

Davies, I. (1966). *African Trade Unions*. Penguin, Harmondsworth.

Deng, F.M. (1971). *Tradition and Modernization: A Challenge for Law among the Dinka of the Sudan*. Yale University, New Haven and London.

Department of Business Development (1974). *Information Paper*. n.p. (mistakenly dated 1973 on the title page).

Department of Labour and Industry (1974). *Submission to the Urban Minimum Wages Board, Part B*, n.p.

Department of Labour, Research and Planning Division (1969). *The Supply of Agreement Labour through the Highland Labour Scheme*. Konedobu.

Department of Lands, Surveys and Mines (1971). *Guide-Lines for Promotion of Indigenous Business*. Department of Lands, Surveys and Mines, Konedobu.

Development Bank (1974). *Annual Report and Financial Statements*. Papua New Guinea Development Bank, Port Moresby.

Diamond, S. (1973). The Rule of Law Versus the Order of Custom. In *The Social Organization of Law* (D. Black and M. Mileski, eds). Seminar Press, New York and London.

Division of Co-operative Development (1974). *Annual Report of the Registrar of Co-operative Societies*. Acting Government Printer, Port Moresby.

Docker, E.W. (1970). *The Blackbirders: The Recruiting of South Seas Labour For Queensland, 1863 – 1907*. Angus and Robertson, Sydney.

Donaldson, M. and Good, K. (1978). Class and Politics in the Eastern Highlands of Papua New Guinea (History of Agriculture Discussion Paper No. 9). University of Papua New Guinea and Department of Primary Industry.

Donaldson, M. and Good, K. (1979). Draft Chapter on the Eastern Highlands (History of Agriculture Discussion Paper No. 30). University of Papua New Guinea and Department of Primary Industry.

Donaldson, M. and Turner, D. (1978). The Foreign Control of Papua New Guinea's Economy and the Reaction of the Independent State (Political Economy Occasional Paper No. 1). University of Papua New Guinea.

Douglas, M. (1969). Is Matriliny Doomed in Africa? In *Man in Africa* (M. Douglas and P.M. Karberry, eds). Tavistock, London.

Douglas, M. (1970) *Purity and Danger: An Analysis of Concepts of Pollution and Taboo*. Penguin, Harmondsworth.

Dumont, L. (1965). The Modern Conception of the Individual: Notes on its Genesis and that of Concomitant Institutions. *Contributions to Indian Sociology* **VIII**, 13 – 61.

Dunning, E. (1972). Dynamics of Racial Stratification: Some Preliminary Observations. *Race* **XIII**, No. 4, 415 – 434.

Dupré, G. and Rey, P. – P. (1973). Reflections on the Pertinence of a Theory of the History of Exchange. *Economy and Society* **2**, No. 2, 131 – 163.

Du Toit, B.M. (1962). Structural Looseness in New Guinea. *Journal of the Polynesian Society* **71**, 397 – 399.

Eggleston, F.W. (1928). The Mandate and the Australian People. In *The Australain Mandate for New Guinea* (F.W. Eggleston, ed.). Macmillan, Melbourne.

Elias, T.O. (1956). *The Nature of African Customary Law*. Manchester University Press, Manchester.

Epstein, A.L. (1967). Urbanization and Social Change in Africa. *Current Anthropology* **8**, 275 – 295.

Epstein, A.L. (1969). *Matupit: Land, Politics, and Change among the Tolai of New Britain*. Australian National University Press, Canberra.

Epstein, A.L. (1973). Law. In *Anthropology in Papua New Guinea: Readings from the Encyclopaedia of Papua and New Guinea* (I. Hogbin, ed.). Melbourne University Press, Carlton.

Epstein, A.L. (1974a). Introduction. In *Contention and Dispute: Aspects of Law and Social Control in Melanesia* (A.L. Epstein, ed.). Australian National University Press, Canberra.

Epstein, A.L. (1974b). Moots on Matupit. In *Contention and Dispute: Aspects of Law and Social Control in Melanesia* (A.L. Epstein, ed.). Australian National University Press, Canberra.

Epstein, T.S. (1964). Personal Capital Formation Among the Tolai of New Britain. In *Capital, Saving and Credit in Peasant Societies* (R. Firth and B.S. Yamey, eds). Allen and Unwin, London.

Epstein, T.S. (1968). *Capitalism, Primitive and Modern: Some Aspects of Tolai Economic Growth*. Australian National University Press, Canberra.

Epstein, S. (1972). The Tolai "Big-Man". *New Guinea* **7**, No. 1, 40 – 60.

Epstein. T.S. (1973). Economy. In *Anthropology in Papua New Guinea: Readings from the Encyclopaedia of Papua New Guinea* (I. Hogbin, ed.). Melbourne University Press, Carlton.

Evans, P. (1977). Multinationals, State-owned Corporations and the Transformation of Imperialism. *Economic Development and Cultural Change* **26**, No. 1, 43 – 64.

Evers, H.–D. (1977). Owning the Means of Subsistence Reproduction: Some Theoretical Notes on the Study of Urban and Rural Landownership. Paper delivered at the Seminar, *Underdevelopment and Subsistence Reproduction in Black Africa*, University of Bielefeld, 26 – 29 May, 1977.

Fairbairn, I.J. (1969). *Namasu: New Guinea's Largest Indigenous-Owned Company* (New Guinea Research Bulletin No. 28). New Guinea Research Unit, The Australian National University, Port Moresby and Canberra.

Fanon, Frantz (1967). *The Wretched of the Earth*. Penguin, Harmondsworth.

Farrall, L. (1977). Coconut Industry. In Papers on Primary Commodities, Part I (History of Agriculture Discussion Paper No. 1). University of Papua New Guinea and Department of Primary Industry.

Feder, E. (1977). Capitalism's Last-Ditch Effort to Save Underdeveloped Agricultures: International Agribusiness, the World Bank and the Rural Poor. *Journal of Contemporary Asia* **7**, No. 1, 56 – 78.

Finkle, J.L. and Gable, R.W. (1966). *Political Development and Social Change*. Wiley, New York and London.

Finney, B.R. (1969). *New Guinean Entrepreneurs* (New Guinea Research Bulletin No. 27). New Guinea Research Unit, The Australian National University, Port Moresby and Canberra.

Finney, B.R. (1973). *Big-Men and Business: Entrepreneurship and Economic Growth in the New Guinea Highlands*. Honolulu, The University Press of Hawaii.

Firth, S.G. (1972). The New Guinea Company, 1885 – 1899: A Case of Unprofitable Imperialism. *Historical Studies* **15**, No. 59, 361 – 377.

Firth, S.G. (1973). *German Recruitment and Employment of Labourers in the Western Pacific before the First World War*. D.Phil. thesis, University of Oxford.

Firth, S. (1977). German Rule: Ideology and Practice. *The Journal of Pacific History* **12**, No. 4, 238 – 241.

Fitzpatrick, P. (1974). Law and Colonialism. In *Catch 19: An Introduction to Politics* (Department of Political and Administrative Studies). University of Papua New Guinea.

Fitzpatrick, P. (1975). Tuki ni Buka: the Formation of a Development Corporation. *Yagl-Ambu* **2**, No. 3, 183 – 195.

Fitzpatrick, P. (1978). "Really Rather Like Slavery": Law and Labour in the Colonial Economy in Papua New Guinea. In *Essays in the Political Economy of*

*Australian Capitalism*, Vol. 3 (E.L. Wheelwright and K. Buckley, eds). Australia and New Zealand Book Company, Brookvale.

Fitzpatrick, P. (1980). The Creation and Containment of the Papua New Guinea Peasantry. *Essays in the Political Economy of Australian Capitalism* Vol. 4 (E.L. Wheelwright and K. Buckley, eds). Australia and New Zealand Book Company, Brookvale.

Fitzpatrick, P. and Blaxter, L. (1973). Informal Sector Discussion Papers Nos. 1, 3, 4 and 5. Department of the Chief Minister and Development Administration.

Fitzpatrick, P. and Blaxter, L. (1975). Colonialism and the Informal Sector. *The Australian and New Zealand Journal of Sociology* 11, No. 3, 42 – 46.

Fitzpatrick, P. and Blaxter, L. (1979). Imposed law in the Containment of Papua New Guinean Economic Ventures. In *The Imposition of Law* (S.B. Burman and B.E. Harrell-Bond, eds). Academic Press, New York and London.

Fitzpatrick, P. and Southwood, J. (1976). The Community Corporation in Papua New Guinea (IASER Discussion Paper No. 5). Institute of Applied Social and Economic Research, Boroko.

Fleckenstein, F. von (1975). Ketarovo: Case Study of a Cattle Project. In *Agricultural Extension in the Village* (Extension Bulletin No. 9) (G.T. Harris and F. von Fleckenstein). Department of Agriculture, Stock and Fisheries, Port Moresby.

Fleckenstein, F. von (1977). Tobacco. In Papers on Primary Commodities, Part II (History of Agriculture Discussion Paper No. 2). University of Papua New Guinea and Department of Primary Industry.

Ford, G.W. (1972). Workers' Organizations. In *Encyclopaedia of Papua and New Guinea*, Vol. 2. Melbourne University Press, Carlton.

Foster-Carter, A. (1974). Neo Marxist Approaches to Development and Underdevelopment. In *Sociology and Development* (E. de Kadt and G. Williams, eds). Tavistock, London.

Foster-Carter, A. (1978). The Modes of Production Controversy. *New Left Review* 107, 47 – 77.

Franck, T.M. (1972). The New Development: Can American Law and Legal Institutions Help Developing Countries? *Wisconsin Law Review* 1972, 3, 768 – 801.

Frank, A.G. (1971a). *Capitalism and Underdevelopment in Latin America*. Penguin, Harmondsworth.

Frank, A.G. (1971b). *Sociology of Development and Underdevelopment of Sociology*. Pluto Press, London.

Frank. A.G. (1974). Dependence is Dead, Long Live Dependence and the Class Struggle: An Answer to Critics. *Latin American Perspectives* 1, No. 1, 87 – 106.

Fraser, A. (1976). Legal Theory and Legal Practice. *Arena* 44, 45, 123 – 156.

Friere, P. (1970). *Pedagogy of the Oppressed*. Seabury Press, New York.

Friere, P. (1972). *Cultural Action for Freedom*. Penguin, Harmondsworth.

Freund, R.P. (1971). Those Enga! *New Guinea* 6, No. 3, 52 – 56.

Fyfe, C. (1973). God on their Side. *New Society*. 5 April, 28 – 29.

Gadiel, D. (1973). *Australia, New Guinea and the International Economy*. Fontana, n.p.

Galanter, M. (1966). The Modernization of Law. *Modernization* (M. Weiner, ed.). Basic Books, New York.

Galanter, M. (1968). The Displacement of Traditional Law in Modern India. *Journal of Social Issues* **xxiv**, No. 4, 65 – 91.

Gammage, B. (1975). The Rabaul Strike, 1929. *Oral History* **III**, No. 2, 2 – 43.

Gardner, J.A. (1978). The "Law and Development" Movement: The "Indirect" Export of American Legal Models to Latin America and their Legal and Social Impact in the "Recipient" and "Exporting" Legal Cultures. Paper delivered at the seminar, *International Symposium: The Social Consequences of Imposed Law*, University of Warwick, 5 – 7 April, 1978.

Gardner, J.A. (in press). *Legal Imperialism: American Lawyers and Foreign Aid in Latin America*. University of Wisconsin Press, Madison.

Garnaut, R., Wright, M. and Curtain, R. (1977). *Employment, Incomes and Migration in Papua New Guinea Towns* (IASER Monograph No. 6). Institute of Applied Social and Economic Research, Boroko.

Geertz, C. (1963). The Integrative Revolution. In *Old Societies and New States: The Quest for Modernity in Asia and Africa* (C. Geertz, ed.). Free Press, New York.

Genovese, E.D. (1975). *Roll, Jordan, Roll: The World the Slaves Made*. Deutsch, London.

Gerritsen, R. (1975). Aspects of the Political Evolution of Rural Papua New Guinea: Towards a Political Economy of the Terminal Peasantry. Paper delivered at Work-in-Progress Seminar, Research School of Social Science, Australian National University, 22 July, 1975.

Gerry, C. and Birkbeck, C. (n.d.). The Petty Commodity Producer in Third World Cities: Petit Bourgeois or "Disguised" Proletarian? Centre for Development Studies, University College of Swansea, Swansea.

Ghai, Y.P. (1976). Notes Towards a Theory of Law and Ideology: Tanzanian Perspectives. *African Law Studies* **13**, 31 – 105.

Ghai, Y.P. (1978). Law and another development. *Development Dialogue* **1978**, 2, 109 – 126.

Ghai, Y.P. (in press). State, Law and Participatory Institutions: The Papua New Guinea Experience.

Ghai, Y.P. and McAuslan, J.P.W.B. (1970). *Public Law and Political Change in Kenya*. Oxford University Press, Nairobi.

Gibbs, H. (1945). *The Laws of the Territory of New Guinea: Their Constitutional Source and Basic Content*. LL.M. thesis, University of Queensland.

Girvan, N. (1970). Multinational Corporations and Dependent Underdevelopment in Mineral-Export Economies. *Social and Economic Studies* **19**, No. 4, 490 – 526.

Glick, L.B. (1973). Sorcery and Witchcraft. In *Anthropology in Papua New Guinea: Readings from the Encyclopaedia of Papua and New Guinea* (I. Hogbin, ed.). Melbourne University Press, Carlton.

Gluckman, M. (1955). *The Judicial Process among the Barotse of Northern Rhodesia*. Manchester University Press, Manchester.

Gluckman, M. (1966). Legal Aspects of Development in Africa: Problems and Research Arising from the Study of Traditional Systems of Law. In *Les Aspects Juridiques de Développment Économique* (A. Tunc, ed.). Libraire Dalloz, Paris.

Good, K. (1979). The Formation of the Peasantry. In *Development and Dependancy: The Political Economy of Papua New Guinea* (K. Good, A. Amarshi and R. Mortimer). Oxford University Press, Melbourne.

Good, K. and Donaldson, M. (1979). The Development of Rural Capitalism in Papua New Guinea: Coffee Production in the Eastern Highlands (History of Agriculture Discussion Paper No. 29). University of Papua New Guinea and Department of Primary Industry.

Gordon, A. (1976). The Future of Plantation Systems after Independence. Paper delivered at the *Tenth Waigani Seminar*, University of Technology, Lae, May, 1976.

Gower, L.C.B. (1969). *The Principles of Modern Company Law*. Stevens and Sons, London.

Gray, G.G. (n.d.). Land Tenure Conversion in the Northern District: The Effects of Land Tenure Conversion at Ombi-Tara. New Guinea Research Unit, roneo.

Gregory, C. (1975). The Concept of Modern Monetary Sector as "Engine for Development" in Underdeveloped Dual Economy Countries. Paper delivered at the Seminar, *Seminar on Industrial Democracy in Papua New Guinea*, University of Papua New Guinea.

Griffin, K. (1969). *Underdevelopment in Spanish America: An Interpretation*. Allen and Unwin, London.

Gunton, R.J. (1974). A Banker's Gamble. In *Problem of Choice: Land in Papua New Guinea's Future* (P.G. Sack, ed.). Australian National University Press and Robert Brown and Associates, Canberra and Port Moresby.

Gutkind, P.C.W. and Wallerstein, I. (1976). Editors' Introduction. In *The Political Economy of Contemporary Africa* (P.C.W. Gutkind and I. Wallerstein, eds). Sage, Beverly Hills and London.

Hager, M.L. (1972). The Role of Lawyers in Developing Countries. *American Bar Association Journal* 58, 33 – 38.

Hale, S. (1978). The Politics of Entrepreneurship in Indian Villages. *Development and Change* **9**, No. 2, 245 – 273.

Harding, T.G. (1971). Wage Labour and Cash Cropping: The Economic Adaptation of New Guinea Copra Producers. *Oceania* **41**, No. 3, 192 – 200.

Harris, G.T. (1976). Some Responses to Population Pressure in the Papua New Guinea Highlands, 1957 – 1974 (Discussion Paper No. 23). Economics Department, University of Papua New Guinea.

Harris, M. (1968). *The Rise of Anthropological Theory: A History of Theories of Culture*. Routledge and Kegan Paul, London.

Harris, M. (1977). *Cows, Pigs, Wars and Witches: The Riddles of Culture*. Fontana, n.p.

Hart, H.L.A. (1961). *The Concept of Law*. Oxford University Press, London.

Hasluck, P. (1976). *A Time for Building: Australian Administration in Papua and New Guinea 1951 – 1963*. Melbourne University Press, Carlton.

Hastings, P. (1969). *New Guinea: Problems and Prospects*. Cheshire, Melbourne.

Hatanaka, S. (1972). *Leadership and Socio-Economic Change in Sinasina, New Guinea Highlands* (New Guinea Research Bulletin No. 45). New Guinea Research Unit, The Australian National University, Canberra and Port Moresby.

Hayek, F. (1944). *The Road to Serfdom*. Routledge and Kegan Paul, London.

Healy, C. (1969). Companies in Papua New Guinea: The Legal Framework. Paper delivered at the *Third Waigani Seminar: Land Tenure and Indigenous Group Enterprise in Melanesia: Legal and Social Implications*, University of Papua New Guinea, 1969.

Herskovits, M.J. (1960). *Economic Anthropology*. Knopf, New York.

Hindess, B. and Hirst, P.G. (1975). *Pre-Capitalist Modes of Production*. Routledge and Kegan Paul, London.

Hirsch, J. (1978). *The State Apparatus and Social Reproduction: Elements of a Theory of the Bourgeois State*. In *State and Capital: A Marxist Debate* (J. Holloway and S. Picciotto, eds). Edward Arnold, London.

Hobsbawm, E.J. (1969). *Industry and Empire*. Penguin, Harmondsworth.

Hogbin, G.R. (1964) *A Survey of Indigenous Rubber Producers in the Kerema Bay Area* (New Guinea Research Bulletin No. 5). New Guinea Research Unit, The Australian National University, Canberra and Port Moresby.

Hogbin, I. (1970). *Social Change*. Melbourne University Press, Carlton.

Horwitz, M.J. (1977). *The Transformation of American Law, 1780 – 1860*. Harvard University Press, Cambridge Mass. and London.

Housing Commission (1975). *National Housing Plan, Part One*. Housing Commission, Ministry of the Interior, Port Moresby.

Howlett, D. (1977). When is a Peasant Not a Peasant: First Thoughts on Rural Proletarianization in Papua New Guinea (History of Agriculture Discussion Paper No. 7). University of Papua New Guinea and Department of Primary Industry.

Howlett, D., Hide, R. and Young, E. with Arba, J., Bi, H. and Kaman, B. (1976). *Chimbu: Issues in Development* (Development Studies Centre Monograph No. 4). The Australian National University, Canberra.

Hudson, W.J. (1971). Introduction. In *Australia and Papua New Guinea* (W.J. Hudson, ed.). Sydney University Press, Sydney.

Hudson, W.J. and Daven, J. (1971). Papua and New Guinea since 1945. In *Australia and Papua New Guinea* (W.J. Hudson, ed.). Sydney University Press, Sydney.

Hunt, A. (1976). Law, State and Class Struggle. *Marxism Today* June, 178 – 187.

Hunt, A. (1978). *The Sociological Movement in Law*. Macmillan, London.

Hunter, G. (1966). *South-east Asia: Race, Culture and Nation*. Oxford University Press, London.

Huttenback, R.A. (1976). *Racism and Empire: White Settlers and Colored Immigrants in the British Self-Governing Colonies, 1830 – 1910*. Cornell University Press, Ithaca and London.

Hymer, S. (1972). The Multinational Corporation and the Law of Uneven Development. In *Economics and World Order: From the 1970's to the 1990's* (J.N. Bhagwati, ed.). Macmillan, New York.

Hymes, D. (1974). The Use of Anthropology: Critical, Political, Personal. In *Reinventing Anthropology* (D. Hymes, ed.). Random House, Vintage Books edition, New York.

ILO (1972). *Employment, Incomes and Equality: A Strategy for Increasing Productive Employment in Kenya*. International Labour Office, Geneva.

Inglis, A. (1974). *"Not a White Woman Safe": Sexual Anxiety and Politics in Port Moresby 1920 – 1934*. Australian National University Press, Canberra.

International Bank for Reconstruction and Development (1965). *The Economic Development of the Territory of Papua and New Guinea*. Johns Hopkins, Baltimore.

Isaac, J.E. (1970). *The Structure of Unskilled Wages and Relativities between Rural and Non Rural Employment in Papua and New Guinea*. Department of Labour, Port Moresby.

Jackman, H. (1972). Co-operatives. In *Encyclopaedia of Papua New Guinea*, Vol. 1. Melbourne University Press, Carlton.

Jackson, G. (1965). *Cattle, Coffee and Land among the Wain* (New Guinea Research Bulletin No. 8). New Guinea Research Unit, The Australian National University, Port Moresby and Canberra.

Jackson, R.T. (1976a). The Social Geography of Urban Papua New Guinea: A Small Start. In *An Introduction to the Urban Geography of Papua New Guinea* (Department of Geography Occasional Paper No. 13) (R. Jackson, ed.). University of Papua New Guinea.

Jackson, R.T. (1976b). Some Conclusions. In *An Introduction to the Urban Geography of Papua New Guinea* (Department of Geography Occasional Paper No. 13) (R. Jackson, ed.). University of Papua New Guinea.

Jackson, R.T., Fitzpatrick, P. and Blaxter, L. (1976). The Law and Urbanization. In *An Introduction to the Urban Geography of Papua New Guinea* (Department of Geography Occasional Paper No. 13) (R. Jackson, ed.). University of Papua New Guinea.

James, R.W. (1974). The Role of the Courts in Attempts to Recover Alienated Land. *Melanesian Law Journal* **2**, No. 2, 270 – 273.

James, R.W. (1975). Developments in Legal Education in the Faculty of Law, University of Papua New Guinea. *Melanesian Law Journal* **3**, No. 2, 185 – 212.

Jeffries, R. (1975). The Labour Aristocracy: Ghana Case Study. *Review of African Political Economy* **3**, 59 – 70.

Jinks, B., Biskup, P. and Nelson, H. (1973). *Readings in New Guinea History*. Angus and Robertson, Sydney.

Johnson, H.G. (1967). *Economic Policies Toward Less Developed Countries.* Allen and Unwin, London.     The Brookings Institution, Washington.

Joyce, R.B. (1971). Australian Interests in New Guinea before 1906. In *Australia and Papua New Guinea* (W.J. Hudson, ed.). Sydney University Press, Sydney.

Kaa, D.J. van de (1970). Estimates of Vital Rates and Future Growth. In *People and Planning in Papua New Guinea* (New Guinea Research Bulletin No. 34) (M. Ward, ed.). New Guinea Research Unit, The Australian National University, Boroko and Canberra.

Kanyeihamba, G.W. (1979). The Impact of the Received Law on Development in Anglophonic Africa. Paper delivered at *The British Sociological Association Annual Conference*, University of Warwick, April, 1979.

Kaputin, J. (1975). The Law: A Colonial Fraud? *New Guinea* **10**, No. 1, 4 – 15.

Kaputin, J.R. and Momis, J. (1974). Press Release, 4 February 1974.

Kassam, F.M. (1974). Laws of Succession in Papua New Guinea: Some Reflections. *Melanesian Law Journal* **2**, No. 1, 5 – 47.

Kay, G. (1975). *Development and Underdevelopment: A Marxist Analysis.* Macmillan, London.

Kemp, T. (1972). The Marxist Theory of Imperialism. In *Studies in the Theory of Imperialism* (R. Owen and B. Sutcliffe, eds). Longman, London.

Kiki, A.M. (1968). *Kiki: Ten Thousand Years in a Lifetime.* Cheshire, Melbourne.

Kiki, A.M. (1970). Development of Trade Unions in the Territory. In *The Politics of Melanesia* (M. Ward, ed.). The Australian National University, Research School of Pacific Studies and the University of Papua New Guinea, Canberra and Port Moresby.

Kerr, J.R. (1968). Law in Papua and New Guinea, 19th Roy Milne Memorial Lecture. Australian Institute of International Affairs, Melbourne.

Klinghoffer, A.J. (1974). The Soviet Union and Africa. In *The Soviet Union and the Developing Nations* (R.E. Kanet, ed.). Johns Hopkins University Press, Baltimore and London.

Knowles, W.H. (1960). Industrial Conflict and Unions. In *Labour Commitment and Social Change in Developing Areas* (W.E. Moore and A.S. Feldman, eds). Social Science Research Council, New York.

Kuper, Leo (1974). *Race, Class and Power: Ideology and Revolutionary Change in Plural Societies.* Duckworth, London.

Laclau, E. (1971). Feudalism and Capitalism in Latin America. *New Left Review* **67**, 19 – 38.

Lambert, J. (1979). The Relationship between Cash Crop Production and Nutritional Status in Papua New Guinea (History of Agriculture Discussion Paper No. 33). University of Papua New Guinea and Department of Primary Industry.

Langmore, J. (1967). Contractors in Port Moresby. In *Papuan Entrepreneurs* (New Guinea Research Bulletin No. 16). New Guinea Research Unit, The Australian National University, Port Moresby and Canberra.

Langmore, J. (1977). Wages. In Aspects of the Rural Economy (History of

Agriculture Discussion Paper No. 4). University of Papua New Guinea and Department of Primary Industry.

Langness, L.L. (1973). Traditional Political Organization. In *Anthropology in Papua New Guinea: Readings from the Encyclopaedia of Papua and New Guinea* (I. Hogbin, ed.). Melbourne University Press, Carlton.

Lasswell, H.D. and McDougal, M.S. (1943). Legal Education and Public Policy. *Yale Law Journal* **52**, 203 – 295.

Law Reform Commission of Papua New Guinea (1976). *Fairness of Transactions* (Working Paper No. 5). Law Reform Commission, Waigani.

Law Reform Commission of Papua New Guinea (1977a). *Annual Report of 1977.* Law Reform Commission n.p.

Law Reform Commission of Papua New Guinea (1977b). *The Role of Customary Law in the Legal System* (Report No. 7). Law Reform Commission, Waigani.

Law Reform Commission of Papua New Guinea (1978). *Law of Succession* (Working Paper No. 12). Law Reform Commission, Waigani.

Law Reform Commission of Papua New Guinea (1979). *Annual Report 1978.* Law Reform Commission, n.p.

Lawrence, P. (1964). *Road Belong Cargo: A Study of Cargo Movement in the Southern Madang District New Guinea.* Melbourne University Press, Carlton.

Lawrence, P. (1970). In *The Rule of Law in an Emerging Society.* International Commission of Jurists, Australian Section, Sydney.

Lea, D.A.M. (1962). *Abelam Land and Sustenance.* Ph.D. thesis, The Australian National University.

Lee, J.M. (1967). *Colonial Development and Good Government: A Study of the Ideas Expressed by the British Official Classes in Planning Decolonization 1939 – 1964.* Clarendon Press, Oxford.

Legge, J.D. (1956). *Australian Colonial Policy: A Survey of Native Administration and European Development in Papua.* Angus and Robertson, Sydney.

Legge, J.D. (1971). The Murray Period: Papua 1906 – 40. In *Australia and Papua New Guinea* (W.J. Hudson, ed.) Sydney University Press, Sydney.

Leibowitz, H. (1976). *Colonial Emancipation in the Pacific and the Caribbean: A Legal and Political Analysis.* Praeger, New York.

Lepani, C. (1976). Planning in Small Dependent Economies—A Case Study of Papua New Guinea. Paper delivered at the seminar *Planning in Small Dependent Economies*, Institute of Development Studies at the University of Sussex, 1976.

Lepervanche, M. de (1973). Social Structure. In *Anthropology in Papua New Guinea: Readings from the Enclyclopaedia of Papua New Guinea* (I. Hogbin, ed.). Melbourne University Press, Carlton.

Levine, H.B. and Levine, M.W. (1979) *Urbanization in Papua New Guinea: A Study of Ambivalent Townsmen.* Cambridge University Press, Cambridge.

Leys, C. (1976). The "Overdeveloped" Post Colonial State: A Re-evaluation. *Review of African Political Economy* **5**, 39 – 48.

Leys, C. (1977). Underdevelopment and Dependency: Critical Notes. *Journal of Contemporary Asia* **7**, 92 – 107.

Lloyd, P.C. (1973). *Classes, Crises and Coups: Themes in the Sociology of Developing Countries*. Paladin, London.

Long, N. (1977). *An Introduction to the Sociology of Rural Development*. Tavistock, London.

Loveday, P. and Wolfers, E.P. (1976). *Parties and Parliament in Papua New Guinea 1964 – 1975* (IASER Monograph No. 5). Institute of Applied Social and Economic Research, Boroko.

Lubett, R. (1977). Business Development. In Aspects of the Rural Economy (History of Agriculture Discussion Paper No. 4). University of Papua New Guinea and Department of Primary Industry.

Luckham, R. (1978). Imperialism, Law and Structural Dependence: The Ghana Legal Profession. *Development and Change* **9**, No. 2, 201 – 243.

Mackellar, M.L. (1975). The Enga Syndrome. *Melanesian Law Journal* 3, No. 2, 213 – 216.

MacTeine, J. and Paliwala, A. (1978). Village Courts in Simbu. n.p., roneo.

Magdoff, H. (1969). *The Age of Imperialism: The Economics of U.S. Foreign Policy*. Monthly Review Press, New York and London.

Maher, R.F. (1961). *New Men of Papua: A Study of Cultural Change*. The University of Wisconsin Press, Madison.

Mair, L.P. (1967). *New Nations*, Weidenfeld and Nicolson, London.

Mair, L.P. (1970). *Australia in New Guinea*. Melbourne University Press, Carlton.

Maitland-Jones, J.F. (1973). *Politics in Ex-British Africa*. Weidenfeld and Nicolson, London.

Mamdani, M. (1976). *Politics and Class Formation in Uganda*. Heinemann, London.

Mandel, E. (1968). *Marxist Economic Theory*. Merlin Press, London.

Mangin, W., ed. (1970). *Peasants in Cities: Readings in the Anthropology of Urbanization*. Houghton Mifflin, Boston.

Manpower Planning Unit (1975). Population, Urbanisation and Employment 1971 – 86 (Discussion Paper No. 1). Central Planning Office, Waigani.

Maquet, J. (1972). Inborn Differences and the Premise of Inequality. In *Race and Social Difference* (P. Baxter and B. Sansom, eds). Penguin, Harmondsworth.

Marcuse, H. (1971). *Soviet Marxism*. Penguin, Harmondsworth.

Markovitz, I.L. (1977). *Power and Class in Africa: An Introduction to Change and Conflict in African Politics*. Prentice-Hall, Englewood Cliffs.

Martin, R.M. (1969). Tribesmen into Trade Unionists: The African Experience and the Papua-New Guinea Prospect. *Journal of Industrial Relations* **11**, No. 2, 125 – 172.

Marx, K. (1973). *Grundrisse: Foundations of the Critique of Political Economy*. Penguin, Harmondsworth.

Marx, K. (1974). *Capital*. Lawrence and Wishart, London.

Marx, K. and Engels, F. (1970). *Selected Works*. Progress Publishers, Moscow.

Mayo, J. (1972). *An Oddity of Empire: An Administrative History of the Protectorate of British New Guinea 1884 – 1888*. M.A. thesis, University of Papua New Guinea.

McCarthy, J.K. (1963). *Patrol into Yesterday*. Cheshire, Melbourne.

McGee, T.G. (1971). *The Urbanization Process in The Third World City*. Bell, London.

McKillop, R.F. (1974a). Problems of Access: Agricultural Extension in the Eastern Highlands of New Guinea. Paper delivered at the Seminar, *Improving Access to Government Services*, University of Papua New Guinea, November, 1974.

McKillop, R.F. (1974b). *The Agricultural Extension Service in Papua New Guinea: Can We Make it More Effective?* (Extension Bulletin No. 5). Department of Agriculture Stock and Fisheries, Port Moresby.

McKillop, R. (1975). Catching the Didiman. *Administration for Development* **3**, 14 – 21.

McKillop, R. (1977a). Cocoa Industry. In Papers on Primary Commodities, Part I (History of Agriculture Discussion Paper No. 1). University of Papua New Guinea and Department of Primary Industry.

McKillop, R. (1977b). Coffee Industry. In Papers on Primary Commodities, Part I (History of Agriculture Discussion Paper No. 1). University of Papua New Guinea and Department of Primary Industry.

McKillop, R. (1977c). Sugar. In Papers on Primary Industry Commodities, Part II (History of Agriculture Discussion Paper No. 2). University of Papua New Guinea and Department of Primary Industry.

McNamara, R.S. (1973). *One Hundred Countries, Two Billion People: The Dimensions of Development*. Pall Mall Press, London.

McSwain, R. (1970). Custom, Kin and Co-operatives. *Journal of the Papua and New Guinea Society* 4, No. 1, 33 – 46.

McSwain, R. (1977). *The Past and Future People: Tradition and Change on a New Guinea Island*. Oxford University Press, Melbourne.

Meggitt, M. (1971). From Tribesmen to Peasants: The Case of the Mae Enga of New Guinea. In *Anthropology in Oceania: Essays Presented to Ian Hogbin* (E.R. Hiatt and C. Jayawardena, eds). Angus and Robertson, Sydney.

Meggitt, M.J. (1974). *Studies in Enga History*. The Oceania Monographs No. 20, Sydney.

Meillassoux, C. (1972). From Reproduction to Production: A Marxist Approach to Economic Anthropology. *Economy and Society* **1**, No. 1, 93 – 105.

Meillassoux, C. (1973). The Social Organization of the Peasantry: The Economic Basis of Kinship. *The Journal of Peasant Studies* **1**, No. 1, 81 – 90.

Melrose Report (1939). Report by R. Melrose Director of District Services and Native Affairs on the Activities of the Wallace Family, November 1939. From the papers of W.R. McNicoll and held in the New Guinea Collection of the Library of the University of Papua Guinea.

Merryman, J.H. (1977). Comparative Law and Social Change: On the Origins,

Style, Decline and Revival of the Law and Development Movement. *The American Journal of Comparative Law* **25**, 457 – 491.

Miles, J. (1956). Native Commercial Agriculture in Papua. *South Pacific* **9**, No. 2, 318 – 327.

Ministry of Labour (1976). *Papua New Guinea National Investment Strategy*. Port Moresby.

Mitchell, D.D. (1976). *Land and Agriculture in Nagovisi Papua New Guinea* (IASER Monograph No. 3). Institute of Applied Social and Economic Research, Boroko.

Mkandawire, P.T. (1977). Employment Strategies in the Third World: A Critique. *Journal of Contemporary Asia* **7**, No. 1, 27 – 43.

Mogu, B. and Bwaleto, K. (1978). A Study of Area Communities and Village Courts in the Kainantu District. *Yagl-Ambu* **5**, No. 1, 87 – 105.

Momis, J. (1973). Bougainville Copper—The Case for Re-negotiation. Paper delivered at the *Seventh Waigani Seminar: Law and Development in Melanesia*, University of Papua New Guinea, 1973.

Morauta, L. (1974). *Beyond the Village: Local Politics in Madang, Papua New Guinea*. Australian National University Press, Canberra.

Morawetz, D. (1967). *Land Tenure Conversion in the Northern District of Papua* (New Guinea Research Bulletin No. 17). New Guinea Research Unit, The Australian National University, Port Moresby and Canberra.

Mortimer, R. (1975). Social Science and the Peasant: A Case of Academic Genocide? University of Papua New Guinea.

Moulik, R. (1970). *A Study of Adoption Process in Relation to Development Bank Loans in the Eastern Highlands*. Department of Information and Extension Services, Port Moresby.

Murray, H. (1931). *The Scientific Method as Applied to Native Labour Problems in Papua*. Government Printer, Port Moresby.

Murray, R. (1971). The Internationalization of Capital and the Nation State. *New Left Review* **67**, 84 – 109.

Murray, R. (1972). Underdevelopment, International Firms, and the International Division of Labour. In *Towards a New World Economy* (sometimes classified under J. Tinbergen). Rotterdam University Press, n.p.

Narakobi, B.M. (1978). Sorcery Among the East Sepiks (Occasional Paper No. 10). Law Reform Commission, Waigani.

Narakobi, C. and Wanji, R. (1976). Inter-Racial Joint Enterprises in Papua New Guinea. *Melanesian Law Journal* **4**, No. 1, 94 – 112.

National Investment and Development Authority (1977). *Investor's Guide to Papua New Guinea*. National Investment and Development Authority, Port Moresby.

National Minimum Wages Board (1976). *Reasons for Decision and Determination*. roneo, n.p.

Nelson, H.N. (1969). European Attitudes in Papua, 1906 – 1914. In *Second*

*Waigani Seminar: The History of Melanesia* (M. Ward, ed.). Research School of Pacific Studies and the University of Papua New Guinea, Canberra and Port Moresby.

Nelson, H. (1974). *Papua New Guinea: Black Unity or Black Chaos?* Penguin, Ringwood.

Nelson, H.N. (1975). *Black, White, Gold: Goldmining in Papua-New Guinea 1878 – 1930.* Ph.D thesis, University of Papua New Guinea. Also (1976). *Black, White and Gold: Goldmining in Papua New Guinea 1878 – 1930.* Australian National University Press, Canberra.

Nelson, H.N. (1976). The Swinging Index: Capital Punishment and British and Australian Adminstrations in Papua and New Guinea 1888 – 1945. Paper delivered at a seminar in the Department of Pacific and Southeast Asian History, Australian National University, 29 September, 1976.

Nettl, J.P. and Robertson, R. (1968). *International Systems and the Modernization of Societies.* Faber, London.

Neumann, F. (1957). *The Democratic and the Authoritarian State: Essays in Political and Legal Theory.* Free Press, Glencoe.

Nicholls, D. (1971). The Lowa Marketing Co-operative Ltd. of Goroka. Paper delivered at the *Fifth Waigani Seminar: Change and Development in Rural Melanesia,* University of Papua New Guinea, 1971.

Nkrumah, K. (1962). Law in Africa. *Journal of African Law* **6,** No. 2, 103 – 108.

Nwabueze, B.O. (1973). *Constitutionalism in the Emergent States.* Hurst, London.

Nwafor, A. (1975). History and the Intelligence of the Disinherited. *The Review of Radical Political Economics* **7,** No. 3, 43 – 54.

O'Brien, D.C. (1972). Modernization, Order and the Erosion of a Democratic Ideal: American Political Science, 1960 – 70. *The Journal of Development Studies* **8,** No. 4, 351 – 378.

O'Connor, A.J. (1970). Indigenous Shareholding: An Analysis. In *The Indigenous Role in Business Enterprise: Three Papers from the Third Waigani Seminar* (New Guinea Research Bulletin No. 35). New Guinea Research Unit, The Australian National University, Port Moresby and Canberra.

Ogan, E. (1972). *Business and Cargo: Socio-Economic Change among the Nasioi of Bougainville* (New Guinea Research Bulletin No. 44). New Guinea Research Unit, The Australian National University, Port Moresby and Canberra.

Okoth-Ogendo, H.W.O. (1979). The Imposition of Property Law in Kenya. In *The Imposition of Law* (S.B. Burman and B.E. Harrell-Bond, eds). Academic Press, New York and London.

O'Neill, N. (1976). The Judges and the Constitution—The First Year. *Melanesian Law Journal* **4,** No. 2, 242 – 258.

Oostermeyer, W.J. and Gray, J. (1967). Twelve Orokaiva Traders. In *Papuan Entrepreneurs* (New Guinea Research Bulletin No. 16). New Guinea Research Unit. The Australian National University, Port Moresby and Canberra.

Oram, N. (1970). Indigenous Housing and Urban Development. In *Port Moresby*

*Urban Development* (New Guinea Research Bulletin No. 37) (J.V. Langmore and N.D. Oram). New Guinea Research Unit, The Australian National University, Port Moresby and Canberra.

Oram, N. (1973) Administration, Development and Public Order. In *Alternative Strategies for Papua New Guinea* (A. Clunies Ross and J. Langmore, eds). Oxford University Press, Melbourne.

Oram, N.D. (1976a). *Colonial Town to Melanesian City: Port Moresby 1884 – 1974*. Australian National University Press, Canberra.

Oram, N. (1976b). Traditional Networks and Modern Association: the Port Moresby Electorates. In *Prelude to Self-Government: Electoral Politics in Papua New Guinea 1972* (D. Stone, ed.). Research School of Pacific Studies and the University of Papua New Guinea at the Australian National University, Canberra.

Overseas Development Group (1973). *A Report on Development Strategies for Papua New Guinea*. Office of Programming and Co-ordination, Port Moresby.

Owen, R. and Sutcliffe, B., eds (1972). *Studies in the Theory of Imperialism*. Longman, London.

Page, J.B. (1964). Notes on Land Law and Custom amongst the Amele Speaking People of the Madang Central Sub-District. Typescript, Madang.

Paliwala, A. (1974). The Bougainville Agreement: Is a Deal a Deal? *Melanesian Law Journal* 2, No. 2, 130 – 150.

Paliwala, A. (1976). Village Courts in Papua New Guinea: Peoples' Courts or Colonial Courts? Paper delivered at the Goroka seminar, *National Goals and Law Reform*, Goroka, May, 1976.

Paliwala, A. (1979). Law and Order in the Village: Papua New Guinea's Village Courts. Paper delivered at the *Cambridge Criminology Conference*, Cambridge, 11 – 13 July, 1979.

Paliwala, A., Zorn, J. and Bayne, P. (1978). Economic Development and the Changing Legal System of Papua New Guinea. *African Law Studies* 16, 3 – 79.

Panoff, M. (1969). Land Tenure among the Maenge of New Britain. Paper delivered at the *Third Waigani Seminar: Land Tenure and Indigenous Group Enterprise in Melanesia: Legal and Social Implications*, University of Papua New Guinea, 1969.

Pashukanis, E.B. (1978). *Law and Marxism: A General Theory*. Ink Links, London.

Paterson, J. (1969). New Guinea's Trade Unions. *New Guinea* 4, No. 1, 26 – 34.

Paul, J.C.N. (1962 – 63). Legal Education in English-Speaking Africa. *Legal Education* 15, 189 – 204.

Petras, J.F. (1975). New Perspectives on Imperialism and Social Classes in the Periphery. *Journal of Contemporary Asia* 5, No. 3, 291 – 308.

Philipp, F. (1971). Beef Cattle Raising by New Guineans. *South Pacific Bulletin* 21, No. 2, 15 – 19.

Ploeg, A. (1971). Some Indigenous Views on the Social and Economic Development of Papua and New Guinea. *Journal of the Papua and New Guinea Society* 5, No. 1, 47 – 62.

Ploeg, A. (1973). Sociological Aspects of Kapore Settlement. In *Hoskins Development: The Role of Oil Palm and Timber* (New Guinea Research Bulletin No. 49). New Guinea Research Unit, The Australian National University, Port Moresby and Canberra.

Ploeg, A. (1979). Recent Developments in Kovai Agriculture (History of Agriculture Working Paper No. 26). University of Papua New Guinea and Department of Primary Industry.

Pooley, B. (1972). The Modernization of Law in Ghana. In *Ghana and the Ivory Coast: Perspectives on Modernization* (P. Foster and A.R. Zolberg, eds). The University of Chicago Press, Chicago and London.

*Post-Courier*, various dates, newspaper, Port Moresby.

Potter, J. (1977). Livestock. In Papers on Primary Commodities, Part II (History of Agriculture Discussion Paper No. 2). University of Papua New Guinea and Department of Primary Industry.

Poulantzas, N. (1973). *Political Power and Social Classes*. New Left Books and Sheed and Ward, London.

Powell, H.A. (1967). Competitive Leadership in Trobriand Political Organization. In *Comparative Political Systems: Studies in the Politics of Pre-Industrial Societies* (R. Cohen and J. Middleton, eds). The Natural History Press, New York.

Power, A.P. (1974). *A Study of Development in Niugini from 1884 to 1940.*M.A. thesis, University of Papua New Guinea.

Public Service Association of Papua New Guinea (n.d.). Submission to National Minimum Wage Enquiry. roneo, n.p.

Public Solicitor (1976). *Public Solicitor of Papua New Guinea, First Annual Report 1975 – 1976*. Port Moresby.

Public Solicitor's File L 413. *Tulu and Navalen Plantations*.

Quinlivan, P.J. (1975). Local Courts in Papua New Guinea: Bringing Justice to the People. In *Lo Bilong ol Manmeri: Crime, Compensation and Village Courts* (J. Zorn and P. Bayne, eds). The University of Papua New Guinea, n.p.

Radi, H. (1971). New Guinea under Mandate. In *Australia and Papua New Guinea* (W.J. Hudson, ed.). Sydney University Press, Sydney.

Reay, M. (1969). But Whose Estates? The Wahgi Smallholders. *New Guinea* 4, No. 3, 64 – 68.

Reay, M. (1974). Changing Conventions of Dispute Settlement in the Minj Area. In *Contention and Dispute: Aspects of Law and Social Control in Melanesia* (A.L. Epstein, ed.). Australian National University Press, Canberra.

Reed, S.W. (1943). *The Making of Modern New Guinea*. The American Philosophical Society, Philadelphia.

Rheinstein, M. (1963). Problems of Law in the New Nations of Africa. In *Old Societies and New States: The Quest for Modernity in Asia and Africa* (C. Geertz, ed.). Free Press, New York.

Rhodes, R.I. (1968). The Disguised Conservatism in Evolutionary Development Theory. *Science and Society* 32, 383 – 412.

Riggs, F.W. (1964). *Administration in Developing Countries: The Theory of Prismatic Society*. Houghton Mifflin, Boston.

Rijswijck, O. van (1966). *The Silanga Resettlement Project* (New Guinea Research Bulletin No. 10). New Guinea Research Unit, The Australian National University, Port Moresby and Canberra.

Robinson, R. (1972). Non-European Foundations of European Imperialism: Sketch for a Theory of Collaboration. In *Studies in the Theory of Imperialism* (R. Owen and B. Sutcliffe, eds). Longman, London.

Roe, M. (1971). Papua-New Guinea and War 1941–5. In *Australia and Papua New Guinea* (W.J. Hudson, ed.). Sydney University Press, Sydney.

Rollins, C.E. (1970). Mineral Development and Economic Growth. In *Imperialism and Underdevelopment: A Reader* (R.I. Rhodes, ed.). Monthly Review Press, New York and London.

Rowley, C.D. (1958). *The Australians in German New Guinea 1914–1921*. Melbourne University Press, Carlton.

Rowley, C.D. (1971). The Occupation of German New Guinea 1914–1921. In *Australia and Papua New Guinea* (W.J. Hudson, ed.). Sydney University Press, Sydney.

Rowley, C.D. (1972). *The New Guinea Villager: A Retrospect from 1964*. Cheshire, Melbourne.

Rudolph, L. and Rudolph, S.H. (1967). *The Modernity of Tradition: Political Development in India*. University of Chicago Press, Chicago and London.

Ruhen, O. (1968). *Mountains in the Clouds*. Horwitz, Melbourne.

Ryan, D. (1963). Taoripi Association: Some Problems of Economic Development in Papua. *Mankind* **6**, No. 1, 11–15.

Sack, P.G. (1973). *Land Between Two Laws: Early European Land Acquisitions in New Guinea*. Australian National University Press, Canberra.

Sack, P. and Sack, B. (1975). *The Land Law of German New Guinea: A Collection of Documents*. Research School of Social Sciences, The Australian National University, Canberra.

Sahlins, M.D. (1966). Poor Man, Rich Man, Big Man, Chief: Political Types in Melanesia. In *Readings in Australian and Pacific Anthropology* (I. Hogbin and L.R. Hiatt, eds). Cambridge University Press and Melbourne University Press, London and New York.

Salisbury, R.F. (1962). *From Stone to Steel: Economic Consequences of Technological Change in New Guinea*. Melbourne University Press, Carlton.

Salisbury, R.F. (1964). Despotism and Australian Administration in the New Guinea Highlands. In *New Guinea: The Central Highlands* (J.B. Watson, ed.). Special Publication. *American Anthropologist* **66**.

Salisbury, R.F. (1970). *Vunamami: Economic Transformation in a Traditional Society*. Melbourne University Press, Carlton.

Sam, P., Passingan, B. and Kanawi, W. (1975). Bringing Law to the People. In *Lo Bilong Ol Manmeri: Crime, Compensation and Village Courts* (J. Zorn and P.

Bayne, eds). University of Papua New Guinea, n.p.

Sankoff, G. (1969). *Wok Bisnis* and Namasu: A Perspective from the Village. In *Namasu: New Guinea's Largest Indigenous-Owned Company* (New Guinea Research Bulletin No. 28) (I.J. Fairbairn). New Guinea Research Unit, The Australian National University, Port Moresby and Canberra.

Sankoff, G. (1972). Cognitive Variability and New Guinea Social Organization: The Buang Dgwa. *American Anthropologist* **74**, No. 3, 555 – 566.

Santos, B. de S. (in press). Science and Politics: Doing Research in Rio's Squatter Settlements. In *Law and Social Enquiry: Case Histories of Research* (R. Luckham, ed.).

Saul, J.S. and Woods, R. (1971). African Peasantries. In *Peasants and Peasant Societies* (T. Shanin, ed.). Penguin, Harmondsworth.

Sawai, C. (1977). Plantation Labour Recruitment in New Guinea in the Period 1922 to 1942. *Yagl-Ambu* **4**, No. 4, 294 – 313.

Scarr, D. (1967). *Fragments of Empire: A History of the Western Pacific High Commission 1877 – 1914.* Australian National University Press, Canberra.

Schwartz, T. (1962). *The Paliau Movement in the Admiralty Islands 1946 – 54.* Anthropological Papers of the American Museum of Natural History 49, No. 2.

Scott, A. Mc (1979). Who Are the Self-Employed? In *Casual Work and Poverty in Third World Cities* (R.J. Bromley and C. Gerry, eds). Wiley, London.

Seddon, D., ed. (1978). *Relations of Production: Marxist Approaches to Economic Anthropology.* Frank Cass, London.

Seddon, N. (1974). Reciprocity, Exchange and Contract. *Melanesian Law Journal* **2**, No. 1, 48 – 65.

Seddon, N. (1975). Legal Problems Facing Trade Unions in Papua New Guinea. *Melanesian Law Journal* **3**, No. 1, 103 – 118.

Seidman, R.B. (1972). Law and Development: A General Model. *Law and Society Review* **6**, 311 – 342.

Seidman, R.B. (1973). Contract Law, the Free Market, and State Intervention: A Jurisprudential Model. *Journal of Economic Issues* **VII**, No. 4, 533 – 575.

Seidman, R.B. (1978). *The State, Law and Development.* Croom Helm, London.

Shand, R.T. (1969). Papua New Guinea. In *Agricultural Development in Asia* (R.T. Shand, ed.). Australian National University Press, Canberra.

Shand, R.T. and Straatmans, W. (1974). *Transition from Subsistence: Cash Crop Development in Papua New Guinea* (New Guinea Research Bulletin No. 54). New Guinea Research Unit, The Australian National University, Port Moresby and Canberra.

Shand, R.T. and Treadgold, M.L. (1971). *The Economy of Papua New Guinea: Projections and Policy Issues.* Research School of Pacific Studies, The Australian National University, Canberra.

Shivji, I.G. (1976). *Class Struggles in Tanzania.* Heinemann, London.

Silikara, J. (1978). The Kabisawali Association. *Yagl-Ambu* **5**, No. 1, 132 – 141.

Simington, M. (1977). The Southwest Pacific Islands in Australian Interwar Defence Planning. *The Australian Journal of Politics and History* **XXIII**, No. 2, 173 – 177.

Simpson, D.R. (1978). The Administrative and Political Development of Local Government in Papua New Guinea to 1964 *Yagl-Ambu*. **5**, No. 1, 21 – 57.

Simpson, S.R. (1971). Land Problems in Papua New Guinea. In *Land Tenure and Economic Development: Problems and Policies in Papua New Guinea* (New Guinea Research Bulletin No. 40) (M. Ward, 1971). New Guinea Research Unit, The Australian National University, Boroko and Canberra.

Sinclair, J.P. (1966). *Behind the Ranges: Patrolling in New Guinea*. Melbourne University Press, Carlton.

Singh, S. (1974). *Co-operatives in Papua New Guinea* (New Guinea Research Bulletin No. 58). New Guinea Research Unit, The Australian National University, Port Moresby and Canberra.

Skeldon, R. (1977a). Regional Associations in Papua New Guinea (IASER Discussion Paper No. 9). Institute of Applied Social and Economic Research, Boroko.

Skeldon, R. (1977b). Internal Migration in Papua New Guinea: A Statistical Description (IASER Discussion Paper No. 11). Institute of Applied Social and Economic Research, Boroko.

Skeldon, R. (1978a). Evolving Patterns of Population Movement in Papua New Guinea with reference to Policy Implications (IASER Discussion Paper No. 17). Institute of Applied Social and Economic Research, Boroko.

Skeldon, R. (1978b). Recent Urban Growth in Papua New Guinea (IASER Discussion Paper No. 21). Institute of Applied Social and Economic Research. Boroko.

Smith, D.W. (1975). *Labour and the Law in Papua New Guinea*. Development Studies Centre, The Australian National University, Canberra.

Smith, M.G. (1974). *Corporations and Society*. Duckworth, London.

Smith, S.S. and Salisbury, R.F. (1961). Notes on Tolai Land Law and Custom. Roneo, Kokopo.

Snyder, F.G. (1978). Legal Innovation and Social Change in a Peasant Community: A Senegalese Village Police. *Africa* **48**, No. 3, 231 – 247.

Somare, M.T. (1975a). Law and the Needs of Papua New Guinea's People. In *Lo Bilong ol Manmeri: Crime, Compensation and Village Courts* (J. Zorn and P. Bayne, eds). University of Papua New Guinea, n.p.

Somare, M. (1975b). *Sana: An Autobiography of Michael Somare*. Niugini, Press, Port Moresby.

Standish, B. (1978a). The "Big Man" Model Reconsidered: Power and Stratification in the Papua New Guinea Highlands. Paper delivered at a *Conference of the Sociological Association of Australia and New Zealand*, University of Queensland, 18 – 21 May, 1978.

Standish, B. (1978b). So Far What Have We Learnt? *Post-Courier* 2nd October 1978, 5.

Standish, B. (1978c). The "Big-man" Model Reconsidered: Power and Stratification in Chimbu (IASER Discussion Paper No. 22). Institute of Applied Social and Economic Research, Boroko.

Standish, B. (n.d.) Independent Papua New Guinea's First National Elections: An Interim Report. Roneo.

Stanner, V.E.H. (1947). *Reconstruction in the South Pacific Islands: A Preliminary Report, Part 1*. Institute of Pacific Relations, New York.

Stevenson, M. A Trade Union in New Guinea. *Oceania* **XXXIX**, 110 – 136.

Stone, D. (1976). The Political Turning Point: The Birth of the National Coalition Government. In *Prelude to Self-Government: Electoral Politics in Papua New Guinea 1972* (D. Stone, ed.). Research School of Pacific Studies and the University of Papua New Guinea at the Australian National University, Canberra.

Strathern, A. (1966). Despots and Directors in the New Guinea Highlands. *Man* n.s. **1**, No. 3, 356 – 367.

Strathern, A. (1971). *The Rope of Moka: Big-Men and Ceremonial Exchange in Mount Hagen, New Guinea*. Cambridge University Press, London.

Strathern, A. (1972a). *One Father, One Blood: Descent and Group Structure Among the Melpa People*. Australian National University Press, Canberra.

Strathern, A. (1972b). The Entrepreneurial Model of Social Change: From Norway to New Guinea. *Ethnology* **XI**, No. 4, 368 – 379.

Strathern, A.J. (1972c). Social Pressures on the Rural Entrepreneur. In *Change and Development in Rural Melanesia*. (M. Ward, ed.). Research School of Pacific Studies, The Australian National University and the University of Papua New Guinea, Canberra and Port Moresby.

Strathern, A. (1977). Contemporary Warfare in the New Guinea Highlands: Revival or Breakdown? *Yagl-Ambu* **4**, No. 3, 135 – 146.

Strathern, M. (1972). *Official and Unofficial Courts: Legal Assumptions and Expectations in a Highlands Community* (New Guinea Research Bulletin No. 47). New Guinea Research Unit and The Australian National University, Port Moresby and Canberra.

Strathern, M. (1975). *No Money on Our Skins: Hagen Migrants in Port Moresby* (New Guinea Research Bulletin No. 61). New Guinea Research Unit, The Australian National University, Port Moresby and Canberra.

Summer, C. (1979). *Reading Ideologies: An Investigation into the Marxist Theory of Ideology and Law*. Academic Press, London and New York.

Sundhaussen, U. (1973). New Guinea's Army: A Political Role? *New Guinea* **8**, No. 2, 29 – 40.

Territory of New Guinea (1914 – 21). *Report . . . on the Administration of the Territory of New Guinea for Years 1914 – 21*.

Territory of New Guinea (1924 – 25). *Report . . . on the Administration of the*

*Territory of New Guinea for Years 1924–25.*

Territory of New Guinea (1950 – 51). *Report . . . on the Administration of the Territory of New Guinea for Years 1950 – 51.*

Territory of New Guinea (1958 – 59). *Report . . . on the Administration of the Territory of New Guinea for Years 1958 – 59.*

Territory of New Guinea (1959 – 60). *Report . . . on the Administration of the Territory of New Guinea for Years 1959 – 60.*

Territory of New Guinea (1960 – 61). *Report . . . on the Administration of New Guinea for Years 1960 – 61.*

Territory of New Guinea (1961 – 62). *Report . . . on the Administration of New Guinea for Years 1961 – 62.*

Territory of Papua (1915 – 16). *Territory of Papua, Annual Report for . . . 1915 – 16.*

Territory of Papua (1919 – 20). *Territory of Papua, Annual Report for . . . 1919 – 20.*

Territory of Papua and New Guinea (1961). *Legislative Council Debates* (5th Council, 3rd Meeting of the First Session) **VI,** No. 3.

Territory of Papua and New Guinea (1965). *House of Assembly Debates* **1,** No. 7.

Territory of Papua and New Guinea (1970). *Report of Board of Enquiry . . . Investigating Rural Minimum Wages . . . Minimum Wage Fixing Machinery and Related Matters.* Department of Labour, n.p.

Thaman, R.R. (1977). Urban Gardening in Papua New Guinea and Fiji. In *The Melanesian Environment* (J.H. Wilson, ed.). Australian National University Press, Canberra.

Thompson, E.P. (1977). *Whigs and Hunters: The Origin of the Black Act.* Penguin, Harmondsworth.

Thompson, E.P. (1978). *The Poverty of Theory and Other Essays.* Merlin Press, London.

Thomsom, J.T. (1975). *Law, Legal Process and Development at the Local Level in Hausa-Speaking Niger: A Trouble Case Analysis of Rural Institutional Inertia.* Ph.D. thesis, Indiana University.

Thomson, J.T. (1979). Capitation in Colonial and Post-Colonial Niger: Analysis of the Effects of an Imposed Head Tax System on Rural Political Organization. In *The Imposition of Law* (S.B. Burman and B.E. Harrell-Bond, eds). Academic Press, New York and London.

To Robert, H. (1967). Papuans and New Guineans in Private Business. *Journal of the Papua and New Guinea Society* **1,** No. 2, 73 – 77.

Townsend, D. (1978). Agricultural Innovation in a Peripheral Area: Finschhafen District of the Morobe Province (History of Agriculture Working Paper No. 22). University of Papua New Guinea and Department of Primary Industry.

Townsend, M.E. (1964). Commercial and Colonial Policies of Imperial Germany. In *Imperialism and Colonialism* (G.H. Nadel and P. Curtis eds). Macmillan, New York.

Trubeck, D.M. (1972). Toward a Social Theory of Law: An Essay on the Study of Law and Development. *Yale Law Journal* **82,** No. 1, 1 – 50.

Trubeck, D.M. and Galanter, M. (1974). Scholars in Self-Estrangement: Some Reflections on the Crisis in Law and Development Studies in the United States. *Wisconsin Law Review* **1974,** 1063 – 1102.

Twining, W. (1964). *The Place of Customary Law in the National Legal Systems of East Africa.* The Law School, The University of Chicago, Chicago.

Unger, R.M. (1976). *Law in Modern Society: Toward a Criticism of Social Theory.* Free Press, New York.

Utrecht, E. (1977). *Papua New Guinea: An Australian Neo-Colony* (Research Monograph No. 6). Transnational Corporations Research Project, Sydney.

Uyassi, M. (1978). *Local Government and Socio-economic Change in the Kainantu District of the Eastern Highlands, Papua New Guinea.* B.A. thesis, University of Papua New Guinea.

Vaitsos, C.V. (1974). *Intercountry Income Distribution and Transnational Enterprises.* Clarendon Press, Oxford.

Valdez, A.L. (1975). Developing the Role of Law in Social Change: Past Endeavours and Future Opportunities in Latin America and the Caribbean. *Lawyer of the Americas* **7,** 1 – 28.

Valentine, C.A. (1973). Changing Indigenous Societies and Cultures. In *Anthropology in Papua New Guinea: Readings From the Encyclopaedia of Papua and New Guinea* (I. Hogbin, ed.). Melbourne University Press, Carlton.

Wallerstein, I. (1974). *The Modern World-System: Capitalist Agriculture and the Origins of the European Economy in the Sixteenth Century.* Academic Press, New York and London.

Wallerstein, I. (1976). The Three Stages of Africa in the World Economy. In *The Political Economy of Contemporary Africa* (P.C.W. Gutkind and I. Wallerstein, eds). Sage, Beverly Hills and London.

Wanji, R. (1977). General Statement of Customary Rules of Succession in the Amele Area, Madang Province, and the Wasera, East Sepik Province (Occasional Paper No. 3). Law Reform Commission, Waigani.

Wanji, R. and Jerewai, A. (n.d.). Law of Succession: Findings from Interview with Public Servants. Typescript of Research for the Law Reform Commission, n.p.

Ward, A.D. (1972). Agrarian Revolution: Handle with Care. *New Guinea* **6,** No. 1, 25 – 34.

Ward, A. (1977). Land Administration: The Key to Social Equality. Paper delivered at the *48th ANZAAS Congress,* Melbourne, 1977.

Ward, A. (1978). Customary Land, Land Registration and Social Equality in Papua New Guinea (History of Agriculture Discussion Paper No. 20). University of Papua New Guinea and Department of Primary Industry.

Ward, R.G. (1971). Internal Migration and Urbanization in Papua New Guinea. In *Population and Growth and Socio-Economic Change* (New Guinea Research Bulletin No. 42) (M. Ward, ed.). New Guinea Research Unit, The Australian National University, Port Moresby and Canberra.

Warren, N. (1978). The Kumara Kommuniti: Politics Short of Policies. *Yagl-Ambu* **5,** No. 1, 106 – 130.

Weeks, J. (1973). Uneven Sectoral Development and the Role of the State. *Bulletin, Institute of Development Studies* **5,** No. 213, 76 – 82.

Wehler, H. – U. (1972). Industrial Growth and Early German Imperialism. In *Studies in the Theory of Imperialism* (R. Owen and B. Sutcliffe, eds). Longman, London.

Whiteman, J. (1973). *Chimbu Family Relationships in Port Moresby* (New Guinea Research Bulletin No. 52). New Guinea Research Unit, The Australian National University, Port Moresby and Canberra.

Whittaker, J.L., Gash, N.G., Hookey, J.F. and Lacey, R.J. (1975). *Documents and Readings in New Guinea History: Prehistory to 1889.* Jacaranda, Milton.

Willis, I. (1974). *Lae: Village and City.* Melbourne University Press, Carlton.

Willis, I. and Adams, B. (1972). What's Wrong with Councils? The Experiment at Lae. *New Guinea* **7,** No. 3, 4 – 26.

Woddis, J. (1967). *Introduction to Neo-Colonialism: The New Imperialism in Asia, Africa and Latin America.* International Publishers, New York, 1967.

Wolf, E.R. (1971). *Peasant Wars of the Twentieth Century.* Faber, London.

Wolfers, E.P. (1972). Trusteeship Without Trust: A Short History of Interracial Relations and the Law in Papua New Guinea. In *Racism: The Australian Experience: A Study of Race Prejudice in Australia*, Vol. 3 (F.S. Stevens, ed.). Australia and New Zealand Book Company, Sydney.

Wolfers, E.P. (1975). *Race Relations and Colonial Rule in Papua New Guinea.* Australia and New Guinea Book Company, Sydney.

Wolpe. H. (1975). The Theory of Internal Colonialism: The South African Case. In *Beyond the Sociology of Development: Economy and Society in Latin America and Africa* (Oxaal, I., Barnett, T. and Booth, D., eds). Routledge and Kegan Paul, London and Boston.

Woolford, D. (1973). The United Party. *New Guinea* **8,** No. 2, 51 – 63.

Woolford, D. (1974). Blacks, Whites . . . and the Awful Press. *New Guinea* **8,** No. 4, 4 – 26.

Worsley, P. (1967). *The Third World.* Weidenfeld and Nicolson, London.

Worsley, P. (1971). *The Trumpet Shall Sound: A Study of "Cargo" Cults in Melanesia.* Granada Publishing, London.

Worsley, R.J. (1966). *The Developing System of Industrial Relations in Papua New Guinea.* Thesis submitted for the degree of Bachelor of Commerce, University of New South Wales.

Wright, E.O. (1976). Class Boundaries in Advanced Capitalist Societies. *New Left Review* **98,** 3 – 41.

Wright. E.O. (1978). *Class, Crisis and the State.* New Left Books, London.

Wright, M. (1975). Towards an Understanding of Being Without Formal Employment in Papua New Guinea Towns (New Guinea Research Unit Discussion Paper No. 9). New Guinea Research Unit, Boroko.

Wright, M., Garnaut, R. and Curtain, R. (1975). Employment and Incomes in Papua New Guinea Towns (New Guinea Research Unit Discussion Paper No. 2). New Guinea Research Unit, Boroko.

Young, M.W. (1974). Private Sanctions and Public Ideology: Some Aspects of Self-Help in Kalauna, Goodenough. In *Contention and Dispute: Aspects of Law and Social Control in Melanesia* (A.L. Epstein, ed.). Australian National University Press, Canberra.

# Index